1000
INDIAN RECIPE
COOKBOOK

AUTHENTIC
EASY TO FOLLOW
RECIPES

D0968029

ARCTURUS

ARCTURUS

This edition published in 2010 by Arcturus Publishing Limited
26/27 Bickels Yard, 151–153 Bermondsey Street,
London SE1 3HA

ISBN: 978-1-84837-483-6
AD001330EN

Content and Design by quadrum™
Quadrum Solutions, Mumbai, India
www.quadrumltd.com • Tel: 91-22-24968212

Printed in the UK

Contents

Introduction

Indian food, like the country itself, varies enormously. Whatever type of food you might be interested in – meat, fish or vegetarian – you will find a recipe to suit your palate and mood. While curry is inevitably associated with India, this term is simply used for meats or vegetables cooked in a spicy sauce, usually eaten with rice or Indian breads. As this collection of a thousand Indian recipes will show you, Indian food is not limited to the familiar restaurant favourites – it is more wide-ranging and complex than you may ever have imagined.

Food is taken very seriously in India and cooking is considered an art. Each Indian state has its own traditions, culture, lifestyle and food. Even individual households may have their own secret recipes for the powders and pastes that form the backbone of the dish. However, what all Indian dishes have in common is the delicate alchemy of spices that gives them their characteristic flavour.

Over the course of history the various invaders who have passed through India have left their influence on its culture and cuisine. Geography and local produce have also played an important role in shaping regional cuisine. The result is dishes so delicious that some of them are legendary!

The recipes that follow have been organized into thirteen chapters. Each chapter includes a variety of recipes chosen to represent the specialities of different regions. In the recipes, you will come across ingredients marked with an asterisk (*). These are ingredients that might not be typically available at the neighbourhood supermarket, but you'll easily find them at your nearest Indian store, or online. A glossary at the back of the book explains what the less familiar ingredients are. Also included is a list of basic cooking techniques that will make the cooking of Indian food simpler.

The recipes in the book are authentic, such as you might encounter in an Indian home – yet they are simple, so if this is the first time that you are going to cook Indian food, relax. All you need to do is turn the pages, pick what tickles your fancy, and create a delicious meal, the Indian way!

PICKLES AND CHUTNEYS

No Indian meal is complete without either a pickle or chutney to add that extra bit of zing to the food. From sweet to savoury to sour, your taste buds will be delighted by the different spices and ingredients that are used here. Chutneys can be dry and spicy, sweet and sour, or all of these together. Some can be stored for a few weeks or months depending on the ingredients while others need to be consumed the very same day. This chapter contains several delightful pickles and chutneys that will add the right touch to your authentic Indian meals.

Green Chilli Pickle

Ingredients
10 green chillies, slit
1 tsp salt
4 tsp ground mustard
1 tsp turmeric
Juice of 2 lemons

Method
- Mix all the ingredients together. Transfer the mixture to a clean, dry jar with a tight lid. Set aside for a day in a cool, dry place.

NOTE: *This can be stored in the refrigerator for a month.*

Sweet Tomato Chutney

Ingredients
2 tsp refined vegetable oil
4 dry red chillies
1 tsp turmeric
2.5cm/1in root ginger, chopped
4 tomatoes, chopped
125g/4½oz sugar
Salt to taste

Method
- Heat the oil in a saucepan. Add the chillies, turmeric and ginger. Fry on a medium heat for 1 minute. Add the remaining ingredients and cook the mixture until it is thick.
- Store in a clean, dry jar.

NOTE: *This can be stored for up to a month in the refrigerator.*

Apple Chutney

Ingredients
250g/9oz apples, peeled
120ml/4fl oz water
2 garlic cloves, crushed
2.5cm/1in root ginger, shredded
120ml/4fl oz malt vinegar
125g/4½oz sugar
Salt to taste

Method
- Slice the apples. Place in a saucepan with all the ingredients.
- Cook on a medium heat till tender.
- Cool and store in an airtight jar.

NOTE: *This can be stored for up to a week in the refrigerator.*

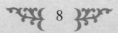

Bengali Mango Pickle

Ingredients
1 tsp salt

½ tsp turmeric

1 tsp chilli powder

150g/5½oz jaggery*

250g/9oz unripe mangoes, chopped into 2.5cm/1in pieces

2 tbsp mustard oil

2 tsp panch phoron*

4 red chillies, slit lengthways

Method
- Mix the salt, turmeric, chilli powder, jaggery and mangoes together. Set aside for 2 hours.
- Heat the oil in a saucepan. Add the panch phoron and the slit red chillies. Let them splutter for 15 seconds.
- Add the mango mixture. Cook on a low heat for 15 minutes, stirring occasionally, until the jaggery turns into a thick syrup.
- Remove from the heat and allow the mixture to cool. Store in a clean, dry jar.

NOTE: *This can be stored in a refrigerator for up to a week.*

Gujarati Sweet Mango Pickle

Ingredients
2 tsp salt

1 tsp turmeric

500g/1lb 2oz unripe mangoes, peeled and grated

400g/14oz sugar

1 tsp asafoetida

1 tbsp chilli powder

2 tsp ground cumin

Method
- Add salt and turmeric to the grated mangoes. Mix well and set aside for an hour.
- Add the sugar and cook the mixture in a sauepan on a low heat till the mixture has a consistency like maple syrup.
- Add the asafoetida, chilli powder and ground cumin. Mix well. Cook for another minute.
- Store in a clean, dry jar.

NOTE: *This can be stored in the refrigerator for a month.*

Ginger Pickle

Ingredients

250g/9oz root ginger, julienned
1 green chilli, finely chopped
3 tbsp refined vegetable oil
¾ tsp mustard seeds
8 curry leaves
1 dry red chilli

100g/3½oz tamarind paste
¼ tsp turmeric
¼ tsp chilli powder
125g/4½oz jaggery*, grated
1 tsp salt
60ml/2fl oz water

Method

• Fry the ginger and green chilli in 2 tbsp oil till brown. Set aside.
• Heat the remaining oil in a saucepan. Add the mustard seeds, curry leaves and red chilli. Let them splutter for 15 seconds.
• Add the fried ginger and green chilli mixture along with all the remaining ingredients. Simmer for 7-8 minutes. Cool and store in an airtight bottle.

NOTE: *This can be stored in the refrigerator for a fortnight.*

Pickled Chicken

Ingredients

1kg/2¼lb unripe chicken, chopped
250ml/8fl oz white vinegar
100ml/3½fl oz mustard oil
2 tsp ginger paste
2 tsp garlic paste
1½ tsp turmeric

1½ tsp chilli powder
2 tsp kalonji seeds*
3 black cardamom pods
8 cloves
Salt to taste

Method

• Mix the chicken with vinegar. Marinate for 3 hours. Pound and set aside.
• Heat the oil in a saucepan. Add the chicken mixture along with all the remaining ingredients. Simmer till the vinegar is absorbed.

NOTE: *This can be stored in the refrigerator for a month.*

Prawn Pickle

Ingredients

1 tsp turmeric

1 tsp chilli powder

1 tsp fenugreek seeds, ground

1 tsp mustard seeds, ground

Salt to taste

1 tbsp white vinegar

250g/9oz prawns, cleaned and de-veined

3 tbsp refined vegetable oil

¼ tsp mustard seeds

¼ tsp fenugreek seeds

¼ tsp asafoetida

Method

- Mix the turmeric, chilli powder, ground fenugreek, ground mustard and salt.
- Add this mixture, along with half the vinegar, to the prawns. Marinate for 2 hours.
- Heat the oil in a saucepan. Add the mustard seeds and fenugreek seeds. Let them splutter for 15 seconds.
- Add the asafoetida and the marinated punripens. Mix well.
- Cook on a low heat for 10 minutes.
- Add the remaining vinegar and continue to cook on a low heat for another 2-3 minutes.
- Remove from the heat and allow it to cool.
- Store in a clean, dry jar.

NOTE: *This can be stored in the refrigerator for a week.*

Onion Chutney

Ingredients

1 large onion, finely sliced

2 tbsp ready-made Indian mango pickle

1 small green chilli

Salt to taste

Method

- Pound all the ingredients into a thick paste.
- Store in a clean, dry jar.

NOTE: *This can be kept in the refrigerator for 2 days.*

Sweet & Sour Lime Pickle

Ingredients

500ml/16fl oz malt vinegar

1½ tsp salt

250ml/8fl oz water

10 large limes, quartered

1cm/½in root ginger, finely sliced

12 garlic cloves, finely sliced

5cm/2in cinnamon

8 cloves

375g/13oz sugar

Method

- Mix the vinegar, salt and half the water in a saucepan. Bring to a boil.
- Add the lime pieces, ginger, garlic, cinnamon and cloves. Cook for 7-8 minutes. Set aside.
- Melt the sugar in the remaining water and simmer till thick. Add the lime mixture. Mix well and remove from the heat.
- Cool and store in a clean, dry jar. Set aside for 3-4 days.

NOTE: *This can be stored in the refrigerator for a month.*

Hot & Sour Chutney

Ingredients

2 tbsp jaggery*, grated

5 tbsp tamarind paste

1 tsp chilli powder

Dash of ground black pepper

1 tsp salt

Pinch of ginger powder

6-7 dates, boiled for 5 minutes and ground to a paste

2 tbsp dates, chopped

1 tbsp raisins

Method

- Mix the grated jaggery with the tamarind paste. Cook the mixture in a saucepan on a low heat for 3-4 minutes. Add all the ingredients, except the chopped dates and raisins. Mix well and cook for 5 minutes.
- Add the chopped dates and raisins. Mix well. Cool and serve.

NOTE: *This can be stored in the refrigerator for a month.*

Cumin Seed Chutney

Ingredients
50g/1¾oz cumin seeds, dry
  roasted (see cooking
  techniques) and ground
1 tsp tamarind paste
1½ tbsp sugar
½ tsp chilli powder
Salt to taste
250ml/8fl oz water

Method
- Mix all the ingredients together. Cook over a low heat for 7-8 minutes until the mixture thickens.
- Allow the mixture to cool and store in a clean, dry jar.

NOTE: *This can be stored in the refrigerator for a week.*

Turnip Pickle

Ingredients
250g/9oz turnips, chopped
  into 2.5cm/1in pieces
240ml/6fl oz water
120ml/¼fl oz refined
  vegetable oil
8 garlic cloves, crushed
1 tbsp ginger paste
240ml/6fl oz malt vinegar
125g/4½oz jaggery*,
  grated
1 tsp chilli powder
4 cloves
5cm/2in cinnamon
2 green cardamom pods
1 tsp mustard seeds,
  ground
1 tbsp salt

Method
- Boil the turnips with the water on a low heat for 15 minutes. Drain and set aside.
- Heat the oil in a saucepan. Fry the garlic and the ginger paste on a low heat till golden brown.
- Add the boiled turnip and all the remaining ingredients. Mix well.
- Cook the mixture until the oil separates.
- Cool and transfer to a clean, dry jar.

NOTE: *This can be stored in a refrigerator for a month.*

Sweet Mango Pickle

Ingredients

500g/1lb 2oz unripe mangoes, peeled and finely sliced

Salt to taste

1 tsp turmeric

120ml/4fl oz refined vegetable oil

2 cloves

2.5cm/1in cinnamon

6 black peppercorns

1 tsp chilli powder

250g/9oz grated jaggery*

5cm/2in root ginger, finely sliced

12 garlic cloves, finely sliced

Method

- Rub the mango slices with the salt and turmeric. Set aside for an hour.
- Squeeze out water by pressing the mango slices between your palms. Set aside.
- Heat the oil in a saucepan. Add the cloves, cinnamon and peppercorns.
- Let them splutter for 15 seconds. Add the mango slices and mix well.
- Add the chilli powder, jaggery, ginger and garlic. Mix well and cook over a low heat till the jaggery melts into a thick syrup.
- Allow the pickle to cool. Store in a dry, clean jar and keep aside for a day.

NOTE: *This can be stored in the refrigerator for a month.*

Carrot Pickle

Ingredients

6½ tbsp refined vegetable oil

1 tsp mustard seeds

1 tsp fenugreek seeds

½ tsp asafoetida

1 tsp turmeric

2 tsp chilli powder

Salt to taste

250g/9oz carrots, thinly sliced

Method

- Heat the oil in a saucepan. Add the mustard seeds, fenugreek seeds, asafoetida, turmeric, chilli powder and the salt. Fry on a low heat for 15 seconds.
- Allow the mixture to cool. Pour over the carrot slices and let stand for 2-3 hours.
- Store in a clean, dry jar.

NOTE: *This can be stored in the refrigerator for a week.*

Green Coconut Chutney

Ingredients

200g/7oz coriander leaves

100g/3½oz grated fresh coconut

2 green chillies

8 garlic cloves

Salt to taste

60ml/2fl oz water

Method

• Grind all the ingredients together. Store in a clean, dry jar.

NOTE: *This can be stored in the refrigerator for 2-3 days.*

Mint Chutney

Ingredients

100g/3½oz fresh mint leaves

1 large onion

3 green chillies

8 garlic cloves

Salt to taste

1 tbsp water

Method

• Grind all the ingredients together. Store in a clean, dry jar
  for 2-3 days.

Peanut Chutney

Ingredients

250g/9oz roasted peanuts

1 tsp chilli powder

2 tsp sugar

Salt to taste

Method

• Grind all the ingredients together. Store in a clean, dry jar
  for 10 days.

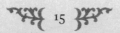

Papaya Chutney

Ingredients
1 tsp salt

2 tsp sugar

200g/7oz grated unripe papaya

2 tbsp refined vegetable oil

1 tsp cumin seeds

8 curry leaves

3 green chillies, slit lengthways

½ tsp turmeric

Method
- Mix the salt and the sugar with the grated papaya. Set aside.
- Heat the oil in a saucepan. Add the cumin seeds, curry leaves, green chillies and turmeric. Let them splutter for 15 seconds.
- Pour this over the grated papaya mixture. Mix well.
- Allow the mixture to cool and then store in a clean, dry jar.

NOTE: *This can be stored in the refrigerator for a week.*

Sweet & Sour Mango Pickle

Ingredients
500g/1lb 2oz unripe mangoes, peeled and chopped into 5cm/2in strips

Salt to taste

125g/4½oz mustard seeds, coarsely ground

3 tbsp water

180g/6½oz grated jaggery*

1 tsp chilli powder

1½ tbsp refined vegetable oil

1 tsp mustard seeds

½ tsp asafoetida

½ tsp turmeric

Method
- Rub the mango slices with salt. Set aside.
- Mix the ground mustard with half a tsp of salt and the water.
- Mix this well with the mango slices, along with the jaggery and chilli powder.
- Heat the oil in a saucepan. Add the mustard seeds, asafoetida and turmeric. Let them splutter for 15 seconds.
- Remove from the heat and pour this oil over the mango mixture. Mix thoroughly.
- Allow to cool and store in a clean, dry jar.

NOTE: *This can be stored in the refrigerator for a month.*

Aubergine Pickle

Ingredients

120ml/4fl oz refined
  vegetable oil

1 tsp mustard seeds

1 tsp fenugreek seeds

2 tsp ground cumin

2.5cm/1in root ginger,
  finely chopped

12 garlic cloves,
  finely chopped

4 green chillies,
  finely chopped

500g/1lb 2oz aubergine,
  chopped into
  2.5cm/1in pieces

125g/4½oz sugar

120ml/4fl oz malt vinegar

Salt to taste

Method

- Heat the oil in a saucepan. Add the mustard seeds, fenugreek seeds and ground cumin.
- Let them splutter for 15 seconds. Add the ginger, garlic and green chillies. Fry on a low heat for a minute.
- Add the aubergine pieces. Mix well to coat with the oil. Cook for 3-4 minutes on a medium heat, stirring well.
- Add the sugar, vinegar and the salt. Cook over a low heat till the aubergine pieces become soft. Allow any extra liquid to evaporate.
- Remove from the heat and cool.
- Store in a clean, dry jar.

NOTE: *This can be stored in the refrigerator for a month.*

Curry Leaves Dry Pickle

Ingredients

25g/scant 1oz curry leaves,
  dry roasted (see cooking
  techniques)

250g/9oz kaala chana*,
  roasted

1 tbsp sugar

8 dry red chillies

Salt to taste

Method

- Dry grind (see cooking techniques) all the ingredients together.
- Store in a clean, dry jar.

NOTE: *This can be stored in the refrigerator for a month.*

Tomato Pickle

Ingredients
240ml/6fl oz refined
vegetable oil

1 tsp mustard seeds

¼ tsp fenugreek seeds

1 tsp cumin seeds

½ tsp turmeric

8 curry leaves

2 tsp ginger paste

2 tsp garlic paste

2 red chillies, slit
lengthways

4 tomatoes, blanched,
skinned and chopped

250ml/8fl oz malt vinegar

250g/9oz sugar

Salt to taste

Method
• Heat the oil in a saucepan. Add the mustard
seeds, fenugreek seeds, cumin seeds,
turmeric, curry leaves, ginger paste, garlic
paste and the red chillies. Fry for 30 seconds.

• Add the tomatoes. Mix well.

• Add the vinegar, sugar and salt. Cook on
a low heat for 20 minutes.

• Remove from the heat and allow the mixture
to cool. Store in clean, dry jar.

NOTE: *This can be stored in the refrigerator
for a month.*

Hot Lime Pickle

Ingredients
60g/2oz turmeric

125g/4½oz chilli powder

1 tsp fenugreek seeds

250g/9oz coarse salt

25 limes, each cut into
8 pieces

Juice of 10 lemons

Method
• Add the turmeric, chilli powder, fenugreek
seeds and salt to the limes. Mix thoroughly.
Transfer to a clean, dry jar.

• Pour the lemon juice over this mixture.

• Seal and set aside in a cool, dry place. Stir
the contents every third day for 15 days.

NOTE: *This can be stored in the refrigerator
for a month.*

Hot & Sweet Mango Chutney

Ingredients

60ml/2fl oz malt vinegar

3-4 dry red chillies, broken into bits

6 cloves

6 black peppercorns

1 tsp cumin seeds

½ tsp kalonji seeds*

250g/9oz sugar

Salt to taste

500g/1lb 2oz unripe mangoes, peeled and diced

5cm/2in root ginger, finely sliced

10 garlic cloves, finely sliced

Method

- In a deep saucepan, heat the vinegar with the chillies, cloves, peppercorns, cumin seeds, kalonji seeds, sugar and salt.
- Simmer for 15 minutes.
- Add the mango pieces, ginger and garlic.
- Simmer till the mango pieces become mushy and most of the vinegar evaporates.
- Cool the mixture and transfer into a clean, dry jar.
- Refrigerate for 2 days before serving.

NOTE: *This can be stored in a refrigerator for a month.*

Jaggery & Date Chutney

Ingredients

4 tbsp tamarind paste

50g/1¾oz jaggery*

8 dates

240ml/6fl oz water

1 tsp chilli powder

1 tsp ground cumin*

¼ tsp dry ginger powder

½ tbsp black salt

Method

- Mix the tamarind paste, jaggery and dates with the water. Set aside for an hour.
- Transfer the mixture to a saucepan and cook for 5-10 minutes on a low heat.
- Add the chilli powder, ground cumin, dry ginger powder and black salt.
- Mix well and cook for another minute.
- Remove from the heat and cool.

NOTE: *This can be stored in the refrigerator for a month.*

Sour Green Mango Pickle

Ingredients

1kg/2¼lb unripe mangoes
1 tbsp fenugreek seeds
1 tbsp fennel seeds
10g/¼oz kalonji seeds*
2 tsp mustard seeds
500ml/16fl oz mustard oil

For the spice mixture:

125g/4½oz chilli powder
2 tsp cumin seeds
2 tsp turmeric
½ tsp asafoetida
Salt to taste

Method

- Chop the mangoes into 2.5cm/1in pieces and pat them dry with a towel.
- Grind all the ingredients for the spice mixture together.
- To this mixture, add the fenugreek seeds, fennel seeds, kalonji seeds, mustard seeds and the mustard oil. Mix well to make a paste.
- Add the dried mango pieces to the paste. Mix well. Cook this mixture in a saucepan on a low heat for 20 minutes.
- Transfer the pickle into a dry jar.

NOTE: *This pickle can be stored in the refrigerator for a month.*

Coconut Chutney

Ingredients

200g/7oz fresh coconut, grated
8 garlic cloves
6 dry red chillies
1½ tsp tamarind paste
Salt to taste
60ml/2fl oz water

Method

- Grind all the ingredients together.
- Store in a clean, dry jar.

NOTE: *This can be stored in the refrigerator for 2-3 days.*

Mango & Chickpea Pickle

Ingredients

500g/1lb 2oz unripe,
  unpeeled mangoes

1 tbsp mustard seeds

2 tbsp fenugreek seeds

1 tbsp chilli powder

½ tbsp turmeric

1 tsp asafoetida

Salt to taste

60g/2oz canned chickpeas

500ml/16fl oz refined
  vegetable oil

Method

- Chop the mangoes into 2.5cm/1in pieces and pat dry with a towel.
- Grind the mustard seeds, fenugreek seeds, chilli powder, turmeric, asafoetida and salt together. Add this to the mango pieces.
- Add the chickpeas and the oil. Cook the mixture in a saucepan on a low heat for 30 minutes.
- Transfer the mixture to a clean, dry porcelain jar.

NOTE: *This can be stored in the refrigerator for a month.*

Dry Garlic Chutney

Ingredients

Salt to taste

2 tsp tamarind paste

For the spice mixture:

20 garlic cloves

200g/7oz desiccated
  coconut

1 tbsp cumin seeds

2 tbsp sesame seeds

5 dry red chillies

60g/2oz peanuts

Method

- Dry roast (see cooking techniques) all the ingredients for the spice mixture. Coarsely grind them along with the salt.
- Add this mixture to the tamarind paste. Mix thoroughly.
- Store in an airtight container and use when required.

NOTE: *This can be stored in the refrigerator for a fortnight.*

Gooseberry Pickle

(Suitable for making only during summer)

Ingredients

2 tbsp mustard oil

1 tsp fennel seeds

1½ tsp mustard seeds, ground

3 cloves

2.5cm/1in cinnamon

8 black peppercorns, ground

1 tsp turmeric

½ tsp chilli powder

Salt to taste

250g/9oz gooseberries, de-seeded and quartered

Method

- Heat the oil in a saucepan. Add all the ingredients, except the gooseberries. Let them splutter for 15 seconds.
- Pour this oil over the gooseberries. Mix thoroughly.
- Transfer the mixture to a clean jar with a tight lid. Keep in a warm place for a week. Shake regularly and place in the sun whenever possible. Make sure that the gooseberries are always immersed in oil.

NOTE: *This can be stored in the refrigerator for a month.*

Mixed Fruit Chutney

Ingredients

2.5cm/1in root ginger, thinly sliced

8 garlic cloves, thinly sliced

60g/2oz plums, stoned and chopped

60g/2oz apricots, stoned and chopped

1 tbsp raisins

2 apples, cored and chopped

250g/9oz brown sugar

240ml/8fl oz malt vinegar

1 tsp garam masala

1 tsp chilli powder

½ tsp caraway seeds

Salt to taste

Method

- Mix all the ingredients together. Cook in a saucepan over a low heat for 10 minutes. Cool and store in a clean, dry jar.

NOTE: *This can be stored in a refrigerator for a month.*

Sweet Cauliflower Pickle

Ingredients

12 garlic cloves

5cm/2in root ginger

2 tbsp mustard oil

2 tbsp brown sugar

120ml/4fl oz malt vinegar

1 tsp mustard seeds, ground

1 tbsp salt

1 tsp chilli powder

1 tsp turmeric

1 tsp garam masala

500g/1lb 2oz cauliflower, steamed (see cooking techniques) and chopped into small pieces

Method

- Pound the garlic and ginger together.
- Heat the oil in a saucepan. Fry this mixture on a low heat till golden brown. Set aside.
- Mix the sugar and vinegar in another saucepan. Cook for 10 minutes on a low heat till thick. Set aside to cool for 5 minutes.
- To the sugar-vinegar mixture, add the fried ginger-garlic mixture and all the remaining ingredients.
- Mix thoroughly. Transfer to an airtight jar. Set aside for a week.

NOTE: *This can be stored in the refrigerator for a month.*

Vinegar Chillies

Ingredients

Salt to taste

250ml/8fl oz white vinegar

25 whole green chillies

Method

- Add the salt to the vinegar. Mix well.
- Pour this mixture over the chillies and transfer them to a clean, dry jar.
- Set aside for 4-5 hours.

NOTE: *This can be stored in the refrigerator for a week.*

Cucumber Pickle

Ingredients
250g/9oz unpeeled cucumber, sliced

Salt to taste

60ml/2fl oz white vinegar

¼ tsp chilli powder

¼ tsp black peppercorns

½ tsp mustard seeds

¼ tsp ground cinnamon

¼ tsp ground cloves

1 tsp sugar

Method
- Rub the cucumber slices with salt and let them stand for 3-4 hours. Drain the excess moisture and set aside.
- Boil the vinegar with the chilli powder, peppercorns, mustard seeds, ground cinnamon, ground cloves and sugar in a saucepan on a low heat for 10 minutes.
- Add the cucumber pieces and simmer for 5 minutes.
- Remove from the heat and allow the pickle to cool completely.
- Store in a clean, dry jar.

NOTE: *This can be stored in the refrigerator for a fortnight.*

Hot Mango Pickle

Ingredients
3 unripe, unpeeled mangoes, chopped into small pieces

1½ tbsp salt

1 tbsp turmeric

500ml/16fl oz refined vegetable oil

2 tsp mustard seeds

1 tsp asafoetida

1 tbsp chilli powder

Method
- Rub the mango pieces with the salt and turmeric. Set aside for 5-6 hours.
- Squeeze out the water from the mango pieces. Leave them to dry for another hour.
- Heat the oil in a saucepan. Add the mustard seeds, asafoetida and chilli powder. Let them splutter for 15 seconds.
- Pour this oil mixture over the mango pieces. The oil should cover the mango pieces.
- Store in a dry jar and set aside for 2-3 days.

NOTE: *This can be stored in the refrigerator for a month.*

SALADS

Salads are a perfect way to add that essential bit of fresh vegetables to one's diet. In India, salads are one of the many side dishes that are served with the main course and there is plenty to choose from. Most homes make a basic shredded cucumber salad commonly known as Koshimbir while there are others that use more exotic ingredients like clams, depending on the region and the season.

Cucumber Salad

Serves 4

Ingredients

4 cucumbers, peeled and finely chopped

25g/scant 1oz coriander leaves, finely chopped

180g/6½oz peanuts, coarsely pounded

2 green chillies, coarsely chopped

1 tsp sugar (optional)

1 tsp lemon juice

Salt to taste

Method
- Mix all the ingredients together.
- Serve chilled.

Potato Salad

Serves 4

Ingredients

4 large potatoes, diced and boiled

1 large onion, finely chopped

1 green chilli, finely chopped

1 tbsp coriander leaves, finely chopped

2 tsp cumin seeds, dry roasted (see cooking techniques) and ground

3 tsp lemon juice

Salt to taste

Method
- Mix all the ingredients together.
- Serve chilled.

Koshimbir

Serves 4

Ingredients

4 tomatoes, finely chopped

2 large onions, finely chopped

10g/¼oz coriander leaves, finely chopped

50g/1¾oz roasted peanuts, coarsely pounded

½ tsp sugar (optional)

1 tsp lemon juice

Salt to taste

Method
- Mix all the ingredients together.
- Serve chilled.

Green Pepper Salad

Serves 4

Ingredients
2 green peppers, roughly chopped
50g/1¾oz pineapple, roughly chopped
50g/1¾oz spring onions, finely chopped
25g/scant 1oz coriander leaves,
  finely chopped
Freshly ground black pepper to taste

2 tsp lemon juice
Salt to taste

Method
- Mix all the ingredients together.
- Serve chilled.

Mint Pasta Salad

Serves 4

Ingredients
100g/3½oz cooked penne pasta
25g/scant 1oz mint leaves, finely
  chopped
1 large potato, diced and boiled
50g/1¾oz spring onions, finely chopped
3 tsp ground cumin, dry roasted
  (see cooking techniques)
½ tsp ground black pepper

1 tbsp lemon juice
Salt to taste

Method
- Mix all the ingredients together.
- Serve chilled.

Mushroom Salad

Serves 4

Ingredients
300g/10oz mushrooms
50g/1¾oz spring onions, thinly sliced
1 red or yellow pepper, thinly sliced
3 tsp ground cumin, dry roasted
  (see cooking techniques)
1 tbsp lemon juice
Salt to taste

Method
- Soak the mushrooms in hot water
  for 5 minutes. Drain and slice.
- Mix with the remaining
  ingredients. Serve chilled.

Egg Salad

Serves 4

Ingredients
1 large onion, finely chopped
10g/¼oz coriander leaves, chopped
2 green chillies, finely chopped
2 tsp lemon juice
1 tsp chaat masala*
Salt to taste
6 hard-boiled eggs, diced

Method
- Mix all the ingredients, except the eggs, together.
- Add the eggs. Mix gently. Serve.

Mixed Fruit Salad

Serves 4

Ingredients
1 apple, diced
50g/1¾oz pineapple, diced
1 pear, diced
6 strawberries, coarsely chopped
2 tsp chaat masala*
2 tsp lemon juice
Salt to taste
Sugar to taste

Method
- Mix all the ingredients together.
- Serve chilled.

Carrot Salad

Serves 4

Ingredients
2 large carrots, grated
3 tbsp peanuts, coarsely powdered
3 green chillies, finely chopped
1 tsp sugar
2 tsp lemon juice
Ground black pepper to taste
1 tbsp coriander leaves, chopped
Salt to taste

Method
- Mix all the ingredients together.
- Serve chilled.

Sprouted Beans Salad

Serves 4

Ingredients

500g/1lb 2oz mung bean sprouts, steamed (see cooking techniques)
1 tomato, finely chopped
2 green chillies, finely chopped
1 large onion, finely chopped
1 tsp sugar

10g/¼oz coriander leaves, chopped
Salt to taste

Method
- Mix all the ingredients together.
- Serve chilled.

Kaala Chana & Peanut Salad

Serves 4

Ingredients

250g/9oz kaala chana*, boiled
250g/9oz roasted peanuts
1 tbsp coriander leaves, finely chopped
1 large onion, finely grated
1 tsp chaat masala*
Juice of 1 lemon

2 green chillies, finely chopped
Salt to taste

Method
- Mix all the ingredients together.
- Serve chilled.

Mixed Salad

Serves 4

Ingredients

125g/4½oz cabbage, grated
1 tomato, finely chopped
1 cucumber, finely chopped
1 carrot, grated
2 tsp chaat masala*
2 tsp lemon juice
Salt to taste

Method
- Mix all the ingredients together.
- Serve chilled.

Cabbage & Pomegranate Salad

Serves 4

Ingredients

Salt to taste

150g/5½oz grated cabbage

200g/7oz pomegranate seeds

1 tbsp coriander leaves,
   finely chopped

1 tsp chaat masala*

2 tsp refined vegetable oil

1 tsp cumin seeds

Method

- Sprinkle the salt on top of the cabbage and set aside for 30 minutes. Squeeze out water from the cabbage by pressing it between your palms.
- Add.the pomegranate seeds, coriander and chaat masala. Set aside.
- Heat the oil in a saucepan. Add the cumin seeds. Let them splutter for 15 seconds. Pour this over the cabbage mixture. Serve chilled.

Fish Salad

Serves 4

Ingredients

½ tsp chilli powder

¾ tsp turmeric

1 tsp tamarind paste

1 tsp ginger paste

1 tsp garlic paste

Salt to taste

500g/1lb 2oz boneless fish or fillets,
   chopped into 5cm/2in pieces

2 tbsp refined vegetable oil

1 large onion, finely sliced

2 tbsp coriander leaves,
   finely chopped

1 tbsp lemon juice

1 tsp chaat masala*

2 green chillies, finely chopped

Method

- Mix the chilli powder, turmeric, tamarind paste, ginger paste, garlic paste and salt together. Marinate the fish with the mixture for 30 minutes.
- Heat the oil in a saucepan. Shallow fry the fish on a medium heat till it is cooked on both sides. Drain on absorbent paper. Allow to cool, then roughly shred the fish.
- Mix thoroughly with all the remaining ingredients. Serve chilled.

Spicy Chicken Salad

Serves 4

Ingredients
600g/1lb 5oz skinned boneless chicken,
  cut into 2.5cm/1in pieces

2 large onions, thinly sliced

3 green chillies, slit lengthwise

1 tsp lemon juice

25g/scant 1oz coriander leaves,
  finely chopped

Salt to taste

For the marinade:
½ tsp chilli powder

1 tsp freshly ground black pepper

½ tsp turmeric

60ml/2fl oz sour cream

1 tsp ginger paste

1 tsp garlic paste

1 tsp ground coriander

1 tsp ground cumin

1 tsp lemon juice

Method
* Mix the marinade ingredients together. Marinate the chicken pieces with this mixture for 30 minutes.
* Grill the chicken for 15 minutes.
* Add the remaining ingredients. Mix well. Serve chilled.

Watermelon Salad

Serves 4

Ingredients
½ watermelon

8 garlic cloves, finely chopped

1 tbsp coriander leaves,
  finely chopped

25g/scant 1oz spring onion, finely
  chopped

Juice of 1 lemon

Salt to taste

Method
* Scoop out the flesh of the watermelon. Carefully deseed and dice. Do not discard the shell.
* Mix the watermelon pieces with the garlic, coriander leaves, spring onion, lemon juice and salt.
* Place this mixture back into the shell. Serve chilled.

Cabbage Salad

Serves 4

Ingredients

50g/1¾oz sprouted mung beans

500g/1lb 2oz cabbage, finely grated

25g/scant 1oz fresh coconut, grated

1 tbsp coriander leaves,
  finely chopped

2 tsp sugar

1 tbsp lemon juice

Salt to taste

2 tsp refined vegetable oil

½ tsp mustard seeds

8 curry leaves

¼ tsp turmeric

3 green chillies, slit lengthways

Method

- In a bowl, mix the mung beans with the cabbage, coconut, coriander leaves, sugar, lemon juice and salt. Set aside.
- Heat the oil in a saucepan. Add the mustard seeds, curry leaves, turmeric and green chillies. Let them splutter for 15 seconds. Pour this over the cabbage mixture. Mix thoroughly.
- Serve chilled.

French Bean Salad

Serves 4

Ingredients

Salt to taste

250g/9oz French beans, finely chopped

1 large onion, finely chopped

1 tsp lemon juice

1 tsp honey

1 tsp ground cumin, dry roasted
  (see cooking techniques)

1 tbsp coriander leaves,
  finely chopped

1 tbsp fresh coconut, grated

Method

- Add the salt to the beans and steam (see cooking techniques) them, keeping them slightly crunchy.
- Mix with all the other ingredients in a bowl.
- Serve at room temperature.

Water Chestnut Salad

Serves 4

Ingredients

1 tbsp refined vegetable oil

½ tsp ginger paste

½ tsp garlic paste

1 red pepper, julienned

1 yellow pepper, julienned

1 green pepper, julienned

50g/1¾oz spring onions, finely chopped

4 green chillies, slit lengthwise

300g/10oz water chestnuts, par-boiled
(see cooking techniques)
and quartered

Salt to taste

¾ tsp ground black pepper

2 tsp soy sauce

Method

- Heat the oil in a saucepan. Add the ginger paste and garlic paste.
  Fry for a few seconds on a medium heat.
- Add all the remaining ingredients. Sauté for 30 seconds.
  Serve immediately.

NOTE: *The salad should be crunchy when it is served.*

Vermicelli & Corn Salad

Serves 4

Ingredients

1 tsp refined vegetable oil

½ tsp cumin seeds

1 large onion, finely chopped

100g/3½oz vermicelli, boiled and
drained

200g/7oz boiled corn

2 tbsp coriander leaves, chopped

2 tsp lemon juice

1 tsp ground cumin, dry roasted
(see cooking techniques)

2 green chillies, finely chopped

Method

- Heat the oil in a saucepan. Add the cumin seeds. Let them splutter for 15
  seconds. Add the onion and fry for a few seconds on a medium heat.
- Add all the remaining ingredients. Toss well. Serve immediately.

Rice Salad

Serves 6

Ingredients

100g/3½oz steamed basmati rice
(see page 519)

125g/4½oz boiled peas

50g/1¾oz cauliflower florets, boiled

50g/1¾oz carrots, diced and boiled

60g/2oz roasted peanuts

1 tbsp lemon juice

1 tsp caster sugar

Salt to taste

2 tsp refined vegetable oil

1 tsp cumin seeds

5-6 curry leaves, roughly torn

2 tbsp coriander leaves,
finely chopped

Method

- Mix the rice, peas, cauliflower florets, carrots, peanuts, lemon juice, sugar and salt together in a bowl. Set aside.
- Heat the oil in a saucepan. Add the cumin seeds and curry leaves. Let them splutter for 15 seconds.
- Pour this over the rice mixture. Toss lightly.
- Garnish with the coriander leaves. Serve immediately.

Daikon Salad

Serves 4

Ingredients

2 daikons, grated

Salt to taste

2 tsp sugar

2 tsp refined vegetable oil

1 tsp mustard seeds

8 curry leaves

2 green chillies, slit lengthways

1 tbsp coriander leaves,
finely chopped

½ tbsp lemon juice

Method

- In a bowl, mix the daikon with the salt and sugar. Set aside.
- Heat the oil in a saucepan. Add the mustard seeds, curry leaves and green chillies. Let them splutter for 15 seconds.
- Pour this oil over the daikon mixture. Add the coriander leaves and lemon juice. Mix thoroughly. Serve chilled.

Peanut & Chickpea Salad

Serves 4

Ingredients

125g/4½oz peanuts

75g/2½oz chickpeas, soaked for 2 hours

60g/2oz kaala chana*, soaked for 2 hours

750ml/1¼fl oz water

1 large green pepper, cored, deseeded and finely chopped

50g/1¾oz coriander leaves, finely chopped

1 large tomato, finely chopped

1 large onion, finely chopped

2 green chillies, finely chopped

2 tsp lemon juice

2 tsp chaat masala*

Salt to taste

Method

- In a saucepan, boil the peanuts, chickpeas and kaala chana with the water on a high heat for 45 minutes.
- Transfer to a bowl. Add the remaining ingredients and mix well.
- Serve chilled.

Rajma Salad

(Kidney Bean Salad)

Serves 4

Ingredients

Salt to taste

2 tbsp malt vinegar

600g/1lb 5oz canned kidney beans

1 large onion, finely chopped

1 tomato, finely chopped

5 cloves

2 green chillies, finely chopped

1 tbsp coriander leaves, finely chopped

Method

- Sprinkle salt and vinegar on top of the kidney beans. Mix well and set aside for 10 minutes.
- Add the remaining ingredients. Mix thoroughly and serve chilled.

Beetroot Salad

Serves 4

Ingredients

250g/9oz beetroot, boiled
and grated

125g/4½oz peanuts,
coarsely pounded

2 tsp lemon juice

1 tbsp coriander leaves,
finely chopped

Salt to taste

2 tsp refined
vegetable oil

1 tsp cumin seeds

2 green chillies, slit
lengthways

Method

• In a bowl, mix the beetroot, peanuts, lemon
juice, coriander leaves and salt. Set aside.

• Heat the oil in a saucepan. Add the cumin
seeds and slit green chillies. Let them
splutter for 15 seconds.

• Pour this mixture over the beetroot mixture.
Mix well.

• Serve chilled.

Paneer Salad

Serves 4

Ingredients

1 green pepper, diced

1 large onion, finely
chopped

125g/4½oz pomegranate
seeds

3 tsp chaat masala*

10g/¼oz coriander leaves,
finely chopped

2 tsp lemon juice

Salt to taste

500g/1lb 2oz paneer*,
diced

Method

• In a bowl, mix all the ingredients thoroughly,
except the paneer.

• Add the paneer pieces gently, making sure
they do not crumble. Mix carefully.

• Serve chilled.

Corn Salad

Serves 24

Ingredients

2 tsp refined vegetable oil

½ tsp cumin seeds

1 large onion, finely chopped

2 green chillies, finely chopped

1 tomato, finely chopped

400g/14oz boiled corn kernels

Salt to taste

2 tsp lemon juice

1 tsp chaat masala*

1 tbsp coriander leaves, finely chopped

Method

- Heat the oil in a saucepan. Add the cumin seeds. Let them splutter for 15 seconds.
- Add the onion and fry for a minute.
- Add the chillies, tomato, corn and salt. Cook for a minute, stirring continuously.
- Add the lemon juice, chaat masala and coriander leaves.
- Serve at room temperature.

Stir-Fried Salad

Serves 4

Ingredients

2 tsp refined vegetable oil

100g/3½oz mushrooms, sliced

100g/3½oz baby corn, sliced lengthwise

1 green pepper, cored, deseeded and sliced

½ tsp ground black pepper

2 green chillies, slit lengthways

Salt to taste

1 tomato, finely sliced

1 tsp lemon juice

Method

- Heat the oil in a saucepan. Add the mushrooms, baby corn and green pepper. Stir-fry on a high heat for 2 minutes.
- Add the remaining ingredients. Cook for another minute on a medium heat. Serve warm.

Spinach Salad

Serves 4

Ingredients

200g/7oz spinach, chopped

1.5 litres/2¾ pints salted hot water

1½ tbsp clear honey

½ tbsp roasted sesame seeds

½ tbsp lemon juice

Salt to taste

Method

- Soak the spinach in the water for 2 minutes and drain completely.
- Add all the remaining ingredients to the spinach. Mix well.
- Serve chilled.

Prawn Salad

Serves 4

Ingredients

250g/9oz prawns, shelled and de-veined

Salt to taste

1 tbsp lemon juice

750 ml/1¼fl oz water

50g/1¾oz spring onions, finely chopped

10g/¼oz coriander leaves, finely chopped

3 tsp chaat masala*

2 green chillies, finely chopped

1 tomato, finely chopped

1 green pepper, finely chopped

Method

- Boil the prawns in a saucepan with the salt, lemon juice and water on a medium heat for 10 minutes. Drain and cool.
- Mix thoroughly with all the other ingredients in a bowl.
- Serve chilled.

RAITA

These yoghurt-based side dishes are integral to a complete Indian meal. The cool yoghurt brings a much-needed respite from the fiery flavours, making raitas a great complement to hot curries. Raitas are made by blending yoghurt with dry spices, fruit and/or vegetables. Some raitas are very sweet like the Mango Raita and some are tangy like the Mixed Fruit Raita. Each region has its own special ingredients and there is a delightful array to choose from.

Pineapple & Honey Raita

Serves 4

Ingredients
250g/9oz pineapple, diced
85g/3oz mixed nuts
  (cashew nuts, pistachios
  and walnuts)
1 tsp honey
450g/1lb yoghurt
Salt to taste

Method
- Mix all the ingredients together in a bowl.
- Serve chilled.

Mango Raita

Serves 4

Ingredients
450g/1lb ripe mangoes,
  peeled and diced
450g/1lb yoghurt
¼ tsp saffron, soaked in
  1 tbsp milk
Salt to taste

Method
- Mix all the ingredients together in a bowl.
- Serve chilled.

Apple Walnut Raita

Serves 4

Ingredients
2 apples, cored and diced
85g/3oz walnuts, chopped
350g/12oz yoghurt
Salt to taste

Method
- Mix all the ingredients together in a bowl.
- Serve chilled.

Bottle Gourd Raita

Serves 4

Ingredients

1 bottle gourd*, peeled and grated
350g/12oz yoghurt
½ tsp ground black pepper

1 tbsp coriander leaves,
  finely chopped
Salt to taste

Method
- Steam (see cooking techniques) the bottle gourd till soft.
- Squeeze out the excess water and mix with the remaining ingredients. Serve chilled.

Cucumber Raita

Serves 4

Ingredients

1 large cucumber, grated
450g/1lb yoghurt
2 green chillies, slit lengthways

1 tbsp ready-made mustard
Salt to taste

Method
- Squeeze out the excess water from the cucumber.
- Add all the remaining ingredients. Mix well. Serve chilled.

Carrot Raita

Serves 4

Ingredients

2 large carrots, finely grated
450g/1lb yoghurt
2 green chillies, slit lengthways

2 tbsp roasted peanuts
1 tsp sugar (optional)
Salt to taste

Method
- Mix all the ingredients well in a bowl. Serve chilled.

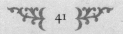

Mustard Raita

Serves 4

Ingredients
450g/1lb yoghurt
2 tsp ground mustard
1 green chilli,
  finely chopped
½ tsp ground
  black pepper
Salt to taste

Method
- In a bowl, whisk the yoghurt with all the other ingredients.
- Serve chilled.

Spring Onion Raita

Serves 4

Ingredients
100g/3½oz spring onions,
  chopped
350g/12oz yoghurt
1 tbsp coriander leaves,
  finely chopped
1 green chilli,
  finely chopped
Salt to taste

Method
- Mix all the ingredients well in a bowl.
- Serve chilled.

Pineapple Raita

Serves 4

Ingredients
100g/3½oz canned
  pineapple pieces, diced
450g/1lb yoghurt
Salt to taste

Method
- Mix all the ingredients well in a bowl.
- Serve chilled.

Potato Raita

Serves 4

Ingredients

2 large potatoes, boiled and diced
450g/1lb yoghurt
1 tsp chaat masala*

1 tbsp coriander leaves, chopped
1 small onion, finely grated (optional)
Salt to taste

Method
• Mix all the ingredients well in a bowl. Serve chilled.

Spinach Raita

Serves 4

Ingredients

100g/3½oz spinach leaves, finely
  chopped
250ml/8fl oz hot water
450g/1lb Greek yoghurt

Pinch of chaat masala*
2 green chillies, slit lengthways
Salt to taste

Method
• Soak the spinach leaves in the hot water for 5 minutes. Drain out the
  water and mix the spinach with the remaining ingredients. Serve chilled.

Mixed Fruit Raita

Serves 4

Ingredients

1 apple, cored and diced
20 green grapes
1 orange, de-seeded and diced

450g/1lb yoghurt
1 tsp chaat masala*
Salt to taste

Method
• Mix all the ingredients well in a bowl. Serve chilled.

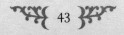

Banana Raita

Serves 4

Ingredients

2 large ripe bananas, peeled
  and sliced

350g/12oz yoghurt

2 tsp caster sugar

¼ tsp grated nutmeg

¼ tsp green cardamom seeds, ground

A pinch of salt

Method

• Mix all the ingredients well in a bowl. Serve chilled.

Guava Raita

Serves 4

Ingredients

1 large ripe guava, peeled and diced

450g/1lb yoghurt

1 tsp ground cumin, dry roasted
  (see cooking techniques)

1 green chilli, slit lengthways

¼ tsp ground black pepper

1 tsp caster sugar

Salt to taste

Method

• Mix all the ingredients well in a bowl. Serve chilled.

Garlic Raita

Serves 4

Ingredients

2 green chillies

5 garlic cloves

450g/1lb yoghurt, whisked

Salt to taste

Method

• Dry roast (see cooking techniques) the chillies till they turn light brown.
  Grind them with the garlic.

• Mix with the remaining ingredients. Serve chilled.

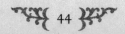

Mixed Vegetable Raita

Serves 4

Ingredients

1 large potato, finely diced and boiled

25g/scant 1oz French beans, finely diced and boiled

25g/scant 1oz carrots, finely diced and boiled

50g/1¾oz boiled peas

450g/1lb yoghurt

½ tsp ground black pepper

1 tbsp coriander leaves, finely chopped

Salt to taste

Method

- Mix all the ingredients well in a bowl. Serve chilled.

Boondi Raita

Serves 4

Ingredients

115g/4oz salted boondi*

450g/1lb yoghurt

½ tsp sugar

½ tsp chaat masala*

Method

- Mix all the ingredients well in a bowl. Serve chilled.

Cauliflower Raita

Serves 4

Ingredients

250g/9oz cauliflower, chopped into tiny florets, or grated

Salt to taste

½ tsp ground black pepper

½ tsp chilli powder

½ tsp ground mustard

450g/1lb yoghurt

1 tsp ghee

½ tsp mustard seeds

Chaat masala* to taste

Method

- Mix the cauliflower with salt and steam (see cooking techniques) the mixture.
- Whisk the pepper, chilli powder, mustard, salt and yoghurt in a bowl.
- Add the cauliflower mixture to the yoghurt mixture and set aside.
- Heat the ghee in a small saucepan. When it begins to smoke, add the mustard seeds. Let them splutter for 15 seconds.
- Add this with the chaat masala to the yoghurt mixture. Serve chilled.

Cabbage Raita

Serves 4

Ingredients

100g/3½oz cabbage, grated

Salt to taste

1 tbsp coriander leaves, finely chopped

2 tsp grated coconut

450g/1lb yoghurt

1 tsp oil

½ tsp mustard seeds

3-4 curry leaves

Method

- Steam (see cooking techniques) the cabbage with salt. Let it cool down.
- Add the coriander leaves, coconut and yoghurt. Mix well. Set aside.
- Heat the oil in a small saucepan. Add the mustard seeds and curry leaves. Let them splutter for 15 seconds.
- Pour this in the yoghurt mixture. Serve chilled.

Beetroot Raita

Serves 4

Ingredients

1 large beetroot, boiled and grated
450g/1lb yoghurt
½ tsp sugar
Salt to taste
1 tsp ghee

½ tsp cumin seeds
1 green chilli, slit lengthways
1 tbsp coriander leaves,
  finely chopped

Method

* Mix the beetroot, yoghurt, sugar and salt in a bowl.
* Heat the ghee in a saucepan. Add the cumin seeds and green chilli.
  Let them splutter for 15 seconds. Add this to the beetroot-yoghurt mixture.
* Transfer to a serving bowl and garnish with the coriander leaves.
* Serve chilled.

Sprouted Pulses Raita

Serves 4

Ingredients

75g/2½oz bean sprouts
75g/2½oz sprouted kaala chana*
75g/2½oz sprouted chickpeas
1 cucumber, finely chopped
10g/¼oz coriander leaves,
  finely chopped

2 tsp chaat masala*
½ tsp sugar
450g/1lb yoghurt

Method

* Steam (see cooking techniques) the bean sprouts for 5 minutes. Set
  aside.
* Boil the kaala chana and chickpeas along with some water on a medium
  heat in a saucepan for 30 minutes. Set aside.
* Mix the bean sprouts with all the remaining ingredients. Mix well. Drain
  and add the kaala chana and chickpeas.
* Serve chilled.

Pasta Pudina Raita

Serves 4

Ingredients
200g/7oz pasta, boiled

1 large cucumber, finely chopped

450g/1lb yoghurt, whisked

2 tsp ready-made mustard

50g/1¾oz mint leaves, finely chopped

Salt to taste

Method
- Mix all the ingredients together. Serve chilled.

Mint Raita

Serves 4

Ingredients
50g/1¾oz mint leaves

25g/scant 1oz coriander leaves

1 green chilli

2 garlic cloves

450g/1lb yoghurt

1 tsp chaat masala*

1 tsp caster sugar

Salt to taste

Method
- Grind together the mint leaves, coriander leaves, green chilli and garlic.
- Mix with the other ingredients in a bowl.
- Serve chilled.

Aubergine Raita

Serves 4

Ingredients
1 large aubergine

450g/1lb yoghurt

1 large onion,
  finely grated

2 green chillies,
  finely chopped

10g/¼oz coriander leaves,
  finely chopped

Salt to taste

Method
- Pierce the aubergine all over with a fork. Roast in the oven at 180°C (350°F, Gas Mark 4) turning it occasionally, till the skin is charred.
- Soak the aubergine in a bowl of water to cool it down. Drain the water and peel off the aubergine skin.
- Mash the aubergine till smooth. Mix with all the other ingredients.
- Serve chilled.

Saffron Raita

Serves 4

Ingredients
350g/12oz yoghurt

1 tsp saffron, soaked in
  2 tbsp milk for
  30 minutes

25g/scant 1oz raisins,
  soaked in water for 2
  hours

75g/2½oz roasted almonds
  and pistachios,
  finely chopped

1 tbsp caster sugar

Method
- In a bowl, whisk the yoghurt with the saffron.
- Add all the other ingredients. Mix well.
- Serve chilled.

Yam Raita

Serves 4

Ingredients

250g/9oz yams*

Salt to taste

¼ tsp chilli powder

¼ tsp ground black pepper

350g/12oz yoghurt

1 tsp ghee

½ tsp cumin seeds

2 green chillies, slit lengthways

1 tbsp coriander leaves, finely chopped

Method

- Peel and grate the yams. Add some salt and steam (see cooking techniques) the mixture till soft. Set aside.
- In a bowl, mix the salt, chilli powder and ground pepper with the yoghurt.
- Add the yam to the yoghurt mixture. Set aside.
- Heat the ghee in a small saucepan. Add the cumin seeds and green chillies. Let them splutter for 15 seconds.
- Add this to the yoghurt mixture. Mix gently.
- Garnish with the coriander leaves. Serve chilled.

Okra Raita

Serves 4

Ingredients

250g/9oz okra, finely chopped

Salt to taste

½ tsp chilli powder

½ tsp turmeric

Refined vegetable oil for deep frying

350g/12oz yoghurt

1 tsp chaat masala*

Method

- Rub the okra pieces with the salt, chilli powder and turmeric.
- Heat the oil in a saucepan. Deep fry the okra on a medium heat for 3-4 minutes. Drain on absorbent paper. Set aside.
- In a bowl, whisk the yoghurt with the chaat masala and salt.
- Add the fried okra to the yoghurt mixture.
- Serve chilled or at room temperature.

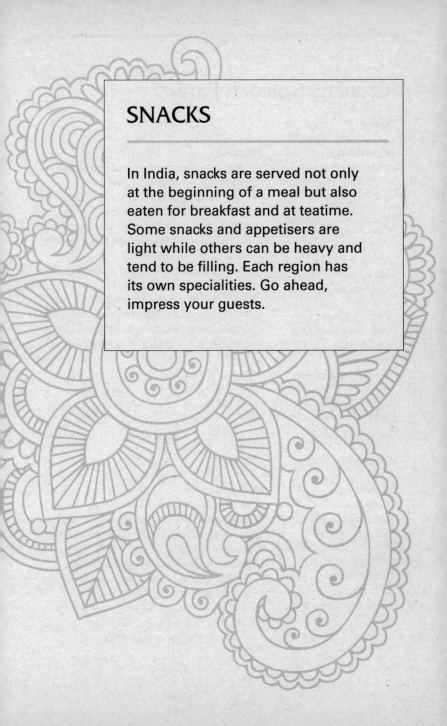

SNACKS

In India, snacks are served not only at the beginning of a meal but also eaten for breakfast and at teatime. Some snacks and appetisers are light while others can be heavy and tend to be filling. Each region has its own specialities. Go ahead, impress your guests.

Crunchy Spinach Patty

Makes 12

Ingredients

1 tbsp refined vegetable oil plus extra for deep frying

1 large onion, finely chopped

50g/1¾oz spinach, boiled and finely chopped

1 tsp garlic paste

1 tsp ginger paste

Salt to taste

300g/10oz paneer*, chopped

2 eggs, whisked

2 tbsp plain white flour

Pepper to taste

Salt to taste

50g/1¾oz breadcrumbs

Method

- Heat the oil in a frying pan. Fry the onion on a medium heat till translucent.
- Add the spinach, garlic paste, ginger paste and salt. Cook for 2-3 minutes.
- Remove from the heat and add the paneer. Mix well and divide into square patties. Cover with foil and refrigerate for 30 minutes.
- Mix the eggs, flour, pepper and salt together to form a smooth batter.
- Heat the remaining oil in a frying pan. Dip each paneer patty into the batter, roll in the breadcrumbs and deep fry till golden brown.
- Serve hot with dry garlic chutney (see page 21).

Rava Dosa
(Semolina Crêpe)

Makes 10-12

Ingredients

100g/3½oz semolina

85g/3oz plain white flour

Pinch of bicarbonate of soda

250g/9oz yoghurt

240ml/8fl oz water

Salt to taste

Refined vegetable oil for greasing

Method

- Blend all the ingredients, except the oil, together to form a batter of a pancake-mix consistency. Set aside for 20-30 minutes.
- Grease and heat a flat pan. Pour 2 tbsp of batter in it. Spread by lifting the pan and rotating it gently.
- Pour some oil around the edges.
- Cook for 3 minutes. Flip and cook till crisp.
- Repeat for the remaining batter.
- Serve hot with coconut chutney (see page 20).

Doodhi Cutlet
(Bottle Gourd Cutlet)

Makes 20

Ingredients

1 tbsp refined vegetable oil plus extra for frying

1 large onion, chopped

4 green chillies, finely chopped

2.5cm/1in root ginger, grated

1 large bottle gourd*, peeled and grated

Salt to taste

2 eggs, whisked

100g/3½oz breadcrumbs

For the white sauce:

2 tbsp margarine/butter

4 tbsp flour

Salt to taste

Pepper to taste

1 tbsp cream

Method

• For the white sauce, heat the margarine/butter in a saucepan. Add all the remaining white sauce ingredients and stir on a medium heat till thick and creamy. Set aside.

• Heat the oil in a frying pan. Fry the onion, green chillies and ginger on a medium heat for 2-3 minutes.

• Add the bottle gourd and salt. Mix well. Cover with a lid and cook for 15-20 minutes on a medium heat.

• Uncover and mash the bottle gourd well. Add the white sauce and half the whisked eggs. Set aside for 20 minutes to harden and set.

• Chop the mixture into cutlets.

• Heat the oil in a saucepan. Dip each cutlet in the remaining whisked egg, roll in the breadcrumbs and deep fry till golden brown.

• Serve hot with sweet tomato chutney (see page 8).

Patra
(Colocasia Leaf Pinwheel)

Makes 20

Ingredients
10 colocasia leaves*
2 tbsp refined vegetable oil
½ tsp mustard seeds
1 tsp sesame seeds
1 tsp cumin seeds
8 curry leaves
2 tbsp coriander leaves,
   finely chopped

For the batter:
250g/9oz besan*
4 tbsp jaggery*, grated
1 tsp tamarind paste
½ tsp ginger paste
½ tsp garlic paste
1 tsp chilli powder
½ tsp turmeric
Salt to taste

Method
* Mix all the batter ingredients to form a thick batter.
* Spread a layer of the batter on each colocasia leaf to cover it completely.
* Place 5 coated leaves one above the other.
* Fold the leaves 2.5cm/1in from each corner to form a square. Roll this square into a cylinder.
* Repeat for the other 5 leaves.
* Steam the rolls (see cooking techniques) for about 20-25 minutes. Set aside to cool.
* Slice each roll into pinwheel-like shapes. Set aside.
* Heat the oil in a saucepan. Add the mustard, sesame seeds, cumin seeds and curry leaves. Let them splutter for 15 seconds.
* Pour this over the pinwheels.
* Garnish with the coriander leaves. Serve hot.

Nargisi Chicken Kebab
(Chicken and Cheese Kebab)

Makes 20-25

Ingredients

500g/1lb 2oz chicken, minced
150g/5½oz grated Cheddar cheese
2 large onions, finely chopped
1 tsp ginger paste
1 tsp garlic paste
1 tsp ground cardamom
2 tsp garam masala

1 tsp ground coriander
½ tsp turmeric
½ tsp chilli powder
Salt to taste
15-20 raisins
Refined vegetable oil for deep frying

Method

- Knead all the ingredients, except the raisins and oil, into a dough.
- Make small dumplings. Place a raisin in the centre of each dumpling.
- Heat the oil in a frying pan. Fry the dumplings on a medium heat till golden brown. Serve hot with mint chutney (see page 15).

Sev Puris with Savoury Topping

Serves 4

Ingredients

24 sev puris*
2 potatoes, diced and boiled
1 large onion, finely chopped
¼ small unripe green mango, finely chopped
120ml/4fl oz hot and sour chutney (see page 12)

4 tbsp mint chutney (see page 15)
1 tsp chaat masala*
Juice of 1 lemon
Salt to taste
150g/5½oz sev*
2 tbsp coriander leaves, chopped

Method

- Arrange the puris on a serving plate.
- Place small portions of the potatoes, onion and mango on each puri.
- Sprinkle the hot and sour chutney and mint chutney on top of each puri.
- Sprinkle the chaat masala, lemon juice and salt on top.
- Garnish with the sev and coriander leaves. Serve immediately.

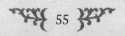

Special Roll

Makes 4

Ingredients

1 tsp yeast

Pinch of sugar

240ml/8fl oz warm water

350g/12oz plain white flour

½ tsp baking powder

2 tbsp butter

1 large onion, finely chopped

2 tomatoes, finely chopped

30g/1oz mint leaves, finely chopped

200g/7oz spinach, boiled

300g/10oz paneer*, diced

Salt to taste

Ground black pepper to taste

125g/4½oz tomato purée

1 egg, whisked

Method

- Dissolve the yeast and sugar in the water.
- Sieve the flour and baking powder together. Mix with the yeast and knead into a dough.
- With a rolling pin, roll out the dough into 2 chapattis. Set aside.
- Heat half the butter in a saucepan. Add the onion, tomatoes, mint leaves, spinach, paneer, salt and black pepper. Sauté on a medium heat for 3 minutes.
- Spread this over 1 chapatti. Pour the tomato purée on top and cover with the other chapatti. Seal the ends.
- Brush the chapattis with the egg and remaining butter.
- Bake in an oven at 150°C (300°F, Gas Mark 2) for 10 minutes. Serve hot.

Fried Colocasia

Serves 4

Ingredients

500g/1lb 2 oz colocasia*
2 tbsp ground coriander
1 tbsp ground cumin
1 tbsp amchoor*
2 tsp besan*

Salt to taste
Refined vegetable oil for frying
Chaat masala*, to taste
1 tbsp coriander leaves, chopped
½ tsp lemon juice

Method

* Boil the colocasia in a saucepan for 15 minutes on a low heat. Cool, peel, cut lengthways and flatten. Set aside.
* Mix the ground coriander, ground cumin, amchoor, besan and salt. Roll the colocasia pieces in this mixture. Set aside.
* Heat the oil in a saucepan. Deep fry the colocasia till crisp, then drain.
* Sprinkle with the remaining ingredients. Serve hot.

Mixed Dhal Dosa
(Mixed Lentil Crêpe)

Makes 8-10

Ingredients

250g/9oz rice, soaked for 5-6 hours
100g/3½oz mung dhal*, soaked for 5-6 hours
100g/3½oz chana dhal*, soaked for 5-6 hours
100g/3½oz urad dhal*, soaked for 5-6 hours

2 tbsp yoghurt
½ tsp bicarbonate of soda
2 tbsp refined vegetable oil plus extra for frying
Salt to taste

Method

* Wet grind (see cooking techniques) the rice and the dhals separately. Mix together. Add the yoghurt, bicarbonate of soda, oil and salt. Whisk till fluffy and light. Set aside for 3-4 hours.
* Grease and heat a flat pan. Pour 2 tbsp of batter over it and spread like a crêpe. Pour some oil around the edges. Cook for 2 minutes. Serve hot.

Makkai Cakes
(Corn Cakes)

Makes 12-15

Ingredients

4 fresh corn cobs

2 tbsp butter

750ml/1¼ pints milk

½ tsp chilli powder

Salt to taste

Ground black pepper to taste

25g/scant 1oz coriander leaves, chopped

50g/1¾oz breadcrumbs

Method

- Remove the kernels from the corn cobs and grind them coarsely.
- Heat the butter in a saucepan and fry the ground corn for 2-3 minutes on a medium heat. Add the milk and simmer till dry.
- Add the chilli powder, salt, black pepper and coriander leaves.
- Add the breadcrumbs and mix well. Divide the mixture into small patties.
- Heat the butter in a frying pan. Shallow fry the patties till golden brown. Serve hot with ketchup.

Hara Bhara Kebab
(Green Vegetable Kebab)

Serves 4

Ingredients

300g/10oz chana dhal*, soaked overnight

2 green cardamom pods

2.5cm/1in cinnamon

Salt to taste

60ml/2fl oz water

200g/7oz spinach, steamed (see cooking techniques) and ground

½ tsp garam masala

¼ tsp mace, grated

Refined vegetable oil to shallow fry

Method

- Drain the dhal. Add the cardamom, cloves, cinnamon, salt and water. Cook in a saucepan on a medium heat till soft. Grind to a paste.
- Add all the remaining ingredients, except the oil. Mix well. Divide the mixture into lemon-sized balls and flatten each into small patties.
- Heat the oil in a frying pan. Shallow fry the patties over a medium heat till golden brown. Serve hot with mint chutney (see page 15).

Fish Pakoda
(Battered Fried Fish)

Makes 12

Ingredients

300g/10oz boneless fish, chopped into 2.5cm/1in pieces

Salt to taste

2 tsp lemon juice

3 tbsp water

250g/9oz besan*

1 tsp garlic paste

2 green chillies, finely chopped

1 tsp garam masala

½ tsp turmeric

Refined vegetable oil for deep frying

Method
- Marinate the fish with the salt and lemon juice for 20 minutes.
- Mix the remaining ingredients, except the oil, to make a thick batter.
- Heat the oil in a saucepan. Dip each piece of fish in the batter and fry till golden. Drain on absorbent paper. Serve hot.

Shammi Kebab
(Mince and Bengal Gram Kebab)

Makes 35

Ingredients

750g/1lb 10oz chicken, minced

600g/1lb 5oz chana dhal*

3 large onions, chopped

1 tsp ginger paste

1 tsp garlic paste

2.5cm/1in cinnamon

4 cloves

2 black cardamom pods

7 peppercorns

1 tsp ground cumin

Salt to taste

450ml/15fl oz water

2 eggs, whisked

Refined vegetable oil for frying

Method
- Mix together all the ingredients, except the eggs and oil. Boil in a saucepan till all the water evaporates. Grind to a thick paste.
- Add the eggs to the paste. Mix well. Divide the mixture into 35 patties.
- Heat the oil in a frying pan. Fry the patties on a low heat till golden.
- Serve hot with mint chutney (see page 15).

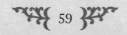

Basic Dhokla
(Basic Steamed Cake)

Makes 18-20

Ingredients
250g/9oz rice
450g/1lb chana dhal*
60g/2oz yoghurt
¼ tsp bicarbonate of soda
6 green chillies, chopped
1cm/½in root ginger, grated
¼ tsp ground coriander
¼ tsp ground cumin
½ tsp turmeric
Salt to taste
½ coconut, grated
150g/5½oz coriander leaves, finely chopped
1 tbsp refined vegetable oil
½ tsp mustard seeds

Method
- Soak the rice and dhal together for 6 hours. Grind coarsely.
- Add the yoghurt and bicarbonate of soda. Mix well. Let the paste ferment for 6-8 hours.
- Add the green chillies, ginger, ground coriander, ground cumin, turmeric and salt to the batter. Mix thoroughly.
- Pour into a 20cm/8in round cake tin. Steam (see cooking techniques) the batter for 10 minutes.
- Cool and chop into square pieces. Sprinkle the grated coconut and coriander leaves over them. Set aside.
- Heat the oil in a saucepan. Add the mustard seeds. Let them splutter for 15 seconds.
- Pour this over the dhoklas. Serve hot.

Adai
(Rice and Lentil Crêpe)

Makes 12

Ingredients
125g/4½oz rice
75g/2½oz urad dhal*
75g/2½oz chana dhal*
75g/2½oz masoor dhal*
75g/2½oz mung dhal*
6 red chillies
Salt to taste
240ml/8fl oz water
Refined vegetable oil for greasing

Method
- Soak the rice with all the dhals overnight.
- Drain the mixture and add the red chillies, salt and water. Grind until smooth.
- Grease and heat a flat pan. Spread 3 tbsp of the batter on it. Cover and cook on a medium heat for 2-3 minutes. Flip and cook the other side.
- Remove carefully with a spatula. Repeat for the rest of the batter. Serve hot.

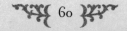

Double Decker Dhokla
(Steamed Double Decker Cake)

Makes 20

Ingredients
500g/1lb 2oz rice
300g/10oz urad beans*
75g/2½oz urad dhal*
75g/2½oz chana dhal*
75g/2½oz masoor dhal*
2 green chillies
500g/1lb 2oz yoghurt
1 tsp chilli powder
½ tsp turmeric
Salt to taste
115g/4oz mint chutney (see page 15)

Method
* Mix the rice and urad beans. Soak overnight.
* Mix all the dhals. Soak overnight.
* Drain and grind the rice mixture and the dhal mixture separately. Set aside.
* Mix the green chillies, yoghurt, chilli powder, turmeric and salt together. Add half of this blend to the rice mixture and add the remaining to the dhal mixture. Allow to ferment for 6 hours.
* Grease a 20cm/8in round cake tin. Pour the rice mixture into it. Sprinkle the mint chutney on top of the rice mixture. Pour the dhal mixture on top.
* Steam (see cooking techniques) for 7-8 minutes. Chop and serve hot.

Ulundu Vada
(Fried Doughnut-shaped Snack)

Makes 12

Ingredients
600g/1lb 5oz urad dhal*, soaked overnight and drained
4 green chillies, finely chopped
Salt to taste
3 tbsp water
Refined vegetable oil for deep frying

Method
* Grind the dhal with the green chillies, salt and water.
* Shape the mixture into doughnuts.
* Heat the oil in a saucepan. Add the vadas and deep fry on a medium heat till brown.
* Drain on absorbent paper. Serve hot with coconut chutney (see page 20).

Bhakar Wadi
(Spicy Gram Flour Pinwheel)

Serves 4

Ingredients

500g/1lb 2oz besan*

175g/6oz wholemeal flour

Salt to taste

Pinch of asafoetida

120ml/4fl oz warm refined vegetable oil plus extra for deep frying

100g/3½oz desiccated coconut

1 tsp sesame seeds

1 tsp poppy seeds

Pinch of sugar

1 tsp chilli powder

25g/scant 1oz coriander leaves, finely chopped

1 tbsp tamarind paste

Method

- Knead the besan, flour, salt, asafoetida, warm oil and enough water into a stiff dough. Set aside.
- Dry roast (see cooking techniques) the coconut, sesame seeds and poppy seeds for 3-5 minutes. Grind to a powder.
- Add the sugar, salt, chilli powder, coriander leaves and tamarind paste to the powder and mix thoroughly to prepare the filling. Set aside.
- Divide the dough into lemon-sized balls. Roll each into a thin disc.
- Spread the filling on each disc so that the filling covers the entire disc. Roll each into a tight cylinder. Seal the edges with a little water.
- Slice the cylinders to get pinwheel-like shapes.
- Heat the oil in a saucepan. Add the pinwheel rolls and fry on a medium heat till crisp.
- Drain on absorbent paper. Store in an airtight container once cooled.

NOTE: *These can be stored for a fortnight.*

Mangalorean Chaat

Serves 4

Ingredients

75g/2½oz chana dhal*

240ml/8fl oz water

Salt to taste

Large pinch of bicarbonate of soda

2 large potatoes, finely chopped and boiled

350g/12oz fresh yoghurt

2 tbsp caster sugar

4 tbsp refined vegetable oil

1 tbsp dried fenugreek leaves

1 tsp ginger paste

1 tsp garlic paste

2 green chillies

1 tsp ground cumin, dry roasted (see cooking techniques)

1 tsp garam masala

1 tbsp amchoor*

1 tsp turmeric

½ tsp chilli powder

150g/5½oz canned chickpeas

1 large onion, finely chopped

2 tbsp coriander leaves, finely chopped

Method

- Cook the dhal with the water, salt and bicarbonate of soda in a saucepan on a medium heat for 30 minutes. Add more water if the dhal feels too dry. Mix the potatoes with the dhal mixture and set aside.
- Whisk the yoghurt with the sugar. Place in the freezer to chill.
- Heat the oil in a saucepan. Add the fenugreek leaves and fry on a medium heat for 3-4 minutes.
- Add the ginger paste, garlic paste, green chillies, ground cumin, garam masala, amchoor, turmeric and chilli powder. Fry for 2-3 minutes, stirring continuously.
- Add the chickpeas. Sauté for 5 minutes, stirring continuously. Add the dhal mixture and mix well.
- Remove from the heat and spread the mixture on a serving platter.
- Pour the sweet yoghurt on top.
- Sprinkle with the onion and coriander leaves. Serve immediately.

Pani Puri

Makes 30

Ingredients
For the puris:
175g/6oz plain white flour

100g/3½oz semolina

Salt to taste

Refined vegetable oil
  for deep frying

For the stuffing:
50g/1¾oz sprouted mung
  beans

150g/5½oz sprouted
  chickpeas

Salt to taste

2 large potatoes, boiled
  and mashed

For the pani:
2 tbsp tamarind paste

100g/3½oz coriander
  leaves, finely chopped

1½ tsp ground cumin, dry
  roasted (see cooking
  techniques)

2-4 green chillies,
  finely chopped

2.5cm/1in root ginger

Rock salt to taste

240ml/8fl oz water

Method
- Knead all the puri ingredients, except the oil, with enough water to form a stiff dough.
- Roll out into small puris of 5cm/2in diameter.
- Heat the oil in a frying pan. Deep fry the puris till light brown. Set aside.
- For the stuffing, parboil the sprouted mung beans and chickpeas with the salt. Mix with the potatoes. Set aside.
- For the pani, grind together all the pani ingredients, except the water.
- Add this mixture to the water. Mix well and set aside.
- To serve, make a hole in each puri and fill it with the stuffing. Pour 3 tbsp of the pani into each and serve immediately.

Stuffed Spinach Egg

Serves 4

Ingredients

200g/7oz spinach

Pinch of bicarbonate
  of soda

1 tbsp refined vegetable oil

1 tsp cumin seeds

6 garlic cloves, crushed

2 green chillies, ground

Salt to taste

8 hard boiled eggs, halved
  lengthways

1 tbsp ghee

1 onion, finely chopped

2.5cm/1in root ginger,
  chopped

Method

- Mix the spinach with the bicarbonate of soda. Steam (see cooking techniques) till tender. Grind and set aside.
- Heat the oil in a saucepan. When it begins to smoke, add the cumin seeds, garlic and green chillies. Stir-fry for a few seconds. Add the steamed spinach and salt.
- Cover with a lid and cook till dry. Set aside.
- Scoop the yolks out from the eggs. Add the egg yolks to the spinach mixture. Mix well.
- Place spoonfuls of the spinach-egg mixture in the hollow egg whites. Set aside.
- Heat the ghee in a small frying pan. Fry the onion and ginger till golden brown.
- Sprinkle this on top of the eggs. Serve hot.

Sada Dosa
(Savoury Rice Crêpe)

Makes 15

Ingredients

100g/3½oz parboiled rice
  (see cooking techniques)

75g/2½oz urad dhal*

½ tsp fenugreek seeds

½ tsp bicarbonate of soda

Salt to taste

125g/4½oz yoghurt,
  whipped

60ml/2fl oz refined
  vegetable oil

Method

- Soak the rice and the dhal together with the fenugreek seeds for 7-8 hours.
- Drain and grind the mixture to a grainy paste.
- Add bicarbonate of soda and salt. Mix well.
- Set aside to ferment for 8-10 hours.
- Add the yoghurt to make the batter. This batter should be thick enough to coat a spoon. Add a little water if needed. Set aside.
- Grease and heat a flat pan. Spread a spoonful of the batter over it to make a thin crêpe. Pour 1 tsp oil on top. Cook until crisp. Repeat for the rest of the batter and serve hot.

Potato Samosa

(Potato Savoury)

Makes 20

Ingredients

175g/6oz plain white flour

Pinch of salt

5 tbsp refined vegetable oil
plus extra for deep frying

100ml/3½fl oz water

1cm/½in root ginger,
grated

2 green chillies,
finely chopped

2 garlic cloves,
finely chopped

½ tsp ground coriander

1 large onion,
finely chopped

2 large potatoes, boiled
and mashed

1 tbsp coriander leaves,
finely chopped

1 tbsp lemon juice

½ tsp turmeric

1 tsp chilli powder

½ tsp garam masala

Salt to taste

Method

- Mix the flour with the salt, 2 tbsp oil and water. Knead into a pliable dough. Cover with a moist cloth and set aside for 15-20 minutes.
- Knead the dough again. Cover with a moist cloth and set aside.
- For the filling, heat 3 tbsp oil in a frying pan. Add the ginger, green chillies, garlic and ground coriander. Fry for a minute on a medium heat, stirring continuously.
- Add the onion and fry till brown.
- Add the potatoes, coriander leaves, lemon juice, turmeric, chilli powder, garam masala and salt. Mix thoroughly.
- Cook on a low heat for 4 minutes, stirring occasionally. Set aside.
- To make the samosas, divide the dough into 10 balls. Roll out into discs of 12cm/5in diameter. Cut each disc into 2 half-moons.
- Run a moist finger along the diameter of a half-moon. Bring the ends together to make a cone.
- Place a tbsp of the filling in the cone and seal by pressing the edges together. Repeat for all the half-moons.
- Heat the oil in a frying pan. Deep fry the samosas, five at a time, over a low heat till light brown. Drain on absorbent paper.
- Serve hot with mint chutney (see page 15).

Hot Kachori

(Fried Dumpling with Lentil Filling)

Makes 15

Ingredients

250g/9oz plain white flour plus 1 tbsp for the patching

5 tbsp refined vegetable oil plus extra for deep frying

Salt to taste

1.4 litres/2½ pints water plus 1 tbsp for patching

300g/10oz mung dhal*, soaked for 30 minutes

½ tsp ground coriander

½ tsp ground fennel

½ tsp cumin seeds

½ tsp mustard seeds

2-3 pinches of asafoetida

1 tsp garam masala

1 tsp chilli powder

Method

- Mix 250g/9oz flour with 3 tbsp oil, salt and 100ml/3½fl oz of the water. Knead into a soft, pliable dough. Set aside for 30 minutes.
- To make the filling, cook the dhal with the remaining water in a saucepan on a medium heat for 45 minutes. Drain and set aside.
- Heat 2 tbsp oil in a saucepan. When it begins to smoke, add the ground coriander, fennel, cumin seeds, mustard seeds, asafoetida, garam masala, chilli powder and salt. Let them splutter for 30 seconds.
- Add the cooked dhal. Mix well and fry for 2-3 minutes, stirring continuously.
- Cool the dhal mixture and divide into 15 lemon-sized balls. Set aside.
- Mix 1 tbsp flour with 1 tbsp water to make a paste for patching. Set aside.
- Divide the dough into 15 balls. Roll out into discs of 12cm/5in diameter.
- Place 1 ball of the filling in the centre of a disc. Seal like a pouch.
- Flatten slightly by pressing it between the palms. Repeat for the remaining discs.
- Heat the oil in a saucepan until it starts smoking. Deep fry the discs till golden brown on the underside. Flip and repeat.
- If a kachori tears while frying, seal it with the patching paste.
- Drain on absorbent paper. Serve hot with mint chutney (see page 15).

Khandvi
(Besan Roll-Ups)

Makes 10-15

Ingredients

60g/2oz besan*
60g/2oz yoghurt
120ml/4fl oz water
1 tsp turmeric
Salt to taste
5 tbsp refined vegetable oil
1 tbsp fresh coconut, grated
1 tbsp coriander leaves,
  finely chopped

½ tsp mustard seeds
2 pinches of asafoetida
8 curry leaves
2 green chillies, finely chopped
1 tsp sesame seeds

Method

- Mix the besan, yoghurt, water, turmeric and salt together.
- Heat 4 tbsp oil in a frying pan. Add the besan mixture and cook, stirring continuously to make sure no lumps are formed.
- Cook till the mixture leaves the sides of the pan. Set aside.
- Grease two 15 × 35cm/6 × 14in non-stick baking trays. Pour in the besan mixture and smooth flat with a palette knife. Allow to set for 10 minutes.
- Cut the mixture into 5cm/2in wide strips. Carefully roll up each strip.
- Place the rolls in a serving dish. Sprinkle the grated coconut and coriander leaves on top. Set aside.
- Heat 1 tbsp oil in a small saucepan. Add the mustard seeds, asafoetida, curry leaves, green chillies and sesame seeds. Let them splutter for 15 seconds.
- Pour this immediately over the besan rolls. Serve hot or at room temperature.

Makkai Squares
(Corn Squares)

Makes 12

Ingredients

2 tsp ghee

100g/3½oz corn kernels, ground

Salt to taste

125g/4½oz boiled peas

3 tbsp refined vegetable oil

8 green chillies, finely chopped

½ tsp cumin seeds

½ tsp mustard seeds

½ tsp garlic paste

½ tbsp ground coriander

½ tbsp ground cumin

175g/6oz maize flour

175g/6oz wholemeal flour

150ml/5fl oz water

Method

* Heat the ghee in a saucepan. When it begins to smoke, fry the corn for 3 minutes. Set aside.
* Add salt to the boiled peas. Mash the peas well. Set aside.
* Heat 2 tbsp oil in a frying pan. Add the green chillies, cumin and mustard seeds. Let them splutter for 15 seconds.
* Add the fried corn, mashed peas, garlic paste, ground coriander and ground cumin. Mix well. Remove from the heat and set aside.
* Mix both the flours together. Add salt and 1 tbsp oil. Add the water and knead into a soft dough.
* Roll out 24 square shapes, each square 10x10cm/4x4in in size.
* Place the corn and peas mixture in the centre of a square and cover with another square. Gently press the edges of the square to seal.
* Repeat for the rest of the squares.
* Grease and heat a frying pan. Roast the squares on the pan till golden brown.
* Serve hot with ketchup.

Dhal Pakwan
(Crispy Bread with Lentils)

Serves 4

Ingredients
600g/1lb 5oz chana dhal*
3 tbsp refined vegetable oil
1 tsp cumin seeds
750ml/1¼ pints water
Salt to taste
½ tsp turmeric
½ tsp amchoor*
10g/¼oz coriander leaves, finely chopped

For the pakwan:
250g/9oz plain white flour
½ tsp cumin seeds
Salt to taste
Refined vegetable oil for deep frying

Method
- Soak the chana dhal for 4 hours. Drain and set aside.
- Heat the oil in a saucepan. Add the cumin seeds. Let them splutter for 15 seconds.
- Add the soaked dhal, water, salt and turmeric. Simmer for 30 minutes.
- Transfer to a serving dish. Sprinkle with the amchoor and coriander leaves. Set aside.
- Knead all the pakwan ingredients, except the oil, with enough water to make a stiff dough.
- Divide into walnut-sized balls. Roll out into thick discs, 10cm/4in in diameter. Pierce all over with a fork.
- Heat the oil in a frying pan. Deep fry the discs till golden. Drain on absorbent paper.
- Serve the pakwans with the hot dhal.

Spicy Sev
(Spicy Gram Flour Flakes)

Serves 4

Ingredients
500g/1lb 2oz besan*
1 tsp ajowan seeds
1 tbsp refined vegetable oil plus extra for deep frying
¼ tsp asafoetida
Salt to taste
200ml/7fl oz water

Method
- Knead the besan with the ajowan seeds, oil, asafoetida, salt and water into a sticky dough.
- Put the dough in a piping bag.
- Heat the oil in a saucepan. Press the dough through the nozzle in the form of noodles into the pan and fry lightly on both sides.
- Drain well and cool before storing.

NOTE: *This can be stored for a fortnight.*

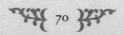

Stuffed Veggie Crescents

Makes 6

Ingredients

350g/12oz plain white flour

6 tbsp warm refined vegetable oil plus extra for deep frying

Salt to taste

1 tomato, sliced

For the filling:

3 tbsp refined vegetable oil

200g/7oz peas

1 carrot, julienned

100g/3½oz French beans, chopped into thin strips

4 tbsp fresh coconut, grated

3 green chillies

2.5cm/1in root ginger, crushed

4 tsp coriander leaves, finely chopped

2 tsp sugar

2 tsp lemon juice

Salt to taste

Method

- First make the filling. Heat the oil in a saucepan. Add the peas, carrot and French beans and fry, stirring continuously, till soft.
- Add all the remaining filling ingredients and mix well. Set aside.
- Mix the flour with the oil and the salt. Knead into a stiff dough.
- Divide the dough into 6 lemon-sized balls.
- Roll each ball into a disc of 10cm/4in diameter.
- Place the vegetable filling on one half of a disc. Fold the other half over to cover the filling and press the edges together to seal.
- Repeat for all the discs.
- Heat the oil in a saucepan. Add the crescents and fry till they are golden brown.
- Arrange them in a round serving dish and garnish with the tomato slices. Serve immediately.

Kachori Usal
(Fried Bread with Chickpeas)

Serves 4

Ingredients
For the pastry:

50g/1¾oz fenugreek leaves
finely chopped

175g/6oz wholemeal flour

2 green chillies,
finely chopped

1 tsp ginger paste

¼ tsp turmeric

100ml/3½fl oz water

Salt to taste

For the filling:

1 tsp refined vegetable oil

250g/9oz mung beans,
boiled

250g/9oz green chickpeas,
boiled

¼ tsp turmeric

½ tsp chilli powder

1 tsp ground coriander

1 tsp ground cumin

Salt to taste

For the sauce:

2 tsp refined vegetable oil

2 large onions,
finely chopped

2 tomatoes, chopped

1 tsp garlic paste

½ tsp garam masala

¼ tsp chilli powder

Salt to taste

Method

- Mix all the pastry ingredients together. Knead into a firm dough. Set aside.
- For the filling, heat the oil in a frying pan and sauté all the filling ingredients on a medium heat for 5 minutes. Set aside.
- For the sauce, heat the oil in a frying pan. Add all the sauce ingredients. Fry for 5 minutes, stirring occasionally. Set aside.
- Divide the dough into 8 portions. Roll out each portion into a disc of 10cm/4in diameter.
- Place some filling in the centre of a disc. Seal like a pouch and smooth to form a stuffed ball. Repeat for all the discs.
- Steam the balls (see cooking techniques) for 15 minutes.
- Add the balls to the sauce and toss to coat. Cook on a low heat for 5 minutes.
- Serve hot.

Dhal Dhokli
(Gujarati Savoury Snack)

Serves 4

Ingredients
For the dhokli:
175g/6oz wholemeal flour

Pinch of turmeric

¼ tsp chilli powder

½ tsp ajowan seeds

1 tsp refined vegetable oil

100ml/3½fl oz water

For the dhal:
2 tbsp refined vegetable oil

3-4 cloves

5cm/2in cinnamon

1 tsp mustard seeds

300g/10oz masoor dhal*,
  cooked and mashed

½ tsp turmeric

Pinch of asafoetida

1 tbsp tamarind paste

2 tbsp grated jaggery*

60g/2oz peanuts

1 tsp ground coriander

1 tsp ground cumin

½ tsp chilli powder

Salt to taste

25g/scant 1oz coriander
  leaves, finely chopped

Method
- Mix all the dhokli ingredients together. Knead to form a firm dough.
- Divide the dough into 5-6 balls. Roll out into thick discs, 6cm/2.4in in diameter. Set aside for 10 minutes to harden.
- Cut out the dhokli discs into diamond-shaped pieces. Set aside.
- For the dhal, heat the oil in a saucepan. Add the cloves, cinnamon and mustard seeds. Let them splutter for 15 seconds.
- Add all the remaining dhal ingredients, except the coriander leaves. Mix well. Cook on a high heat till the dhal starts boiling.
- Add the dhokli pieces to the boiling dhal. Continue to cook over a low heat for 10 minutes.
- Garnish with the coriander leaves. Serve hot.

Misal

(Healthy Sprouted Beans Snack)

Serves 4

Ingredients

3-4 tbsp refined vegetable oil

½ tsp mustard seeds

¼ tsp asafoetida

6 curry leaves

1 tsp ginger paste

1 tsp garlic paste

25g/scant 1oz coriander leaves, ground in a blender

1 tsp chilli powder

1 tsp tamarind paste

2 tsp grated jaggery*

Salt to taste

300g/10oz sprouted mung beans, boiled

2 large potatoes, diced and boiled

500ml/16fl oz water

300g/10oz Bombay Mix*

1 large tomato, finely chopped

1 large onion, finely chopped

25g/scant 1oz coriander leaves, finely chopped

4 slices of bread

For the spice mixture:

1 tsp cumin seeds

2 tsp coriander seeds

2 cloves

3 peppercorns

¼ tsp ground cinnamon

Method

* Grind together all the ingredients of the spice mixture. Set aside.
* Heat the oil in a saucepan. Add the mustard seeds, asafoetida and curry leaves. Let them splutter for 2-3 minutes.
* Add the ginger paste, garlic paste, ground coriander leaves, chilli powder, tamarind paste, jaggery and salt. Mix well and cook for 3-4 minutes.
* Add the ground spice mixture. Sauté for 2-3 minutes.
* Add the sprouted beans, potatoes and water. Mix well and simmer for 15 minutes.
* Transfer to a serving bowl and sprinkle with the Bombay Mix, chopped tomato, chopped onion and coriander leaves on top.
* Serve hot with a slice of bread on the side.

Pandori
(Mung Dhal Snack)

Makes 12

Ingredients

1 green chilli, halved lengthways

Salt to taste

1 tsp bicarbonate of soda

¼ tsp asafoetida

250g/9oz whole mung dhal*, soaked for 4 hours

2 tsp refined vegetable oil

2 tsp coriander leaves, finely chopped

Method

- Add the green chilli, salt, bicarbonate of soda and asafoetida to the dhal. Grind to a paste.
- Grease a 20cm/8in round cake tin with the oil and pour the dhal paste in it. Steam (see cooking techniques) for 10 minutes.
- Set the steamed dhal mixture aside for 10 minutes. Once cool, cut into 2.5cm/1in pieces.
- Garnish with the coriander leaves. Serve hot with green coconut chutney (see page 15).

Vegetable Adai
(Vegetable, Rice and Lentil Crêpe)

Makes 8

Ingredients

100g/3½oz parboiled rice (see cooking techniques)

150g/5½oz masoor dhal*

75g/2½oz urad dhal*

3-4 red chillies

¼ tsp asafoetida

Salt to taste

4 tbsp water

1 onion, finely chopped

½ carrot, finely chopped

50g/1¾oz cabbage, finely chopped

4-5 curry leaves

10g/¼oz coriander leaves, finely chopped

4 tsp refined vegetable oil

Method

- Soak the rice and the dhals together for about 20 minutes.
- Drain and add the red chillies, asafoetida, salt and water. Grind to a coarse paste.
- Add the onion, carrot, cabbage, curry leaves and coriander leaves. Mix well to make a batter with a consistency similar to sponge cake batter. Add more water if the consistency is not right.
- Grease a flat pan. Pour a spoonful of the batter. Spread with the back of a spoon to make a thin crêpe.
- Pour half a tsp oil around the crêpe. Flip to cook both sides.
- Repeat for the rest of the batter. Serve hot with coconut chutney (see page 20).

Spicy Corn on the Cob

Serves 4

Ingredients
8 corn cobs
Salted butter to taste
Salt to taste
2 tsp chaat masala*
2 lemons, halved

Method
- Roast the corns cobs on a charcoal grill or open flame till golden brown all over.
- Rub the butter, salt, chaat masala and the lemons on each cob.
- Serve immediately.

Mixed Vegetable Chop

Makes 12

Ingredients
Salt to taste
¼ tsp ground black pepper
4-5 large potatoes, boiled and mashed
2 tbsp refined vegetable oil plus extra for deep frying
1 small onion, finely chopped
½ tsp garam masala
1 tsp lemon juice
100g/3½oz frozen mixed vegetables
2-3 green chillies, finely chopped
50g/1¾oz coriander leaves, finely chopped
250g/9oz arrowroot powder
150ml/5fl oz water
100g/3½oz breadcrumbs

Method
- Add the salt and black pepper to the potatoes. Mix well and divide into 12 balls. Set aside.
- For the filling, heat 2 tbsp oil in a frying pan. Fry the onion on a medium heat till translucent.
- Add the garam masala, lemon juice, mixed vegetables, green chillies and coriander leaves. Mix well and cook on a medium heat for 2-3 minutes. Mash well and set aside.
- Flatten the potato balls with greased palms.
- Place some filling mixture on eacn potato patty. Seal to make oblong-shaped chops. Set aside.
- Mix the arrowroot powder with enough water to form a thin batter.
- Heat the oil in a frying pan. Dip the chops in the batter, roll in the breadcrumbs and deep fry on a medium heat till golden brown.
- Drain and serve hot.

Idli Upma
(Steamed Rice Cake Snack)

Serves 4

Ingredients
5 tbsp refined vegetable oil

½ tsp mustard seeds

½ tsp cumin seeds

1 tsp urad dhal*

2 green chillies, slit
  lengthways

8 curry leaves

Pinch of asafoetida

¼ tsp turmeric

8 idlis (see page 130),
  crushed

2 tsp caster sugar

1 tbsp coriander leaves,
  finely chopped

Salt to taste

Method
- Heat the oil in a saucepan. Add the mustard
  seeds, cumin seeds, urad dhal, green chillies,
  curry leaves, asafoetida and turmeric. Let
  them splutter for 30 seconds.
- Add the crushed idlis, caster sugar, coriander
  and salt. Mix gently.
- Serve immediately.

Dhal Bhajiya
(Batter Fried Lentil Balls)

Makes 15

Ingredients
250/9oz mung dhal*,
  soaked for 2-3 hours

2 green chillies,
  finely chopped

2 tbsp coriander leaves,
  finely chopped

1 tsp cumin seeds

Salt to taste

Refined vegetable oil for
  deep frying

Method
- Drain the dhal and grind coarsely.
- Add the chillies, coriander leaves, cumin
  seeds and salt. Mix well.
- Heat the oil in a frying pan. Add small
  portions of the dhal mixture and fry over a
  medium heat till golden brown.
- Serve hot with mint chutney (see page 15).

Masala Papad
(Poppadoms Topped with Spices)

Makes 8

Ingredients

2 tomatoes, finely chopped
2 large onions, finely chopped
3 green chillies, finely chopped
10g/¼oz coriander leaves, chopped

2 tsp lemon juice
1 tsp chaat masala*
Salt to taste
8 poppadoms

Method
* Mix all the ingredients, except the poppadoms, in a bowl.
* Roast the poppadoms on a high heat, turning each side. Make sure you don't burn them.
* Spread the vegetable mixture over each poppadom. Serve immediately.

Vegetable Sandwich

Makes 6

Ingredients

12 bread slices
50g/1¾oz butter
100g/3½oz mint chutney (see page 15)
1 large potato, boiled and
  thinly sliced
1 tomato, thinly sliced

1 large onion, thinly sliced
1 cucumber, thinly sliced
Chaat masala* to taste
Salt to taste

Method
* Butter the bread slices and apply a thin coat of mint chutney on each.
* Place a layer of potato, tomato, onion and cucumber slices on 6 bread slices.
* Sprinkle with some chaat masala and salt.
* Cover with the remaining bread slices and cut as desired. Serve immediately.

Sprouted Mung Bean Rolls

Makes 8

Ingredients

175g/6oz wholemeal flour

2 tbsp plain white flour

½ tsp caster sugar

75ml/ 2½fl oz water

50g/1¾oz frozen peas

25g/scant 1oz sprouted mung beans

2 tbsp refined vegetable oil

50g/1¾oz spinach, finely chopped

1 small tomato, finely chopped

1 small onion, finely chopped

30g/1oz cabbage leaves, finely chopped

1 tsp ground cumin

1 tsp ground coriander

¼ tsp ginger paste

¼ tsp garlic paste

60ml/2fl oz cream

Salt to taste

750g/1lb 10oz yoghurt

Method

* Mix the wholemeal flour, plain white flour, sugar and water. Knead into a stiff dough. Set aside.
* Boil the peas and mung beans in minimum water. Drain and set aside.
* Heat the oil in a saucepan. Add the spinach, tomato, onion and cabbage. Fry, stirring occasionally, till the tomato turns pulpy.
* Add the peas and mung beans mixture along with all remaining ingredients, except the dough. Cook on a medium heat till dry. Set aside.
* Make thin chapattis (see page 549) with the dough.
* On one side of each chapatti, place the cooked mixture lengthways in the centre, and roll up. Serve with mint chutney (see page15) and yoghurt.

Chutney Sandwich

Makes 6

Ingredients

12 bread slices

½ tsp butter

6 tbsp mint chutney (see page 15)

4 tomatoes, sliced

Method

* Butter all the bread slices. Spread the mint chutney on 6 slices.
* Place the tomatoes over the mint chutney and cover with another buttered slice. Serve immediately.

Chatpata Gobhi
(Tangy Cauliflower Snack)

Serves 4

Ingredients

500g/1lb 2oz cauliflower florets

Salt to taste

1 tsp ground black pepper

1 tbsp refined vegetable oil

1 tbsp lemon juice

Method
- Steam (see cooking techniques) the cauliflower florets for 10 minutes. Set aside to cool.
- Mix the steamed florets thoroughly with the remaining ingredients. Spread the cauliflower on a flameproof dish and grill for 5-7 minutes, or till it turns brown. Serve hot.

Sabudana Vada
(Sago Cutlet)

Makes 12

Ingredients

300g/10oz sago

125g/4½oz peanuts, roasted and crushed coarsely

2 large potatoes, boiled and mashed

5 green chillies, crushed

Salt to taste

Refined vegetable oil for deep frying

Method
- Soak the sago for 5 hours. Drain thoroughly and set aside for 3-4 hours.
- Mix the sago with all the ingredients, except the oil. Knead well.
- Grease your palms and make twelve patties with the mixture.
- Heat the oil in a frying pan. Deep fry 3-4 patties at a time on a medium heat till golden brown.
- Drain on absorbent paper. Serve hot with mint chutney (see page 15).

Bread Upma
(Bread Snack)

Serves 4

Ingredients

2 tbsp refined vegetable oil

½ tsp mustard seeds

½ tsp cumin seeds

3 green chillies, slit lengthways

½ tsp turmeric

¼ tsp asafoetida

2 onions, finely chopped

2 tomatoes, finely chopped

Salt to taste

2 tsp sugar

3-4 tbsp water

15 bread slices, broken into bits

1 tbsp coriander leaves, chopped

Method

- Heat the oil in a frying pan. Add the mustard seeds, cumin seeds, green chillies, turmeric and asafoetida. Let them splutter for 15 seconds.
- Add the onions and sauté till translucent. Add the tomatoes, salt, sugar and water. Bring to boil on a medium heat.
- Add the bread and mix well. Simmer for 2-3 minutes, stirring occasionally.
- Garnish with the coriander leaves. Serve hot.

Spicy Khaja
(Spicy Flour Dumplings with Ginger)

Makes 25-30

Ingredients

500g/1lb 2oz besan*

85g/3oz plain white flour

2 tsp chilli powder

½ tsp ajowan seeds

½ tsp cumin seeds

1 tbsp coriander leaves, chopped

Salt to taste

200ml/7fl oz water

1 tbsp refined vegetable oil plus extra for deep frying

Method

- Knead all the ingredients, except the oil for frying, into a soft dough.
- Make 25-30 balls of 10cm/4in diameter. Prick all over with a fork.
- Allow to dry on a clean cloth for 25-30 minutes.
- Deep fry till golden brown. Drain, cool and store for up to 15 days.

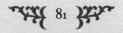

Crispy Potato

Serves 4

Ingredients

500g/1lb 2oz Greek yoghurt

1 tsp ginger paste

1 tsp garlic paste

1 tsp garam masala

1 tsp ground cumin, dry roasted
(see cooking techniques)

1 tbsp mint leaves, chopped

½ tbsp coriander leaves, chopped

Salt to taste

2 tbsp refined vegetable oil

4-5 potatoes, peeled and julienned

Method

- Whisk the yoghurt in a bowl. Add all the ingredients, except the oil and the potatoes. Mix well.
- Marinate the potatoes with the yoghurt for 3-4 hours in the refrigerator.
- Pour the oil in a grilling pan and arrange the marinated potatoes on it.
- Grill for 10 minutes. Turn the potatoes and grill for another 8-10 minutes till crispy. Serve hot.

Dhal Vada

(Fried Mixed Lentil Patties)

Makes 15

Ingredients

300g/10oz whole masoor dhal*

150g/5½oz masoor dhal*

1 large onion, finely chopped

2.5cm/1in root ginger, finely chopped

3 green chillies, finely chopped

¼ tbsp asafoetida

Salt to taste

Refined vegetable oil for frying

Method

- Mix the dhals together. Place in a colander and pour water in them. Set aside for an hour. Pat dry with a towel.
- Grind the dhals into a paste. Add all the remaining ingredients, except the oil. Mix well and shape the mixture into patties.
- Heat the oil in a frying pan. Deep fry the patties on a medium heat till golden brown. Serve hot with mint chutney (see page 15).

Spicy Banana Fritters

Serves 4

Ingredients

4 unripe bananas
125g/4½oz besan*
75ml/2½fl oz water
½ tsp chilli powder

¼ tsp turmeric
½ tsp amchoor*
Salt to taste
Refined vegetable oil for deep frying

Method

- Steam (see cooking techniques) the bananas in their skin for 7-8 minutes. Peel and slice. Set aside.
- Mix all the remaining ingredients, except the oil, to form a thick batter. Set aside.
- Heat the oil in a frying pan. Dip the banana slices in the batter and deep fry on a medium heat till golden brown.
- Serve hot with mint chutney (see page 15).

Masala Dosa
(Crêpe with Spicy Potato Filling)

Makes 10-12

Ingredients

2 tbsp refined vegetable oil
½ tbsp urad dhal*
½ tsp cumin seeds
½ tsp mustard seeds
2 large onions, finely sliced

¼ tsp turmeric
Salt to taste
2 large potatoes, boiled and chopped
1 tbsp coriander leaves, chopped
Fresh sada dosa (see page 65)

Method

- Heat the oil in a saucepan. Add the urad dhal, cumin and mustard seeds. Let them splutter for 15 seconds. Add the onions and fry till translucent.
- Add the turmeric, salt, potatoes and coriander leaves. Mix well and remove from the heat.
- Place a tbsp of this potato mixture in the centre of each sada dosa.
- Fold into a triangle to cover the potato mixture. Serve hot with coconut chutney (see page 20).

Soy Kebab

Makes 2

Ingredients

500g/1lb 2oz soy nuggets, soaked overnight

1 onion, finely chopped

3-4 garlic cloves

2.5cm/1in root ginger

1 tsp lemon juice

2 tsp coriander leaves, chopped

2 tbsp almonds, soaked and flaked

½ tsp garam masala

½ tsp chilli powder

1 tsp chaat masala

Refined vegetable oil for shallow frying

Method

- Drain the soy nuggets. Add all the remaining ingredients, except the oil. Grind into a thick paste and refrigerate for 30 minutes.
- Divide the mixture into walnut-sized balls and flatten them.
- Heat the oil in a frying pan. Add the kebabs and shallow fry till golden brown. Serve hot with mint chutney (see page 15).

Semolina Idli

(Semolina Cake)

Makes 12

Ingredients

4 tsp refined vegetable oil

150g/5½oz semolina

120ml/4fl oz sour cream

¼ tsp mustard seeds

¼ tsp cumin seeds

5 green chillies, chopped

1cm/½in root ginger, shredded

4 tbsp coriander leaves, finely chopped

Salt to taste

4-5 curry leaves

Method

- Heat 1 tsp oil in a saucepan. Add the semolina and fry for 30 seconds. Add the sour cream. Set aside.
- Heat the remaining oil in a frying pan. Add the mustard seeds, cumin seeds, green chillies, ginger, coriander leaves, salt and curry leaves. Stir-fry for 2 minutes.
- Add this to the semolina mixture. Set aside for 10 minutes.
- Pour the semolina mixture into greased idli moulds or cupcake moulds. Steam (see cooking techniques) for 15 minutes. Remove from the moulds. Serve hot.

Egg & Potato Cutlet

Serves 4

Ingredients

4 hard boiled eggs,
mashed

2 potatoes, boiled and
mashed

½ tsp ground black pepper

2 green chillies, chopped

1cm/½in root ginger,
finely chopped

2 garlic cloves,
finely chopped

½ tsp lemon juice

Salt to taste

Refined vegetable oil for
shallow frying

Method

- Mix together all the ingredients, except the oil.
- Divide into walnut-sized balls and press to form cutlets.
- Heat the oil in a saucepan. Add the cutlets and shallow fry till golden brown.
- Serve hot.

Chivda

(Beaten Rice Mixture)

Serves 4

Ingredients

2 tbsp refined vegetable oil

1 tsp mustard seeds

½ tsp cumin seeds

½ tsp turmeric

8 curry leaves

750g/1lb 10oz poha*

125g/4½oz peanuts

75g/2½oz chana dhal*,
roasted

1 tbsp caster sugar

Salt to taste

Method

- Heat the oil in a saucepan. Add the mustard seeds, cumin seeds, turmeric and curry leaves. Let them splutter for 15 seconds.
- Add all the remaining ingredients and stir-fry for 4-5 minutes on a low heat.
- Allow to cool completely. Store in an airtight container.

NOTE: *This can be stored for up to 15 days.*

Bread Bhajjia
(Bread Fritters)

Serves 4

Ingredients
85g/3oz maize flour
1 onion, finely chopped
½ tsp chilli powder
1 tsp ground coriander
Salt to taste
75ml/2½fl oz water
8 slices of bread, quartered
Refined vegetable oil
  for deep frying

Method
- Mix all the ingredients, except the bread and oil, to make a thick batter.
- Heat the oil in a frying pan. Dip the bread pieces in the batter and fry till golden brown.
- Serve hot with ketchup or mint chutney (see page 15).

Egg Masala

Serves 4

Ingredients
2 small onions, chopped
2 green chillies, chopped
2 tbsp refined vegetable oil
1 tsp ginger paste
1 tsp garlic paste
1 tsp chilli powder
½ tsp turmeric
1 tsp ground coriander
1 tsp ground cumin
½ tsp garam masala
2 tomatoes,
  finely chopped
2 tbsp besan*
Salt to taste
25g/scant 1oz coriander
  leaves, finely chopped
8 eggs, boiled and halved

Method
- Grind the chopped onions and green chillies together to make a coarse paste.
- Heat the oil in a saucepan. Add this paste along with the ginger paste, garlic paste, chilli powder, turmeric, ground coriander, ground cumin and garam masala. Mix well and fry for 3 minutes, stirring continuously.
- Add the tomatoes and sauté for 4 minutes.
- Add the besan and salt. Mix well and sauté for another minute.
- Add the coriander leaves and sauté for another 2-3 minutes on a medium heat.
- Add the eggs and mix gently. The masala should cover the eggs well on all sides. Cook over a low heat for 3-4 minutes.
- Serve hot.

Prawn Pakoda

(Fried Prawn Snack)

Serves 4

Ingredients

250g/9oz prawns, shelled and de-veined

Salt to taste

375g/13oz besan*

1 tsp ginger paste

1 tsp garlic paste

½ tsp turmeric

1 tsp garam masala

150ml/5fl oz water

Refined vegetable oil for deep frying

Method

- Marinate the prawns with the salt for 20 minutes.
- Add the remaining ingredients, except the oil.
- Add enough water to form a thick batter.
- Heat the oil in a saucepan. Add small spoonfuls of the batter and fry on a medium heat till golden brown. Drain on absorbent paper.
- Serve hot with mint chutney (see page 15).

Cheese Crunchies

Serves 6

Ingredients

2 tbsp plain white flour

240ml/8fl oz milk

4 tbsp butter

1 medium-sized onion, finely chopped

Salt to taste

150g/5½oz goat's cheese, drained

150g/5½oz Cheddar cheese, grated

12 bread slices

2 eggs, whisked

Method

- Mix the flour, milk and 1 tsp butter in a saucepan. Bring to a boil, taking care that no lumps are formed. Simmer till the mixture thickens. Set aside.
- Heat the remaining butter in a saucepan. Fry the onion on a medium heat till soft.
- Add the salt, goat's cheese, Cheddar cheese and the flour mixture. Mix well and set aside.
- Butter the bread slices. Spread a spoonful of the cheese mixture on 6 slices and cover with the other 6 slices.
- Brush the tops of these sandwiches with the whisked egg.
- Bake in a preheated oven at 180°C (350°F/ Gas Mark 6) for 10-15 minutes till golden brown. Serve hot with ketchup.

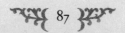

Mysore Bonda
(South Indian Fried Flour Dumpling)

Makes 12

Ingredients

175g/6oz plain white flour
1 small onion, finely chopped
1 tbsp rice flour
120ml/4fl oz sour cream

Pinch of bicarbonate of soda
2 tbsp coriander leaves, chopped
Salt to taste
Refined vegetable oil for deep frying

Method
- Make the batter by mixing all the ingredients, except the oil, together. Set aside for 3 hours.
- Heat the oil in a frying pan. Drop spoonfuls of the batter into it and deep fry on a medium heat till golden brown. Serve hot with ketchup.

Radhaballabhi
(Bengali Savoury Rolls)

Makes 12-15

Ingredients

4 tbsp mung dhal*
4 tbsp chana dhal*
4 cloves
3 green cardamom pods

½ tsp cumin seeds
3 tbsp ghee plus extra for deep frying
Salt to taste
350g/12oz plain white flour

Method
- Soak the dhals overnight. Drain the water and grind to a paste. Set aside.
- Grind the cloves, cardamom and cumin seeds together.
- Heat 1 tbsp ghee in a frying pan. Fry the ground spices for 30 seconds. Add the dhal paste and salt. Stir-fry on a medium heat till dry. Set aside.
- Knead the flour with 2 tbsp ghee, salt and enough water to make a stiff dough. Divide into lemon-sized balls. Roll into discs and place scoops of the fried dhal in the centre of each. Seal like a pouch.
- Roll the pouches into thick puris, each 10cm/4in in diameter. Set aside.
- Heat the ghee in a saucepan. Deep fry the puris till golden brown.
- Drain on absorbent paper and serve hot.

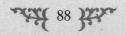

Medu Vada
(Fried Lentil Cakes)

Serves 4

Ingredients

300g/10oz urad dhal*, soaked for 6
  hours

Salt to taste

¼ tsp asafoetida

8 curry leaves

1 tsp cumin seeds

1 tsp ground black pepper

Refined vegetable for deep frying

Method
- Drain the urad dhal and grind into a thick, dry paste.
- Add all the remaining ingredients, except the oil, and mix well.
- Wet your palms. Make a lemon-sized ball with the batter, flatten it and make a hole in the centre like a doughnut. Repeat for rest of the batter.
- Heat the oil in a frying pan. Deep fry the vadas till golden brown.
- Serve hot with sambhar (see page 179).

Tomato Omelette

Makes 10

Ingredients

2 large tomatoes, finely chopped

180g/6½oz besan*

85g/3oz wholemeal flour

2 tbsp semolina

1 large onion, finely chopped

½ tsp ginger paste

½ tsp garlic paste

¼ tsp turmeric

½ tsp chilli powder

1 tsp ground coriander

½ tsp ground cumin, dry roasted
  (see cooking techniques)

25g/scant 1oz coriander leaves, chopped

Salt to taste

120ml/4fl oz water

Refined vegetable for greasing

Method
- Mix together all the ingredients, except the oil, to make a thick batter.
- Grease and heat a flat pan. Spread a spoonful of the batter on it.
- Sprinkle some oil around the omelette, cover with a lid and cook on a medium heat for 2 minutes. Flip and repeat. Repeat for the remaining batter.
- Serve hot with tomato ketchup or mint chutney (see page 15).

Egg Bhurji
(Spicy Scrambled Egg)

Serves 4

Ingredients

4 tbsp refined vegetable oil

½ tsp cumin seeds

2 large onions, finely chopped

8 garlic cloves, finely chopped

½ tsp turmeric

3 green chillies, finely chopped

2 tomatoes, finely chopped

Salt to taste

8 eggs, whisked

10g/¼oz coriander leaves, chopped

Method

• Heat the oil in a saucepan. Add the cumin seeds. Let them splutter for 15 seconds. Add the onions and fry them on a medium heat till translucent.

• Add the garlic, turmeric, green chillies and tomatoes. Stir-fry for 2 minutes. Add the eggs and cook, stirring continuously, till the eggs are done.

• Garnish with the coriander leaves and serve hot.

Egg Cutlet

Makes 8

Ingredients

240ml/8fl oz refined vegetable oil

1 large onion, finely chopped

1 tsp ginger paste

1 tsp garlic paste

Salt to taste

½ tsp ground black pepper

2 large potatoes, boiled and mashed

8 hard boiled eggs, halved

1 egg, whisked

100g/3½oz breadcrumbs

Method

• Heat the oil in a saucepan. Add the onion, ginger paste, garlic paste, salt and black pepper. Fry on a medium heat till brown.

• Add the potatoes. Fry for 2 minutes.

• Scoop out the egg yolks and add them to the potato mixture. Mix well.

• Fill the hollowed eggs with the potato-egg yolk mixture.

• Dip these in the whisked egg and roll in the breadcrumbs. Set aside.

• Heat the oil in a frying pan. Deep fry the eggs till golden. Serve hot.

Jhal Mudi
(Spicy Puffed Rice)

Serves 5-6

Ingredients

300g/10oz kurmure*
1 cucumber, finely chopped
125g/4½oz boiled chana*
1 large potato, boiled and finely chopped
125g/4½oz roasted peanuts
1 large onion, finely chopped

25g/scant 1oz coriander leaves, finely chopped
4-5 tbsp mustard oil
1 tbsp ground cumin, dry roasted
2 tbsp lemon juice
Salt to taste

Method
- Toss all the ingredients together to mix well. Serve immediately.

Tofu Tikka

Makes 15

Ingredients

300g/10oz tofu, chopped into 5cm/2in pieces
1 green pepper, diced
1 tomato, diced
1 large onion, diced
1 tsp chaat masala*

250g/9oz Greek yoghurt
½ tsp garam masala
½ tsp turmeric
1 tsp garlic paste
1 tsp lemon juice
Salt to taste
1 tbsp refined vegetable oil

For the marinade:
25g/scant 1oz coriander leaves, ground
25g/scant 1oz mint leaves, ground

Method
- Mix the marinade ingredients together. Marinate the tofu with the mixture for 30 minutes.
- Grill with the pepper, tomato and onion pieces for 20 minutes, turning occasionally.
- Sprinkle chaat masala on top. Serve hot with mint chutney (see page 15).

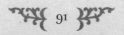

Aloo Kabli

(Spicy Potato, Chickpea and Tamarind Mix)

Serves 4

Ingredients

3 large potatoes, boiled
  and finely diced

250g/9oz white peas*, boiled

1 large onion, finely chopped

1 green chilli, finely chopped

2 tsp tamarind paste

2 tsp dry roasted (see cooking
  techniques) cumin seeds, ground

10g/¼oz coriander leaves, chopped

Salt to taste

Method

- Mix all the ingredients together in a bowl. Mash lightly.
- Serve chilled or at room temperature.

Masala Omelette

Makes 6

Ingredients

8 eggs, whisked

1 large onion, finely chopped

1 tomato, finely chopped

4 green chillies, finely chopped

2-3 garlic cloves, finely chopped

2.5cm/1in root ginger, finely chopped

3 tbsp coriander leaves,
  finely chopped

1 tsp chaat masala*

½ tsp turmeric

Salt to taste

6 tbsp refined vegetable oil

Method

- Mix together all the ingredients, except the oil, and mix well.
- Heat a frying pan and spread 1 tbsp oil on it. Spread one-sixth of the egg mixture over it.
- Once it has set, flip the omelette and cook the other side on a medium heat.
- Repeat for the rest of the batter.
- Serve hot with ketchup or mint chutney (see page 15).

Masala Peanuts

Serves 4

Ingredients

500g/1lb 2oz roasted peanuts

1 large onion, finely chopped

3 green chillies, finely chopped

25g/scant 1oz coriander leaves,
  finely chopped

1 large potato, boiled and chopped

1 tsp chaat masala*

1 tbsp lemon juice

Salt to taste

Method

• Toss all the ingredients together to mix well. Serve immediately.

Kothmir Wadi
(Fried Coriander Balls)

Makes 20-25

Ingredients

100g/3½oz coriander leaves,
  finely chopped

250g/9oz besan*

45g/1½oz rice flour

3 green chillies, finely chopped

½ tsp ginger paste

½ tsp garlic paste

1 tbsp sesame seeds

1 tsp turmeric

1 tsp ground coriander

1 tsp sugar

¼ tsp asafoetida

¼ tsp bicarbonate of soda

Salt to taste

150ml/5fl oz water

Refined vegetable oil to grease
  plus extra for shallow frying

Method

• In a bowl, mix together all the ingredients, except the oil. Add some water to make a thick batter.

• Grease a 20cm/8in round cake tin with oil and pour the batter into it.

• Steam (see cooking techniques) for 10-15 minutes. Set aside for 10 minutes to cool. Chop the steamed mixture into square pieces.

• Heat the oil in a frying pan. Shallow fry the pieces till golden brown on both sides. Serve hot.

Rice and Corn Rolls

Serves 4

Ingredients

100g/3½oz steamed rice (see page 519), mashed

200g/7oz boiled corn kernels

125g/4½oz besan*

1 large onion, finely chopped

1 tsp garam masala

½ tsp chilli powder

10g/¼oz coriander leaves, chopped

Juice of 1 lemon

Salt to taste

Refined vegetable oil for deep frying

Method

• Mix all the ingredients, except the oil, together.
• Heat the oil in a saucepan. Drop small spoonfuls of the mixture in the oil and fry till golden brown on all sides.
• Drain on absorbent paper. Serve hot.

Dahi Cutlet

(Yoghurt Cutlet)

Serves 4

Ingredients

600g/1lb 5oz Greek yoghurt

Salt to taste

3 tbsp coriander leaves, chopped

6 green chillies, finely chopped

200g/7oz breadcrumbs

1 tsp garam masala

2 tsp walnuts, chopped

2 tbsp plain white flour

½ tsp bicarbonate of soda

90ml/3fl oz water

Refined vegetable oil for deep frying

Method

• Mix the yoghurt with the salt, coriander leaves, chillies, breadcrumbs and garam masala. Divide into lemon-sized portions.
• Press some chopped walnuts into the centre of each portion. Set aside.
• Mix the flour, bicarbonate of soda and enough water to make a thin batter. Dip the cutlets in the batter and set aside.
• Heat the oil in a saucepan. Deep fry the cutlets till golden brown.
• Serve hot with mint chutney (see page 15).

Uthappam
(Rice Pancake)

Makes 12

Ingredients

500g/1lb 2oz rice
150g/5½oz urad dhal*
2 tsp fenugreek seeds

Salt to taste
12 tbsp refined vegetable oil

Method

* Mix all the ingredients, except the oil, together. Soak in water for 6-7 hours. Drain and grind into a fine paste. Set aside for 8 hours to ferment.
* Heat a frying pan and spread 1 tsp oil over it.
* Pour in a large tbsp of batter. Spread like a pancake.
* Cook over a low heat for 2-3 minutes. Flip and repeat.
* Repeat for the rest of the batter. Serve hot.

Koraishutir Kochuri
(Bread Stuffed with Peas)

Serves 4

Ingredients

175g/6oz plain white flour
¾ tsp salt
2 tbsp ghee plus extra for deep frying
500g/1lb 2oz frozen peas

2.5cm/1in root ginger
4 small green chillies
2 tbsp fennel seeds
¼ tsp asafoetida

Method

* Knead the flour with ¼ tsp salt and 2 tbsp ghee. Set aside.
* Grind the peas, ginger, chillies and fennel to a fine paste. Set aside.
* Heat a tsp of ghee in a saucepan. Fry the asafoetida for 30 seconds.
* Add the peas paste and ½ tsp salt. Stir-fry for 5 minutes. Set aside.
* Divide the dough into 8 balls. Flatten and fill each with the pea mixture. Seal like a pouch and flatten again. Roll out into round discs.
* Heat the ghee in a saucepan. Add the stuffed discs and fry on a medium heat till golden brown. Drain on absorbent paper and serve hot.

Kanda Vada
(Onion Cutlet)

Serves 4

Ingredients

4 large onions, sliced
4 green chillies, finely chopped
10g/¼oz coriander leaves, chopped
¾ tsp garlic paste
¾ tsp ginger paste

½ tsp turmeric
Pinch of bicarbonate of soda
Salt to taste
250g/9oz besan*
Refined vegetable oil for deep frying

Method

- Mix all the ingredients, except the oil. Knead and set aside for 10 minutes.
- Heat the oil in a saucepan. Add spoonfuls of the mixture to the oil and deep fry on a medium heat till golden brown. Serve hot.

Aloo Tuk
(Spicy Potato Snack)

Serves 4

Ingredients

8-10 baby potatoes, parboiled
Salt to taste
Refined vegetable oil for frying
2 tbsp mint chutney (see page 15)
2 tbsp sweet tomato chutney
  (see page 8)

1 large onion, finely chopped
2-3 green chillies, finely chopped
1 tsp black salt, powdered
1 tsp chaat masala*
Juice of 1 lemon

Method

- Press the potatoes gently to slightly flatten them. Sprinkle with the salt.
- Heat the oil in a saucepan. Add the potatoes and shallow fry till they are golden brown on all sides.
- Transfer the potatoes to a serving platter. Sprinkle the mint chutney and the sweet tomato chutney over them.
- Sprinkle the onion, green chillies, black salt, chaat masala and lemon juice on top. Serve immediately.

Coconut Cutlet

Makes 10

Ingredients

200g/7oz fresh coconut, grated
2.5cm/1in root ginger
4 green chillies
2 large onions, finely chopped
50g/1¾oz coriander leaves
4-5 curry leaves

Salt to taste
2 large potatoes, boiled and mashed
2 eggs, whisked
100g/3½oz breadcrumbs
Refined vegetable oil for deep frying

Method

- Grind the coconut, ginger, chillies, onions, coriander leaves and curry leaves together. Set aside.
- Add salt to the potatoes and mix it well.
- Make lemon-sized potato balls and flatten them on your palm.
- Place some ground coconut mixture in the centre of each cutlet. Seal them like a pouch and gently flatten again.
- Dip each cutlet in the whisked egg and roll in the breadcrumbs.
- Heat the oil in a saucepan. Deep fry the cutlets till golden brown.
- Drain on absorbent paper and serve hot with mint chutney (see page 15).

Mung Sprout Dhokla
(Steamed Mung Sprout Cake)

Makes 20

Ingredients

200g/7oz sprouted mung beans
150g/5½oz mung dhal*
2 tbsp sour cream

Salt to taste
2 tbsp grated carrot
Refined vegetable oil for greasing

Method

- Mix the mung beans, mung dhal and the sour cream. Grind together into a smooth paste. Ferment for 3-4 hours. Add the salt and set aside.
- Grease a 20cm/8in round cake tin. Pour the dhal mixture in it. Sprinkle the carrots on top and steam (see cooking techniques) for 7 minutes.
- Chop into pieces and serve hot.

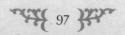

Paneer Pakoda

(Batter Fried Paneer)

Serves 4

Ingredients

2½ tsp chilli powder

1¼ tsp amchoor*

250g/9oz paneer*, cut into large pieces

8 tbsp besan*

Salt to taste

Pinch of bicarbonate of soda

150ml/5fl oz water

Refined vegetable oil for deep frying

Method

- Mix 1 tbsp chilli powder and the amchoor. Marinate the paneer pieces with the mixture for 20 minutes.
- Mix the besan with the remaining chilli powder, salt, bicarbonate of soda and sufficient water to make the batter.
- Heat the oil in a saucepan. Dip each paneer piece in the batter and deep fry on a medium heat till golden brown.
- Serve hot with mint chutney (see page 15).

Indian Meat Loaf

Serves 4

Ingredients

500g/1lb 2oz beef mince

200g/7oz bacon rashers

½ tsp ginger paste

½ tsp garlic paste

2 green chillies, finely chopped

½ tsp ground black pepper

¼ tsp nutmeg, grated

Juice of 1 lemon

Salt to taste

2 eggs, whisked

Method

- In a saucepan, mix together all the ingredients, except the eggs.
- Cook on a high heat till the mixture is dry. Set aside to cool.
- Add the whisked eggs and mix well. Pour into a 20 x 10cm/8 x 4in cake tin.
- Steam the mixture (see cooking techniques) for 15-20 minutes. Allow to cool for 10 minutes. Cut into slices and serve hot.

Paneer Tikka
(Paneer Patty)

Serves 4

Ingredients

250g/9oz paneer*, chopped into 12 pieces

2 tomatoes, quartered and
   pulp removed

2 green peppers, cored and quartered

2 medium-sized onions, quartered

3-4 cabbage leaves, shredded

1 small onion, finely sliced

For the marinade:

1 tsp ginger paste

1 tsp garlic paste

250g/9oz Greek yoghurt

2 tbsp single cream

Salt to taste

Method
- Mix the marinade ingredients together. Marinate the paneer, tomatoes, peppers and onions with this mixture for 2-3 hours.
- Skewer them one after the other and grill on a charcoal grill till the paneer pieces are brown.
- Garnish with the cabbage and onion. Serve hot.

Paneer Cutlet

Makes 10

Ingredients

1 tbsp ghee

2 large onions, finely chopped

2.5cm/1in root ginger, grated

2 green chillies, finely chopped

4 garlic cloves, finely chopped

3 potatoes, boiled and mashed

300g/10oz goat's cheese, drained

1 tbsp plain white flour

3 tbsp coriander leaves, chopped

50g/1¾oz breadcrumbs

Salt to taste

Refined vegetable oil for frying

Method
- Heat the ghee in a saucepan. Add the onions, ginger, chillies and garlic. Fry, stirring frequently, till the onion turns brown. Remove from the heat.
- Add the potatoes, goat's cheese, flour, coriander leaves, breadcrumbs and salt. Mix thoroughly and shape the mixture into cutlets.
- Heat the oil in a saucepan. Shallow fry the cutlets till golden. Serve hot.

Dhal ke Kebab

(Dhal Kebab)

Makes 12

Ingredients

600g/1lb 5oz masoor dhal*

1.2 litres/2 pints water

Salt to taste

3 tbsp coriander leaves, chopped

3 tbsp cornflour

3 tbsp breadcrumbs

1 tsp garlic paste

Refined vegetable oil for deep frying

Method

- Cook the dhal with the water and salt in a saucepan on a medium heat for 30 minutes. Drain the excess water and mash the cooked dhal with a wooden spoon.
- Add all the remaining ingredients, except the oil. Mix well and shape the mixture into 12 patties.
- Heat the oil in a saucepan. Deep-fry the patties till golden brown. Drain on absorbent paper and serve hot.

Savoury Rice Balls

Serves 4

Ingredients

100g/3½oz steamed rice (see page 519)

125g/4½oz besan*

125g/4½oz yoghurt

½ tsp chilli powder

¼ tsp turmeric

1 tsp garam masala

Salt to taste

Refined vegetable oil for deep frying

Method

- Mash the rice with a wooden spoon. Add all the remaining ingredients, except the oil, and mix thoroughly. This should make a batter with a cake-mix consistency. Add water if required.
- Heat the oil in a frying pan. Add spoonfuls of the batter and deep fry on a medium heat till golden brown.
- Drain on absorbent paper and serve hot.

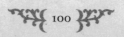

Nutritious Roti Roll

Serves 4

Ingredients
For the filling:
1 tsp cumin seeds
1 tsp butter
1 boiled potato, mashed
1 boiled egg, finely chopped
1 tbsp coriander leaves, chopped
½ tsp chilli powder
Pinch of ground black pepper

Pinch of garam masala
1 tbsp green onions, finely chopped
Salt to taste

For the roti:
85g/3oz wholemeal flour
1 tsp refined vegetable oil
Pinch of salt

Method
- Mix all the ingredients for the filling together and mash well. Set aside.
- Mix all the ingredients for the roti. Knead into a pliable dough.
- Make walnut-sized balls of the dough and roll each into discs.
- Spread the mashed stuffing thinly and evenly on each disc. Roll each disc into a tight roll.
- Roast the rolls lightly on a hot frying pan. Serve hot.

Chicken Mint Kebab

Makes 20

Ingredients
500g/1lb 2oz minced chicken
50g/1¾oz mint leaves, finely chopped
4 green chillies, finely chopped
1 tsp ground coriander
1 tsp ground cumin
Juice of 1 lemon

1 tsp ginger paste
1 tsp garlic paste
1 egg, whisked
1 tbsp cornflour
Salt to taste
Refined vegetable oil for frying

Method
- Mix together all the ingredients, except the oil. Knead into a soft dough.
- Divide the dough into 20 portions and flatten each.
- Heat the oil in a frying pan. Shallow fry the kebabs on a medium heat till golden brown. Serve hot with mint chutney (see page 15).

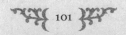

Masala Crisps

Serves 4

Ingredients

200g/7oz plain salted potato crisps

2 onions, finely chopped

10g/¼oz coriander leaves,
  finely chopped

2 tsp lemon juice

1 tsp chaat masala*

Salt to taste

Method

- Crumble the crisps. Add all the ingredients and toss to mix thoroughly.
- Serve immediately.

Mixed Vegetable Samosa
(Mixed Vegetable Savoury)

Makes 10

Ingredients

2 tbsp refined vegetable oil plus extra
  for deep frying

1 large onion, finely chopped

175g/6oz ginger paste

1 tsp ground cumin, dry roasted
  (see cooking techniques)

Salt to taste

2 potatoes, boiled and finely diced

125g/4½oz cooked peas

For the pastry:

175g/6oz plain white flour

Pinch of salt

2 tbsp refined vegetable oil

100ml/3½fl oz water

Method

- Heat 2 tbsp oil in a frying pan. Add the onion, ginger and ground cumin. Fry for 3-5 minutes, stirring continuously.
- Add the salt, potatoes and peas. Mix thoroughly and mash. Set aside.
- Make dough cones with the pastry ingredients, like in the Potato Samosa recipe (see page 66).
- Fill each cone with 1 tbsp potato-peas mixture and seal the edges.
- Heat the oil in a frying pan and deep fry the cones till golden brown.
- Drain and serve hot with ketchup or mint chutney (see page 15).

Mince Rolls

Makes 12

Ingredients

500g/1lb 2oz lamb mince

2 green chillies, finely chopped

2.5cm/1in root ginger, finely chopped

2 garlic cloves, finely chopped

1 tsp garam masala

1 large onion, finely chopped

25g/scant 1oz coriander leaves, chopped

1 egg, whisked

Salt to taste

50g/1¾oz breadcrumbs

Refined vegetable oil for shallow frying

Method

- Mix together all the ingredients, except the breadcrumbs and the oil. Divide the mixture into 12 cylindrical portions. Roll in the breadcrumbs. Set aside.
- Heat the oil in a frying pan. Shallow fry the rolls on a low heat till golden brown on all sides.
- Serve hot with green coconut chutney (see page 15).

Golli Kebab

(Vegetable Finger Rolls)

Makes 12

Ingredients

1 large carrot, finely chopped

50g/1¾oz French beans, chopped

50g/1¾oz cabbage, finely chopped

1 small onion, grated

1 tsp garlic paste

2 green chillies

Salt to taste

½ tsp caster sugar

½ tsp amchoor*

50g/1¾oz breadcrumbs

125g/4½oz besan*

Refined vegetable oil for frying

Method

- Mix together all the ingredients, except the oil. Shape into 12 cylinders.
- Heat the oil in a frying pan. Deep fry the cylinders till golden brown.
- Serve hot with ketchup.

Mathis
(Deep Fried Savouries)

Makes 25

Ingredients

350g/12oz plain white flour
200ml/7fl oz warm water
1 tbsp ghee
1 tsp ajowan seeds

1 tbsp ghee
Salt to taste
Refined vegetable oil
 for deep frying

Method
- Mix together all the ingredients, except the oil. Knead into pliable dough.
- Divide the dough into 25 portions. Roll each portion into a disc, 5cm/2in in diameter. Prick the discs with a fork and set aside for 30 minutes.
- Heat the oil in a saucepan. Deep fry the discs till they turn pale golden.
- Drain on absorbent paper. Cool and store in an air-tight container.

Poha Pakoda

Serves 4

Ingredients

100g/3½oz poha*
500ml/16fl oz water
125g/4½oz peanuts, coarsely pounded
½ tsp ginger paste
½ tsp garlic paste
2 tsp lemon juice
1 tsp sugar

1 tsp ground coriander
½ tsp ground cumin
10g/¼oz coriander leaves,
 finely chopped
Salt to taste
Refined vegetable oil for deep frying

Method
- Soak the poha in the water for 15 minutes. Drain and mix with all the remaining ingredients, except the oil. Form walnut-sized balls.
- Heat the oil in a frying pan. Deep fry the poha balls on a medium heat till they turn golden brown.
- Drain on absorbent paper. Serve hot with mint chutney (see page 15).

Hariyali Murgh Tikka
(Green Chicken Tikka)

Serves 4

Ingredients

650g/1lb 6oz boneless chicken, chopped into 5cm/2in pieces

Refined vegetable oil for basting

For the marinade:

Salt to taste

125g/4½oz yoghurt

1 tbsp ginger paste

1 tbsp garlic paste

25g/scant 1oz mint leaves, ground

25g/scant 1oz coriander leaves, ground

50g/1¾oz spinach, ground

2 tbsp garam masala

3 tbsp lemon juice

Method

- Mix the marinade ingredients together. Marinate the chicken with this mixture for 5-6 hours in the refrigerator. Remove from the refrigerator at least an hour before cooking.
- Grill the chicken pieces on skewers or a grilling tray basted with oil. Cook till the chicken turns brown on all sides. Serve hot.

Boti Kebab
(Bite-sized Lamb Kebab)

Makes 20

Ingredients

500g/1lb 2oz boneless lamb, chopped into small pieces

1 tsp ginger paste

2 tsp garlic paste

2 tsp green chillies

½ tbsp ground coriander

½ tbsp ground cumin

¼ tsp turmeric

1 tsp chilli powder

¾ tsp garam masala

Juice of 1 lemon

Salt to taste

Method

- Mix all the ingredients thoroughly and set aside for 3 hours.
- Skewer the lamb pieces. Cook over a charcoal grill for 20 minutes till golden brown. Serve hot.

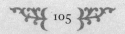

Chaat

(Savoury Potato Snack)

Serves 4

Ingredients

Refined vegetable oil for frying

4 medium-sized potatoes, boiled, peeled and cut into 2.5cm/1in pieces

½ tsp chilli powder

Salt to taste

1 tsp ground cumin, dry roasted (see cooking techniques)

1½ tsp chaat masala*

1 tsp lemon juice

2 tbsp hot and sweet mango chutney (see page 19)

1 tbsp mint chutney (see page 15)

10g/¼oz coriander leaves, chopped

1 large onion, finely chopped

Method

- Heat the oil in a frying pan. Deep fry the potatoes on a medium heat till golden brown on all sides. Drain on absorbent paper.
- In a bowl, toss the potatoes with the chilli powder, salt, ground cumin, chaat masala, lemon juice, hot and sweet mango chutney and mint chutney. Garnish with the coriander leaves and onion. Serve immediately.

Coconut Dosa

(Coconut Rice Crêpe)

Makes 10-12

Ingredients

250g/9oz rice, soaked for 4 hours

100g/3½oz poha*, soaked for 15 minutes

100g/3½oz steamed rice (see page 519)

50g/1¾oz fresh coconut, grated

50g/1¾oz coriander leaves, chopped

Salt to taste

12 tsp refined vegetable oil

Method

- Grind all the ingredients, except the oil, together to form a thick batter.
- Grease and heat a flat pan. Pour a spoonful of the batter and spread with the back of a spoon to make a thin crêpe. Pour a tsp of oil over it. Cook until crisp. Repeat for the remaining batter.
- Serve hot with coconut chutney (see page 20).

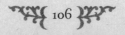

Dry Fruit Patties

Makes 8

Ingredients

50g/1¾oz mixed dry fruits,
  finely chopped

2 tbsp hot and sweet mango chutney
  (see page 19)

4 large potatoes, boiled and mashed

2 green chillies, finely chopped

1 tbsp cornflour

Salt to taste

Refined vegetable oil for frying

Method

- Mix the dry fruits with the hot and sweet mango chutney. Set aside.
- Mix the potatoes, green chillies, cornflour and salt.
- Divide the mixture into 8 lemon-sized balls. Flatten them by gently pressing them between your palms.
- Place a little dry fruit mix in the centre of each and seal like a pouch. Flatten once more to form patties.
- Heat the oil in a frying pan. Add the patties and shallow fry on a medium heat till golden brown on all sides. Serve hot.

Cooked Rice Dosa

Makes 10-12

Ingredients

100g/3½oz steamed rice (see page 519)

250g/9oz besan*

3-4 green chillies, finely chopped

1 onion, finely chopped

50g/1¾oz coriander leaves, chopped

8 curry leaves, finely chopped

Pinch of asafoetida

3 tbsp yoghurt

Salt to taste

150ml/5fl oz water

12 tsp refined vegetable oil

Method

- Mix all the ingredients together. Mash lightly and add a little water to make a thick batter.
- Grease and heat a flat pan. Pour a spoonful of the batter over it and spread to make a thin crêpe. Pour a tsp of oil around it. Cook until crisp. Repeat for the remaining batter.
- Serve hot with coconut chutney (see page 20).

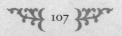

Unripe Banana Patties

Makes 10

Ingredients

6 unripe bananas, boiled and mashed

3 green chillies, finely chopped

1 small onion, finely chopped

¼ tsp turmeric

1 tbsp cornflour

1 tsp ground coriander

1 tsp ground cumin

1 tsp lemon juice

½ tsp ginger paste

½ tsp garlic paste

Salt to taste

Refined vegetable oil for
  shallow frying

Method

- Mix together all the ingredients, except the oil. Knead well.
- Divide into 10 equal balls. Flatten into patties.
- Heat the oil in a frying pan. Add a few patties at a time and fry till golden brown on all sides.
- Serve hot with ketchup or mint chutney (see page 15).

Sooji Vada

(Fried Semolina Snack)

Makes 25-30

Ingredients

200g/7oz semolina

250g/9oz yoghurt

1 large onion, chopped

2.5cm/1in root ginger, grated

8 curry leaves

4 green chillies, finely chopped

½ fresh coconut, ground

Salt to taste

Refined vegetable oil for deep frying

Method

- Mix together all the ingredients, except the oil, to make a thick batter. Set aside.
- Heat the oil in a frying pan. Gently add spoonfuls of the batter and fry on a medium heat till golden brown.
- Drain on absorbent paper. Serve hot with mint chutney (see page 15).

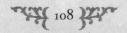

Sweet 'n' Sour Savoury Bites

Makes 20

Ingredients

2 tbsp refined vegetable oil

1 tsp mustard seeds

1 tsp sesame seeds

7-8 curry leaves

2 tbsp coriander leaves,
  finely chopped

For the muthias:

200g/7oz steamed rice (see page 519)

50g/1¾oz cabbage, grated

1 medium-sized carrot, grated

125g/4½oz frozen peas, defrosted
  and mashed

4 green chillies, finely chopped

1 tsp ginger paste

1 tsp garlic paste

2 tbsp caster sugar

2 tbsp lemon juice

Pinch of turmeric

1 tsp garam masala

3 tbsp tomato sauce

Salt to taste

Method

• Mix all the muthia ingredients together in a bowl. Knead well.

• Transfer this mixture to a greased 20cm/8in round cake tin and spread evenly.

• Place the tin in a steamer and steam (see cooking techniques) for 15-20 minutes. Set aside to cool for 15 minutes. Cut into diamond-shaped pieces. Set aside.

• Heat the oil in a saucepan. Add the mustard seeds, sesame seeds and curry leaves. Let them splutter for 15 seconds.

• Pour this directly over the muthias. Garnish with the coriander and serve hot.

Prawn Patties

Serves 4

Ingredients

2 tbsp refined vegetable oil plus
for frying

1 onion, finely chopped

2.5cm/1in root ginger, finely chopped

2 garlic cloves, finely chopped

250g/9oz prawns, cleaned and de-veined

1 tsp garam masala

Salt to taste

1 tsp lemon juice

2 tbsp coriander leaves, chopped

5 large potatoes, boiled and mashed

100g/3½oz breadcrumbs

Method

- Heat 2 tbsp oil in a frying pan. Add the onion and fry till translucent.
- Add the ginger and garlic and sauté on a medium heat for a minute.
- Add the prawns, garam masala and salt. Cook for 5-7 minutes.
- Add the lemon juice and coriander leaves. Mix well and set aside.
- Add salt to the potatoes and shape into patties. Place a little prawn mixture on each patty. Seal into pouches and flatten. Set aside.
- Heat the oil in a saucepan. Roll the patties in breadcrumbs and shallow fry till golden brown. Serve hot.

Reshmi Kebab
(Chicken Kebab in Creamy Marinade)

Makes 10-12

Ingredients

250ml/8fl oz sour cream

1 tsp ginger paste

1 tsp garlic paste

1 tsp salt

1 egg, whisked

120ml/4fl oz double cream

500g/1lb 2oz boneless chicken, chopped

Method

- Mix the sour cream, ginger paste and garlic paste together. Add the salt, egg and cream to make a thick paste.
- Marinate the chicken with this mixture for 2-3 hours.
- Skewer the pieces and cook on a charcoal grill till light brown.
- Serve hot.

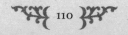

Cracked Wheat Delight

Makes 15

Ingredients

250g/9oz cracked wheat, lightly roasted

150g/5½oz mung dhal*

300ml/10fl oz water

125g/4½oz frozen peas

60g/2oz carrots, grated

1 tbsp roasted peanuts

1 tbsp tamarind paste

1 tsp garam masala

1 tsp chilli powder

¼ tsp turmeric

1 tsp salt

1 tbsp coriander leaves, chopped

Method

- Soak the cracked wheat and mung dhal in the water for 2-3 hours.
- Add the remaining ingredients, except the coriander leaves, and mix well.
- Pour the mixture into a 20cm/8in round cake tin. Steam (see cooking techniques) for 10 minutes.
- Cool and cut into pieces. Garnish with the coriander. Serve with green coconut chutney (see page 15).

Methi Dhokla

(Steamed Fenugreek Cake)

Makes 12

Ingredients

200g/7oz short-grained rice

150g/5½oz urad dhal*

Salt to taste

25g/scant 1oz fenugreek leaves, chopped

2 tsp green chillies

1 tbsp sour cream

Refined vegetable oil for greasing

Method

- Soak the rice and dhal together for 6 hours.
- Grind into a thick paste and set aside to ferment for 8 hours.
- Add the remaining ingredients. Mix well and ferment for 6-7 hours more.
- Grease a 20cm/8in round cake tin. Pour the batter into the tin and steam (see cooking techniques) for 7-10 minutes.
- Serve hot with any sweet chutney.

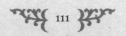

Peas Patties

Makes 12

Ingredients

2 tbsp refined vegetable oil plus extra
  for deep frying

1 tsp cumin seeds

600g/1lb 5oz cooked peas, mashed

1½ tsp amchoor*

1½ tsp ground coriander

Salt to taste

½ tsp ground black pepper

6 potatoes, boiled and mashed

2 bread slices

Method

* Heat 2 tbsp oil in a saucepan. Add the cumin seeds. After 15 seconds, add the peas, amchoor and coriander. Fry for 2 minutes. Set aside.
* Add salt and pepper to the potatoes. Set aside.
* Dip the bread slices in water. Squeeze out the extra water by pressing them between your palms. Remove the crusts and add the slices to the potato mix. Mix well. Divide the mixture into lemon-sized balls.
* Flatten each ball and place a tbsp of the peas mixture in the centre. Seal like a pouch and flatten again.
* Heat the oil in a frying pan. Deep fry the patties till golden. Serve hot.

Nimki

(Crispy Flour Triangle)

Makes 20

Ingredients

500g/1lb 2oz besan*

75g/2½oz ghee

1 tsp salt

1 tsp cumin seeds

1 tsp ajowan seeds

200ml/7fl oz water

Salt to taste

Refined vegetable oil for deep frying

Method

* Mix together all the ingredients, except the oil. Knead into a stiff dough.
* Make walnut-sized balls. Roll out into thin discs. Cut in half and fold into triangles.
* Heat the oil in a frying pan. Deep fry the triangles on a medium heat till golden brown. Cool and store in an airtight container for up to 8 days.

Dahi Pakoda Chaat
(Fried Lentil Dumplings in Yoghurt)

Serves 4

Ingredients

200g/7oz mung dhal*
200g/7oz urad dhal*
1cm/½in root ginger, chopped
3 tbsp chopped coriander leaves
Salt to taste
Refined vegetable oil for deep frying
125g/4½oz sweet tomato chutney
(see page 8)

125g/4½oz mint chutney (see page 15)
175g/6oz yoghurt, whisked
½ tsp black salt
1 tbsp ground cumin, dry roasted (see cooking techniques)
3 tbsp Bombay Mix*

Method

- Soak the dhals together for 4-5 hours. Drain and add the ginger, 2 tbsp coriander leaves and the salt. Grind to make a coarse batter. Set aside.
- Heat the oil in a saucepan. When it begins to smoke, add spoonfuls of the batter to it. Fry till golden brown. Drain on absorbent paper.
- Arrange the fried pakodas in a serving dish. Sprinkle the mint chutney, sweet tomato chutney and yoghurt over the pakodas. Sprinkle with the remaining ingredients. Serve immediately.

Kutidhal Dhokla
(Broken Lentil Cake)

Makes 20

Ingredients

250g/8oz mung dhal*
150ml/5fl oz sour cream

Salt to taste
1 tsp ginger paste

Method

- Soak the dhal in the sour cream for 4-5 hours. Grind to a thick paste.
- Add the salt and ginger paste. Mix well.
- Pour into a 20cm/8in round cake tin and steam (see cooking techniques) for 10 minutes.
- Set aside to cool for 10 minutes. Chop into bite-sized pieces and serve hot.

Ghugni
(Spicy Bengal Gram)

Serves 5-6

Ingredients

600g/1lb 5oz chana dhal*, soaked
  overnight

450ml/15fl oz water

Pinch of bicarbonate of soda

Salt to taste

2 tbsp ghee

400g/14oz fresh coconut, finely chopped

2 tbsp mustard oil

1 large onion, finely chopped

½ tsp turmeric

1 tsp ground cumin

½ tsp ginger paste

2 green chillies, finely chopped

2 bay leaves

1 tsp sugar

¼ tsp ground cinnamon

¼ tsp ground cardamom

¼ tsp ground cloves

2 tbsp lemon juice

Method

- In a saucepan, mix the chana dhal with the water, bicarbonate of soda and salt. Cook for 30 minutes on a medium heat. Set aside.
- Heat 1 tbsp ghee in a frying pan. Deep fry the coconut pieces. Set aside.
- Heat the mustard oil in a frying pan. Fry the onion on a medium heat till brown.
- Add the turmeric, ground cumin, ginger paste and green chillies. Fry for 3 minutes.
- Add the cooked dhal, fried coconut pieces, bay leaves and the sugar. Mix thoroughly.
- Sprinkle with the cinnamon, cardamom, cloves, lemon juice and the remaining ghee. Mix well to coat.
- Serve hot with puris (see page 552) or as it is.

Instant Dosa
(Instant Rice Crêpe)

Makes 10-12

Ingredients

85g/3oz rice flour
45g/1½oz wholemeal flour
45g/1½oz plain white flour
25g/scant 1oz semolina
60g/2oz besan*

1 tsp ground cumin
4 green chillies, finely chopped
2 tbsp sour cream
Salt to taste
120ml/4fl oz refined vegetable oil

Method
- Mix together all the ingredients, except the oil, with enough water to make a thick batter of a pouring consistency.
- Heat a frying pan and pour a tsp of the oil in it. Pour 2 tbsp of the batter and spread with the back of a spoon to make a crêpe.
- Cook on a low heat till the underside is brown. Flip and repeat.
- Remove carefully with a spatula. Repeat for the remaining batter.
- Serve hot with any chutney.

Sweet Potato Roll

Makes 15-20

Ingredients
4 large sweet potatoes, steamed (see cooking techniques) and mashed
175g/6oz rice flour
4 tbsp honey
20 cashew nuts, lightly roasted and chopped

20 raisins
Salt to taste
2 tsp sesame seeds
Ghee for deep frying

Method
- Mix together all the ingredients, except the ghee and the sesame seeds.
- Make walnut-sized balls and roll in the sesame seeds to coat.
- Heat the ghee in a frying pan. Deep fry the balls on a medium heat till golden brown. Serve hot.

Potato Pancake

Makes 30

Ingredients

6 large potatoes, 3 grated plus 3 boiled and mashed

2 eggs

2 tbsp plain white flour

½ tsp freshly ground black pepper

1 small onion, finely chopped

120ml /4fl oz milk

60ml/2fl oz refined vegetable oil

1 tsp salt

2 tbsp oil

Method

- Mix together all the ingredients, except the oil, to form a thick batter.
- Heat a flat pan and spread the oil on it. Drop 2-4 large spoonfuls of the batter and spread like a pancake.
- Cook each side on a medium heat for 3-4 minutes till the pancake is golden and crisp around the edges.
- Repeat for the remaining batter. Serve hot.

Murgh Malai Kebab
(Creamy Chicken Kebab)

Makes 25-30

Ingredients

1 tsp ginger paste

1 tsp garlic paste

2 green chillies

25g/scant 1oz coriander leaves, finely chopped

3 tbsp cream

1 tsp plain white flour

125g/4½oz Cheddar cheese, grated

1 tsp salt

500g/1lb 2oz boneless chicken, finely chopped

Method

- Mix together all the ingredients, except the chicken.
- Marinate the chicken pieces with the mixture for 4-6 hours.
- Arrange in an ovenproof dish and bake in an oven at 165°C (325°F, Gas Mark 4) for about 20-30 minutes, till the chicken turns light brown.
- Serve hot with mint chutney (see page 15).

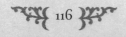

Keema Puffs

(Mince-stuffed Savouries)

Makes 12

Ingredients

250g/9oz plain white flour
½ tbsp salt
½ tsp baking powder
1 tbsp ghee
100ml/3½fl oz water
2 tbsp refined vegetable oil
2 medium-sized onions, finely chopped
¾ tsp ginger paste
¾ tsp garlic paste
6 green chillies, finely chopped

1 large tomato, finely chopped
½ tsp turmeric
½ tsp chilli powder
1 tsp garam masala
125g/4½oz frozen peas
4 tbsp yoghurt
2 tbsp water
50g/1¾oz coriander leaves, finely chopped
500g/1lb 2oz chicken, minced

Method

- Sieve together the flour, salt and baking powder. Add the ghee and water. Knead to form a dough. Set aside for 30 minutes and knead once again. Set aside.
- Heat the oil in a saucepan. Add the onions, ginger paste, garlic paste and green chillies. Fry for 2 minutes on a medium heat.
- Add the tomato, turmeric, chilli powder, garam masala and some salt. Mix well and cook for 5 minutes, stirring frequently.
- Add the peas, yoghurt, water, coriander leaves and the minced chicken. Mix well. Cook for 15 minutes, stirring occasionally, till the mixture becomes dry. Set aside.
- Roll out the dough into one big disc. Cut into a square shape, then cut 12 small rectangles out of the square.
- Place the mince mixture in the centre of each rectangle and roll like a candy wrapper.
- Bake in an oven at 175°C (350°F, Gas Mark 4) for 10 minutes. Serve hot.

Egg Pakoda
(Fried Egg Snack)

Makes 20

Ingredients

3 eggs, whisked

3 bread slices, quartered

125g/4½oz Cheddar cheese, grated

1 onion, finely chopped

3 green chillies, finely chopped

1 tbsp coriander leaves chopped

½ tsp ground black pepper

½ tsp chilli powder

Salt to taste

Refined vegetable oil for deep frying

Method

- Mix together all the ingredients, except the oil.
- Heat the oil in a frying pan. Add spoonfuls of the mixture. Fry on a medium heat till golden brown.
- Drain on absorbent paper. Serve hot.

Egg Dosa
(Egg and Rice Crêpe)

Makes 12-14

Ingredients

150g/5½oz urad dhal*

100g/3½oz steamed rice (see page 519)

Salt to taste

4 eggs, whisked

Ground black pepper to taste

25g/scant 1oz onion, finely chopped

2 tbsp coriander leaves chopped

1 tbsp refined vegetable oil

1 tbsp butter

Method

- Soak the dhal and rice together for 4 hours. Add salt and grind to a thick batter. Let it ferment overnight.
- Grease and heat a flat pan. Spread 2 tbsp of the batter over it.
- Pour 3 tbsp of the egg over the batter. Sprinkle pepper, onion and coriander leaves. Pour some oil around the edges and cook for 2 minutes. Flip carefully and cook for 2 more minutes.
- Repeat for the rest of the batter. Place a knob of butter on each dosa and serve hot with coconut chutney (see page 20).

Khasta Kachori
(Spicy Fried Lentil Dumpling)

Makes 12-15

Ingredients

200g/7oz besan*
300g/10oz plain white flour
Salt to taste
200ml/7fl oz water
2 tbsp refined vegetable oil plus
  for deep frying
Pinch of asafoetida
225g/8oz mung dhal*, soaked
  for an hour and drained
1 tsp turmeric
1 tsp ground coriander

4 tsp fennel seeds
2-3 cloves
1 tbsp coriander leaves,
  finely chopped
3 green chillies, finely chopped
2.5cm/1in root ginger, finely chopped
1 tbsp mint leaves, finely chopped
¼ tsp chilli powder
1 tsp amchoor*

Method

- Knead the besan, flour and some salt with enough water into a stiff dough. Set aside.
- Heat the oil in a saucepan. Add the asafoetida and let it splutter for 15 seconds. Add the dhal and fry for 5 minutes on a medium heat, stirring continuously.
- Add the turmeric, ground coriander, fennel seeds, cloves, coriander leaves, green chillies, ginger, mint leaves, chilli powder and amchoor. Mix well and cook for 10-12 minutes. Set aside.
- Divide the dough into lemon-sized balls. Flatten them and roll out into small discs, 12.5cm/5in in diameter.
- Place a spoonful of the dhal mixture in the centre of each disc. Seal like a pouch and flatten into puris. Set aside.
- Heat the oil in a saucepan. Deep fry the puris till they puff up.
- Serve hot with green coconut chutney (see page 15).

Mixed Legume Dhokla
(Steamed Mixed Legume Cake)

Makes 20

Ingredients
125g/4½oz whole mung beans*
125g/4½oz kaala chana*
60g/2oz Turkish gram
50g/1¾oz dry green peas
75g/2½oz urad beans*
2 tsp green chillies
Salt to taste

Method
- Soak together the mung beans, kaala chana, Turkish gram and dry green peas. Soak the urad beans separately. Set aside for 6 hours.
- Grind all the soaked ingredients together to make a thick batter. Ferment for 6 hours.
- Add the green chillies and salt. Mix well and pour into a 20cm/8in round cake tin and steam (see cooking techniques) for 10 minutes.
- Cut into diamond shapes. Serve with mint chutney (see page 15).

Frankie

Makes 10-12

Ingredients
1 tsp chaat masala*
½ tsp garam masala
½ tsp ground cumin
4 large potatoes, boiled and mashed
Salt to taste
10-12 chapattis (see page 549)
Refined vegetable oil for greasing
2-3 green chillies, chopped finely and soaked in some white vinegar
2 tbsp coriander leaves, finely chopped
1 onion, finely chopped

Method
- Mix together the chaat masala, garam masala, ground cumin, potatoes and salt. Knead well and set aside.
- Heat a frying pan and place a chapatti on it.
- Spread a little oil on the chapatti and flip it to fry one side. Repeat for the other side.
- Spread a layer of the potato mixture evenly on the hot chapatti.
- Sprinkle a few green chillies, coriander leaves and onion.
- Roll up the chapatti so that the potato mixture is inside.
- Dry roast (see cooking techniques) the roll on the frying pan till golden brown and serve hot.

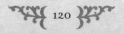

Besan & Cheese Delight

Makes 25

Ingredients
2 eggs
250g/9oz Cheddar cheese, grated
1 tsp ground black pepper
1 tsp ground mustard
½ tsp chilli powder
60ml/2fl oz refined vegetable oil

For the besan mix:
50g/1¾oz semolina, dry roasted
  (see cooking techniques)
375g/13oz besan*
200g/7oz cabbage, grated
1 tsp ginger paste
1 tsp garlic paste
Pinch of baking powder
Salt to taste

Method
- Whisk 1 egg thoroughly. Add the Cheddar cheese, pepper, ground mustard and chilli powder. Mix well and set aside.
- Mix the besan mix ingredients together. Transfer to a 20cm/8in round cake tin and steam (see cooking techniques) for 20 minutes. When cooled, cut into 25 pieces and spread the egg-cheese mixture over each.
- Heat the oil in a saucepan. Deep fry the pieces on a medium heat till golden brown. Serve hot with green coconut chutney (see page 15).

Chilli Idli

Serves 4

Ingredients
3 tbsp refined vegetable oil
1 tsp mustard seeds
1 small onion, sliced
½ tsp garam masala
1 tbsp ketchup
4 idlis (see page 130), chopped
Salt to taste
2 tbsp coriander leaves

Method
- Heat the oil in a saucepan. Add the mustard seeds. Let them splutter for 15 seconds.
- Add all the remaining ingredients, except the coriander leaves. Mix well.
- Cook on a medium heat for 4-5 minutes, tossing gently. Garnish with the coriander leaves. Serve hot.

Spinach Canapé

Makes 10

Ingredients

2 tbsp butter

10 bread slices, quartered

2 tbsp ghee

1 onion, finely chopped

300g/10oz spinach, finely chopped

Salt to taste

125g/4½oz goat's cheese, drained

4 tbsp Cheddar cheese, grated

Method

- Butter both sides of the bread pieces and bake in a preheated oven at 200°C (400°F, Gas Mark 6) for 7 minutes. Set aside.
- Heat the ghee in a saucepan. Fry the onion till brown. Add the spinach and salt. Cook for 5 minutes. Add the goat's cheese and mix well.
- Spread the spinach mixture on the toasted bread pieces. Sprinkle some grated Cheddar cheese on top and bake in an oven at 130°C (250°F, Gas Mark ½) till the cheese melts. Serve hot.

Paushtik Chaat

(Healthy Snack)

Serves 4

Ingredients

3 tsp refined vegetable oil

½ tsp cumin seeds

2.5cm/1in root ginger, crushed

1 small potato, boiled and chopped

1 tsp garam masala

Salt to taste

Ground black pepper to taste

250g/9oz mung beans, cooked

300g/10oz canned kidney beans

300g/10oz canned chickpeas

10g/¼oz coriander leaves, chopped

1 tsp lemon juice

Method

- Heat the oil in a saucepan. Add the cumin seeds. Let them splutter for 15 seconds.
- Add the ginger, potato, garam masala, salt and pepper. Sauté on a medium heat for 3 minutes. Add the mung beans, kidney beans and chickpeas. Cook on a medium heat for 8 minutes.
- Garnish with the coriander leaves and lemon juice. Serve chilled.

Cabbage Roll

Serves 4

Ingredients

1 tbsp plain white flour

3 tbsp water

Salt to taste

2 tbsp refined vegetable oil plus for deep frying

1 tsp cumin seeds

100g/3½oz frozen, mixed vegetables

1 tbsp single cream

2 tbsp paneer*

¼ tsp turmeric

1 tsp chilli powder

1 tsp ground coriander

1 tsp ground cumin

8 big cabbage leaves, soaked in hot water for 2-3 minutes and drained

Method

- Mix the flour, water and salt to form a thick paste. Set aside.
- Heat the oil in a saucepan. Add the cumin seeds and let them splutter for 15 seconds. Add all the remaining ingredients, except the cabbage leaves. Cook on a medium heat for 2-3 minutes, stirring frequently.
- Place spoonfuls of this mixture in the centre of each cabbage leaf. Fold the leaves up and seal the ends with the flour paste.
- Heat the oil in a frying pan. Dip the cabbage rolls in the flour paste and deep fry. Serve hot.

Tomato Bread

Makes 4

Ingredients

1½ tbsp refined vegetable oil

150g/5½oz tomato purée

3-4 curry leaves

2 green chillies, finely chopped

Salt to taste

2 large potatoes, boiled and sliced

6 bread slices, shredded

10g/¼oz coriander leaves, chopped

Method

- Heat the oil in a saucepan. Add the tomato purée, curry leaves, green chillies and salt. Cook for 5 minutes.
- Add the potatoes and the bread. Cook on a low heat for 5 minutes.
- Garnish with the coriander leaves. Serve hot.

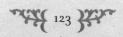

Corn & Cheese Balls

Makes 8-10

Ingredients

200g/7oz sweet corn

250g/9oz Mozzarella cheese, grated

4 large potatoes, boiled and mashed

2 green chillies, finely chopped

2.5cm/1in root ginger, finely chopped

1 tbsp coriander leaves, chopped

1 tsp lemon juice

50g/1¾oz breadcrumbs

Salt to taste

Refined vegetable oil for
   deep frying

50g/1¾oz semolina

Method

* In a bowl, mix together all the ingredients, except the oil and the semolina. Divide into 8-10 balls.
* Heat the oil in a saucepan. Roll the balls in the semolina and deep fry on a medium heat till golden brown. Serve hot.

Corn Flakes Chivda
(Roasted Corn Flakes Snack)

Makes 500g/1lb 2oz

Ingredients

250g/9oz peanuts

150g/5½oz chana dhal*

100g/3½oz raisins

125g/4½oz cashew nuts

200g/7oz cornflakes

60ml/2fl oz refined vegetable oil

7 green chillies, slit

25 curry leaves

½ tsp turmeric

2 tsp sugar

Salt to taste

Method

* Dry roast (see cooking techniques) the peanuts, chana dhal, raisins, cashew nuts and cornflakes till crisp. Set aside.
* Heat the oil in a saucepan. Add the green chillies, curry leaves and turmeric. Sauté on a medium heat for a minute.
* Add the sugar, salt and all the roasted ingredients. Stir-fry for 2-3 minutes.
* Cool and store in an airtight container for up to 8 days.

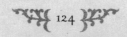

Nut Roll

Makes 20-25

Ingredients

140g/5oz plain white flour
240ml/8fl oz milk
1 tbsp butter
Salt to taste
Ground black pepper to taste
½ tbsp coriander leaves, finely chopped

3-4 tbsp Cheddar cheese, grated
¼ tsp nutmeg, grated
125g/4½oz cashew nuts, coarsely ground
125g/4½oz peanuts, coarsely ground
50g/1¾oz breadcrumbs
Refined vegetable oil for deep frying

Method

- Mix 85g/3oz flour with the milk in a saucepan. Add the butter and cook the mixture, stirring continuously, on a low heat till it is thick.
- Add the salt and pepper. Let the mixture cool for 20 minutes.
- Add the coriander leaves, Cheddar cheese, nutmeg, cashew nuts and peanuts. Mix thoroughly. Set aside.
- Sprinkle half the breadcrumbs on a tray.
- Drop teaspoonfuls of the flour mixture over the breadcrumbs and make rolls. Set aside.
- Mix the remaining flour with enough water to make a thin batter. Dip the rolls in the batter and roll them again in breadcrumbs.
- Heat the oil in a saucepan. Deep fry the rolls on a medium heat till light brown.
- Serve hot with ketchup or green coconut chutney (see page 15).

Cabbage Rolls with Mince

Makes 12

Ingredients

1 tbsp refined vegetable
   oil plus extra for frying

2 onions, finely chopped

2 tomatoes, finely chopped

½ tbsp ginger paste

½ tbsp garlic paste

2 green chillies, sliced

½ tsp turmeric

½ tsp chilli powder

¼ tsp ground black pepper

500g/1lb 2oz chicken, minced

200g/7oz frozen peas

2 small potatoes, diced

1 big carrot, diced

Salt to taste

25g/scant 1oz coriander leaves,
   finely chopped

12 large cabbage leaves, parboiled
   (see cooking techniques)

2 eggs whisked

100g/3½oz breadcrumbs

Method

- Heat 1 tbsp oil in a saucepan. Fry the onions till translucent.
- Add the tomatoes, ginger paste, garlic paste, green chillies, turmeric, chilli powder and pepper. Mix well and fry for 2 minutes on a medium heat.
- Add the chicken mince, peas, potatoes, carrots, salt and coriander leaves. Simmer for 20-30 minutes, stirring occasionally. Cool the mixture for 20 minutes.
- Place spoonfulls of the mince mixture in a cabbage leaf and roll it. Repeat for the remaining leaves. Secure the rolls with a toothpick.
- Heat the oil in a saucepan. Dip the rolls in the egg, coat with the breadcrumbs and fry till golden brown.
- Drain and serve hot.

Pav Bhaji
(Spicy Vegetables with Bread)

Serves 4

Ingredients

2 large potatoes, boiled

200g/7oz frozen, mixed vegetables
(green peppers, carrots, cauliflower
and peas)

2 tbsp butter

1½ tsp garlic paste

2 large onions, grated

4 large tomatoes, chopped

250ml/8fl oz water

2 tsp pav bhaji masala*

1½ tsp chilli powder

¼ tsp turmeric

Juice of 1 lemon

Salt to taste

1 tbsp coriander leaves, chopped

Butter to roast

4 hamburger buns, slit into half

1 large onion, finely chopped

Small slices of lemon

Method

- Mash the vegetables well. Set aside.
- Heat the butter in a saucepan. Add the garlic paste and onions and fry till the onions turn brown. Add the tomatoes and fry, stirring occasionally, on a medium heat for 10 minutes.
- Add the mashed vegetables, water, pav bhaji masala, chilli powder, turmeric, lemon juice and salt. Simmer till the gravy is thick. Mash and cook for 3-4 minutes, stirring continuously. Sprinkle the coriander leaves and mix well. Set aside.
- Heat a flat pan. Spread some butter on it and roast the hamburger buns till crisp on both sides.
- Serve the vegetables mixture hot with the buns, with the onion and lemon slices on the side.

Soy Cutlet

Makes 10

Ingredients

300g/10oz mung dhal*, soaked for
4 hours

Salt to taste

400g/14oz soy granules, soaked in warm
water for 15 minutes

1 large onion, finely chopped

2-3 green chillies, finely chopped

1 tsp amchoor*

1 tsp garam masala

2 tbsp coriander leaves, chopped

150g/5½oz paneer* or tofu, grated

Refined vegetable oil for deep frying

Method

- Do not drain the dhal. Add the salt and cook in a saucepan on a medium
  heat for 40 minutes. Set aside.
- Drain the soy granules. Mix with the dhal and grind into a thick paste.
- In a non-stick saucepan, mix this paste with all the remaining ingredients,
  except the oil. Cook on a low heat till dry.
- Divide the mixture into lemon-sized balls and shape into cutlets.
- Heat the oil in a saucepan. Fry the cutlets till golden brown.
- Serve hot with mint chutney (see page 15).

Corn Bhel

(Spicy Corn Snack)

Serves 4

Ingredients

200g/7oz boiled corn kernels

100g/3½oz spring onions, finely
chopped

1 potato, boiled, peeled and
finely chopped

1 tomato, finely chopped

1 cucumber, finely chopped

10g/¼oz coriander leaves, chopped

1 tsp chaat masala*

2 tsp lemon juice

1 tbsp mint chutney (see page 15)

Salt to taste

Method

- In a bowl, toss all the ingredients together to mix thoroughly.
- Serve immediately.

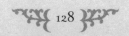

Methi Gota

(Fried Fenugreek Dumpling)

Makes 20

Ingredients

500g/1lb 2oz besan*

45g/1½oz wholemeal flour

125g/4½oz yoghurt

4 tbsp refined vegetable oil
plus extra for frying

2 tsp bicarbonate of soda

50g/1¾oz fresh fenugreek leaves,
finely chopped

50g/1¾oz coriander leaves,
finely chopped

1 ripe banana, peeled and mashed

1 tbsp coriander seeds

10-15 black peppercorns

2 green chillies

½ tsp ginger paste

½ tsp garam masala

Pinch of asafoetida

1 tsp chilli powder

Salt to taste

Method

* Mix the besan, flour and yoghurt together.
* Add 2 tbsp oil and the bicarbonate of soda. Set aside to ferment for 2-3 hours.
* Add all the remaining ingredients, except the oil. Mix well to make a thick batter.
* Heat 2 tbsp oil and add to the batter. Mix well and set aside for 5 minutes.
* Heat the remaining oil in a saucepan. Drop small spoonfuls of the batter into the oil and fry till golden brown.
* Drain on absorbent paper. Serve hot.

Idli

(Steamed Rice Cake)

Serves 4

Ingredients

500g/1lb 2oz rice, soaked overnight
300g/10oz urad dhal*, soaked overnight
1 tbsp salt

Pinch of bicarbonate of soda
Refined vegetable oil for greasing

Method

- Drain the rice and the dhal and grind together.
- Add the salt and bicarbonate of soda. Set aside for 8-9 hours to ferment.
- Grease cupcake moulds. Pour the rice-dhal mixture into them such that each is half-full. Steam (see cooking techniques) for 10-12 minutes.
- Scoop the idlis out. Serve hot with coconut chutney (see page 20).

Idli Plus

(Steamed Rice Cake with Seasoning)

Serves 6

Ingredients

500g/1lb 2oz rice, soaked overnight
300g/10oz urad dhal*, soaked overnight
1 tbsp salt
¼ tsp turmeric
1 tbsp caster sugar

Salt to taste
1 tbsp refined vegetable oil
½ tsp cumin seeds
½ tsp mustard seeds

Method

- Drain the rice and the dhal and grind together.
- Add the salt and set aside for 8-9 hours to ferment.
- Add the turmeric, sugar and salt. Mix well and set aside.
- Heat the oil in a saucepan. Add the cumin and mustard seeds. Let them splutter for 15 seconds.
- Add the rice-dhal mixture. Cover with a lid and simmer for 10 minutes.
- Uncover and flip the mixture. Cover again and simmer for 5 minutes.
- Pierce the idli with a fork. If the fork comes out clean, the idli is done.
- Cut into pieces and serve hot with coconut chutney (see page 20).

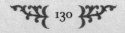

Masala Sandwich

Makes 6

Ingredients

2 tsp refined vegetable oil
1 small onion, finely chopped
¼ tsp turmeric
1 large tomato, finely chopped
1 large potato, boiled and mashed
1 tbsp boiled peas

1 tsp chaat masala*
Salt to taste
10g/¼oz coriander leaves, chopped
50g/1¾oz butter
12 bread slices

Method

- Heat the oil in a saucepan. Add the onion and fry till translucent.
- Add the turmeric and tomato. Stir-fry on a medium heat for 2-3 minutes.
- Add the potato, peas, chaat masala, salt and coriander leaves. Mix well and cook for a minute on a low heat. Set aside.
- Butter the bread slices. Place a layer of the vegetable mixture on six slices. Cover with the remaining slices and grill for 10 minutes. Turn over and grill again for 5 minutes. Serve hot.

Mint Kebab

Makes 8

Ingredients

10g/¼oz mint leaves, finely chopped
500g/1lb 2oz goat's cheese, drained
2 tsp cornflour
10 cashew nuts, roughly chopped
½ tsp ground black pepper

1 tsp amchoor*
Salt to taste
Refined vegetable oil for frying

Method

- Mix together all the ingredients, except the oil. Knead into a soft but firm dough. Divide into 8 lemon-sized balls and flatten them.
- Heat the oil in a saucepan. Deep fry the kebabs on a medium heat till golden brown.
- Serve hot with mint chutney (see page 15).

Vegetable Sevia Upma

(Vegetable Vermicelli Snack)

Serves 4

Ingredients

5 tbsp refined vegetable oil

1 large green pepper, finely chopped

¼ tsp mustard seeds

2 green chillies, slit lengthways

200g/7oz vermicelli

8 curry leaves

Salt to taste

Pinch of asafoetida

50g/1¾oz French beans, finely chopped

1 carrot, finely chopped

50g/1¾oz frozen peas

1 large onion, finely chopped

25g/scant 1oz coriander leaves, finely chopped

Juice of 1 lemon (optional)

Method

* Heat 2 tbsp oil in a saucepan. Fry the green pepper for 2-3 minutes. Set aside.
* Heat 2 tbsp oil in another saucepan. Add the mustard seeds. Let them splutter for 15 seconds.
* Add the green chillies and the vermicelli. Fry for 1-2 minutes on a medium heat, stirring occasionally. Add the curry leaves, salt and asafoetida.
* Sprinkle with a little water and add the fried green pepper, French beans, carrot, peas and onion. Mix well and cook for 3-4 minutes on a medium heat.
* Cover with a lid and cook for another minute.
* Sprinkle the coriander leaves and the lemon juice on top. Serve hot with coconut chutney (see page 20).

Bhel
(Puffed Rice Snack)

Serves 4-6

Ingredients

2 large potatoes, boiled and diced

2 large onions, finely chopped

125g/4½oz roasted peanuts

2 tbsp ground cumin, dry roasted
(see cooking techniques)

300g/10oz Bhel Mix

250g/9oz hot and sweet mango chutney
(see page 19)

60g/2oz mint chutney (see page 15)

Salt to taste

25g/scant 1oz coriander leaves, chopped

Method

- Mix the potatoes, onions, peanuts and ground cumin with the Bhel Mix.
  Add both the chutneys and salt. Toss to mix.
- Top with the coriander leaves. Serve immediately.

Sabudana Khichdi
(Sago Snack with Potato and Peanuts)

Serves 6

Ingredients

300g/10oz sago

250ml/8fl oz water

250g/9oz peanuts, coarsely ground

Salt to taste

2 tsp caster sugar

25g/scant 1oz coriander leaves, chopped

2 tbsp refined vegetable oil

1 tsp cumin seeds

5-6 green chillies, finely chopped

100g/3½oz potatoes, boiled and
chopped

Method

- Soak the sago overnight in the water. Add the peanuts, salt, caster sugar
  and coriander leaves and mix well. Set aside.
- Heat the oil in a saucepan. Add the cumin seeds and green chillies.
  Fry for about 30 seconds.
- Add the potatoes and fry for 1-2 minutes on a medium heat.
- Add the sago mix. Stir and mix well.
- Cover with a lid and cook on a low heat for 2-3 minutes. Serve hot.

Simple Dhokla
(Simple Steamed Cake)

Makes 25

Ingredients

250g/9oz chana dhal*, soaked overnight and drained

2 green chillies

1 tsp ginger paste

Pinch of asafoetida

½ tsp bicarbonate of soda

Salt to taste

2 tbsp refined vegetable oil

½ tsp mustard seeds

4-5 curry leaves

4 tbsp fresh coconut, grated

10g/¼oz coriander leaves, chopped

Method

- Grind the dhal to a coarse paste. Allow to ferment for 6-8 hours.
- Add the green chillies, ginger paste, asafoetida, bicarbonate of soda, salt, 1 tbsp of the oil and a little water. Mix well.
- Grease a 20cm/8in round cake tin and fill it with the batter.
- Steam (see cooking techniques) for 10-12 minutes. Set aside.
- Heat the remaining oil in a saucepan. Add the mustard seeds and curry leaves. Let them splutter for 15 seconds.
- Pour this over the dhoklas. Garnish with the coconut and coriander leaves. Cut into pieces and serve hot.

Jaldi Potato

Serves 4

Ingredients

2 tsp refined vegetable oil

1 tsp cumin seeds

1 green chilli, chopped

½ tsp black salt

1 tsp amchoor*

1 tsp ground coriander

4 large potatoes, boiled and diced

2 tbsp coriander leaves, chopped

Method

- Heat the oil in a saucepan. Add the cumin seeds and let them splutter for 15 seconds.
- Add all the remaining ingredients. Mix well. Cook on a low heat for 3-4 minutes. Serve hot.

Orange Dhokla
(Orange Steamed Cake)

Makes 25

Ingredients

50g/1¾oz semolina
250g/9oz besan*
250ml/8fl oz sour cream
Salt to taste
100ml/3½fl oz water
4 garlic cloves
1cm/½in root ginger
3-4 green chillies
100g/3½oz carrots, grated

¾ tsp bicarbonate of soda
¼ tsp turmeric
Refined vegetable oil
  for greasing
1 tsp mustard seeds
10-12 curry leaves
50g/1¾oz grated coconut
25g/scant 1oz coriander leaves,
  finely chopped

Method

• Mix together the semolina, besan, sour cream, salt and water. Set aside to ferment overnight.
• Grind the garlic, ginger and chillies together.
• Add to the fermented batter along with the carrot, bicarbonate of soda and turmeric. Mix well.
• Grease a 20cm/8in round cake tin with a little oil. Pour the batter in it. Steam (see cooking techniques) for about 20 minutes. Cool and chop into pieces.
• Heat some oil in a saucepan. Add the mustard seeds and curry leaves. Fry them for 30 seconds. Pour this over the dhokla pieces.
• Garnish with the coconut and coriander leaves. Serve hot.

Cabbage Muthia
(Steamed Cabbage Nuggets)

Serves 4

Ingredients

250g/9oz wholemeal flour
100g/3½oz shredded cabbage
½ tsp ginger paste
½ tsp garlic paste
Salt to taste

2 tsp sugar
1 tbsp lemon juice
2 tbsp refined vegetable oil
1 tsp mustard seeds
1 tbsp coriander leaves, chopped

Method

- Mix the flour, cabbage, ginger paste, garlic paste, salt, sugar, lemon juice and 1 tbsp oil. Knead into a pliable dough.
- Make 2 long rolls with the dough. Steam (see cooking techniques) for 15 minutes. Cool and cut into slices. Set aside.
- Heat the remaining oil in a saucepan. Add the mustard seeds. Let them splutter for 15 seconds.
- Add the sliced rolls and fry on a medium heat till brown. Garnish with the coriander leaves and serve hot.

Rava Dhokla
(Steamed Semolina Cake)

Makes 15-18

Ingredients

200g/7oz semolina
240ml/8fl oz sour cream
2 tsp green chillies

Salt to taste
1 tsp red chilli powder
1 tsp ground black pepper

Method

- Mix the semolina and sour cream together. Ferment for 5-6 hours.
- Add the green chillies and salt. Mix well.
- Place the semolina mixture in a 20cm/8in round cake tin. Sprinkle with the chilli powder and pepper. Steam (see cooking techniques) for 10 minutes.
- Cut into pieces and serve hot with mint chutney (see page 15).

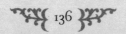

Chapatti Upma

(Quick Chapatti Snack)

Serves 4

Ingredients

6 left-over chapattis (see page 549), broken into small bits

2 tbsp refined vegetable oil

¼ tsp mustard seeds

10-12 curry leaves

1 medium-sized onion, chopped

2-3 green chillies, finely chopped

¼ tsp turmeric

Juice of 1 lemon

1 tsp sugar

Salt to taste

10g/¼oz coriander leaves, chopped

Method

* Heat the oil in a saucepan. Add the mustard seeds. Let them splutter for 15 seconds.
* Add the curry leaves, onion, chillies and turmeric. Sauté on a medium heat till the onion turns light brown. Add the chapattis.
* Sprinkle the lemon juice, sugar and salt. Mix well and cook on a medium heat for 5 minutes. Garnish with the coriander leaves and serve hot.

Mung Dhokla

(Steamed Mung Cake)

Makes about 20

Ingredients

250g/9oz mung dhal*, soaked for 2 hours

150ml/5fl oz sour cream

2 tbsp water

Salt to taste

2 grated carrots or 25g/scant 1oz grated cabbage

Method

* Drain the dhal and grind it.
* Add the sour cream and water and ferment for 6 hours. Add the salt and mix well to make the batter.
* Grease a 20cm/8in round cake tin and pour the batter in it. Sprinkle with the carrots or cabbage. Steam (see cooking techniques) for 7-10 minutes.
* Cut into pieces and serve with mint chutney (see page 15).

Mughlai Meat Cutlet
(Rich Meat Cutlet)

Makes 12

Ingredients

1 tsp ginger paste

1 tsp garlic paste

Salt to taste

500g/1lb 2oz boneless lamb, chopped

240ml/8fl oz water

1 tbsp ground cumin

¼ tsp turmeric

Refined vegetable oil for frying

2 eggs, whisked

50g/1¾oz breadcrumbs

Method

- Mix the ginger paste, garlic paste and salt. Marinate the lamb with this mixture for 2 hours.
- In a saucepan, cook the lamb with the water on a medium heat till tender. Reserve the stock and set the lamb aside.
- Add the cumin and turmeric to the stock. Mix well.
- Transfer the stock to a saucepan and simmer till the water evaporates. Marinate the lamb again with this mixture for 30 minutes.
- Heat the oil in a saucepan. Dip each lamb piece in the whisked egg, roll in the breadcrumbs and fry till light brown. Serve hot.

Masala Vada
(Spicy Fried Dumpling)

Makes 15

Ingredients

300g/10oz chana dhal*, soaked in
  500ml/16fl oz water for 3-4 hours

50g/1¾oz onion, finely chopped

25g/scant 1oz coriander leaves, chopped

25g/scant 1oz dill leaves, finely chopped

½ tsp cumin seeds

Salt to taste

3 tbsp refined vegetable oil plus extra
  for deep frying

Method

- Coarsely grind the dhal. Mix with all the ingredients, except the oil.
- Add 3 tbsp of oil to the dhal mixture. Make round, flat patties.
- Heat the remaining oil in a frying pan. Deep fry the patties. Serve hot.

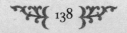

Cabbage Chivda
(Cabbage and Beaten Rice Snack)

Serves 4

Ingredients

100g/3½oz cabbage, finely chopped
Salt to taste
3 tbsp refined vegetable oil
125g/4½oz peanuts
150g/5½oz chana dhal*, roasted
1 tsp mustard seeds
Pinch of asafoetida

200g/7oz poha*, soaked in water
1 tsp ginger paste
4 tsp sugar
1½ tbsp lemon juice
25g/scant 1oz coriander leaves, chopped

Method

- Mix the cabbage with the salt and set aside for 10 minutes.
- Heat 1 tbsp oil in a frying pan. Fry the peanuts and chana dhal for 2 minutes on a medium heat. Drain and set aside.
- Heat the remaining oil in a frying pan. Fry the mustard seeds, asafoetida and cabbage for 2 minutes. Sprinkle a little water, cover with a lid and cook on a low heat for 5 minutes. Add the poha, ginger paste, sugar, lemon juice and salt. Mix well and cook for 10 minutes.
- Garnish with the coriander leaves, fried peanuts and dhal. Serve hot.

Bread Besan Bhajji
(Bread and Gram Flour Snack)

Makes 32

Ingredients

175g/6oz besan*
1250ml/5fl oz water
½ tsp ajowan seeds

Salt to taste
Refined vegetable oil for deep frying
8 bread slices, halved

Method

- Make a thick batter by mixing the besan with the water. Add the ajowan seeds and salt. Whisk well.
- Heat the oil in a frying pan. Dip the bread pieces in the batter and fry till golden brown. Serve hot.

Methi Seekh Kebab
(Skewered Mint Kebab with Fenugreek Leaves)

Makes 8-10

Ingredients

100g/3½oz fenugreek leaves, chopped

3 large potatoes, boiled and mashed

1 tsp ginger paste

1 tsp garlic paste

4 green chillies, finely chopped

1 tsp ground cumin

1 tsp ground coriander

½ tsp garam masala

Salt to taste

2 tbsp breadcrumbs

Refined vegetable oil for basting

Method

* Mix together all the ingredients, except the oil. Shape into patties.
* Skewer and cook on a charcoal grill, basting with the oil and turning occasionally. Serve hot.

Jhinga Hariyali
(Green Prawn)

Makes 20

Ingredients

Salt to taste

Juice of 1 lemon

20 prawns, shelled and de-veined (retain the tail)

75g/2½oz mint leaves, finely chopped

75g/2½oz coriander leaves, chopped

1 tsp ginger paste

1 tsp garlic paste

Pinch of garam masala

1 tbsp refined vegetable oil

1 small onion, sliced

Method

* Rub salt and lemon juice on the prawns. Set aside for 20 minutes.
* Grind together 50g/1¾oz mint leaves, 50g/1¾oz coriander leaves, ginger paste, garlic paste and the garam masala.
* Add to the prawns and set aside for 30 minutes. Sprinkle the oil on top.
* Skewer the prawns and cook on a charcoal grill, turning occasionally.
* Garnish with the remaining coriander and mint leaves, and the sliced onion. Serve hot.

Methi Adai
(Fenugreek Crêpe)

Makes 20-22

Ingredients

100g/3½oz rice
100g/3½oz urad dhal*
100g/3½oz mung dhal*
100g/3½oz chana dhal*
100g/3½oz masoor dhal*
Pinch of asafoetida

6-7 curry leaves
Salt to taste
50g/1¾oz fresh fenugreek leaves, chopped
Refined vegetable oil for greasing

Method

- Soak the rice and dhals together for 3-4 hours.
- Drain the rice and dhal and add the asafoetida, curry leaves and the salt to them. Grind coarsely and set aside to ferment for 7 hours. Add the fenugreek leaves.
- Grease a frying pan and heat it. Add a tbsp of the fermented mixture and spread to form a pancake. Pour some oil around the edges and cook on a medium heat for 3-4 minutes. Flip and cook for 2 more minutes.
- Repeat for the rest of the batter. Serve hot with coconut chutney (see page 20).

Peas Chaat

Serves 4

Ingredients

2 tsp refined vegetable oil
½ tsp cumin seeds
300g/10oz canned green peas
½ tsp amchoor*

¼ tsp turmeric
¼ tsp garam masala
1 tsp lemon juice
5cm/2in root ginger, peeled and julienned

Method

- Heat the oil in a saucepan. Add the cumin seeds and let them splutter for 15 seconds. Add the peas, amchoor, turmeric and garam masala. Mix well and cook for 2-3 minutes, stirring occasionally.
- Garnish with the lemon juice and the ginger. Serve hot.

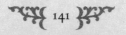

Shingada
(Bengali Savoury)

Makes 8-10

Ingredients
2 tbsp refined vegetable oil plus
  extra for deep frying
1 tsp cumin seeds
200g/7oz boiled peas
2 potatoes, boiled and chopped
1 tsp ground coriander
Salt to taste

For the pastry:
350g/12oz plain white flour
¼ tsp salt
A little water

Method
- Heat 2 tbsp oil in a saucepan. Add the cumin seeds. Let them splutter for 15 seconds. Add the peas, potatoes, ground coriander and salt. Mix well and fry on a medium heat for 5 minutes. Set aside.
- Make dough cones with the pastry ingredients, like in the Potato Samosa recipe (see page 66). Fill the cones with the vegetable mixture and seal.
- Heat the remaining oil in a frying pan. Deep fry the cones on a medium heat till golden brown. Serve hot with mint chutney (see page 15).

Onion Bhajia
(Onion Fritters)

Makes 20

Ingredients
250g/9oz besan*
4 large onions, thinly sliced
Salt to taste
½ tsp turmeric
150ml/5fl oz water
Refined vegetable oil for frying

Method
- Mix the besan, onions, salt and turmeric together. Add the water and mix well.
- Heat the oil in a frying pan. Add spoonfuls of the mixture and deep fry till golden. Drain on absorbent paper and serve hot.

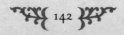 142

Bagani Murgh
(Chicken in Cashew Paste)

Makes 12

Ingredients

500g/1lb 2oz boneless chicken, diced
1 small onion, sliced
1 tomato, sliced
1 cucumber, sliced

For the marinade:
6-7 cashew nuts, ground to a paste
2 tbsp single cream

1 tsp ginger paste
1 tsp garlic paste
2 green chillies, finely chopped
10g/¼oz mint leaves, ground
10g/¼oz coriander leaves, ground
Salt to taste

Method
- Mix the marinade ingredients together. Marinate the chicken with this mixture for 4-5 hours.
- Skewer and cook on a charcoal grill, turning occasionally.
- Garnish with the onion, tomato and cucumber. Serve hot.

Potato Tikki
(Potato Patties)

Makes 12

Ingredients

4 large potatoes, boiled and mashed
1 tsp ginger paste
1 tsp garlic paste
Juice of 1 lemon
1 large onion, finely chopped

25g/scant 1oz coriander leaves, chopped
¼ tsp chilli powder
Salt to taste
2 tbsp rice flour
3 tbsp refined vegetable oil

Method
- Mix the potatoes with the ginger paste, garlic paste, lemon juice, onion, coriander leaves, chilli powder and salt. Knead well. Shape into patties.
- Dust the patties with rice flour.
- Heat the oil in a frying pan. Shallow fry the patties on a medium heat till golden brown. Drain and serve hot with mint chutney (see page 15).

Batata Vada
(Batter Fried Potato Dumpling)

Makes 12-14

Ingredients

1 tsp refined vegetable oil plus extra for deep frying

½ tsp mustard seeds

½ tsp urad dhal*

½ tsp turmeric

5 potatoes, boiled and mashed

Salt to taste

Juice of 1 lemon

250g/9oz besan*

Pinch of asafoetida

120ml/4fl oz water

Method

- Heat 1 tsp oil in a frying pan. Add the mustard seeds, urad dhal and turmeric. Let them splutter for 15 seconds.
- Pour this over the potatoes. Also add salt and lemon juice. Mix well.
- Divide the potato mixture into walnut-sized balls. Set aside.
- Mix the besan, asafoetida, salt and water to make the batter.
- Heat the remaining oil in a frying pan. Dip the potato balls in the batter and deep fry till golden. Drain and serve with mint chutney (see page 15).

Mini Chicken Kebab

Makes 8

Ingredients

350g/12oz chicken, minced

125g/4½oz besan*

1 large onion, finely chopped

½ tsp ginger paste

½ tsp garlic paste

1 tsp lemon juice

¼ tsp green cardamom powder

1 tbsp coriander leaves, chopped

Salt to taste

1 tbsp sesame seeds

Method

- Mix together all the ingredients, except the sesame seeds.
- Divide the mixture into small balls and sprinkle with sesame seeds.
- Bake in an oven at 190°C (375°F; Gas Mark 5) for 25 minutes. Serve hot with mint chutney (see page 15).

Lentil Rissole

Makes 12

Ingredients

2 tbsp refined vegetable oil plus
  extra for shallow frying

2 small onions, finely chopped

2 carrots, finely chopped

600g/1lb 5oz masoor dhal*

500ml/16fl oz water

2 tbsp ground coriander

Salt to taste

25g/scant 1oz coriander leaves, chopped

100g/3½oz breadcrumbs

2 tbsp plain white flour

1 egg, whisked

Method

- Heat 1 tbsp oil in a frying pan. Add the onions and carrots and fry on a medium heat for 2-3 minutes, stirring frequently. Add the masoor dhal, water, ground coriander and salt. Simmer for 30 minutes, stirring.
- Add the coriander leaves and half the breadcrumbs. Mix well.
- Mould into sausage shapes and coat with the flour. Dip the rissoles in the whisked egg and roll in the remaining breadcrumbs. Set aside.
- Heat the remaining oil. Shallow fry the rissoles till golden, flipping once. Serve hot with green coconut chutney (see page 15).

Nutritious Poha

Serves 4

Ingredients

1 tbsp refined vegetable oil

125g/4½oz peanuts

1 onion, finely chopped

¼ tsp turmeric

Salt to taste

1 potato, boiled and chopped

200g/7oz poha*, soaked for 5 minutes
  and drained

1 tsp lemon juice

1 tbsp coriander leaves, chopped

Method

- Heat the oil in a saucepan. Fry the peanuts, onion, turmeric and salt on a medium heat for 2-3 minutes.
- Add the potato and poha. Stir-fry on a low heat till evenly mixed.
- Garnish with the lemon juice and coriander leaves. Serve hot.

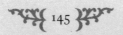 145

Beans Usal

(Beans in Spicy Gravy)

Serves 4

Ingredients

300g/10oz masoor dhal*, soaked in hot
  water for 20 minutes

¼ tsp turmeric

Salt to taste

50g/1¾oz French beans, finely chopped

240ml/8fl oz water

1 tbsp refined vegetable oil

¼ tsp mustard seeds

A few curry leaves

Salt to taste

Method

- Mix the dhal, turmeric and salt together. Grind to a coarse paste.
- Steam (see cooking techniques) for 20-25 minutes. Set aside to cool for 20 minutes. Crumble the mixture with your fingers. Set aside.
- Cook the French beans with the water and a little salt in a saucepan on a medium heat till soft. Set aside.
- Heat the oil in a saucepan. Add the mustard seeds. Let them splutter for 15 seconds. Add the curry leaves and the crumbled dhal.
- Stir-fry for about 3-4 minutes on a medium heat till soft. Add the cooked beans and mix well. Serve hot.

Bread Chutney Pakoda

Serves 4

Ingredients

250g/9oz besan*

150ml/5fl oz water

½ tsp ajowan seeds

125g/4½oz mint chutney (see page 15)

12 slices of bread

Refined vegetable oil for deep frying

Method

- Mix the besan with the water to make a batter of a pancake-mix consistency. Add the ajowan seeds and whisk lightly. Set aside.
- Spread the mint chutney on a bread slice and place another on top. Repeat for all the bread slices. Cut them diagonally into half.
- Heat the oil in a frying pan. Dip the sandwiches in the batter and fry on a medium heat till golden brown. Serve hot with ketchup.

Methi Khakra Delight
(Fenugreek Snack)

Makes 16

Ingredients

50g/1¾oz fresh fenugreek leaves, finely chopped

300g/10oz wholemeal flour

1 tsp chilli powder

¼ tsp turmeric

½ tsp ground coriander

1 tbsp refined vegetable oil

Salt to taste

120ml/4fl oz water

Method

- Mix all the ingredients together. Knead into a soft but firm dough.
- Divide the dough into 16 lemon-sized balls. Roll out into very thin discs.
- Heat a flat pan. Place the discs on the flat pan and cook till crisp. Repeat for the other side. Store in an airtight container.

Green Cutlet

Makes 12

Ingredients

200g/7oz spinach, finely chopped

4 potatoes, boiled and mashed

200g/7oz mung dhal*, boiled and mashed

25g/scant 1oz coriander leaves, chopped

2 green chillies, finely chopped

1 tsp garam masala

1 large onion, finely chopped

Salt to taste

1 tsp garlic paste

1 tsp ginger paste

Refined vegetable oil for frying

250g/9oz breadcrumbs

Method

- Mix the spinach and potatoes together. Add the mung dhal, coriander leaves, green chillies, garam masala, onion, salt, garlic paste and ginger paste. Knead well.
- Divide the mixture into walnut-sized portions and shape each into cutlets.
- Heat the oil in a frying pan. Roll the cutlets in the breadcrumbs and shallow fry till golden brown. Serve hot.

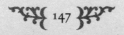

Handvo

(Savoury Semolina Cake)

Serves 4

Ingredients

100g/3½oz semolina

125g/4½oz besan*

200g/7oz yoghurt

25g/scant 1oz bottle gourd, grated

1 carrot, grated

25g/scant 1oz green peas

½ tsp turmeric

½ tsp chilli powder

½ tsp ginger paste

½ tsp garlic paste

1 green chilli, finely chopped

Salt to taste

Pinch of asafoetida

½ tsp bicarbonate of soda

4 tbsp refined vegetable oil

¾ tsp mustard seeds

½ tsp sesame seeds

Method

* Mix the semolina, besan and yoghurt in a saucepan. Add the grated bottle gourd and carrot and the peas.
* Add the turmeric, chilli powder, ginger paste, garlic paste, green chilli, salt and asafoetida to make the batter. It should have the consistency of a cake batter. If not, add a few tablespoons of water.
* Add the bicarbonate of soda and stir well. Set aside.
* Heat the oil in a saucepan. Add the mustard and sesame seeds. Let them splutter for 15 seconds.
* Pour the batter in the saucepan. Cover with a lid and cook on a low heat for 10-12 minutes.
* Uncover and flip the set batter carefully, using a spatula. Cover again and cook on a low heat for 15 more minutes.
* Pierce with a fork to check if done. If cooked, the fork will come out clean. Serve hot.

Ghugra
(Crescents with Savoury Vegetable Centres)

Serves 4

Ingredients

5 tbsp refined vegetable oil plus extra for deep frying

Pinch of asafoetida

400g/14oz canned peas, ground

250ml/8fl oz water

Salt to taste

5cm/2in root ginger, finely chopped

2 tsp lemon juice

1 tbsp coriander leaves, chopped

350g/12oz wholemeal flour

Method
- Heat 2 tbsp oil in a saucepan. Add the asafoetida. When it splutters, add the peas and 120ml/4fl oz water. Cook on a medium heat for 3 minutes.
- Add the salt, ginger and lemon juice. Mix well and cook for another 5 minutes. Sprinkle the coriander leaves on top and set aside.
- Knead the flour with the salt, remaining water and 3 tbsp oil. Divide into small balls and roll out into round discs of 10cm/4in diameter.
- Place some pea mixture on each disc so that half the disc is covered with the mixture. Fold the other half over to make a 'D' shape. Seal by pressing the edges together.
- Heat the oil. Fry the ghugras on a medium heat till golden. Serve hot.

Banana Kebab

Makes 20

Ingredients

6 green bananas

1 tsp ginger paste

250g/9oz besan*

25g/scant 1oz coriander leaves, chopped

½ tsp chilli powder

1 tsp amchoor*

Juice of 1 lemon

Salt to taste

240ml/8fl oz refined vegetable oil for shallow frying

Method
- Boil the bananas in their skins for 10-15 minutes. Drain and peel.
- Mix with the remaining ingredients, except the oil. Shape into patties.
- Heat the oil in a frying pan. Shallow fry the patties till golden. Serve hot.

Vegetable Patties

Makes 12

Ingredients

2 tbsp arrowroot powder

4-5 large potatoes, boiled and grated

1 tbsp refined vegetable oil plus
  extra for frying

125g/4½oz besan*

25g/scant 1oz fresh coconut, grated

4-5 cashew nuts

3-4 raisins

125g/4½oz frozen peas, boiled

2 tsp dried pomegranate seeds

2 tsp coarsely ground coriander

1 tsp fennel seeds

½ tsp ground black pepper

½ tsp chilli powder

1 tsp amchoor*

½ tsp rock salt

Salt to taste

Method

- Knead together the arrowroot, potatoes and 1 tbsp of oil. Set aside.
- To make the filling, mix the remaining ingredients, except the oil.
- Divide the potato dough into round patties. Place a spoonful of the filling in the centre of each patty. Seal them like a pouch and flatten.
- Heat the remaining oil in a saucepan. Shallow fry the patties over a low heat till golden brown. Serve hot.

Sprouted Beans Bhel

(Savoury Snack with Sprouted Beans)

Serves 4

Ingredients

100g/3½oz sprouted mung beans, boiled

250g/9oz kaala chana*, boiled

3 large potatoes, boiled and chopped

2 large tomatoes, finely chopped

1 medium-sized onion, chopped

Salt to taste

For the garnish:

2 tbsp mint chutney (see page 15)

2 tbsp hot and sweet mango chutney
  (see page 19)

4-5 tbsp yoghurt

100g/3½ oz potato crisps, crushed

10g/¼oz coriander leaves, chopped

Method

- Mix all the ingredients together, except the garnish ingredients.
- Garnish in the order that the ingredients are listed. Serve immediately.

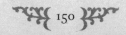

Aloo Kachori
(Fried Potato Dumpling)

Makes 15

Ingredients
350g/12oz wholemeal flour

1 tbsp refined vegetable oil plus extra for deep frying

1 tsp ajowan seeds

Salt to taste

5 potatoes, boiled and mashed

2 tsp chilli powder

1 tbsp coriander leaves, chopped

Method
- Knead the flour, 1 tbsp oil, ajowan seeds and salt together. Divide into lime-sized balls. Flatten each between your palms and set aside.
- Mix together the potatoes, chilli powder, coriander leaves and some salt.
- Place a portion of this mixture in the centre of each patty. Seal by pinching the edges together.
- Heat the oil in a frying pan. Deep fry the kachoris on a medium heat till golden brown. Drain and serve hot.

Diet Dosa
(Diet Crêpe)

Makes 12

Ingredients
300g/10oz mung dhal*, soaked in 250ml/8fl oz water for 3-4 hours

3-4 green chillies

2.5cm/1in root ginger

100g/3½oz semolina

1 tbsp sour cream

50g/1¾oz coriander leaves, chopped

6 curry leaves

Refined vegetable oil for greasing

Salt to taste

Method
- Mix the dhal with the green chillies and ginger. Grind together.
- Add the semolina and sour cream. Mix well. Add the coriander leaves, curry leaves and enough water to make a thick batter.
- Grease a flat pan and heat it. Pour 2 tbsp batter on it and spread with the back of a spoon. Cook for 3 minutes on a low heat. Flip and repeat.
- Repeat for the remaining batter. Serve hot.

Nutri Roll

Makes 8-10

Ingredients

200g/7oz spinach, finely chopped

1 carrot, finely chopped

125g/4½oz frozen peas

50g/1¾oz sprouted mung beans

3-4 large potatoes, boiled and mashed

2 large onions, finely chopped

½ tsp ginger paste

½ tsp garlic paste

1 green chilli, finely chopped

½ tsp amchoor*

Salt to taste

½ tsp chilli powder

3 tbsp coriander leaves, finely chopped

Refined vegetable oil for shallow frying

8-10 chapattis (see page 549)

2 tbsp hot and sweet mango chutney (see page 19)

Method

- Steam (see cooking techniques) the spinach, carrots, peas and mung beans together.
- Mix the steamed vegetables with the potatoes, onions, ginger paste, garlic paste, green chilli, amchoor, salt, chilli powder and coriander leaves. Knead well to make a smooth mixture.
- Shape the mixture into small cutlets.
- Heat the oil in a saucepan. Shallow fry the cutlets on a medium heat till golden brown. Drain and set aside.
- Spread some hot and sweet mango chutney over a chapatti. Place a cutlet in the centre and roll the chapatti up.
- Repeat for all the chapattis. Serve hot.

Sabudana Palak Doodhi Uttapam

(Sago, Spinach and Bottle Gourd Pancake)

Makes 20

Ingredients

1 tsp toor dhal*

1 tsp mung dhal*

1 tsp urad beans*

1 tsp masoor dhal*

3 tsp rice

100g/3½ oz sago, coarsely
  ground

50g/1¾oz spinach, steamed
  (see cooking techniques)
  and ground

¼ bottle gourd*, grated

125g/4½oz besan*

½ tsp ground cumin

1 tsp mint leaves,
  finely chopped

1 green chilli,
  finely chopped

½ tsp ginger paste

Salt to taste

100ml/3½fl oz water

Refined vegetable oil
  for frying

Method

- Grind together the toor dhal, mung dhal, urad beans, masoor dhal and rice. Set aside.
- Soak the sago for 3-5 minutes. Drain completely.
- Mix with the ground dhal-and-rice mixture.
- Add the spinach, bottle gourd, besan, ground cumin, mint leaves, green chilli, ginger paste, salt and enough water to make a thick batter. Set aside for 30 minutes.
- Grease a frying pan and heat it. Pour 1 tbsp batter in the pan and spread it with the back of a spoon.
- Cover and cook on a medium heat till the underside is light brown. Flip and repeat.
- Repeat for the remaining batter. Serve hot with tomato ketchup or green coconut chutney (see page 15).

Poha

Serves 4

Ingredients

150g/5½oz poha*

1½ tbsp refined vegetable oil

½ tsp cumin seeds

½ tsp mustard seeds

1 large potato, finely chopped

2 large onions, finely sliced

5-6 green chillies, finely chopped

8 curry leaves, roughly chopped

¼ tsp turmeric

45g/1½oz roasted peanuts (optional)

25g/scant 1oz fresh coconut, grated or scraped

10g/¼oz coriander leaves, finely chopped

1 tsp lemon juice

Salt to taste

Method

- Wash the poha well. Drain the water completely and set the poha aside in a colander for 15 minutes.
- Gently loosen the poha lumps with your fingers. Set aside.
- Heat the oil in a saucepan. Add the cumin and mustard seeds. Let them splutter for 15 seconds.
- Add the chopped potatoes. Stir-fry on a medium heat for 2-3 minutes. Add the onions, green chillies, curry leaves and turmeric. Cook till the onions are translucent. Remove from the heat.
- Add the poha, roasted peanuts and half of the grated coconut and coriander leaves. Toss to mix thoroughly.
- Sprinkle the lemon juice and salt. Cook on a low heat for 4-5 minutes.
- Garnish with the remaining coconut and coriander leaves. Serve hot.

Vegetable Cutlet

Makes 10-12

Ingredients

2 onions, finely chopped

5 garlic cloves

¼ tsp fennel seeds

2-3 green chillies

10g/¼oz coriander leaves, finely chopped

2 large carrots, finely chopped

1 large potato, finely chopped

1 small beetroot, finely chopped

50g/1¾oz French beans, finely chopped

50g/1¾oz green peas

900ml/1½ pints water

Salt to taste

¼ tsp turmeric

2-3 tbsp besan*

1 tbsp refined vegetable oil plus extra for deep frying

50g/1¾oz breadcrumbs

Method

- Grind 1 onion, the garlic, fennel seeds, green chillies and coriander leaves together into a smooth paste. Set aside.
- Mix the carrots, potato, beetroot, French beans and peas together in a saucepan. Add 500ml/16fl oz water, salt and turmeric and cook on a medium heat till the vegetables are soft.
- Mash the vegetables thoroughly and set aside.
- Mix the besan and the remaining water together to form a smooth batter. Set aside.
- Heat 1 tbsp oil in a saucepan. Add the remaining onion and fry till translucent.
- Add the onion-garlic paste and fry for a minute on a medium heat, stirring continuously.
- Add the mashed vegetables and mix thoroughly.
- Remove from the heat and set aside to cool.
- Divide this mixture into 10-12 balls. Flatten between your palms to make patties.
- Dip the patties in the batter and roll in the breadcrumbs.
- Heat the oil in a frying pan. Shallow fry the patties till golden brown on both sides.
- Serve hot with ketchup.

Soy Bean Uppit

(Soy Bean Snack)

Serves 4

Ingredients

1½ tbsp refined vegetable oil

½ tsp mustard seeds

2 green chillies, finely chopped

2 red chillies, finely chopped

Pinch of asafoetida

1 large onion, finely chopped

2.5cm/1in root ginger, julienned

10 garlic cloves, finely chopped

6 curry leaves

100g/3½oz soy bean semolina*, dry roasted (see cooking techniques)

100g/3½oz semolina, dry roasted (see cooking techniques)

200g/7oz peas

500ml/16fl oz hot water

¼ tsp turmeric

1 tsp sugar

1 tsp salt

1 large tomato, finely chopped

2 tbsp coriander leaves, finely chopped

15 raisins

10 cashew nuts

Method

- Heat the oil in a saucepan. Add the mustard seeds. Let them splutter for 15 seconds.
- Add the green chillies, red chillies, asafoetida, onion, ginger, garlic and curry leaves. Fry on a medium heat for 3-4 minutes, stirring frequently.
- Add the soy bean semolina, semolina and the peas. Cook till both the kinds of the semolina turn golden brown.
- Add the hot water, turmeric, sugar and salt. Cook over a medium heat till the water dries up.
- Garnish with the tomato, coriander leaves, raisins and cashew nuts.
- Serve hot.

Upma

(Semolina Breakfast Dish)

Serves 4

Ingredients

1 tbsp ghee
150g/5½oz semolina
1 tbsp refined vegetable oil
¼ tsp mustard seeds
1 tsp urad dhal*
3 green chillies, slit lengthways
8-10 curry leaves
1 medium-sized onion,
  finely chopped

1 medium-sized tomato,
  finely chopped
750ml/1¼ pints water
1 heaped tsp sugar
Salt to taste
50g/1¾oz canned peas (optional)
25g/scant 1oz coriander leaves,
  finely chopped

Method

- Heat the ghee in a frying pan. Add the semolina and fry, stirring frequently, till the semolina turns golden brown. Set aside.
- Heat the oil in a saucepan. Add the mustard seeds, urad dhal, green chillies and curry leaves. Fry till the urad dhal turns brown.
- Add the onion and fry on a low heat till translucent. Add the tomato and fry for another 3-4 minutes.
- Add the water and mix well. Cook on a medium heat till the mixture starts boiling. Stir well.
- Add the sugar, salt, semolina and peas. Mix well.
- Cook on a low heat, stirring continuously for 2-3 minutes.
- Garnish with the coriander leaves. Serve hot.

Vermicelli Upma
(Vermicelli with Onion)

Serves 4

Ingredients

3 tbsp refined vegetable oil

1 tsp mung dhal*

1 tsp urad dhal*

¼ tsp mustard seeds

8 curry leaves

10 peanuts

10 cashew nuts

1 medium potato, finely chopped

1 large carrot, finely chopped

2 green chillies, finely chopped

1cm/½ in root ginger, finely chopped

1 large onion, finely chopped

1 tomato, finely chopped

50g/1¾oz frozen peas

Salt to taste

1 litre/1¾ pints water

200g/7oz vermicelli

2 tbsp ghee

Method

- Heat the oil in a saucepan. Add the mung dhal, urad dhal, mustard seeds and curry leaves. Let them splutter for 30 seconds.
- Add the peanuts and cashew nuts. Fry on a medium heat till golden brown.
- Add the potato and carrot. Fry for 4-5 minutes.
- Add the chillies, ginger, onion, tomato, peas and salt. Cook on a medium heat, stirring frequently, till the vegetables are tender.
- Add the water and bring to a boil. Stir well.
- Add the vermicelli while stirring continuously to make sure no lumps are formed.
- Cover with a lid and cook on a low heat for 5-6 minutes.
- Add the ghee and mix well. Serve hot.

Bonda

(Potato Chop)

Makes 10

Ingredients

5 tbsp refined vegetable oil plus extra for deep frying

½ tsp mustard seeds

2.5mm/1in root ginger, finely chopped

2 green chillies, finely chopped

50g/1¾oz coriander leaves, finely chopped

1 large onion, finely chopped

4 medium-sized potatoes, boiled and mashed

1 large carrot, finely chopped and boiled

125g/4½oz canned peas

Pinch of turmeric

Salt to taste

1 tsp lemon juice

250g/9oz besan*

200ml/7fl oz water

½ tsp baking powder

Method

- Heat 4 tbsp oil in a saucepan. Add the mustard seeds, ginger, green chillies, coriander leaves and onion. Fry on a medium heat, stirring occasionally, till the onion turns brown.
- Add the potatoes, carrot, peas, turmeric and salt. Cook on a low heat for 5-6 minutes, stirring occasionally.
- Sprinkle lemon juice and divide the mixture into 10 balls. Set aside.
- Mix the the besan, water and baking powder with 1 tbsp oil to make the batter.
- Heat the oil in a saucepan. Dip each potato ball in the batter and deep fry on a medium heat till golden brown.
- Serve hot.

Instant Dhokla

(Instant Steamed Savoury Cake)

Makes 15-20

Ingredients

250g/9oz besan*

1 tsp salt

2 tbsp sugar

2 tbsp refined vegetable oil

½ tbsp lemon juice

240ml/8fl oz water

1 tbsp baking powder

1 tsp mustard seeds

2 green chillies, slit lengthways

A few curry leaves

1 tbsp water

2 tbsp coriander leaves, finely chopped

1 tbsp fresh coconut, grated

Method

- Mix together the besan, salt, sugar, 1 tbsp oil, lemon juice and water to make a smooth batter.
- Grease a 20cm/8in round cake tin.
- Add the baking powder to the batter. Mix well and pour immediately in the greased tin. Steam (see cooking techniques) for 20 minutes.
- Pierce with a fork to check if done. If the fork does not come out clean, steam again for 5-10 minutes. Set aside.
- Heat the remaining oil in a saucepan. Add the mustard seeds. Let them splutter for 15 seconds.
- Add the green chillies, curry leaves and water. Cook on a low heat for 2 minutes.
- Pour this mixture over the dhokla and allow it to soak up the liquid.
- Garnish with the coriander leaves and grated coconut.
- Cut into squares and serve with mint chutney (see page 15).

DHAL

Dhals – or lentils – complete an Indian meal, always eaten with rice or Indian breads. Most regions have specific ways of cooking dhals. In Bengal, dhals are sometimes cooked with a fish head and in other regions, fresh vegetables are added for extra flavour. As India's population has a large number of vegetarians, dhals are considered to be the source of protein to supplement the lack of meat and fish in their diets.

Dhal Maharani
(Black Lentils and Kidney Beans)

Serves 4

Ingredients

150g/5½oz urad dhal*

2 tbsp kidney beans

1.4 litres/2½ pints water

Salt to taste

1 tbsp refined vegetable oil

½ tsp cumin seeds

1 large onion, finely chopped

3 medium-sized tomatoes, chopped

1 tsp ginger paste

½ tsp garlic paste

½ tsp chilli powder

½ tsp garam masala

120ml/4fl oz fresh single cream

Method

- Soak the urad dhal and kidney beans together overnight. Drain and cook together in a saucepan with the water and salt for 1 hour on a medium heat. Set aside.
- Heat the oil in a saucepan. Add the cumin seeds. Let them splutter for 15 seconds.
- Add the onion and fry on a medium heat till golden brown.
- Add the tomatoes. Mix well. Add the ginger paste and garlic paste. Fry for 5 minutes.
- Add the cooked dhal and beans mixture, chilli powder and garam masala. Mix well.
- Add the cream. Simmer for 5 minutes, stirring frequently.
- Serve hot with naan (see page 565) or steamed rice (see page 519).

Milagu Kuzhambu
(Split Red Gram in a Pepper Sauce)

Serves 4

Ingredients
2 tsp ghee
2 tsp coriander seeds
1 tbsp tamarind paste
1 tsp ground black pepper
¼ tsp asafoetida
Salt to taste
1 tbsp toor dhal*, cooked
1 litre/1¾ pints water
¼ tsp mustard seeds
1 green chilli, chopped
¼ tsp turmeric
10 curry leaves

Method
- Heat a few drops of ghee in a saucepan. Add the coriander seeds and fry on a medium heat for 2 minutes. Cool and grind.
- Mix with the tamarind paste, pepper, asafoetida, salt and dhal in a large saucepan.
- Add the water. Mix well and bring to a boil on a medium heat. Set aside.
- Heat the remaining ghee in a saucepan. Add the mustard seeds, green chilli, turmeric and curry leaves. Let them splutter for 15 seconds.
- Add this to the dhal. Serve hot.

Dhal Hariyali
(Leafy Vegetables with Split Bengal Gram)

Serves 4

Ingredients
300g/10oz toor dhal*
1.4 litres/2½ pints water
Salt to taste
2 tbsp ghee
1 tsp cumin seeds
1 onion, finely chopped
½ tsp ginger paste
½ tsp garlic paste
½ tsp turmeric
50g/1¾oz spinach, chopped
10g/¼oz fenugreek leaves, finely chopped
25g/scant 1oz coriander leaves

Method
- Cook the dhal with the water and salt in a saucepan for 45 minutes, stirring frequently. Set aside.
- Heat the ghee in a saucepan. Add the cumin seeds, onion, ginger paste, garlic paste and turmeric. Fry for 2 minutes on a low heat, stirring continuously.
- Add the spinach, fenugreek leaves and the coriander leaves. Mix well and simmer for 5-7 minutes.
- Serve hot with steamed rice (see page 519).

Dhalcha

(Split Bengal Gram with Lamb)

Serves 4

Ingredients

150g/5½oz chana dhal*
150g/5½oz toor dhal*
2.8 litres/5 pints water
Salt to taste
2 tbsp tamarind paste
2 tbsp refined vegetable
  oil
4 large onions, chopped
5cm/2in root ginger,
  grated
10 garlic cloves, pounded
750g/1lb 10oz lamb,
  chopped
1.4 litres/2½ pints water
3-4 tomatoes, chopped
1 tsp chilli powder
1 tsp turmeric
1 tsp garam masala
20 curry leaves
25g/scant 1oz coriander
  leaves, finely chopped

Method

- Cook the dhals with the water and salt for 1 hour on a medium heat. Add the tamarind paste and mash well. Set aside.
- Heat the oil in a saucepan. Add the onions, ginger and garlic. Fry on a medium heat till brown. Add the lamb and stir constantly till brown.
- Add water and simmer till the lamb is tender.
- Add the tomatoes, chilli powder, turmeric and salt. Mix well. Cook for another 7 minutes.
- Add the dhal, garam masala and curry leaves. Mix well. Simmer for 4-5 minutes.
- Garnish with the coriander leaves. Serve hot.

Tarkari Dhalcha

(Split Bengal Gram with Vegetables)

Serves 4

Ingredients

150g/5½oz chana dhal*
150g/5½oz toor dhal*
Salt to taste
3 litres/5¼ pints water
10g/¼oz mint leaves
10g/¼oz coriander leaves
2 tbsp refined vegetable oil
½ tsp mustard seeds
½ tsp cumin seeds
Pinch of fenugreek seeds
Pinch of kalonji seeds*
2 dry red chillies
10 curry leaves
½ tsp ginger paste
½ tsp garlic paste
½ tsp turmeric
1 tsp chilli powder
1 tsp tamarind paste
500g/1lb 2oz pumpkin,
  finely diced

Method

- Cook both the dhals with the salt, 2.5 litres/4 pints of water and half the mint and coriander in a saucepan on a medium heat for 1 hour. Grind into a thick paste. Set aside.
- Heat the oil in a saucepan. Add the mustard, cumin, fenugreek and kalonji seeds. Let them splutter for 15 seconds.
- Add the red chillies and curry leaves. Fry on a medium heat for 15 seconds.
- Add the dhal paste, ginger paste, garlic paste, turmeric, chilli powder and tamarind paste. Mix well. Cook on a medium heat, stirring frequently, for 10 minutes.
- Add the remaining water and the pumpkin. Simmer till the pumpkin is cooked.
- Add the remaining mint and coriander leaves. Cook for 3-4 minutes.
- Serve hot.

Dhokar Dhalna

(Fried Dhal Cubes in Curry)

Serves 4

Ingredients

600g/1lb 5oz chana dhal*, soaked overnight

120ml/4fl oz water

Salt to taste

4 tbsp refined vegetable oil plus extra for deep frying

3 green chillies, chopped

½ tsp asafoetida

2 large onions, finely chopped

1 bay leaf

1 tsp ginger paste

1 tsp garlic paste

1 tsp chilli powder

¾ tsp turmeric

1 tsp garam masala

1 tbsp coriander leaves, finely chopped

Method

- Grind the dhal with the water and some salt to a thick paste. Set aside.
- Heat 1 tbsp oil in a saucepan. Add the green chillies and asafoetida. Let them splutter for 15 seconds. Stir in the dhal paste and some more salt. Mix well.
- Spread this mixture on a tray to cool. Cut into 2.5cm/1in pieces.
- Heat the oil for deep frying in a saucepan. Fry the pieces till golden brown. Set aside.
- Heat 2 tbsp oil in a saucepan. Fry the onions till brown. Grind them to a paste and set aside.
- Heat the remaining 1 tbsp oil in a saucepan. Add the bay leaf, fried dhal pieces, the fried onion paste, ginger paste, garlic paste, chilli powder, turmeric and garam masala. Add enough water to cover the dhal pieces. Mix well and simmer for 7-8 minutes.
- Garnish with the coriander leaves. Serve hot.

Varan

(Simple Split Red Gram Dhal)

Serves 4

Ingredients
300g/10oz toor dhal*
2.4 litres/4 pints water
¼ tsp asafoetida
½ tsp turmeric
Salt to taste

Method
- Cook all the ingredients in a saucepan for about 1 hour on a medium heat.
- Serve hot with steamed rice (see page 519).

Sweet Dhal

(Sweet Split Red Gram)

Serves 4-6

Ingredients
300g/10oz toor dhal*
2.5 litres/4 pints water
Salt to taste
¼ tsp turmeric
A large pinch of asafoetida
½ tsp chilli powder
5cm/2in piece of jaggery*
2 tsp refined vegetable oil
¼ tsp cumin seeds
¼ tsp mustard seeds
2 dry red chillies
1 tbsp coriander leaves, finely chopped

Method
- Wash and cook the toor dhal with the water and salt in a saucepan on a low heat for 1 hour.
- Add the turmeric, asafoetida, chilli powder, and jaggery. Cook for 5 minutes. Mix thoroughly. Set aside.
- In a small saucepan, heat the oil. Add the cumin seeds, mustard seeds and the dry red chillies. Let them splutter for 15 seconds.
- Pour this in the dhal and mix well.
- Garnish with the coriander leaves. Serve hot.

Sweet & Sour Dhal

(Sweet and Sour Split Red Gram)

Serves 4-6

Ingredients
300g/10oz toor dhal*
2.4 litres/4 pints water
Salt to taste
¼ tsp turmeric
¼ tsp asafoetida
1 tsp tamarind paste
1 tsp sugar
2 tsp refined vegetable oil
½ tsp mustard seeds
2 green chillies
8 curry leaves
1 tbsp coriander leaves,
  finely chopped

Method
- Cook the toor dhal in a saucepan with the water and salt on a medium heat for 1 hour.
- Add the turmeric, asafoetida, tamarind paste and sugar. Cook for 5 minutes. Set aside.
- In a small saucepan, heat the oil. Add the mustard seeds, green chillies and curry leaves. Let them splutter for 15 seconds.
- Pour this seasoning in the dhal.
- Garnish with the coriander leaves.
- Serve hot with steamed rice (see page 519) or chapattis (see page 549).

Mung-ni-Dhal

(Split Green Gram)

Serves 4

Ingredients
300g/10oz mung dhal*
1.9 litres/3½ pints water
Salt to taste
¼ tsp turmeric
½ tsp ginger paste
1 green chilli,
  finely chopped
¼ tsp sugar
1 tbsp ghee
½ tsp sesame seeds
1 small onion, chopped
1 garlic clove, chopped

Method
- Boil the mung dhal with the water and salt in a saucepan on a medium heat for 30 minutes.
- Add the turmeric, ginger paste, green chilli and sugar. Stir well.
- Add 120ml/4fl oz water if the dhal is dry. Simmer for 2-3 minutes and set aside.
- Heat the ghee in a small saucepan. Add the sesame seeds, onion and garlic. Fry them for 1 minute, stirring continuously.
- Add this to the dhal. Serve hot.

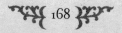

Dhal with Onion & Coconut

(Split Red Gram with Onion and Coconut)

Serves 4-6

Ingredients
300g/10oz toor dhal*
2.8 litres/5 pints water
2 green chillies, chopped
1 small onion, chopped
Salt to taste
¼ tsp turmeric
1½ tsp vegetable oil
½ tsp mustard seeds
1 tbsp coriander leaves,
  finely chopped
50g/1¾oz fresh coconut,
  grated

Method
- Boil the toor dhal with water, green chillies, onion, salt and turmeric in a saucepan on a medium heat for 1 hour. Set aside.
- Heat the oil in a saucepan. Add the mustard seeds. Let them splutter for 15 seconds.
- Pour this in the dhal and mix well.
- Garnish with the coriander leaves and coconut. Serve hot.

Dahi Kadhi

(Yoghurt-based Curry)

Serves 4

Ingredients
1 tbsp besan*
250g/9oz yoghurt
750ml/1¼ pints water
2 tsp sugar
Salt to taste
½ tsp ginger paste
1 tbsp refined vegetable oil
¼ tsp mustard seeds
¼ tsp cumin seeds
¼ tsp fenugreek seeds
8 curry leaves
10g/¼oz coriander leaves,
  finely chopped

Method
- Mix the besan with the yoghurt, water, sugar, salt and ginger paste in a large saucepan. Stir well to make sure no lumps form.
- Cook the mixture on a medium heat till it starts to thicken, stirring frequently. Bring to the boil. Set aside.
- Heat the oil in a saucepan. Add the mustard seeds, cumin seeds, fenugreek seeds and curry leaves. Let them splutter for 15 seconds.
- Pour this oil on top of the besan mixture.
- Garnish with the coriander leaves. Serve hot.

Spinach Dhal

(Spinach with Split Green Gram)

Serves 4

Ingredients

300g/10oz mung dhal*
1.9 litres/3½ pints water
Salt to taste
1 large onion, chopped
6 garlic cloves, chopped
¼ tsp turmeric
100g/3½oz spinach,
 chopped
½ tsp amchoor*
Pinch of garam masala
½ tsp ginger paste
1 tbsp refined vegetable oil
1 tsp cumin seeds
2 tbsp coriander leaves,
 finely chopped

Method

- Cook the dhal with the water and salt in a saucepan on a medium heat for 30-40 minutes.
- Add the onion and garlic. Cook for 7 minutes.
- Add the turmeric, spinach, amchoor, garam masala and ginger paste. Mix thoroughly.
- Simmer till the dhal is soft and all the spices have been absorbed. Set aside.
- Heat the oil in a saucepan. Add the cumin seeds. Let them splutter for 15 seconds.
- Pour this on top of the dhal.
- Garnish with the coriander leaves. Serve hot

Tawker Dhal

(Sour Split Red Lentil with Unripe Mango)

Serves 4

Ingredients

300g/10oz toor dhal*
2.4 litres/4 pints water
1 unripe mango, stoned
 and quartered
½ tsp turmeric
4 green chillies
Salt to taste
2 tsp mustard oil
½ tsp mustard seeds
1 tbsp coriander leaves,
 finely chopped

Method

- Boil the dhal with the water, mango pieces, turmeric, green chillies and salt for an hour. Set aside.
- Heat the oil in a saucepan and add the mustard seeds. Let them splutter for 15 seconds.
- Add this to the dhal. Simmer till thick.
- Garnish with the coriander leaves. Serve hot with steamed rice (see page 519).

Basic Dhal

(Split Red Gram with Tomato)

Serves 4

Ingredients

300g/10oz toor dhal*
1.2 litres/2 pints water
Salt to taste
¼ tsp turmeric
½ tbsp refined vegetable oil
¼ tsp cumin seeds
2 green chillies, slit lengthways
1 medium-sized tomato, finely chopped
1 tbsp coriander leaves, finely chopped

Method

- Cook the toor dhal with the water and salt in a saucepan for 1 hour on a medium heat.
- Add the turmeric and mix well.
- If the dhal is too thick, add 120ml/4fl oz water to it. Mix well and set aside.
- Heat the oil in a saucepan. Add the cumin seeds and let them splutter for 15 seconds. Add the green chillies and tomato. Fry for 2 minutes.
- Add this to the dhal. Mix and simmer for 3 minutes.
- Garnish with the coriander leaves. Serve hot with steamed rice (see page 519).

Maa-ki-Dhal

(Rich Black Gram)

Serves 4

Ingredients

240g kaali dhal*
125g/4½oz kidney beans
2.8 litres/5 pints water
Salt to taste
3.5cm/1½in root ginger, julienned
1 tsp chilli powder
3 tomatoes, puréed
1 tbsp butter
2 tsp refined vegetable oil
1 tsp cumin seeds
2 tbsp single cream

Method

- Soak the dhal and the kidney beans together overnight.
- Cook with the water, salt and ginger in a saucepan for 40 minutes on a medium heat.
- Add the chilli powder, tomato purée and butter. Simmer for 8-10 minutes. Set aside.
- Heat the oil in a saucepan. Add the cumin seeds. Let them splutter for 15 seconds.
- Add this to the dhal. Mix well.
- Add the cream. Serve hot with steamed rice (see page 519).

Dhansak
(Spicy Parsi Split Red Gram)

Serves 4

Ingredients
3 tbsp refined vegetable oil
1 large onion, finely chopped
2 large tomatoes, chopped
½ tsp turmeric
½ tsp chilli powder
1 tbsp dhansak masala*
1 tbsp malt vinegar
Salt to taste

For the dhal mixture:
150g/5½oz toor dhal*
75g/2½oz mung dhal*
75g/2½oz masoor dhal*
1 small aubergine, quartered
7.5cm/3in piece of pumpkin, quartered
1 tbsp fresh fenugreek leaves
1.4 litres/2½ pints water
Salt to taste

Method
- Cook the ingredients for the dhal mixture together in a saucepan on a medium heat for 45 minutes. Set aside.
- Heat the oil in a saucepan. Fry the onions and tomatoes on a medium heat for 2-3 minutes.
- Add the dhal mixture and all the remaining ingredients. Mix well and cook on a medium heat for 5-7 minutes. Serve hot.

Masoor Dhal

Serves 4

Ingredients
300g/10oz masoor dhal*
Salt to taste
Pinch of turmeric
1.2 litres/2 pints water

2 tbsp refined vegetable oil
6 garlic cloves, crushed
1 tsp lemon juice

Method
- Cook the dhal, salt, turmeric and water in a saucepan on a medium heat for 45 minutes. Set aside.
- Heat the oil in a frying pan and fry the garlic till brown. Add to the dhal and sprinkle with the lemon juice. Mix well. Serve hot.

Panchemel Dhal
(Five Lentil Mix)

Serves 4

Ingredients

75g/2½oz mung dhal*
1 tbsp chana dhal*
1 tbsp masoor dhal*
1 tbsp toor dhal*
1 tbsp urad dhal*
750ml/1¼ pints water
½ tsp turmeric

Salt to taste
1 tbsp ghee
1 tsp cumin seeds
Pinch of asafoetida
½ tsp garam masala
1 tsp ginger paste

Method

- Cook the dhals with the water, turmeric and salt in a saucepan for 1 hour on a medium heat. Stir well. Set aside.
- Heat the ghee in a saucepan. Fry the remaining ingredients for 1 minute.
- Add this to the dhal, mix well and simmer for 3-4 minutes. Serve hot.

Cholar Dhal
(Split Bengal Gram)

Serves 4

Ingredients

600g/1lb 5oz chana dhal*
2.4 litres/5 pints water
Salt to taste
3 tbsp ghee
½ tsp cumin seeds
½ tsp turmeric

2 tsp sugar
3 cloves
2 bay leaves
2.5cm/1in cinnamon
2 green cardamom pods
15g/½oz coconut, chopped and fried

Method

- Cook the dhal with the water and salt in a saucepan on a medium heat for 1 hour. Set aside.
- Heat 2 tbsp ghee in a saucepan. Add all the ingredients, except the coconut. Let them splutter for 20 seconds. Add the cooked dhal and cook, stirring well for 5 minutes. Add the coconut and 1 tbsp ghee. Serve hot.

Dilpasand Dhal
(Special Lentils)

Serves 4

Ingredients

60g/2oz urad beans*
2 tbsp kidney beans
2 tbsp chickpeas
2 litres/3½ pints water
¼ tsp turmeric
2 tbsp ghee

2 tomatoes, blanched and puréed
2 tsp ground cumin, dry roasted
  (see cooking techniques)
125g/4½oz yoghurt, whisked
120ml/4fl oz single cream
Salt to taste

Method

- Mix both the beans, chickpeas and water. Soak in a saucepan for 4 hours. Add the turmeric and cook for 45 minutes on a medium heat. Set aside.
- Heat the ghee in a saucepan. Add all the remaining ingredients and cook on a medium heat till the ghee separates.
- Add the beans and chickpeas mixture. Simmer till dry. Serve hot.

Dhal Masoor
(Split Red Lentils)

Serves 4

Ingredients

1 tbsp ghee
1 tsp cumin seeds
1 small onion, finely chopped
2.5cm/1in root ginger, finely chopped
6 garlic cloves, finely chopped
4 green chillies, slit lengthways

1 tomato, peeled and puréed
½ tsp turmeric
300g/10oz masoor dhal*
1.5 litres/2¾ pints water
Salt to taste
2 tbsp coriander leaves

Method

- Heat the ghee in a saucepan. Add the cumin seeds, onion, ginger, garlic, chillies, tomato and turmeric. Fry for 5 minutes, stirring frequently.
- Add the dhal, water and salt. Simmer for 45 minutes. Garnish with the coriander leaves. Serve hot with steamed rice (see page 519).

Dhal with Aubergine

(Lentils with Aubergine)

Serves 4

Ingredients

300g/10oz toor dhal*

1.5 litre/2¾ pints water

Salt to taste

1 tbsp refined vegetable oil

50g/1¾oz aubergines, diced

2.5cm/1in cinnamon

2 green cardamom pods

2 cloves

1 large onion, finely chopped

2 large tomatoes, finely chopped

½ tsp ginger paste

½ tsp garlic paste

1 tsp ground coriander

½ tsp turmeric

10g/¼oz coriander leaves, to garnish

Method

- Boil the dhal with the water and salt in a saucepan for 45 minutes on a medium heat. Set aside.
- Heat the oil in a saucepan. Add all the remaining ingredients, except the coriander leaves. Fry for 2-3 minutes, stirring constantly.
- Add the mixture to the dhal. Simmer for 5 minutes. Garnish and serve.

Yellow Dhal Tadka

Serves 4

Ingredients

300g/10oz mung dhal*

1 litre/1¾ pints water

¼ tsp turmeric

Salt to taste

3 tsp ghee

½ tsp mustard seeds

½ tsp cumin seeds

½ tsp fenugreek seeds

2.5cm/1in root ginger, finely chopped

4 garlic cloves, finely chopped

3 green chillies, slit lengthways

8 curry leaves

Method

- Cook the dhal with the water, turmeric and salt in a saucepan for 45 minutes on a medium heat. Set aside.
- Heat the ghee in a saucepan. Add all the remaining ingredients. Fry them for 1 minute and pour on top of the dhal. Mix well and serve hot.

Rasam

(Spicy Tamarind-based Soup)

Serves 4

Ingredients

2 tbsp tamarind paste

750ml/1¼ pints water

8-10 curry leaves

2 tbsp chopped coriander leaves

Pinch of asafoetida

Salt to taste

2 tsp ghee

½ tsp mustard seeds

For the spice mixture:

2 tsp coriander seeds

2 tbsp toor dhal*

1 tsp cumin seeds

4-5 peppercorns

1 dried red chilli

Method

- Dry roast (see cooking techniques) and grind the spice mixture ingredients together.
- Mix the spice mixture with all the ingredients, except the ghee and the mustard seeds. Cook for 7 minutes on a medium heat in a saucepan.
- Heat the ghee in another saucepan. Add the mustard seeds and let them splutter for 15 seconds. Pour this directly in the rasam. Serve hot.

Simple Mung Dhal

Serves 4

Ingredients

300g/10oz mung dhal*

1 litre/1¾ pints water

Pinch of turmeric

Salt to taste

2 tbsp refined vegetable oil

1 large onion, finely chopped

3 green chillies, finely chopped

2.5cm/1in root ginger, finely chopped

5 curry leaves

2 tomatoes, finely chopped

Method

- Cook the dhal with the water, turmeric and salt in a saucepan for 30 minutes on a medium heat. Set aside.
- Heat the oil in a saucepan. Add all the remaining ingredients. Fry for 3-4 minutes. Add this to the dhal. Simmer till thick. Serve hot.

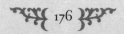

Whole Green Mung

Serves 4

Ingredients

250g/9oz mung beans, soaked overnight
1 litre/1¾ pints water
½ tbsp refined vegetable oil
½ tsp cumin seeds
6 curry leaves
1 large onion, finely chopped
½ tsp garlic paste

½ tsp ginger paste
3 green chillies, finely chopped
1 tomato, finely chopped
¼ tsp turmeric
Salt to taste
120ml/4fl oz milk

Method

- Cook the beans with the water in a saucepan for 45 minutes on a medium heat. Set aside.
- Heat the oil in a saucepan. Add the cumin seeds and curry leaves.
- After 15 seconds, add the cooked beans and all the remaining ingredients. Mix well and simmer for 7-8 minutes. Serve hot.

Dahi Kadhi with Pakoras
(Yoghurt-based Curry with Fried Dumplings)

Serves 4

Ingredients
For the pakora:
125g/4½oz besan*
¼ tsp cumin seeds
2 tsp chopped onions
1 chopped green chilli
½ tsp grated ginger
Pinch of turmeric

2 green chillies, finely chopped
½ tsp ajowan seeds
Salt to taste
Oil for deep frying

For the kadhi:
Dahi Kadhi (see page 169)

Method

- In a bowl, mix all the pakora ingredients, except the oil, with enough water to form a thick batter. Fry spoonfuls in hot oil till golden brown.
- Cook the kadhi and add the pakoras to it. Simmer for 3-4 minutes.
- Serve hot with steamed rice (see page 519).

177

Sweet Unripe Mango Dhal

(Split Red Gram with Unripe Mango)

Serves 4

Ingredients

300g/10oz toor dhal*

2 green chillies, slit lengthways

2 tsp jaggery*, grated

1 small onion, sliced

Salt to taste

¼ tsp turmeric

1.5 litres/2¾ pints water

1 unripe mango, peeled and chopped

1½ tsp refined vegetable oil

½ tsp mustard seeds

1 tbsp coriander leaves, for garnish

Method

- Mix all the ingredients, except the oil, mustard seeds and coriander leaves, in a saucepan. Cook for 30 minutes on a medium heat. Set aside.
- Heat the oil in a saucepan. Add the mustard seeds. Let them splutter for 15 seconds. Pour this on top of the dhal. Garnish and serve hot.

Malai Dhal

(Split Black Gram with Cream)

Serves 4

Ingredients

300g/10oz urad dhal*, soaked for 4 hours

1 litre/1¾ pints water

500ml/16fl oz milk, boiled

1 tsp turmeric

Salt to taste

½ tsp amchoor*

2 tbsp single cream

1 tbsp ghee

1 tsp cumin seeds

2.5cm/1in root ginger, finely chopped

1 small tomato, finely chopped

1 small onion, finely chopped

Method

- Cook the dhal with the water on a medium heat for 45 minutes.
- Add the milk, turmeric, salt, amchoor and cream. Mix well and cook for 3-4 minutes. Set aside.
- Heat the ghee in a saucepan. Add the cumin seeds, ginger, tomato and onion. Fry for 3 minutes. Add this to the dhal. Mix well and serve hot.

Sambhar

(Mixed Lentils and Vegetables cooked with special spices)

Serves 4

Ingredients

300g/10oz toor dhal*
1.5 litres/2¾ pints water
Salt to taste
1 tbsp refined vegetable oil
1 large onion, thinly sliced
2 tsp tamarind paste
¼ tsp turmeric
1 green chilli, roughly chopped
1½ tsp sambhar powder*
2 tbsp coriander leaves, finely chopped

For the seasoning:

1 green chilli, slit lengthways
1 tsp mustard seeds
½ tsp urad dhal*
8 curry leaves
¼ tsp asafoetida

Method

- Mix all the ingredients of the seasoning together. Set aside.
- Cook the toor dhal with the water and salt in a saucepan on a medium heat for 40 minutes. Mash well. Set aside.
- Heat the oil in a saucepan. Add the seasoning ingredients. Let them splutter for 20 seconds.
- Add the cooked dhal and all the remaining ingredients, except the coriander leaves. Cook on a low heat for 8-10 minutes.
- Garnish with the coriander leaves. Serve hot.

Three Dhals
(Mixed Lentils)

Serves 4

Ingredients

150g/5½oz toor dhal*

75g/2½oz masoor dhal*

75g/2½oz mung dhal*

1 litre/1¾ pints water

1 large tomato, finely chopped

1 small onion, finely chopped

4 garlic cloves, finely chopped

6 curry leaves

Salt to taste

¼ tsp turmeric

2 tbsp refined vegetable oil

½ tsp cumin seeds

Method

- Soak the dhals in the water for 30 minutes. Cook with the remaining ingredients, except the oil and cumin, for 45 minutes on a medium heat.
- Heat the oil in a saucepan. Add the cumin seeds. Let them splutter for 15 seconds. Pour this on top of the dhal. Mix well. Serve hot.

Methi-Drumstick Sambhar
(Fenugreek and Drumsticks with Split Red Gram)

Serves 4

Ingredients

300g/10oz toor dhal*

1 litre/1¾ pints water

Pinch of turmeric

Salt to taste

2 Indian drumsticks*, chopped

1 tsp refined vegetable oil

¼ tsp mustard seeds

1 red chilli, halved

¼ tsp asafoetida

10g/¼oz fresh fenugreek leaves, chopped

1¼ tsp sambhar powder*

1¼ tsp tamarind paste

Method

- Mix the dhal, water, turmeric, salt and drumsticks in a saucepan. Cook for 45 minutes on a medium heat. Set aside.
- Heat the oil in a pan. Add all the remaining ingredients and stir-fry for 2-3 minutes. Add this to the dhal and simmer for 7-8 minutes. Serve hot.

Dhal Shorba
(Lentil Soup)

Serves 4

Ingredients

300g/10oz toor dhal*

Salt to taste

1 litre/1¾ pints water

1 tbsp refined vegetable oil

2 large onions, sliced

4 garlic cloves, crushed

50g/1¾oz spinach leaves, finely chopped

3 tomatoes, finely chopped

1 tsp lemon juice

1 tsp garam masala

Method
- Cook the dhal, salt and water in a saucepan on a medium heat for 45 minutes. Set aside.
- Heat the oil. Fry the onions on a medium heat till brown. Add all the remaining ingredients and cook for 5 minutes, stirring frequently.
- Add this to the dhal mixture. Serve hot.

Yummy Mung
(Whole Mung)

Serves 4

Ingredients

250g/9oz mung beans

2.5 litres/4 pints water

Salt to taste

2 medium-sized onions, chopped

3 green chillies, chopped

¼ tsp turmeric

1 tsp chilli powder

1 tsp lemon juice

1 tbsp refined vegetable oil

½ tsp cumin seeds

6 garlic cloves, crushed

Method
- Soak the mung beans in the water for 3-4 hours. Cook in a saucepan with the salt, onions, green chillies, turmeric and chilli powder on a medium heat for 1 hour.
- Add the lemon juice. Simmer for 10 minutes. Set aside.
- Heat the oil in a saucepan. Add the cumin seeds and garlic. Fry for 1 minute on a medium heat. Pour this in the mung mixture. Serve hot.

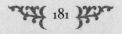

Masala Toor Dhal
(Spicy Split Red Gram)

Serves 4

Ingredients

300g/10oz toor dhal*
1.5 litres/2¾ pints water
Salt to taste
½ tsp turmeric
1 tbsp refined vegetable oil
½ tsp mustard seeds
8 curry leaves
¼ tsp asafoetida

½ tsp ginger paste
½ tsp garlic paste
1 green chilli, finely chopped
1 onion, finely chopped
1 tomato, finely chopped
2 tsp lemon juice
2 tbsp coriander leaves, to garnish

Method
- Cook the dhal with the water, salt and turmeric in a saucepan for 45 minutes on a medium heat. Set aside.
- Heat the oil in a saucepan. Add all the ingredients, except the lemon juice and coriander leaves. Fry for 3-4 minutes on a medium heat. Pour this on top of the dhal.
- Add the lemon juice and coriander leaves. Mix well. Serve hot.

Dry Yellow Mung Dhal
(Dry Yellow Gram)

Serves 4

Ingredients

300g/10oz mung dhal*, soaked for 1 hour
250ml/8fl oz water
¼ tsp turmeric
Salt to taste

1 tbsp ghee
1 tsp amchoor*
1 tbsp coriander leaves, chopped
1 small onion, finely chopped

Method
- Cook the dhal with the water, turmeric and salt in a saucepan for 45 minutes on a medium heat.
- Heat the ghee and pour it on top of the dhal. Sprinkle the amchoor, coriander leaves and the onion on top. Serve hot.

Whole Urad

(Whole Black Gram)

Serves 4

Ingredients

300g/10oz urad beans*, washed
Salt to taste
1.25 litres/2½ pints water
¼ tsp turmeric
½ tsp chilli powder
½ tsp dried ginger powder
¾ tsp garam masala

1 tbsp ghee
½ tsp cumin seeds
1 large onion, finely chopped
2 tbsp coriander leaves,
  finely chopped

Method

- Cook the urad beans with the salt and water in a saucepan for
  45 minutes on a medium heat.
- Add the turmeric, chilli powder, ginger powder and garam masala.
  Mix well and simmer for 5 minutes. Set aside.
- Heat the ghee in a saucepan. Add the cumin seeds and let them splutter
  for 15 seconds. Add the onion and fry it on a medium heat till brown.
- Add the onion mixture to the dhal and mix well. Simmer for 10 minutes.
- Garnish with the coriander leaves. Serve hot.

Dhal Fry

(Split Red Gram with Fried Spices)

Serves 4

Ingredients

300g/10oz toor dhal*

1.5 litres/2¾ pints water

½ tsp turmeric

Salt to taste

2 tbsp ghee

½ tsp mustard seeds

½ tsp cumin seeds

½ tsp fenugreek seeds

2.5cm/1in root ginger, finely chopped

2-3 garlic cloves, finely chopped

2 green chillies, finely chopped

1 small onion, finely chopped

1 tomato, finely chopped

Method

- Cook the dhal with the water, turmeric and salt in a saucepan for 45 minutes over a medium heat. Stir well. Set aside.
- Heat the ghee in a saucepan. Add the mustard seeds, cumin seeds and fenugreek seeds. Let them splutter for 15 seconds.
- Add the ginger, garlic, green chillies, onion and tomato. Fry on a medium heat for 3-4 minutes, stirring frequently. Add this to the dhal. Serve hot.

Peppery Mung Dhal

Serves 4

Ingredients

225g/8oz mung dhal*

Salt to taste

2 green chillies, finely chopped

Pinch of turmeric

1.25 litres/2½ pints water

1 tsp lemon juice

½ tsp ground black pepper

Method

- Mix the dhal, salt, green chillies, turmeric and water in a saucepan. Cook on a medium heat for 45 minutes.
- Add the lemon juice and pepper. Mix well. Serve hot.

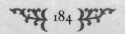

Dhal Bukhara

(Creamy Whole Black Gram)

Serves 4-6

Ingredients

600g/1lb 5oz urad dhal*, soaked
  overnight

2 tbsp kidney beans, soaked overnight

2 litres/3½ pints water

Salt to taste

3 tbsp butter

1 tsp cumin seeds

1 large onion, finely chopped

2.5cm/1in root ginger, finely chopped

2 garlic cloves, finely chopped

1 tsp chilli powder

1 tbsp ground coriander

4 tomatoes, blanched and chopped

½ tsp garam masala

2 tbsp fresh single cream

2 tbsp yoghurt

3 tbsp ghee

2.5cm/1in root ginger, julienned

2 green chillies, slit lengthways

1 tbsp coriander leaves,
  finely chopped

Method

- Do not drain the dhal and the kidney beans. Mix with the water and salt in a saucepan. Cook for one hour on a medium heat. Mash gently and set aside.
- In a small frying pan, melt the butter. Add the cumin seeds. Let them splutter for 15 seconds.
- Add the onion, ginger, garlic, chilli powder, coriander and tomatoes. Cook on a low heat for 7-8 minutes, stirring occasionally.
- Add the garam masala, cream, yoghurt and ghee. Mix well. Cook for 2-3 minutes.
- Add this mixture to the dhal. Simmer for 10 minutes.
- Garnish with the ginger, green chillies and coriander leaves. Serve hot with steamed rice (see page 519), chapatti (see page 549) or naan (see page 565).

Methi Dhal
(Split Red Gram with Fenugreek)

Serves 4

Ingredients

50g/1¾oz fresh fenugreek leaves, finely chopped

Salt to taste

300g/10oz toor dhal*

1.5 litres/2¾ pints water

1 large onion, finely chopped

2 tomatoes, finely chopped

2 tsp tamarind paste

1 green chilli, slit lengthways

¼ tsp turmeric

¾ tsp chilli powder

2 tbsp fresh coconut, grated

1 tbsp jaggery*, grated

For the seasoning:

2 tsp refined vegetable oil

½ tsp mustard seeds

6 curry leaves

8 cloves, pounded

Method

- Rub the fenugreek leaves with some salt and set aside.
- Cook the toor dhal with the water and salt in a saucepan for 45 minutes on a medium heat.
- Add the fenugreek leaves along with the onion, tomatoes, tamarind paste, green chilli, turmeric, chilli powder, coconut and jaggery. Mix thoroughly. Add some more water if needed. Simmer for 5 minutes.
- Remove from the heat. Mash well and set aside.
- Heat the oil in a saucepan. Add the mustard seeds, curry leaves and cloves. Let them splutter for 15 seconds. Pour this on top of the dhal. Serve hot.

VEGETABLES

Vegetables in India are not side dishes but form an integral part of the meal. They can be steamed, fried or cooked in a sauce. Each seasonal vegetable has unique spices with which it is cooked, depending on the weather. This chapter has several interesting combinations and curries that are guaranteed to set your mouth watering.

Malai Koftas
(Dumplings in Sweet Sauce)

Serves 4

Ingredients

2.5cm/1in cinnamon

6 green cardamom pods

¼ tsp ground nutmeg

6 cloves

3 tsp freshly ground white pepper

3.5cm/1½in root ginger, grated

½ tsp turmeric

2 garlic cloves, crushed

2½ tsp sugar

Salt to taste

120ml/4fl oz water

3 tbsp ghee

360ml/12fl oz milk

120ml/4fl oz single cream

1 tbsp Cheddar cheese, grated

1 tbsp coriander leaves, finely chopped

For the koftas:

50g/1¾oz khoya*

50g/1¾oz paneer*

4 large potatoes, boiled and mashed

4-5 green chillies, finely chopped

1cm/½in root ginger, grated

1 tsp coriander, chopped

½ tsp cumin seeds

Salt to taste

20g/¾oz raisins

20g/¾oz cashew nuts

Method

- For the koftas, knead together all the kofta ingredients, except the raisins and cashew nuts, to form a soft dough.
- Divide this dough into walnut-sized balls. Press 2-3 raisins and cashew nuts into the centre of each ball.
- Bake the balls in an oven at 200°C (400°F/ Gas Mark 6) for 5 minutes. Set them aside.
- For the sauce, dry roast (see cooking techniques) the cinnamon, cardamom, nutmeg and cloves together in a frying pan on a low heat for 1 minute. Grind and set aside.
- Grind the pepper, ginger, turmeric, garlic, sugar and salt with the water. Set aside.
- Heat the ghee in a saucepan. Add the cinnamon-cardamom mixture. Fry it on a medium heat for a minute.
- Add the pepper-ginger mixture. Fry for 5-7 minutes, stirring occasionally.
- Add the milk and cream. Simmer for 15 minutes, stirring occasionally.
- Place the warm koftas in a casserole dish.
- Pour the sauce over the koftas and garnish with the cheese and coriander leaves. Serve hot.
- Alternatively, after pouring the sauce over the koftas, bake in a pre-heated oven at 200°C (400°F, Gas Mark 6) for 5 minutes. Garnish with the cheese and the coriander leaves. Serve hot.

Aloo Palak

(Potatoes Cooked with Spinach)

Serves 6

Ingredients

300g/10oz spinach,
  chopped and steamed

2 green chillies, slit
  lengthways

4 tbsp ghee

2 large potatoes, boiled
  and diced

½ tsp cumin seeds

2.5cm/1in root ginger,
  julienned

2 large onions,
  finely chopped

3 tomatoes,
  finely chopped

1 tsp chilli powder

½ tsp ground cinnamon

½ tsp ground cloves

¼ tsp turmeric

½ tsp garam masala

½ tsp wholemeal flour

1 tsp lemon juice

Salt to taste

½ tbsp butter

Large pinch of asafoetida

Method

● Coarsely grind the spinach with the green chillies in a blender. Set aside.

● Heat the ghee in a saucepan. Add the potatoes and fry them on a medium heat till light brown and crisp. Drain them and set aside.

● In the same ghee, add the cumin seeds. Let them splutter for 15 seconds.

● Add the ginger and onions. Fry them on a medium heat for 2-3 minutes.

● Add the remaining ingredients, except the butter and asafoetida. Cook the mixture on a medium heat for 3-4 minutes, stirring at regular intervals.

● Add the spinach and potatoes. Mix well and simmer for 2-3 minutes. Set the mixture aside.

● Heat the butter in a small saucepan. Add the asafoetida. Let it splutter for 5 seconds.

● Pour this mixture immediately over the aloo palak. Mix gently. Serve hot.

NOTE: *You can replace the potatoes with fresh peas or corn kernels.*

Dum ka Karela

(Slow Cooked Bitter Gourd)

Serves 4

Ingredients

12 bitter gourds*
Salt to taste
500ml/16fl oz water
1 tsp turmeric
1 tsp ginger paste
1 tsp garlic paste
Butter for basting
  and greasing

For the filling:

1 tbsp fresh coconut,
  chopped
60g/2oz peanuts
1 tbsp sesame seeds
1 tsp cumin seeds
2 large onions
2.5cm/1in root ginger,
  julienned
2 tsp jaggery*, grated
1½ tsp ground coriander
1 tsp chilli powder
Salt to taste
150g/5½oz paneer*, grated

For the seasoning:

3 tbsp refined vegetable oil
10 curry leaves
½ tsp cumin seeds
½ tsp mustard seeds
¼ tsp fenugreek seeds

Method

- Make a single slit in the bitter gourds lengthways, taking care that the bases remain intact. Deseed them. Rub them with salt and set aside for 1 hour.
- Mix the water with the turmeric, ginger paste, garlic paste and some salt in a saucepan and cook on a medium heat for 5-7 minutes. Add the bitter gourds. Cook till they are soft. Drain and set aside.
- For the filling, dry roast (see cooking techniques) all the filling ingredients, except the paneer. Mix the dry roasted mixture with 60ml/2fl oz water. Grind to a fine paste.
- Add the paneer. Mix it thoroughly with the ground paste. Set aside.
- Heat the oil in a frying pan. Add the seasoning ingredients. Let them splutter for 15 seconds.
- Pour this over the filling mixture. Mix well. Divide the filling into 12 equal portions.
- Stuff a portion in each bitter gourd. Arrange them on a greased baking tray with the stuffed side facing up. Punch a few holes in a sheet of foil and seal the tray with it.
- Bake the bitter gourds in an oven at 140°C (275°F, Gas Mark 1) for 30 minutes, basting them at regular intervals. Serve hot.

Navratna Curry

(Rich Mixed Vegetable Curry)

Serves 4

Ingredients

100g/3½oz French beans
2 large carrots
100g/3½oz cauliflower
200g/7oz peas
360ml/12fl oz water
4 tbsp ghee plus extra
  for deep frying
2 potatoes, chopped
150g/5½oz paneer*,
  chopped into pieces
2 tomatoes, puréed
2 large green peppers,
  chopped into long strips
150g/5½oz cashew nuts
250g/9oz raisins
2 tsp sugar
Salt to taste
200g/7oz yoghurt, whisked
2 pineapple slices,
  chopped
A few cherries

For the spice mixture:

6 garlic cloves
2 green chillies
4 dry red chillies
2.5cm/1in root ginger
2 tsp coriander seeds
1 tsp cumin seeds
1 tsp black cumin seeds
3 green cardamom pods

Method

- Dice the French beans, carrots and cauliflower. Mix them with the peas and water. Cook this mixture in a saucepan on a medium heat for 7-8 minutes. Set aside.
- Heat the ghee for deep frying in a pan. Add the potatoes and paneer. Deep-fry them on a medium heat till they turn golden brown. Drain them and set aside.
- Grind together all the ingredients of the spice mixture into a paste. Set aside.
- Heat 4 tbsp ghee in a frying pan.
  Add the spice paste. Fry it on a medium heat for 1-2 minutes, stirring constantly.
- Add the tomato purée, peppers, cashew nuts, raisins, sugar and salt. Mix well.
- Add the cooked vegetables, fried paneer and potatoes and the yoghurt. Stir till the yoghurt and tomato purée coat the remaining ingredients. Simmer for 10-15 minutes.
- Decorate the Navratna curry with the pineapple slices and cherries. Serve hot.

Mixed Vegetable Kofta in Tomato Curry

Serves 4

Ingredients
For the kofta:

125g/4½oz frozen corn

125g/4½oz frozen peas

60g/2oz French beans, chopped

60g/2oz carrots, finely chopped

375g/13oz besan*

½ tsp chilli powder

Pinch of turmeric

1 tsp amchoor*

1 tsp ground coriander

½ tsp ground cumin

Salt to taste

Refined vegetable oil for deep frying

For the curry:

4 tomatoes, finely chopped

2 tsp tomato paste

1 tsp ground ginger

½ tsp chilli powder

¼ tsp sugar

¼ tsp ground cinnamon

2 cloves

Salt to taste

1 tbsp paneer*, grated

25g/scant 1oz coriander leaves, finely chopped

Method

- For the kofta, mix the corn, peas, French beans and carrots together in a saucepan. Parboil (see cooking techniques) the mixture.
- Knead the parboiled mixture with the remaining kofta ingredients, except the oil, to form a soft dough. Divide the dough into lemon-sized balls.
- Heat the oil in a frying pan. Add the kofta balls. Deep fry them on a medium heat till they turn golden brown. Drain the koftas and set them aside.
- For the curry, mix together all the curry ingredients, except the paneer and coriander leaves, in a saucepan.
- Cook this mixture for 15 minutes on a medium heat, stirring frequently.
- Add the koftas gently to the curry, 15 minutes before serving.
- Garnish with the paneer and coriander leaves. Serve hot.

Muthias in White Sauce

(Paneer and Fenugreek Dumplings in White Sauce)

Serves 4

Ingredients

1 tbsp cashew nuts

1 tbsp lightly roasted peanuts

1 slice white bread

1 medium-sized onion, finely chopped

2.5cm/1in root ginger

3 green chillies

1 tsp poppy seeds, soaked in 2 tbsp milk for 1 hour

2 tbsp ghee

240ml/6fl oz milk

1 tsp caster sugar

Pinch of ground cinnamon

Pinch of ground cloves

120ml/4fl oz single cream

Salt to taste

200g/7oz yoghurt

For the muthias:

300g/10oz paneer*, crumbled

1 tbsp finely chopped fenugreek leaves

1 tbsp plain white flour

Salt to taste

Chilli powder to taste

Ghee for deep frying

Method

- Knead together all the muthia ingredients, except the ghee, to form a soft dough. Divide the dough into walnut-sized balls.
- Heat the ghee in a frying pan. Add the balls and deep fry them on a medium heat till they turn golden brown. Set aside.
- Grind together the cashew nuts, roasted peanuts and bread with enough water to form a paste. Set the mixture aside.
- Grind together the onion, ginger, chillies and poppy seeds with enough water to form a paste. Set the mixture aside.
- Heat the ghee in a frying pan. Add the onion-ginger mixture. Fry till it turns brown.
- Add all the remaining ingredients and the cashew-peanut paste. Mix well. Simmer for 15 minutes, stirring frequently.
- Add the muthias. Mix gently. Serve hot.

Brown Curry

Serves 4

Ingredients

2 green cardamom pods

2 cloves

2 black peppercorns

1cm/½in cinnamon

1 bay leaf

2 dry red chillies

1 tsp wholemeal flour

2 tbsp refined vegetable oil

1 large onion, sliced

1 tsp cumin seeds

Pinch of asafoetida

1 large green pepper,
   julienned

2.5cm/1in root ginger,
   julienned

4 garlic cloves, pounded

½ tsp chilli powder

¼ tsp turmeric

1 tsp ground coriander

2 large tomatoes,
   finely chopped

1 tbsp tamarind paste

Salt to taste

1 tbsp coriander leaves,
   finely chopped

Method

- Grind together the cardamom, cloves, peppercorns, cinnamon, bay leaf and red chillies to a fine powder. Set aside.
- Dry roast (see cooking techniques) the flour to a light pink, stirring continuously. Set aside.
- Heat the oil in a saucepan. Add the onion. Fry on a medium heat till it turns brown. Drain and grind to a fine paste. Set aside.
- Heat the same oil and add the cumin seeds. Let them splutter for 15 seconds.
- Add the asafoetida, green pepper, ginger and garlic. Stir-fry for a minute.
- Add the remaining ingredients, except the coriander leaves. Mix well.
- Add the ground cardamom-clove mixture, the dry roasted flour and the onion paste. Mix well.
- Simmer for 10-15 minutes.
- Garnish with the coriander leaves. Serve hot.

NOTE: *This curry goes well with vegetables like baby potatoes in their skin, peas and stir-fried aubergine pieces.*

Diamond Curry

Serves 4

Ingredients

2-3 tbsp refined vegetable oil

2 large onions, ground to a paste

1 tsp ginger paste

1 tsp garlic paste

2 large tomatoes, puréed

1-2 green chillies

½ tsp turmeric

1 tbsp ground cumin

½ tsp garam masala

½ tsp sugar

Salt to taste

250ml/8fl oz water

For the diamonds:

250g/9oz besan*

200ml/7fl oz water

1 tbsp refined vegetable oil

1 pinch asafoetida

½ tsp cumin seeds

25g/scant 1oz coriander leaves, finely chopped

2 green chillies, finely chopped

Salt to taste

Method

- For the sauce, heat the oil in a saucepan. Add the onion paste. Fry the paste on a medium heat till it turns translucent.
- Add the ginger paste and garlic paste. Fry for a minute.
- Add the remaining ingredients, except the diamond ingredients. Mix well. Cover with a lid and simmer the mixture for 5-7 minutes. Set the sauce aside.
- To make the diamonds, mix the besan with water carefully to form a thick batter. Avoid forming lumps. Set aside.
- Heat the oil in a saucepan. Add the asafoetida and cumin seeds. Let them splutter for 15 seconds.
- Add the besan batter and all the remaining diamond ingredients. Stir continuously on a medium heat till the mixture leaves the sides of the pan.
- Grease a 15 × 35cm/6 × 14in non-stick baking tray. Pour in the batter and smooth flat with a palette knife. Allow to set for 20 minutes. Chop into diamond shapes.
- Add the diamonds to the sauce. Serve hot.

Vegetable Stew

Serves 4

Ingredients

1 tbsp plain white flour

3 tbsp refined vegetable oil

4 cloves

2.5cm/1in cinnamon

2 green cardamom pods

1 small onion, diced

1cm/½in root ginger, chopped

2-5 green chillies, slit lengthways

10 curry leaves

150g/5½oz frozen, mixed vegetables

600ml/1 pint coconut milk

Salt to taste

1 tbsp vinegar

1 tsp ground black pepper

1 tsp mustard seeds

1 shallot, chopped

Method

* Mix the flour with enough water to form a thick paste. Set aside.
* Heat 2 tbsp oil in a saucepan. Add the cloves, cinnamon and cardamom. Let them splutter for 30 seconds.
* Add the onion, ginger, chillies and curry leaves. Stir-fry the mixture on a medium heat for 2-3 minutes.
* Add the vegetables, coconut milk and salt. Stir for 2-3 minutes.
* Add the flour paste. Cook for 5-7 minutes, stirring continuously.
* Add the vinegar. Mix well. Simmer for another minute. Set the stew aside.
* Heat the remaining oil in a saucepan. Add the pepper, mustard seeds and shallot. Fry for 1 minute.
* Pour this mixture over the stew. Serve hot.

Mushroom & Pea Curry

Serves 4

Ingredients

2 green chillies

1 tbsp poppy seeds

2 green cardamom pods

1 tbsp cashew nuts

1cm/½in root ginger

½ tbsp ghee

1 large onion,
  finely chopped

4 garlic cloves,
  finely chopped

400g/14oz mushrooms,
  sliced

200g/7oz canned peas

Salt to taste

1 tbsp yoghurt

1 tbsp single cream

10g/¼oz coriander leaves,
  finely chopped

Method

- Grind together the green chillies, poppy seeds, cardamom, cashew nuts and ginger to form a thick paste. Set aside.
- Heat the ghee in a saucepan. Add the onion. Fry on a medium heat till translucent.
- Add the garlic and the ground green chillies-poppy seeds mixture. Stir-fry for 5-7 minutes.
- Add the mushrooms and peas. Stir-fry for 3-4 minutes.
- Add the salt, yoghurt and cream. Mix well. Simmer for 5-7 minutes, stirring occasionally.
- Garnish with the coriander leaves. Serve hot.

Navratan Korma

(Spicy Mixed Vegetables)

Serves 4

Ingredients

1 tsp cumin seeds

2 tsp poppy seeds

3 green cardamom pods

1 large onion,
finely chopped

25g/scant 1oz coconut,
shredded

3 green chillies, slit
lengthways

3 tbsp ghee

15 cashew nuts

3 tbsp butter

400g/14oz canned peas

2 carrots, boiled
and chopped

1 small apple,
finely chopped

2 pineapple slices,
finely chopped

125g/4½oz yoghurt

60ml/2fl oz single cream

120ml/4fl oz tomato
ketchup

20 raisins

Salt to taste

1 tbsp Cheddar cheese,
grated

1 tbsp coriander leaves,
finely chopped

2 glacé cherries

Method

- Grind together the cumin seeds and the poppy seeds to a fine powder. Set aside.
- Grind together the cardamom, onion, coconut and green chillies to a thick paste. Set aside.
- Heat the ghee. Add the cashew nuts. Fry them on a medium heat till they turn golden brown. Drain and set them aside. Do not discard the ghee.
- Add the butter to the ghee and heat the mixture for a minute, stirring thoroughly.
- Add the cardamom-onion mixture. Stir-fry on a medium heat for 2 minutes.
- Add the peas, carrots, apple and pineapple. Stir-fry the mixture for 5-6 minutes.
- Add the cumin-poppy seeds mixture. Cook for another minute on a low heat.
- Add the yoghurt, cream, ketchup, raisins and salt. Stir the mixture on a low heat for 7-8 minutes.
- Garnish the korma with the cheese, coriander leaves, cherries and the fried cashew nuts. Serve hot.

Sindhi Sai Bhaji*

(Sindhi Spicy Vegetables)

Serves 4

Ingredients

3 tbsp refined vegetable oil

1 large onion, chopped

3 green chillies, slit lengthways

6 garlic cloves, finely chopped

1 carrot, finely chopped

1 large green pepper, finely chopped

1 small cabbage, finely chopped

1 large potato, finely chopped

1 aubergine, finely chopped

100g/3½oz okra, chopped

100g/3½oz French beans, finely chopped

150g/5½oz spinach leaves, finely chopped

100g/3½oz coriander leaves, finely chopped

300g/10oz masoor dhal*, soaked for 30 minutes and drained

150g/5½oz mung dhal*, soaked for 30 minutes and drained

750ml/1¼ pints water

1 tsp chilli powder

1 tsp ground coriander

½ tsp turmeric

1 tsp salt

1 tomato

½ tbsp ghee

Pinch of asafoetida

Method

- Heat the oil in a large saucepan. Add the onion. Fry on a medium heat till translucent.
- Add the green chillies and garlic. Fry for another minute.
- Add all the remaining ingredients, except the tomato, ghee and asafoetida. Mix thoroughly. Cover with a lid and cook on a low heat for 10 minutes, stirring at regular intervals.
- Place the whole tomato on top of the vegetable mixture, cover again and continue to cook the mixture for 30 minutes.
- Remove from the heat and blend the contents coarsely. Set the bhaji aside.
- Heat the ghee in a saucepan. Add the asafoetida. Let it splutter for 10 seconds. Pour directly over the bhaji. Stir the mixture thoroughly. Serve hot.

Nawabi Beetroot

(Rich Beetroot)

Serves 4

Ingredients

500g/1lb 2oz medium-sized beetroots, peeled

125g/4½oz yoghurt

120ml/4fl oz single cream

Salt to taste

2.5cm/1in root ginger, julienned

100g/3½oz fresh peas

1 tbsp lemon juice

1 tbsp refined vegetable oil

2 tbsp butter

1 large onion, grated

6 garlic cloves, crushed

1 tsp chilli powder

Pinch of turmeric

1 tsp garam masala

250g/9oz Cheddar cheese, grated

50g/1¾oz coriander leaves, finely chopped

Method

- Hollow out the beetroots. Do not discard the scooped out portions. Set aside.
- Mix together 2 tbsp yoghurt, 2 tbsp cream and salt.
- Toss the hollowed beetroots in this mixture to coat them well.
- Steam (see cooking techniques) these beetroots on a medium heat for 5-7 minutes. Set aside.
- Mix the scooped out portions of the beetroots with the ginger, peas, lemon juice and salt.
- Heat the oil in a saucepan. Add the beetroot-ginger mixture. Stir-fry on a medium heat for 4-5 minutes.
- Stuff the steamed beetroots with this mixture. Set aside.
- Heat the butter in a saucepan. Add the onion and garlic. Fry them on a medium heat till the onion turns translucent.
- Add the remaining cream, the chilli powder, turmeric and garam masala. Stir well. Cook for 4-5 minutes.
- Add the stuffed beetroots, the remaining yoghurt and the cheese. Simmer for 2-3 minutes and add the coriander leaves. Serve hot.

Baghara Baingan

(Hot and Tangy Aubergine)

Serves 4

Ingredients

1 tbsp coriander seeds

1 tbsp poppy seeds

1 tbsp sesame seeds

½ tsp cumin seeds

3 dry red chillies

100g/3½oz fresh coconut, grated

3 large onions, finely chopped

2.5cm/1in root ginger

5 tbsp refined vegetable oil

500g/1lb 2oz aubergines, chopped

8 curry leaves·

½ tsp turmeric

½ tsp chilli powder

3 green chillies, slit lengthways

8 curry leaves

1½ tsp tamarind paste

250ml/8fl oz water

Salt to taste

Method

- Dry roast (see cooking techniques) the coriander seeds, poppy seeds, sesame seeds, cumin seeds and red chillies for 1-2 minutes. Set aside.
- Grind together the coconut, 1 onion and the ginger to form a thick paste. Set aside.
- Heat half the oil in a saucepan. Add the aubergines. Fry them on a medium heat for 5 minutes, turning occasionally. Drain and set them aside.
- Heat the remaining oil in a saucepan. Add the curry leaves and the remaining onions. Fry them on a medium heat till the onions turn brown.
- Add the coconut paste. Stir-fry for a minute.
- Add the remaining ingredients. Mix well. Cook on a low heat for 3-4 minutes.
- Add the dry roasted coriander seeds-poppy seeds mixture. Mix well. Continue to cook for 2-3 minutes.
- Add the fried aubergines. Stir the mixture thoroughly. Cook for 3-4 minutes. Serve hot.

Steamed Carrot Kofta

Serves 4

Ingredients

2 tbsp refined vegetable oil
2 large onions, grated
6 tomatoes,
  finely chopped
1 tbsp yoghurt
1 tsp garam masala

For the kofta:

2 large carrots, grated
125g/4½oz besan*
125g/4½oz wholemeal
  flour
150g/5½oz cracked wheat
1 tsp garam masala
½ tsp turmeric
1 tsp chilli powder
¼ tsp citric acid
½ tsp bicarbonate of soda
2 tsp refined vegetable oil
Salt to taste

For the paste:

3 tsp coriander seeds
1 tsp cumin seeds
4 black peppercorns
3 cloves
5cm/2in cinnamon
2 green cardamom pods
3 tsp fresh coconut, grated
6 red chillies
Salt to taste
2 tbsp water

Method

- Knead all the kofta ingredients with enough water into a soft dough. Divide the dough into walnut-sized balls.
- Steam (see cooking techniques) the balls in a steamer on a medium heat for 7-8 minutes. Set aside.
- Mix together all the paste ingredients except the water. Dry roast (see cooking techniques) the mixture on a medium heat for 2-3 minutes.
- Add water to the mixture and grind to form a smooth paste. Set aside.
- Heat the oil in a saucepan. Add the grated onions. Fry on a medium heat till they turn translucent.
- Add the tomatoes, yoghurt, garam masala and the ground paste. Sauté the mixture for 2-3 minutes.
- Add the steamed balls. Mix well. Cook the mixture on a low heat for 3-4 minutes, stirring at regular intervals. Serve hot.

Dhingri Shabnam

(Paneer Dumplings Stuffed with Mushroom)

Serves 4

Ingredients

450g/1lb paneer*

125g/4½oz plain white flour

60ml/2fl oz water

Refined vegetable oil plus extra for deep frying

¼ tsp garam masala

For the filling:

100g/3½oz button mushrooms

1 tsp unsalted butter

8 cashew nuts, chopped

16 raisins

2 tbsp khoya*

1 tbsp paneer*

1 tbsp coriander leaves, finely chopped

1 green chilli, chopped

For the sauce:

2 tbsp refined vegetable oil

¼ tsp fenugreek seeds

1 onion, finely chopped

1 tsp garlic paste

1 tsp ginger paste

¼ tsp turmeric

7-8 cashew nuts, ground

50g/1¾oz yoghurt

1 large onion, ground to a paste

750ml/1¼ pints water

Salt to taste

Method

- Knead together the paneer and flour with 60ml/2fl oz water to form a soft dough. Divide the dough into 8 balls. Flatten into discs. Set aside.
- For the filling, slice the mushrooms.
- Heat the butter in a frying pan. Add the sliced mushrooms. Stir-fry them on a medium heat for a minute.
- Remove from the heat and mix with the remaining filling ingredients.
- Divide this mixture into 8 equal portions.
- Place one filling portion on each paneer-flour disc. Seal into pouches and smooth into balls to make the koftas.
- Heat the oil for deep frying in a frying pan. Add the koftas. Deep fry them on a medium heat till they turn golden brown. Drain and set them aside.
- For the sauce, heat 2 tbsp of oil in a saucepan. Add the fenugreek seeds. Let them splutter for 15 seconds.
- Add the onion. Sauté on a medium heat till translucent.
- Add the remaining sauce ingredients. Mix well. Simmer for 8-10 minutes.
- Remove from the heat and strain the sauce through a soup strainer into a separate saucepan.
- Gently add the koftas to the strained sauce.
- Simmer this mixture for 5 minutes, stirring gently.
- Sprinkle the garam masala on top of the dhingri shabnam. Serve hot.

Mushroom Xacutti

(Spicy Mushroom in Goan Curry)

Serves 4

Ingredients

4 tbsp refined vegetable oil

3 red chillies

2 large onions,
finely chopped

1 coconut, grated

2 tsp coriander seeds

4 black peppercorns

½ tsp turmeric

1 tsp poppy seeds

2.5cm/1in cinnamon

2 cloves

2 green cardamom pods

½ tsp cumin seeds

½ tsp fennel seeds

5 garlic cloves, crushed

Salt to taste

2 tomatoes,
finely chopped

1 tsp tamarind paste

500g/1lb 2oz mushrooms,
chopped

1 tbsp coriander leaves,
finely chopped

Method

● Heat 3 tbsp oil in a saucepan. Add the red chillies. Sauté them on a medium heat for 20 seconds.

● Add the onions and coconut. Fry the mixture till it turns brown. Set aside.

● Heat a saucepan. Add the coriander seeds, peppercorns, turmeric, poppy seeds, cinnamon, cloves, cardamom, cumin seeds and fennel seeds. Dry roast (see cooking techniques) the mixture for 1-2 minutes, stirring constantly.

● Add the garlic and the salt. Mix well. Dry roast for another minute. Remove from the heat and grind to form a smooth mixture.

● Heat the remaining oil. Add the tomatoes and tamarind paste. Fry this mixture on a medium heat for a minute.

● Add the mushrooms. Sauté for 2-3 minutes.

● Add the coriander seeds-peppercorns mixture and the onion-coconut mixture. Mix well. Stir-fry on a low heat for 3-4 minutes.

● Garnish the mushroom xacutti with the coriander leaves. Serve hot.

Paneer & Corn Curry

Serves 4

Ingredients

3 cloves

2.5cm/1in cinnamon

3 black peppercorns

1 tbsp broken
cashew nuts

1 tbsp poppy seeds

3 tbsp warm milk

2 tbsp refined vegetable oil

1 large onion, grated

2 bay leaves

½ tsp ginger paste

½ tsp garlic paste

1 tsp red chilli powder

4 tomatoes, puréed

125g/4½oz yoghurt,
whisked

2 tbsp single cream

1 tsp sugar

½ tsp garam masala

250g/9oz paneer*, chopped

200g/7oz sweetcorn
kernels, cooked

Salt to taste

2 tbsp coriander leaves

Method

- Grind together the cloves, cinnamon and peppercorns to a fine powder. Set aside.
- Soak the cashew nuts and poppy seeds in the warm milk for 30 minutes. Set aside.
- Heat the oil in a saucepan. Add the onion and bay leaves. Fry them on a medium heat for a minute.
- Add the ground clove-cinnamon-peppercorn powder and the cashew nut-poppy seeds-milk mixture.
- Add the ginger paste, garlic paste and the red chilli powder. Mix well. Fry for a minute.
- Add the tomatoes. Stir-fry the mixture on a low heat for 2-3 minutes.
- Add the yoghurt, cream, sugar, garam masala, paneer, sweetcorn kernels and salt. Stir the mixture thoroughly. Cook on a low heat for 7-8 minutes, stirring at regular intervals.
- Garnish the curry with the coriander leaves. Serve hot.

Basant Bahar

(Spicy Green Tomatoes in Sauce)

Serves 4

Ingredients

500g/1lb 2oz green
   tomatoes

1 tsp refined vegetable oil

Pinch of asafoetida

3 small onions,
   finely chopped

10 garlic cloves, crushed

250g/9oz besan*

1 tsp fennel seeds

1 tsp ground coriander

¼ tsp turmeric

¼ tsp garam masala

½ tsp chilli powder

1 tsp lemon juice

Salt to taste

For the sauce:

3 onions, roasted (see
   cooking techniques)

2 tomatoes, roasted (see
   cooking techniques)

1cm/½in root ginger

2 green chillies

1 tsp yoghurt

1 tsp single cream

Pinch of asafoetida

1 tsp cumin seeds

2 bay leaves

Salt to taste

2 tsp refined vegetable oil

150g/5½oz soft goat's
   cheese, crumbled

1 tbsp coriander leaves,
   finely chopped

Method

- With a knife, make a cross on the top half of a tomato and slit it, leaving the bottom half intact. Repeat this for all the tomatoes. Set aside.
- Heat the oil in a saucepan. Add the asafoetida. Let it splutter for 10 seconds.
- Add the onions and garlic. Fry them on a medium heat till the onions turn translucent.
- Add the besan, fennel seeds, ground coriander, turmeric, garam masala and chilli powder. Continue to fry for 1-2 minutes.
- Add the lemon juice and salt. Mix well. Remove from the heat and stuff this mixture into the slit tomatoes. Set the stuffed tomatoes aside.
- Grind together all the sauce ingredients except the oil, goat's cheese and the coriander leaves to a smooth paste. Set aside.
- Heat 1 tsp of the oil. Add the goat's cheese. Fry it on a medium heat till it turns golden brown. Set aside.
- Heat the remaining oil in another saucepan. Add the ground sauce paste. Cook the mixture on a medium heat for 4-5 minutes, stirring at regular intervals.
- Add the stuffed tomatoes. Mix well. Cover the saucepan with a lid and cook the mixture on a medium heat for 4-5 minutes.
- Sprinkle the coriander leaves and the fried goat's cheese on top of the basant bahar. Serve hot.

Palak Kofta

(Spinach Dumplings in Sauce)

Serves 4

Ingredients
For the kofta:

300g/10oz spinach, finely chopped

1cm/½in root ginger

1 green chilli

1 garlic clove

Salt to taste

½ tsp garam masala

30g/1oz goat's cheese, drained

2 tbsp besan*, roasted (see cooking techniques)

4 tbsp refined vegetable oil plus extra for deep frying

For the sauce:

½ tsp cumin seeds

2.5cm/1in root ginger

2 garlic cloves

¼ tsp coriander seeds

2 small onions, ground

Pinch of chilli powder

¼ tsp turmeric

½ tomato, puréed

Salt to taste

120ml/4fl oz water

2 tbsp single cream

1 tbsp finely chopped coriander leaves

Method

- To prepare the koftas, mix the spinach, ginger, green chilli, garlic and salt in a saucepan. Cook this mixture on a medium heat for 15 minutes. Drain and grind to a smooth paste.
- Knead this paste with all the remaining kofta ingredients, except the oil, into a firm dough. Divide this dough into walnut-sized balls.
- Heat the oil for deep frying in a saucepan. Add the balls. Deep fry them on a medium heat till they turn golden brown. Drain and set them aside.
- To prepare the sauce, grind together the cumin seeds, ginger, garlic and coriander seeds. Set aside.
- Heat 4 tbsp oil in a saucepan. Add the ground onions. Fry on a low heat till brown. Add the cumin-ginger paste. Fry for another minute.
- Add the chilli powder, turmeric and tomato purée. Mix well. Continue to fry for 2-3 minutes.
- Add the salt and water. Mix well. Cover with a lid and simmer for 5-6 minutes, stirring at regular intervals.
- Uncover and add the koftas. Simmer for 5 more minutes.
- Garnish with the cream and the coriander leaves. Serve hot.

Cabbage Kofta
(Cabbage Dumplings in Sauce)

Serves 4

Ingredients
For the kofta:
100g/3½oz cabbage, grated

4 large potatoes, boiled

1 tsp cumin seeds

1 tsp ginger paste

2 green chillies,
  finely chopped

1 tsp lemon juice

Salt to taste

Refined vegetable oil
  for deep frying

For the sauce:
1 tbsp butter

3 small onions,
  finely chopped

4 garlic cloves

4-6 tomatoes,
  finely chopped

¼ tsp turmeric

1 tsp chilli powder

1 tsp sugar

250ml/8fl oz water

Salt to taste

1 tbsp coriander leaves,
  finely chopped

Method
- Knead together all the kofta ingredients, except the oil to form a soft dough. Divide the dough into walnut-sized balls.
- Heat the oil in a saucepan. Deep fry the balls on a medium heat till golden brown. Drain and set aside.
- To prepare the sauce, heat the butter in a saucepan. Add the onions and garlic. Fry them on a medium heat till they turn golden brown.
- Add the tomatoes, turmeric and chilli powder. Stir-fry the mixture for 4-5 minutes.
- Add the sugar, water and salt. Mix well. Cover with a lid and simmer for 6-7 minutes.
- Add the fried kofta balls. Simmer for 5-6 minutes.
- Garnish the cabbage kofta with the coriander leaves. Serve hot.

Koottu
(Unripe Banana Curry)

Serves 4

Ingredients

2 tbsp fresh coconut, grated

½ tsp cumin seeds

2 green chillies

1 tbsp long-grained rice, soaked for 15 minutes

500ml/16fl oz water

200g/7oz unripe banana, peeled and diced

Salt to taste

2 tsp coconut oil

½ tsp mustard seeds

½ tsp urad dhal*

Pinch of asafoetida

8-10 curry leaves

Method

- Grind together the coconut, cumin seeds, green chillies and rice with 4 tbsp of the water to form a smooth paste. Set aside.
- Mix the banana with the remaining water and salt. Cook this mixture in a saucepan on a medium heat for 10-12 minutes.
- Add the coconut-cumin seeds paste. Cook for 2-3 minutes. Set aside.
- Heat the oil in a saucepan. Add the mustard seeds, urad dhal, asafoetida and curry leaves. Let them splutter for 30 seconds.
- Pour this mixture in the banana curry. Mix well. Serve hot.

NOTE: *You can also replace the unripe banana with white ash gourd or snake gourd.*

Paneer Butter Masala

Serves 4

Ingredients

Refined vegetable oil for frying

500g/1lb 2oz paneer*, chopped

1 large carrot, finely chopped

100g/3½oz French beans, finely chopped

200g/7oz frozen peas

3 green chillies, ground

Salt to taste

1 tbsp coriander leaves, finely chopped

For the sauce:

2.5cm/1in root ginger

4 garlic cloves

4 green chillies

1 tsp cumin seeds

3 tbsp butter

2 small onions, grated

4 tomatoes, puréed

1 tsp cornflour

300g/10oz yoghurt

2 tsp sugar

½ tsp garam masala

250ml/8fl oz water

Salt to taste

Method

- Heat the oil in a saucepan. Add the paneer pieces. Deep fry them on a medium heat till they turn golden brown. Drain and set them aside.
- Mix the carrot, French beans and peas together. Steam (see cooking techniques) this mixture in a steamer on a medium heat for 8-10 minutes.
- Add the green chillies and salt. Mix well. Set aside.
- To prepare the sauce, grind together the ginger, garlic, green chillies and cumin seeds to a smooth paste.
- Heat the butter in a saucepan. Add the onions. Fry them on a medium heat till they turn translucent.
- Add the ginger-garlic paste and the tomatoes. Fry for another minute.
- Add the cornflour, yoghurt, sugar, garam masala, water and salt. Stir the mixture for 4-5 minutes.
- Add the steamed vegetable mixture and the fried paneer. Mix well. Cover with a lid and cook the mixture on a low heat for 2-3 minutes.
- Garnish the paneer butter masala with the coriander leaves. Serve hot.

Mor Kolambu

(South Indian Style Mixed Vegetables)

Serves 4

Ingredients

2 tsp coconut oil

2 medium-sized aubergines, diced

2 Indian drumsticks*, chopped

100g/3½oz pumpkin*, diced

100g/3½oz okra

Salt to taste

200g/7oz yoghurt

250ml/8fl oz water

10 curry leaves

For the spice mixture:

2 tbsp mung dhal*, soaked for 10 minutes

1 tbsp coriander seeds

½ tsp cumin seeds

4-5 fenugreek seeds

½ tsp mustard seeds

½ tsp basmati rice

2 tsp fresh coconut, grated

Method

- Mix all the ingredients of the spice mixture together. Set aside.
- Heat the coconut oil in a saucepan. Add the aubergines, drumsticks, pumpkin, okra and salt. Fry this mixture on a medium heat for 4-5 minutes.
- Add the spice mixture. Stir-fry for 4-5 minutes.
- Add the yoghurt and water. Mix well. Cover with a lid and simmer for 7-8 minutes.
- Garnish the mor kolambu with the curry leaves. Serve hot.

Aloo Gobhi aur Methi ka Tuk

(Sindhi Style Potato, Cauliflower and Fenugreek)

Serves 4

Ingredients

500ml/16fl oz water

Salt to taste

4 large unpeeled potatoes, chopped into 5cm/2in pieces

20g/¾oz fresh fenugreek leaves

3 tbsp refined vegetable oil

1 tbsp mustard seeds

2-4 curry leaves

1 tbsp ginger paste

1 tsp garlic paste

800g/1¾lb cauliflower florets

1 tsp chilli powder

1 tsp amchoor*

½ tsp ground cumin

½ tsp coarsely ground black pepper

Large pinch of dried fenugreek leaves

2 tbsp fresh pomegranate seeds

Method

- Put the water in a saucepan, add salt and bring to the boil.
- Add the potatoes and cook them till they turn soft. Drain the potatoes and set them aside.
- Rub the fresh fenugreek leaves with salt to reduce their bitterness. Wash and drain the leaves. Set aside.
- Heat the oil in a saucepan. Add the mustard seeds and curry leaves. Let them splutter for 15 seconds.
- Add the ginger paste and garlic paste. Fry the mixture on a medium heat for a minute.
- Add the cauliflower florets, chilli powder, amchoor, ground cumin, pepper and the dried fenugreek leaves. Continue to fry for 3-4 minutes.
- Add the potatoes and the fresh fenugreek leaves. Stir-fry the mixture on a low heat for 7-8 minutes.
- Garnish with the pomegranate seeds. Serve hot.

Avial

(South Indian Mixed Vegetables)

Serves 4

Ingredients

400g/14oz plain yoghurt

1 tsp cumin seeds

100g/3½oz fresh coconut, grated

Salt to taste

4 tsp coriander leaves, finely chopped

750ml/1¼ pints water

100g/3½oz pumpkin*, chopped

200g/7oz mixed frozen vegetables

¼ tsp turmeric

4 green chillies, slit lengthways

120ml/4fl oz refined vegetable oil

¼ tsp mustard seeds

10 curry leaves

Pinch of asafoetida

2 dried red chillies

Method

- Whisk the yoghurt with the cumin seeds, coconut, salt, coriander leaves and 250ml/8fl oz water. Set aside.
- Mix the pumpkin and the mixed vegetables with the salt, 500ml/16fl oz water and turmeric in a deep saucepan. Cook this mixture on a medium heat for 10-15 minutes. Set aside.
- Add the yoghurt mixture and the green chillies and simmer for 10 minutes, stirring frequently. Set aside.
- Heat the oil in a saucepan. Add the remaining ingredients. Let them splutter for 30 seconds.
- Pour this in the vegetable mixture. Mix well. Simmer for 1-2 minutes.
- Serve hot.

Buttermilk Curry

Serves 4

Ingredients

400g/14oz yoghurt

250ml/8fl oz water

3 tsp besan*

2 green chillies, slit lengthways

10 curry leaves

Salt to taste

1 tbsp ghee

½ tsp cumin seeds

6 garlic cloves, crushed

2 cloves

2 red chillies

Pinch of asafoetida

½ tsp turmeric

1 tsp chilli powder

2 tbsp coriander leaves, finely chopped

Method

- Mix the yoghurt, water and besan thoroughly in a saucepan. Make sure that no lumps are formed.
- Add the green chillies, curry leaves and salt. Cook this mixture on a low heat for 5-6 minutes, stirring occasionally. Set aside.
- Heat the ghee in a saucepan. Add the cumin seeds and garlic. Fry them on a medium heat for a minute.
- Add the cloves, red chillies, asafoetida, turmeric and chilli powder. Mix well. Fry this mixture for 1 minute.
- Pour this in the yoghurt curry. Simmer for 4-5 minutes.
- Garnish the curry with the coriander leaves. Serve hot.

Cauliflower Cream Curry

Serves 4

Ingredients

1 tsp cumin seeds

3 green chillies, slit
lengthways

1cm/½in root ginger,
grated

150g/5½oz ghee

500g/1lb 2oz cauliflower
florets

3 large potatoes, diced

2 tomatoes,
finely chopped

125g/4½oz frozen peas

2 tsp sugar

750ml/1¼ pints water

Salt to taste

250ml/8fl oz single cream

1 tsp garam masala

25g/scant 1oz coriander
leaves, finely chopped

Method

- Grind the cumin seeds, green chillies and ginger to a paste. Set aside.
- Heat the ghee in a saucepan. Add the cauliflower and potatoes. Deep fry them on a medium heat till they turn golden brown.
- Add the cumin-chilli paste. Fry for 2-3 minutes.
- Add the tomatoes and peas. Mix well. Fry this mixture for 3-4 minutes.
- Add the sugar, water, salt and cream. Stir thoroughly. Cover with a lid and simmer for 10-12 minutes.
- Sprinkle the garam masala and the coriander leaves on top of the curry. Serve hot.

Peas Usal
(Peas Masala)

Serves 3

Ingredients

1 tbsp refined vegetable oil

¼ tsp mustard seeds

¼ tsp cumin seeds

¼ tsp chilli powder

¼ tsp garam masala

2 green chillies, slit lengthways

500g/1lb 2oz fresh peas

2 tbsp water

Salt to taste

1 tbsp fresh coconut, grated

10g/¼oz coriander leaves, finely chopped

Method

- Heat the oil in a saucepan. Add the mustard seeds and cumin seeds. Let them splutter for 15 seconds.
- Add the chilli powder, garam masala and green chillies. Fry the mixture on a medium heat for a minute.
- Add the peas, water and salt. Mix well. Cook the mixture on a low heat for 7-8 minutes.
- Garnish with the coconut and coriander leaves. Serve hot.

Aloo Posto
(Potato with Poppy Seeds)

Serves 4

Ingredients

2 tbsp mustard oil

1 tsp cumin seeds

4 tbsp poppy seeds, ground

4 green chillies, chopped

½ tsp turmeric

Salt to taste

6 potatoes, boiled and diced

2 tbsp coriander leaves, finely chopped

Method

- Heat the oil in a saucepan. Add the cumin seeds. Let them splutter for 15 seconds.
- Add the ground poppy seeds, green chillies, turmeric and salt. Sauté the mixture for a few seconds.
- Add the potatoes. Toss well. Fry the mixture for 3-4 minutes.
- Garnish with the coriander leaves. Serve hot.

Palak Paneer

(Paneer in Spinach Sauce)

Serves 4

Ingredients

1 tbsp refined vegetable oil

50g/1¾oz paneer*, diced

1 tsp cumin seeds

1 green chilli, slit lengthways

1 small onion, finely chopped

200g/7oz spinach, steamed and ground

1 tsp lemon juice

Sugar to taste

Salt to taste

Method

- Heat the oil in a saucepan. Add the paneer and fry till golden brown. Drain and set aside.
- To the same oil, add the cumin seeds, green chilli and onion. Fry them on a medium heat till the onion turns brown.
- Add the remaining ingredients. Stir the mixture thoroughly. Cook for 5 minutes.
- Let this mixture cool for a while. Grind to a coarse paste in a food processor.
- Transfer to a saucepan and add the fried paneer pieces. Stir lightly. Cook on a low heat for 3-4 minutes. Serve hot.

Matar Paneer

(Peas and Paneer)

Serves 4

Ingredients

1½ tbsp ghee

250g/9oz paneer*, chopped

2 bay leaves

½ tsp chilli powder

¼ tsp turmeric

1 tsp ground coriander

½ tsp ground cumin

400g/14oz cooked peas

2 large tomatoes, blanched

5 cashew nuts, ground to a paste

2 tbsp Greek yoghurt

Salt to taste

Method

- Heat half the ghee in a saucepan. Add the paneer pieces and fry them on a medium heat till they turn golden brown. Set aside.
- Heat the remaining ghee in a saucepan. Add the bay leaves, chilli powder, turmeric, coriander and cumin. Let them splutter for 30 seconds.
- Add the peas and tomatoes. Fry for 2-3 minutes.
- Add the cashew nut paste, yoghurt, salt and the fried paneer pieces. Mix well. Simmer the mixture for 10 minutes, stirring occasionally. Serve hot.

Dahi Karela

(Fried Bitter Gourd in Yoghurt)

Serves 4

Ingredients

250g/9oz bitter gourd*, peeled and slit
  lengthways

Salt to taste

1 tsp amchoor*

2 tbsp refined vegetable oil plus extra
  for deep frying

2 large onions, finely chopped

½ tsp garlic paste

½ tsp ginger paste

400g/14oz yoghurt

1½ tsp ground coriander

1 tsp chilli powder

½ tsp turmeric

½ tsp garam masala

250ml/8fl oz water

Method

- Marinate the bitter gourd with the salt and amchoor for an hour. Heat the oil for deep frying in a saucepan. Add the gourd. Deep fry on a medium heat till golden brown. Drain and set aside.
- Heat 2 tbsp oil in a saucepan. Add the onions, garlic paste and ginger paste. Fry on a medium heat till the onions are brown.
- Add the remaining ingredients and the bitter gourd. Mix well. Cook the mixture on a low heat for 7-8 minutes. Serve hot.

Tomato Curry with Vegetables

Serves 4

Ingredients

3 tbsp refined vegetable oil

Pinch of mustard seeds

Pinch of cumin seeds

Pinch of asafoetida

8 curry leaves

4 green chillies, finely chopped

200g/7oz mixed frozen vegetables

750g/1lb 10oz tomatoes, puréed

4 tbsp besan*

Salt to taste

Method

- Heat the oil in a saucepan. Add the mustard seeds, cumin seeds, asafoetida, curry leaves and chillies. Let them splutter for 15 seconds.
- Add the vegetables, tomato purée, besan and salt. Mix well. Cook on a low heat for 8-10 minutes, stirring occasionally. Serve hot.

Doodhi with Chana Dhal
(Bottle Gourd in Gram Dhal)

Serves 4

Ingredients

1 tsp refined vegetable oil

¼ tsp mustard seeds

500g/1lb 2oz bottle gourd*, diced

1 tbsp chana dhal*, soaked for
  1 hour and drained

2 tomatoes, finely chopped

Pinch of turmeric

2 tsp jaggery*, grated

½ tsp chilli powder

Salt to taste

120ml/4fl oz water

10g/¼oz coriander leaves,
  finely chopped

Method

- Heat the oil in a saucepan. Add the mustard seeds. Let them splutter for 15 seconds.
- Add the remaining ingredients, except the water and coriander leaves. Mix well. Fry for 4-5 minutes. Add the water. Simmer for 30 minutes.
- Garnish with the coriander leaves. Serve hot.

Tomato chi Bhaji*
(Tomato Curry)

Serves 4

Ingredients

250g/9oz roasted peanuts

3 green chillies

6 large tomatoes, blanched and sliced

1½ tbsp tamarind paste

1 tbsp jaggery*, grated

1 tsp garam masala

1 tsp ground cumin

½ tsp chilli powder

Salt to taste

1 tbsp coriander leaves,
  finely chopped

Method

- Grind together the peanuts and green chillies to form a smooth paste.
- Mix with the remaining ingredients, except the coriander leaves. Cook this mixture in a saucepan on a medium heat for 5-6 minutes.
- Garnish the bhaji with the coriander leaves. Serve hot.

Dry Potatoes

Serves 4

Ingredients

1 tbsp refined vegetable oil

½ tsp mustard seeds

3 green chillies, slit lengthways

8-10 curry leaves

¼ tsp asafoetida

¼ tsp turmeric

Salt to taste

500g/1lb 2oz potatoes, boiled and diced

10g/¼oz coriander leaves,
finely chopped

Method

• Heat the oil in a saucepan. Add the mustard seeds. Let them splutter for 15 seconds.

• Add the green chillies, curry leaves, asafoetida, turmeric and salt. Fry this mixture on a medium heat for a minute.

• Add the potatoes. Toss well. Cover with a lid and cook for 5 minutes.

• Garnish the potato mixture with the coriander leaves. Serve hot.

Stuffed Okra

Serves 4

Ingredients

1 tbsp ground coriander

6 garlic cloves

50g/1¾oz fresh coconut, finely grated

1cm/½in root ginger

4 green chillies

6 tbsp besan*

1 large onion, finely chopped

1 tsp ground cumin

½ tsp chilli powder

½ tsp turmeric

Salt to taste

750g/1lb 10oz large okra, slit halfway

60ml/2fl oz refined vegetable oil

Method

• Grind the coriander, garlic, coconut, ginger and green chillies to a smooth paste. Mix this paste with the remaining ingredients, except the okra and the oil.

• Stuff this mixture into the okras.

• Heat the oil in a frying pan. Add the stuffed okra. Deep fry on a medium heat till brown, turning occasionally. Serve hot.

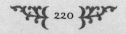

Masala Okra

Serves 4

Ingredients

2 tbsp refined vegetable oil

2 garlic cloves, finely chopped

½ tsp chilli powder

¼ tsp turmeric

½ tsp ground coriander

½ tsp ground cumin

600g/1lb 5oz okra, chopped

Salt to taste

Method

- Heat the oil in a saucepan. Add the garlic. Fry on a medium heat till brown. Add the remaining ingredients, except the okra and salt. Mix well. Fry this mixture for 1-2 minutes.
- Add the okra and salt. Stir-fry the mixture on a low heat for 3-4 minutes. Serve hot.

Simla Matar

(Green Pepper and Pea Curry)

Serves 4

Ingredients

2 tbsp refined vegetable oil

3 small onions, finely chopped

2 green chillies, finely chopped

1 tsp ginger paste

1 tsp garlic paste

2 large green peppers, diced

600g/1lb 5oz frozen peas

250ml/8fl oz water

Salt to taste

1 tbsp fresh coconut, grated

½ tsp ground cinnamon

Method

- Heat the oil in a saucepan. Add the onions. Fry them on a medium heat till they turn brown.
- Add the green chillies, ginger paste and garlic paste. Fry for 1-2 minutes.
- Add the peppers and peas. Continue to fry for 5 minutes.
- Add the water and salt. Mix well. Cover with a lid and simmer for 8-10 minutes.
- Garnish with coconut and cinnamon. Serve hot.

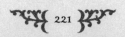

French Beans

Serves 4

Ingredients

3 tbsp refined vegetable oil
¼ tsp cumin seeds
¼ tsp turmeric
½ tsp chilli powder
1 tsp ground coriander
1 tsp ground cumin

1 tsp sugar
Salt to taste
500g/1lb 2oz French beans, finely chopped
120ml/4fl oz water

Method

- Heat the oil in a saucepan. Add the cumin seeds and turmeric. Let them splutter for 15 seconds.
- Add the remaining ingredients, except the water. Mix well.
- Add the water. Cover with a lid. Simmer for 10-12 minutes. Serve hot.

Masala Drumsticks

Serves 4

Ingredients

2 tbsp refined vegetable oil
2 small onions, finely chopped
½ tsp ginger paste
1 tomato, finely chopped
1 green chilli, finely chopped
1 tsp ground cumin
1 tsp ground coriander
½ tsp turmeric

¾ tsp chilli powder
4 Indian drumsticks*, chopped into 5cm/2in pieces
Salt to taste
250ml/8fl oz water
1 tbsp coriander leaves, finely chopped

Method

- Heat the oil in a saucepan. Add the onions and ginger paste. Fry them on a medium heat till the onions turn translucent.
- Add the remaining ingredients, except the water and coriander leaves. Mix well. Fry for 5 minutes. Add the water. Stir thoroughly. Cover with a lid. Simmer for 10-15 minutes.
- Garnish the masala drumsticks with the coriander leaves. Serve hot.

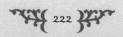

Dry Spicy Potato

Serves 4

Ingredients

750g/1lb 10oz potatoes, boiled and diced

½ tsp chaat masala*

½ tsp chilli powder

¼ tsp turmeric

3 tbsp refined vegetable oil

1 tsp white sesame seeds

2 dry red chillies, quartered

Salt to taste

½ tsp ground cumin, dry roasted (see cooking techniques)

10g/¼oz coriander leaves, finely chopped

Juice of ½ lemon

Method

- Toss the potatoes with the chaat masala, chilli powder and turmeric till the spices coat the potatoes. Set aside.
- Heat the oil in a saucepan. Add the sesame seeds and red chillies. Let them splutter for 15 seconds.
- Add the potatoes and salt. Mix well. Cook on a low heat for 7-8 minutes. Sprinkle the remaining ingredients on top. Serve hot.

Khatte Palak

(Tangy Spinach)

Serves 4

Ingredients

3 tbsp refined vegetable oil

1 large onion, grated

½ tsp ginger paste

½ tsp garlic paste

400g/14oz spinach, finely chopped

2 green chillies, finely chopped

½ tsp turmeric

1 tsp ground cumin

Salt to taste

125g/4½oz yoghurt, whisked

Method

- Heat the oil in a saucepan. Add the onion, ginger paste and garlic paste. Fry this mixture on a medium heat till the onions are translucent.
- Add the remaining ingredients, except the yoghurt. Mix thoroughly. Cook on a low heat for 7-8 minutes.
- Add the yoghurt. Mix well. Simmer for 4-5 minutes. Serve hot.

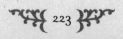

Mixed Three-in-One Vegetables

Serves 4

Ingredients

4 tbsp refined vegetable oil

¼ tsp mustard seeds

¼ tsp fenugreek seeds

300g/10oz okra, diced

2 green peppers, cored and chopped

2 tomatoes, finely chopped

2 large cucumbers, finely chopped

½ tsp chilli powder

¼ tsp turmeric

Salt to taste

Method

- Heat the oil in a saucepan. Add the mustard and fenugreek seeds. Let them splutter for 15 seconds.
- Add the okra. Fry on a medium heat for 7 minutes. Add the remaining ingredients. Mix well. Cook on a low heat for 5-6 minutes. Serve hot.

Potato in Yoghurt Sauce

Serves 4

Ingredients

120ml/4fl oz water

3 tbsp refined vegetable oil

1 tsp cumin seeds

1 tsp mustard seeds

1cm/½in root ginger, grated

2 garlic cloves, crushed

3 large potatoes, boiled and chopped

200g/7oz yoghurt, whisked

¼ tsp wholemeal flour

1 tsp salt

For the spice mixture:

1 tsp chilli powder

½ tsp ground coriander

¼ tsp turmeric

¼ tsp garam masala

Pinch of asafoetida

Method

- Mix the spice mixture ingredients with half the water. Set aside.
- Heat the oil in a saucepan. Add the cumin and mustard seeds. Let them splutter for 15 seconds. Add the ginger and garlic. Fry them on a medium heat for a minute.
- Add the spice mixture and all the remaining ingredients. Stir thoroughly. Simmer for 10-12 minutes. Serve hot.

Stuffed Aubergines

Serves 4

Ingredients

10 small aubergines

1 large onion, finely chopped

3 tbsp fresh coconut, grated

1 tsp ground cumin

1 tsp chilli powder

50g/1¾oz coriander leaves, chopped

Juice of 1 lemon

Salt to taste

3 tbsp refined vegetable oil

Method

- Make a cross with a knife at one end of each aubergine and slit, not severing the other end. Set aside.
- Mix the remaining ingredients, except the oil. Stuff this mixture in the slit aubergines.
- Heat the oil in a frying pan. Add the aubergines and fry them on a medium heat for 3-4 minutes. Cover and cook for 10 minutes, carefully turning the aubergines occasionally. Serve hot.

Sarson ka Saag

(Mustard Greens in Sauce)

Serves 4

Ingredients

3 tbsp refined vegetable oil

100g/3½oz mustard leaves, chopped

200g/7oz spinach, finely chopped

3 green chillies, slit lengthways

1cm/½in root ginger, julienned

2 garlic cloves, crushed

Salt to taste

250ml/8fl oz water

2 tbsp ghee

Blob of butter

Method

- Heat the oil in a saucepan. Add the mustard leaves, spinach and green chillies. Fry them on a medium heat for a minute.
- Add the ginger, garlic, salt and water. Mix well. Simmer for 10 minutes.
- Purée the mixture in a blender until smooth.
- Transfer to a saucepan and cook on a medium heat for 15 minutes.
- Garnish with the butter. Serve hot.

Shahi Paneer
(Paneer in Rich Sauce)

Serves 4

Ingredients

4 tbsp refined vegetable oil

500g/1lb 2oz paneer*, chopped

2 large onions, ground to a paste

1 tsp ginger paste

1 tsp garlic paste

1 tsp chilli powder

300g/10oz tomato purée

200g/7oz yoghurt, whisked

250ml/8fl oz single cream

Salt to taste

Method

- Heat 1 tbsp oil in a saucepan. Add the paneer pieces. Fry them on a medium heat till they turn golden brown. Drain and set aside.
- Add the remaining oil in the same pan. Add the onions, ginger paste and garlic paste. Fry for a minute. Add the paneer and the remaining ingredients. Cook for 5 minutes, stirring occasionally. Serve hot.

Tandoori Potato

Serves 4

Ingredients

16 large potatoes, peeled

Refined vegetable oil to deep fry

3 tbsp finely chopped tomatoes

1 tbsp coriander leaves, chopped

1 tsp garam masala

100g/3½oz Cheddar cheese, grated

Salt to taste

Juice of 2 lemons

Method

- Scoop out the potatoes. Reserve the flesh and the hollowed parts.
- Heat the oil in a frying pan. Add the hollowed potatoes. Fry them on a medium heat till they turn golden brown. Set aside.
- To the same oil, add the scooped potatoes and all the remaining ingredients, except the lemon juice. Sauté on a low heat for 5 minutes.
- Stuff this mixture inside the hollow potatoes.
- Bake the stuffed potatoes in an oven at 200°C (400°F, Gas Mark 6) for 5 minutes.
- Sprinkle the lemon juice on top of the potatoes. Serve hot.

Corn Curry

Serves 4

Ingredients

1 large potato, boiled and mashed	Salt to taste
500g/1lb 2oz tomato purée	1 tsp garam masala
3 tbsp refined vegetable oil	1 tsp chilli powder
8 curry leaves	3 tsp sugar
2 tbsp besan*	250ml/8fl oz water
1 tsp ginger paste	4 corn on the cobs, chopped into
½ tsp turmeric	3 pieces each and boiled

Method

- Mix the potato mash thoroughly with the tomato purée. Set aside.
- Heat the oil in a saucepan. Add the curry leaves. Let them crackle for 10 seconds. Add the besan and ginger paste. Fry on a low heat till brown.
- Add the potato-tomato mixture and all the remaining ingredients except the corn. Simmer for 3-4 minutes.
- Add the corn pieces. Mix well. Simmer for 8-10 minutes. Serve hot.

Masala Green Pepper

Serves 4

Ingredients

1½ tbsp refined vegetable oil	1 large onion, finely chopped
1 tsp garam masala	1 tomato, finely chopped
¼ tsp turmeric	4 large green peppers, julienned
½ tsp ginger paste	125g/4½oz yoghurt
½ tsp garlic paste	Salt to taste

Method

- Heat the oil in a saucepan. Add the garam masala, turmeric, ginger paste and garlic paste. Fry this mixture on a medium heat for 2 minutes.
- Add the onion. Fry till it is translucent.
- Add the tomato and green peppers. Fry for 2-3 minutes. Add the yoghurt and salt. Mix well. Cook for 6-7 minutes. Serve hot.

No-oil Bottle Gourd

Serves 4

Ingredients

500g/1lb 2oz bottle gourd*, skinned and chopped

2 tomatoes, finely chopped

1 large onion, finely chopped

1 tsp ginger paste

1 tsp garlic paste

2 green chillies, finely chopped

½ tsp ground coriander

½ tsp ground cumin

25g/scant 1oz coriander leaves, finely chopped

120ml/4fl oz water

Salt to taste

Method

* Mix all the ingredients together. Cook in a saucepan on a low heat for 20 minutes. Serve hot.

Okra with Yoghurt

Serves 4

Ingredients

3 tbsp refined vegetable oil

½ tsp cumin seeds

500g/1lb 2oz okra, chopped

½ tsp chilli powder

¼ tsp turmeric

2 green chillies, slit lengthways

1 tsp ginger, julienned

200g/7oz yoghurt

1 tsp besan*, dissolved in 1 tbsp water

Salt to taste

1 tbsp coriander leaves, finely chopped

Method

* Heat the oil in a saucepan. Add the cumin seeds. Let them splutter for 15 seconds.
* Add the okra, chilli powder, turmeric, green chillies and ginger.
* Cook on a low heat for 20 minutes, stirring occasionally.
* Add the yoghurt, besan mixture and salt. Cook for 5 minutes.
* Garnish the okra with the coriander leaves. Serve hot.

Sautéed Karela

(Sautéed Bitter Gourd)

Serves 4

Ingredients

4 medium-sized bitter gourds*
Salt to taste
1½ tbsp refined vegetable oil
½ tsp mustard seeds
½ tsp turmeric

½ tsp ginger paste
½ tsp garlic paste
2 large onions, finely chopped
½ tsp chilli powder
¾ tsp jaggery*, grated

Method

• Peel the bitter gourds and slit into halves, lengthways. Discard the seeds and thinly slice each half. Add the salt and set aside for 20 minutes. Squeeze out the water. Set aside again.
• Heat the oil in a saucepan. Add the mustard seeds. Let them splutter for 15 seconds.
• Add the remaining ingredients and fry them on a medium heat for 2-3 minutes. Add the bitter gourd. Mix well. Cook for 5 minutes on a low heat. Serve hot.

Cabbage with Peas

Serves 4

Ingredients

1 tbsp refined vegetable oil
1 tsp mustard seeds
2 green chillies, slit lengthways
¼ tsp turmeric

400g/14oz cabbage, finely shredded
125g/4½oz fresh peas
Salt to taste
2 tbsp desiccated coconut

Method

• Heat the oil in a saucepan. Add the mustard seeds and green chillies. Let them splutter for 15 seconds.
• Add the remaining ingredients, except the coconut. Cook on a low heat for 10 minutes.
• Add the coconut. Mix well. Serve hot.

Potatoes in Tomato Sauce

Serves 4

Ingredients

2 tbsp refined vegetable oil

1 tsp cumin seeds

Pinch of asafoetida

½ tsp turmeric

4 large potatoes, boiled and diced

4 tomatoes, finely chopped

1 tsp chilli powder

Salt to taste

1 tbsp coriander leaves, chopped

Method

- Heat the oil in a saucepan. Add the cumin seeds, asafoetida and turmeric. Let them splutter for 15 seconds.
- Add the remaining ingredients, except the coriander leaves. Mix well. Cook on a low heat for 10 minutes. Garnish with the coriander leaves. Serve hot.

Matar Palak

(Peas and Spinach)

Serves 4

Ingredients

400g/14oz spinach, steamed and chopped

2 green chillies

4-5 tbsp refined vegetable oil

1 tsp cumin seeds

1 pinch of asafoetida

1 tsp turmeric

1 large onion, finely chopped

1 tomato, finely chopped

1 large potato, diced

Salt to taste

200g/7oz green peas

Method

- Grind together the spinach and chillies to a fine paste. Set aside.
- Heat the oil in a saucepan. Add the cumin seeds, asafoetida and turmeric. Let them splutter for 15 seconds.
- Add the onion. Fry on a medium heat till it turns translucent.
- Add the remaining ingredients. Mix well. Cook on a low heat for 7-8 minutes, stirring occasionally.
- Add the spinach paste. Simmer for 5 minutes. Serve hot.

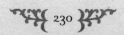

Masala Cabbage

(Spicy Cabbage)

Serves 4

Ingredients

3 tbsp refined vegetable oil

1 tsp cumin seeds

¼ tsp turmeric

1 tsp garlic paste

1 tsp ginger paste

1 large onion, finely chopped

1 tomato, finely chopped

½ tsp chilli powder

Salt to taste

400g/14oz cabbage, finely chopped

Method

- Heat the oil in a saucepan. Add the cumin seeds and turmeric. Let them splutter for 15 seconds. Add the garlic paste, ginger paste and onion. Fry on a medium heat for 2-3 minutes.
- Add the tomato, chilli powder, salt and cabbage. Mix well. Cover with a lid and cook on a low heat for 10-15 minutes. Serve hot.

Aubergine Curry

Serves 4

Ingredients

4 green chillies

2.5cm/1in root ginger

50g/1¾oz coriander leaves, chopped

3 tbsp refined vegetable oil

1 tsp mung dhal*

1 tsp urad dhal*

1 tsp cumin seeds

½ tsp mustard seeds

500g/1lb 2oz small aubergines, chopped into 5cm/2in pieces

½ tsp turmeric

1 tsp tamarind paste

Salt to taste

250ml/8fl oz water

Method

- Grind together the green chillies, ginger and coriander leaves. Set aside.
- Heat the oil in a saucepan. Add the mung dhal, urad dhal, cumin seeds and mustard seeds. Let them splutter for 20 seconds.
- Add the remaining ingredients and the chilli-ginger paste. Mix well. Cover with a lid and simmer for 10 minutes, stirring occasionally. Serve hot.

Simla Mirch ka Bharta

(Spicy Peppers)

Serves 4

Ingredients

3 medium-sized green peppers
3 medium-sized red peppers
3 tbsp refined vegetable oil
2 large onions, finely chopped
6 garlic cloves, finely chopped
2.5cm/1in root ginger, finely chopped

½ tsp chilli powder
¼ tsp turmeric
2 tomatoes, chopped
1 tsp salt
1 tbsp coriander leaves, chopped

Method

- Grill the green and red peppers for 5-6 minutes. Turn frequently to ensure that they are evenly grilled.
- Peel the charred skin, remove the stalks and seeds and chop the peppers into small pieces. Set aside.
- Heat the oil in a saucepan. Add the onions, garlic and ginger. Fry them on a medium heat till the onions are brown.
- Add the chilli powder, turmeric, tomatoes and salt. Sauté the mixture for 4-5 minutes.
- Add the peppers. Mix well. Cover with a lid and cook on a low heat for 30 minutes.
- Garnish the vegetables with the coriander leaves. Serve hot.

Quick Bottle Gourd Curry

Serves 4

Ingredients

1 medium-sized bottle gourd*, peeled
 and chopped

1 large onion, finely chopped

60g/2oz tomatoes, finely chopped

4-5 garlic cloves, chopped

1 tbsp ketchup

1 tbsp dry fenugreek leaves

½ tsp turmeric

¼ tsp freshly ground black pepper

2 tbsp milk

Salt to taste

1 tbsp coriander leaves, chopped

Method

- Cook all the ingredients, except the coriander leaves, in a saucepan on a
  medium heat for 20 minutes, stirring occasionally. Cover with a lid.
- Stir the mixture thoroughly. Garnish with the coriander leaves. Serve hot.

Kaala Chana Curry

(Black Chickpea Curry)

Serves 4

Ingredients

250g/9oz kaala chana*, soaked
 overnight

Pinch of bicarbonate of soda

Salt to taste

1 litre/1¾ pints water

1 small onion

2.5cm/1in root ginger

1 tbsp ghee

1 tomato, diced

½ tsp turmeric

½ tsp chilli powder

8-10 curry leaves

1 tbsp tamarind paste

Method

- Mix the chana with the bicarbonate of soda, salt and half the water. Cook
  in a saucepan on a medium heat for 45 minutes. Mash and set aside.
- Grind the onion and ginger to a paste.
- Heat the ghee in a saucepan. Add the onion-ginger paste and fry till it
  turns brown.
- Add the chana mixture and the remaining ingredients. Mix well. Simmer
  for 8-10 minutes, stirring occasionally. Serve hot.

Kalina

(Mixed Vegetables in Milk)

Serves 4

Ingredients

750ml/1¼ pints milk

2 unripe bananas, peeled and chopped

250g/9oz bottle gourd*, chopped

100g/3½oz cabbage, grated

2 tomatoes, chopped

1 large green pepper, chopped

1 tsp tamarind paste

1 tsp ground coriander

1 tsp ground cumin

2 tsp chilli powder

2 tsp jaggery*, grated

100g/3½oz coriander leaves, finely chopped

2 tbsp khoya*

Salt to taste

1 tbsp coriander leaves, finely chopped

Method

- Heat the milk in a saucepan on a medium heat till it begins to boil. Add the banana and bottle gourd. Mix well. Cook for 5 minutes.
- Add the remaining ingredients, except the coriander leaves. Mix well. Simmer for 8-10 minutes, stirring frequently.
- Garnish the kalina with the coriander leaves. Serve hot.

Tandoori Cauliflower

Serves 4

Ingredients

1½ tsp chilli powder

1½ tsp garam masala

Juice of 2 lemons

100g/3½oz yoghurt

Black salt to taste

1 kg cauliflower florets

Method

- Mix together all the ingredients, except the cauliflower. Then marinate the cauliflower with this mixture for 4 hours.
- Bake in a pre-heated oven at 200°C (400°F, Gas Mark 6) for 5-7 minutes. Serve hot.

Spicy Kaala Chana

Serves 4

Ingredients

500g/1lb 2oz kaala chana*, soaked overnight
500ml/16fl oz water
Salt to taste
3 tbsp refined vegetable oil
Pinch of asafoetida
½ tsp mustard seeds
1 tsp cumin seeds

2 cloves
1cm/½in cinnamon
¼ tsp turmeric
1 tsp ground coriander
1 tsp ground cumin
½ tsp garam masala
1 tsp tamarind paste
1 tbsp coriander leaves, chopped

Method

- Cook the chana with the water and salt in a saucepan on a medium heat for 20 minutes. Set aside.
- Heat the oil in a saucepan. Add the asafoetida and mustard seeds. Let them splutter for 15 seconds. Add the cooked chana and the remaining ingredients, except the coriander leaves. Simmer for 10-15 minutes.
- Garnish the spicy kaala chana with coriander leaves. Serve hot.

Tur Dhal Kofta

(Split Red Gram Dumplings)

Serves 4

Ingredients

600g/1lb 5oz masoor dhal*, soaked overnight
3 green chillies, finely chopped
3 tbsp coriander leaves, chopped
60g/2oz coconut, grated

3 tbsp cumin seeds
Pinch of asafoetida
Salt to taste
Refined vegetable oil for deep frying

Method

- Wash and grind the dhal coarsely. Knead thoroughly with the remaining ingredients, except the oil, to a soft dough. Divide into walnut-sized balls.
- Heat the oil in a saucepan. Add the balls and deep fry them on a low heat till they turn golden brown. Drain the koftas and serve hot.

Shahi Cauliflower

(Rich Cauliflower)

Serves 4

Ingredients

8 garlic cloves

2.5cm/1in root ginger

½ tsp turmeric

2 large onions, grated

4 tsp poppy seeds

2 tbsp ghee

200g/7oz yoghurt, whisked

5 tomatoes, finely chopped

200g/7oz canned peas

1 tsp sugar

2 tbsp fresh single cream

Salt to taste

250ml/8fl oz water

500g/1lb 2oz cauliflower florets, deep fried

8 small potatoes, deep fried

Method

- Grind together the garlic, ginger, turmeric, onions and poppy seeds to a fine paste. Set aside.
- Heat 1 tbsp ghee in a saucepan. Add the poppy paste. Stir-fry for 5 minutes. Add the remaining ingredients, except the cauliflower and potatoes. Cook on a low heat for 4 minutes.
- Add the cauliflower and potatoes. Simmer for 15 minutes and serve hot.

Okra Gojju

(Okra Compote)

Serves 4

Ingredients

500g/1lb 2oz okra, sliced

Salt to taste

2 tbsp refined vegetable oil plus extra for deep frying

1 tsp mustard seeds

Pinch of asafoetida

200g/7oz yoghurt

250ml/8fl oz water

Method

- Toss the okra with salt. Heat the oil in a saucepan and deep fry the okra on a medium heat till golden brown. Set aside.
- Heat 2 tbsp oil. Add the mustard and asafoetida. Let them splutter for 15 seconds. Add the okra, yoghurt and water. Mix well. Serve hot.

Yam in Green Sauce

Serves 4

Ingredients

300g/10oz yam*, thinly sliced
1 tsp chilli powder
1 tsp amchoor*
½ tsp ground black pepper
Salt to taste
Refined vegetable oil for deep frying

Pinch of bicarbonate of soda
3 green chillies
2 tsp wholemeal flour
Salt to taste
3 tbsp refined vegetable oil
1cm/½in root ginger, julienned
1 small onion, finely chopped
Pinch of ground cinnamon
Pinch of ground cloves

For the sauce:

400g/14oz spinach, chopped
100g/3½oz bottle gourd*, grated

Method

- Toss the yam slices with the chilli powder, amchoor, pepper and salt.
- Heat the oil in a saucepan. Add the yam slices. Deep fry them on a medium heat till they turn golden brown. Drain and set aside.
- For the sauce, mix the spinach, bottle gourd and bicarbonate of soda. Steam (see cooking techniques) the mixture in a steamer on a medium heat for 10 minutes.
- Grind this mixture along with the green chillies, flour and salt to a semi-smooth paste. Set aside.
- Heat the oil in a saucepan. Add the ginger and onion. Fry on a medium heat till the onion is brown. Add the ground cinnamon, ground cloves, and the spinach mixture. Mix well. Cook on a medium heat for 8-10 minutes, stirring occasionally.
- Add the yam to this green sauce. Mix well. Cover with a lid and simmer for 4-5 minutes. Serve hot.

Simla Mirch ki Sabzi

(Dry Green Pepper)

Serves 4

Ingredients

2 tbsp refined vegetable oil

2 large onions, finely chopped

¾ tsp ginger paste

¾ tsp garlic paste

1 tsp ground coriander

¼ tsp turmeric

½ tsp garam masala

½ tsp chilli powder

2 tomatoes, finely chopped

Salt to taste

4 large green peppers, chopped

1 tbsp coriander leaves,
 finely chopped

Method

- Heat the oil in a saucepan. Add the onions, ginger paste and garlic paste. Fry on a medium heat till the onions are brown.
- Add all the remaining ingredients, except the coriander leaves. Mix well. Stir-fry the mixture on a low heat for 10-15 minutes.
- Garnish with the coriander leaves. Serve hot.

Cauliflower Curry

Serves 4

Ingredients

3 tbsp refined vegetable oil

1 tsp cumin seeds

¼ tsp turmeric

1 tsp ginger paste

1 tsp ground coriander

1 tsp chilli powder

200g/7oz tomato purée

1 tsp powdered sugar

Salt to taste

400g/14oz cauliflower florets

120ml/4fl oz water

Method

- Heat the oil in a saucepan. Add the cumin seeds. Let them splutter for 15 seconds.
- Add the remaining ingredients, except the water. Mix well. Add the water. Cover with a lid and simmer for 12-15 minutes. Serve hot.

Haaq
(Spinach Curry)

Serves 4

Ingredients

1cm/½ in root ginger, julienned
1 tsp fennel seeds, crushed
2 tbsp refined vegetable oil
2 dried red chillies
¼ tsp asafoetida

1 green chilli, slit lengthways
Salt to taste
400g/14oz spinach, finely chopped
500ml/16fl oz water

Method
- Dry roast (see cooking techniques) the ginger and fennel seeds. Set aside.
- Heat the oil in a saucepan. Add the red chillies, asafoetida, green chilli and salt. Fry this mixture on a medium heat for 1 minute.
- Add the ginger-fennel seed mixture. Fry for a minute. Add the spinach and water. Cover with a lid and simmer for 8-10 minutes. Serve hot.

Dry Cauliflower

Serves 4

Ingredients

3 tbsp refined vegetable oil
1 tsp cumin seeds
¼ tsp turmeric
2 green chillies, finely chopped
1 tsp ginger paste
½ tsp caster sugar

400g/14oz cauliflower florets
Salt to taste
60ml/2fl oz water
10g/¼oz coriander leaves, chopped

Method
- Heat the oil in a saucepan. Add the cumin seeds. Let them splutter for 15 seconds.
- Add the turmeric, green chillies, ginger paste and caster sugar. Fry on a medium heat for a minute. Add the cauliflower, salt and water. Mix well. Cover with a lid and simmer for 12-15 minutes.
- Garnish with the coriander leaves. Serve hot.

Vegetable Korma
(Mixed Vegetables)

Serves 4

Ingredients

3 tbsp refined vegetable oil

1cm/½in cinnamon

2 cloves

2 green cardamom pods

2 large onions, finely chopped

¼ tsp turmeric

½ tsp ginger paste

½ tsp garlic paste

Salt to taste

300g/10oz mixed frozen vegetables

250ml/8fl oz water

1 tsp poppy seeds

Method

- Heat the oil in a saucepan. Add the cinnamon, cloves and cardamom. Let them splutter for 30 seconds.
- Add the onions, turmeric, ginger paste, garlic paste and salt. Fry the mixture on a medium heat for 2-3 minutes, stirring continuously.
- Add the vegetables and water. Mix well. Cover with a lid and simmer for 5-6 minutes, stirring occasionally.
- Add the poppy seeds. Mix well. Simmer for 2 more minutes. Serve hot.

Fried Aubergine

Serves 4

Ingredients

500g/1lb 2oz aubergine, sliced

4 tbsp refined vegetable oil

For the marinade:

1 tsp chilli powder

½ tsp ground black pepper

½ tsp turmeric

1 tsp amchoor*

Salt to taste

1 tbsp rice flour

Method

- Mix the marinade ingredients together. Marinate the aubergine slices with this mixture for 10 minutes.
- Heat the oil in a frying pan. Add the aubergine slices. Fry them on a low heat for 7 minutes. Flip the slices and fry again for 3 minutes. Serve hot.

Red Tomato Curry

Serves 4

Ingredients

1 tbsp peanuts, dry roasted
  (see cooking techniques)

1 tbsp cashew nuts, roasted
  (see cooking techniques)

4 tomatoes, chopped

1 small green pepper, chopped

3 tbsp refined vegetable oil

1 tsp ginger paste

1 tsp garlic paste

1 large onion, chopped

1½ tsp garam masala

¼ tsp turmeric

½ tsp sugar

Salt to taste

Method

- Mix the peanuts and cashew nuts together and grind them. Set aside.
- Grind the tomatoes and green pepper together. Set aside.
- Heat the oil in a frying pan. Add the ginger paste and garlic paste. Fry on a medium heat for a minute. Add the onion, garam masala, turmeric, sugar and salt. Fry the mixture for 2-3 minutes.
- Add the peanut-cashew nut mixture and the tomato-pepper mixture. Mix well. Cover with a lid and simmer for 15 minutes. Serve hot.

Aloo Matar Curry

(Potato and Pea Curry)

Serves 4

Ingredients

1½ tbsp refined vegetable oil

1 tsp cumin seeds

1 large onion, finely chopped

½ tsp turmeric

1 tsp ground coriander

1 tsp ground cumin

1 tsp chilli powder

200g/7oz tomato purée

Salt to taste

2 large potatoes, chopped

400g/14oz peas

120ml/4fl oz water

Method

- Heat the oil in a saucepan. Add the cumin seeds. Let them splutter for 15 seconds. Add the onion. Fry it on a medium heat till it turns brown.
- Add the remaining ingredients. Simmer for 15 minutes. Serve hot.

Badshahi Baingan

(Royal Style Aubergine)

Serves 4

Ingredients

8 small aubergines
Salt to taste
30g/1oz ghee
2 large onions, sliced
1 tbsp cashew nuts
1 tbsp raisins
1 tsp ginger paste

1 tsp garlic paste
1 tsp ground coriander
1 tsp garam masala
¼ tsp turmeric
200g/7oz yoghurt
1 tsp coriander leaves, chopped

Method

- Halve the aubergines lengthways. Rub salt on them and set them aside for 10 minutes. Squeeze out excess moisture and set aside again.
- Heat the ghee in a saucepan. Add the onions, cashew nuts and raisins. Fry them on a medium heat till golden brown. Drain and set aside.
- To the same ghee, add the aubergines and fry them on a medium heat till they are tender. Drain and set aside.
- Add the ginger paste and garlic paste to the same ghee. Fry for a minute. Stir in the remaining ingredients. Cook for 7-8 minutes on a medium heat.
- Add the aubergines. Simmer for 2 minutes. Garnish with the fried onions, cashew nuts and raisins. Serve hot.

Potatoes in Garam Masala

Serves 4

Ingredients

3 tbsp refined vegetable oil
1 large onion, finely chopped
10 garlic cloves, finely chopped
½ tsp turmeric

1 tsp garam masala
Salt to taste
3 large potatoes, boiled and diced
240ml/6fl oz water

Method

- Heat the oil in a saucepan. Add the onion and garlic. Fry for 2 minutes.
- Add the remaining ingredients and mix well. Serve hot.

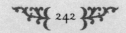

Tamilian Korma
(Tamil-style Mixed Vegetables)

Serves 4

Ingredients

4 tbsp refined vegetable oil

1 tsp cumin seeds

2 large potatoes, chopped

2 large carrots, chopped

100g/3½oz French beans, chopped

Salt to taste

For the spice mixture:

100g/3½oz fresh coconut, shredded

4 green chillies

100g/3½oz coriander leaves, chopped

1 tsp poppy seeds

1 tsp ginger paste

1 tsp turmeric

Method

- Grind all the spice mixture ingredients to a smooth paste. Set aside.
- Heat the oil. Add the cumin seeds. Let them splutter for 15 seconds.
- Add the remaining ingredients and the ground spice mixture. Cook for 15 minutes on a low heat, stirring occasionally. Serve hot.

Dry Aubergine with Onion & Potato

Serves 4

Ingredients

3 tbsp refined vegetable oil

1 tsp mustard seeds

300g/10oz aubergines, chopped

¼ tsp turmeric

3 small onions, finely chopped

2 large potatoes, boiled and diced

1 tsp chilli powder

1 tsp amchoor*

Salt to taste

Method

- Heat the oil in a saucepan. Add the mustard seeds. Let them splutter for 15 seconds.
- Add the aubergines and turmeric. Fry on a low heat for 10 minutes.
- Add the remaining ingredients. Mix well. Cover with a lid and simmer for 10 minutes. Serve hot.

Koftas Lajawab
(Cheese Dumplings in Sauce)

Serves 4

Ingredients
3 tbsp refined vegetable oil
3 large onions, grated
2.5cm/1in root ginger, ground
3 tomatoes, puréed
1 tsp turmeric
Salt to taste
120ml/4fl oz water

For the koftas:
400g/14oz Cheddar cheese, mashed
250g/9oz cornflour
½ tsp freshly ground black pepper
1 tsp garam masala
Salt to taste
Refined vegetable oil for deep frying

Method
- Mix all the kofta ingredients, except the oil, together. Divide into walnut-sized balls. Heat the oil in a saucepan. Add the koftas. Deep fry them on a medium heat till they turn golden brown. Drain and set aside.
- Heat 3 tbsp oil in a saucepan. Add the onions and fry till brown.
- Add the remaining ingredients and mix thoroughly. Cook for 8 minutes, stirring occasionally. Add the koftas to this sauce and serve hot.

Teekha Baingan Masala
(Hot Aubergine)

Serves 4

Ingredients
2 tbsp refined vegetable oil
3 large onions, ground
10 garlic cloves, crushed
2.5cm/1in root ginger, grated

1 tsp tamarind paste
2 tbsp garam masala
Salt to taste
500g/1lb 2oz small aubergines, chopped

Method
- Heat 2 tbsp oil in a saucepan. Add the onions. Fry on a medium heat for 3 minutes. Add the garlic, ginger, tamarind, garam masala and salt. Mix well.
- Add the aubergines. Mix well. Cover with a lid and cook on a low heat for 15 minutes, stirring occasionally. Serve hot.

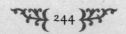

Vegetable Kofta
(Vegetable Dumplings in Creamy Sauce)

Serves 4

Ingredients

6 large potatoes, peeled and chopped

3 large carrots, peeled and chopped

Salt to taste

Flour for coating

2 tbsp refined vegetable oil plus extra for deep frying

3 large onions, finely sliced

4 garlic cloves, finely chopped

2.5cm/1in root ginger, finely chopped

4 cloves, ground

½ tsp turmeric

2 tomatoes, puréed

1 tsp chilli powder

4 tbsp double cream

25g/scant 1oz coriander leaves, chopped

Method

- Boil the potatoes and carrots in salted water for 15 minutes. Drain and reserve the stock. Add salt to the vegetables and mash them.
- Divide the mash into lemon-sized balls. Coat with the flour and deep fry the koftas in the oil on a medium heat till golden brown. Set aside.
- Heat 2 tbsp of the oil in a saucepan. Add the onions, garlic, ginger, cloves and turmeric. Fry on a medium heat for 4-5 minutes. Add the tomatoes, chilli powder and the vegetable stock. Simmer for 4 minutes.
- Add the koftas. Garnish with the cream and coriander leaves. Serve hot.

Dry Pumpkin

Serves 4

Ingredients

3 tbsp refined vegetable oil

1 tsp cumin seeds

¼ tsp turmeric

¾ tsp ground coriander

Salt to taste

750g/1lb 10oz pumpkin, chopped

60ml/2fl oz water

Method

- Heat the oil in a saucepan. Add the cumin seeds and turmeric. Let them splutter for 15 seconds.
- Add the remaining ingredients. Mix well. Cover with a lid and simmer for 15 minutes. Serve hot.

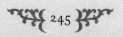

Mixed Vegetables with Fenugreek

Serves 4

Ingredients

4-5 tbsp refined vegetable oil
1 tsp mustard seeds
½ tsp fenugreek seeds
2 large onions, finely chopped
2 large sweet potatoes, diced
4 small aubergines, diced
2 large green peppers, diced
3 large potatoes, diced
100g/3½oz French beans, chopped

½ tsp turmeric
1 tsp chilli powder
2 tbsp tamarind paste
1 tbsp coriander leaves, chopped
8-10 curry leaves
1 tsp sugar
Salt to taste
750ml/1¼ pints water

Method

- Heat the oil in a saucepan. Add the mustard and fenugreek seeds. Let them splutter for 15 seconds. Add the onions. Fry till translucent.
- Add the remaining ingredients, except the water. Mix well. Add the water. Simmer for 20 minutes. Serve hot.

Dum Gobhi

(Slow Cooked Cauliflower)

Serves 4

Ingredients

2.5cm/1in root ginger, julienned
2 tomatoes, finely chopped
¼ tsp turmeric
1 tbsp yoghurt

½ tsp garam masala
Salt to taste
800g/1¾lb cauliflower florets

Method

- Mix together all the ingredients, except the cauliflower florets.
- Place the cauliflower florets in a saucepan and pour this mixture over it. Cover with a lid and simmer for 20 minutes, stirring occasionally. Serve hot.

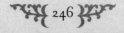

Chhole

(Chickpea Curry)

Serves 5

Ingredients

375g/13oz chickpeas, soaked overnight

1 litre/1¾ pints water

Salt to taste

1 tomato, finely chopped

3 small onions, finely chopped

1½ tbsp coriander leaves, finely
   chopped

2 tbsp refined vegetable oil

1 tsp cumin seeds

1 tsp ginger paste

1 tsp garlic paste

2 bay leaves

1 tsp sugar

1 tsp chilli powder

½ tsp turmeric

1 tbsp ghee

4 green chillies, slit lengthways

½ tsp ground cinnamon

½ tsp ground clove

Juice of 1 lemon

Method

- Mix the chickpeas with half the water and the salt. Cook this mixture in a saucepan on a medium heat for 30 minutes. Remove from the heat and drain the chickpeas.
- Grind 2 tbsp of the chickpeas with half of the tomato, one onion and half the coriander leaves to a fine paste. Set aside.
- Heat the oil in a large saucepan. Add the cumin seeds. Let them splutter for 15 seconds.
- Add the remaining onions, the ginger paste and the garlic paste. Fry this mixture on a medium heat till the onions are brown.
- Add the remaining tomato along with the bay leaves, sugar, chilli powder, turmeric and the chickpea-tomato paste. Fry this mixture on a medium heat for 2-3 minutes.
- Add the remaining chickpeas with the remaining water. Simmer for 8-10 minutes. Set aside.
- Heat the ghee in a small saucepan. Add the green chillies, ground cinnamon and clove. Let them splutter for 30 seconds. Pour this mixture over the chickpeas. Mix well. Sprinkle the lemon juice and the remaining coriander leaves on top of the chhole. Serve hot.

Aubergine Curry with Onion & Potato

Serves 4

Ingredients

3 tbsp refined vegetable oil

2 large onions, finely chopped

1 tsp ginger paste

1 tsp garlic paste

1 tsp ground coriander

1 tsp ground cumin

1 tsp chilli powder

¼ tsp turmeric

120ml/4fl oz water

Salt to taste

250g/9oz small aubergines

250g/9oz baby potatoes, halved

50g/1¾oz coriander leaves,
   finely chopped

Method

- Heat the oil in a saucepan. Add the onions. Fry till they turn translucent.
- Add the remaining ingredients, except the coriander leaves. Mix well. Simmer for 15 minutes.
- Garnish with the coriander leaves. Serve hot.

Simple Bottle Gourd

Serves 4

Ingredients

½ tbsp ghee

1 tsp cumin seeds

2 green chillies, slit lengthways

750g/1lb 10oz bottle gourd*, chopped

Salt to taste

120ml/4fl oz milk

1 tbsp desiccated coconut

10g/¼oz coriander leaves,
   finely chopped

Method

- Heat the ghee in a saucepan. Add the cumin seeds and green chillies. Let them splutter for 15 seconds.
- Add the bottle gourd, salt and milk. Simmer for 10-12 minutes.
- Add the remaining ingredients. Mix well. Serve hot.

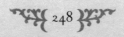

Mixed Vegetable Curry

Serves 4

Ingredients

3 tbsp refined vegetable oil

1 tsp cumin seeds

1 tsp ground coriander

½ tsp ground cumin

1 tsp chilli powder

¼ tsp turmeric

½ tsp sugar

1 carrot, chopped into strips

1 large potato, diced

200g/7oz French beans, chopped

50g/1¾oz cauliflower florets

Salt to taste

200g/7oz tomato purée

120ml/4fl oz water

10g/¼oz coriander leaves, finely chopped

Method

- Heat the oil in a saucepan. Add the cumin seeds, ground coriander and ground cumin. Let them splutter for 15 seconds.
- Add the remaining ingredients, except the coriander leaves. Mix thoroughly. Simmer for 15 minutes.
- Garnish the curry with the coriander leaves. Serve hot.

Dry Mixed Vegetables

Serves 4

Ingredients

3 tbsp refined vegetable oil

1 tsp cumin seeds

1 tsp ground coriander

½ tsp ground cumin

¼ tsp turmeric

1 carrot, julienned

1 large potato, diced

200g/7oz French beans, chopped

60g/2oz cauliflower florets

Salt to taste

120ml/4fl oz water

10g/¼oz coriander leaves, chopped

Method

- Heat the oil in a saucepan. Add the cumin seeds. Let them splutter for 15 seconds.
- Add the remaining ingredients, except the coriander leaves. Mix thoroughly and cook for 15 minutes on a low heat.
- Garnish with the coriander leaves and serve hot.

Dry Potatoes & Peas

Serves 4

Ingredients
3 tbsp refined vegetable oil
1 tsp cumin seeds
½ tsp turmeric
1 tsp garam masala

2 large potatoes, boiled and diced
400g/14oz cooked peas
Salt to taste

Method
- Heat the oil in a saucepan. Add the cumin seeds and turmeric. Let them splutter for 15 seconds.
- Add the remaining ingredients. Stir-fry on a medium heat for 5 minutes. Serve hot.

Dhokar Dhalna
(Bengal Gram Curry)

Serves 4

Ingredients
300g/10oz chana dhal*, soaked overnight
2 tbsp mustard oil
1 tsp cumin seeds
Salt to taste
5cm/2in cinnamon

4 green cardamom pods
6 cloves
½ tsp turmeric
½ tsp sugar
250ml/8fl oz water
3 large potatoes, diced and fried

Method
- Grind the chana dhal with enough water to form a smooth paste. Set aside.
- Heat half the oil in a saucepan. Add half the cumin seeds. Let them splutter for 15 seconds. Add the dhal paste and the salt. Fry for 2-3 minutes. Drain and spread on a large plate and allow to set. Chop into 2.5cm/1in pieces. Set aside.
- Fry these dhal pieces in the remaining oil till golden brown. Set aside.
- In the same oil, add the remaining ingredients, except the potatoes. Cook for 2 minutes. Add the potatoes and the dhal pieces. Mix well. Cook on a low heat for 4-5 minutes. Serve hot.

Spicy Fried Potatoes

Serves 4

Ingredients

250ml/8fl oz refined vegetable oil

3 large potatoes, chopped into thin
  strips

½ tsp chilli powder

1 tsp freshly ground black pepper

Salt to taste

Method

- Heat the oil in a saucepan. Add the potato strips. Deep fry them on a medium heat till they turn golden brown.
- Drain and toss well with the remaining ingredients. Serve hot.

Pumpkin with Boiled Gram

Serves 4

Ingredients

1 tbsp refined vegetable oil

1 tsp cumin seeds

½ tsp turmeric

500g/1lb 2oz pumpkin, chopped into
  pieces

125g/4½oz kaala chana*, cooked

1 tsp ground coriander

1 tsp ground cumin

1 tsp chilli powder

Salt to taste

120ml/4fl oz water

10g/¼oz coriander leaves,
  finely chopped

Method

- Heat the oil in a saucepan. Add the cumin seeds and turmeric. Let them splutter for 15 seconds.
- Add the remaining ingredients, except the water and coriander leaves. Fry the mixture on a medium heat for 2-3 minutes.
- Add the water. Mix well. Cover with a lid and simmer for 15 minutes, stirring occasionally.
- Garnish with the coriander leaves. Serve hot.

Dum Aloo
(Slow Cooked Potatoes)

Serves 4

Ingredients

1 tbsp refined vegetable oil

500g/1lb 2oz baby potatoes, boiled and peeled

Salt to taste

1 tsp tamarind paste

For the paste:

½ tsp chilli powder

¼ tsp turmeric

¼ tsp black peppercorns

2 tsp coriander seeds

1 black cardamom

2.5cm/1in cinnamon

2 cloves

6 garlic cloves

Method

* Grind the paste ingredients together. Heat the oil in a frying pan. Add the paste. Fry on a medium heat for 10 minutes.
* Add the remaining ingredients. Mix well. Cook for 8 minutes. Serve hot.

Vegetable Makkhanwala
(Vegetables in Butter)

Serves 4

Ingredients

120ml/4fl oz single cream

½ tsp plain white flour

120ml/4fl oz milk

4 tbsp ketchup

1 tbsp butter

2 large onions, finely chopped

500g/1lb 2oz mixed frozen vegetables

1 tsp garam masala

½ tsp chilli powder

Salt to taste

Method

* Mix the cream, flour, milk and ketchup. Set aside.
* Heat the butter in a saucepan. Add the onions. Fry them on a medium heat till they turn translucent.
* Add the vegetables, garam masala, chilli powder, salt and the cream-flour mixture. Mix well. Simmer for 10-12 minutes. Serve hot.

French Beans with Mung Dhal

Serves 4

Ingredients

1 tbsp refined vegetable oil
1 tsp mustard seeds
¼ tsp turmeric
2 green chillies, slit lengthways
400g/14oz French beans, chopped

3 tbsp mung dhal*, soaked for
  30 minutes and drained
Salt to taste
120ml/4fl oz water
2 tbsp coriander leaves, chopped

Method

- Heat the oil in a saucepan. Add the mustard seeds, turmeric and green chillies. Let them splutter for 15 seconds.
- Add the remaining ingredients, except the water and coriander leaves. Mix well. Add the water. Simmer for 15 minutes.
- Add the coriander leaves and serve hot.

Spicy Potato with Yoghurt Sauce

Serves 4

Ingredients

1 tsp besan*, mixed with 4 tbsp water
200g/7oz yoghurt
750g/1lb 10oz potatoes, boiled and diced
½ tsp chaat masala*
½ tsp ground cumin, dry roasted
  (see cooking techniques)
½ tsp chilli powder

¼ tsp turmeric
1 tbsp refined vegetable oil
1 tsp white sesame seeds
2 dried red chillies, quartered
Salt to taste
10g/¼oz coriander leaves, finely
  chopped

Method

- Whisk the besan paste with the yoghurt. Set aside.
- Toss the potatoes with the chaat masala, ground cumin, chilli powder and turmeric. Set aside.
- Heat the oil in a saucepan. Add the sesame seeds and chilli pieces. Let them splutter for 15 seconds.
- Add the potatoes, yoghurt mixture and salt. Mix well. Simmer for 4-5 minutes. Garnish with the coriander leaves. Serve hot.

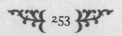

Stuffed Green Pepper

Serves 4

Ingredients

4 tbsp refined vegetable oil

1 large onion, ground

½ tsp ginger paste

½ tsp garlic paste

1 tsp garam masala

2 large potatoes, boiled and mashed

50g/1¾oz boiled peas

1 small carrot, boiled and chopped

Pinch of asafoetida

Salt to taste

8 small green peppers, cored

Method

- Heat ½ tbsp oil in a frying pan. Add the onion and fry till translucent.
- Add the remaining ingredients, except the peppers. Mix well. Fry for 3-4 minutes.
- Stuff this mixture into the peppers. Set aside.
- Heat the remaining oil in a frying pan. Add the stuffed peppers. Fry them on a low heat for 7-10 minutes, turning occasionally. Serve hot.

Doi Phulkopi Aloo
(Bengali Style Cauliflower and Potato in Yoghurt)

Serves 4

Ingredients

300g/10oz yoghurt

¼ tsp turmeric

1 tsp sugar

Salt to taste

200g/7oz cauliflower florets

4 potatoes, diced and lightly fried

2 tbsp mustard oil

5cm/2in cinnamon

4 green cardamom pods

6 cloves

2 bay leaves

Method

- Mix the yoghurt, turmeric, sugar and salt. Marinate the cauliflower and potatoes with this mixture for 20 minutes.
- Heat the oil in a saucepan. Fry the remaining ingredients for 1-2 minutes.
- Add the marinated vegetables. Cook on a low heat for 6-7 minutes. Serve hot.

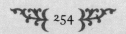

Green Pepper with Besan

Serves 4

Ingredients

4 tbsp refined vegetable oil

½ tsp mustard seeds

500g/1lb 2oz green peppers, cored and chopped

½ tsp turmeric

½ tsp ground coriander

½ tsp ground cumin

500g/1lb 2oz besan*, mixed with 120ml/4fl oz water

1 tsp sugar

Salt to taste

1 tbsp coriander leaves

Method

- Heat the oil in a saucepan. Add the mustard seeds. Let them splutter for 15 seconds.
- Add the green peppers, turmeric, ground coriander and ground cumin. Stir well. Cover with lid and simmer for 5-7 minutes.
- Add the besan, sugar and salt. Stir till the besan coats the peppers. Garnish with the coriander leaves. Serve hot.

Aubergine with Peas

Serves 4

Ingredients

2 tbsp refined vegetable oil

½ tsp mustard seeds

Pinch of asafoetida

½ tsp turmeric

2 large onions, finely chopped

2 tomatoes, finely chopped

1 tsp sugar

Salt to taste

120ml/4fl oz water

300g/10oz small aubergines, chopped

400g/14oz fresh green peas

25g/scant 1oz coriander leaves

Method

- Heat the oil in a saucepan. Add the mustard seeds, asafoetida and turmeric. Let them splutter for 15 seconds.
- Add the onions. Fry till they turn brown. Add the tomatoes, sugar, salt, water, aubergines and peas. Mix well. Cover with a lid. Simmer for 10 minutes.
- Garnish with the coriander leaves. Serve hot.

Bandakopir Ghonto
(Bengali Style Cabbage with Peas)

Serves 4

Ingredients

2 tbsp mustard oil

1 tsp cumin seeds

4 green chillies, chopped

½ tsp turmeric

1 tsp sugar

150g/5½oz cabbage, finely sliced

400g/14oz frozen peas

Salt to taste

¼ tsp ground cinnamon

¼ tsp ground cardamom

¼ tsp ground cloves

Method

- Heat the oil in a saucepan. Add the cumin seeds and green chillies. Let them splutter for 15 seconds.
- Add the turmeric, sugar, cabbage, peas and salt. Mix well. Cover with a lid and cook on a low heat for 8-10 minutes.
- Garnish with the ground cinnamon, cardamom and cloves. Serve hot.

Bhaja Mashlar Begun
(Fried Masala Aubergine)

Serves 4

Ingredients

4 tbsp mustard oil

3 dry red chillies

¼ tsp fenugreek seeds

400g/14oz long aubergines, diced

2 green chillies, finely chopped

200g/7oz Greek yoghurt

1 tsp sugar

½ tsp turmeric

1 tsp ground cumin, dry roasted
  (see cooking techniques)

Salt to taste

Method

- Heat the oil in a saucepan. Add the red chillies and fenugreek seeds. Let them splutter for 15 seconds.
- Add the aubergines and green chillies. Fry them for 4-5 minutes.
- Add the remaining ingredients. Mix well. Cook on a low heat for 7-8 minutes. Serve hot.

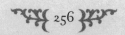

Zunka
(Spicy Gram Flour Curry)

Serves 4

Ingredients

750g/1lb 10oz besan*, dry roasted
  (see cooking techniques)
400ml/14fl oz water
4 tbsp refined vegetable oil
½ tsp mustard seeds
½ tsp cumin seeds

½ tsp turmeric
3-4 green chillies, slit lengthways
10 garlic cloves, crushed
3 small onions, finely chopped
1 tsp tamarind paste
Salt to taste

Method

* Mix the besan with enough water to form a thick paste. Set aside.
* Heat the oil in a saucepan. Add the mustard and cumin seeds.
  Let them splutter for 15 seconds. Add the remaining ingredients.
  Fry for a minute. Add the besan paste and stir continuously on a
  low heat till thick. Serve hot.

Turnip Curry

Serves 4

Ingredients

3 tsp poppy seeds
3 tsp sesame seeds
3 tsp coriander seeds
3 tsp fresh coconut, grated
125g/4½oz yoghurt
120ml/4fl oz refined vegetable oil

2 large onions, finely chopped
1½ tsp chilli powder
1 tsp ginger paste
1 tsp garlic paste
400g/14oz turnips, chopped
Salt to taste

Method

* Dry roast (see cooking techniques) the poppy, sesame and coriander
  seeds and the coconut for 1-2 minutes. Grind to a paste.
* Whisk this paste with the yoghurt. Set aside.
* Heat the oil in a saucepan. Add the remaining ingredients. Fry them on a
  medium heat for 5 minutes. Add the yoghurt mixture. Simmer for 7-8
  minutes. Serve hot.

Chhaner Dhalna

(Bengali Style Paneer)

Serves 4

Ingredients

2 tbsp mustard oil plus extra for
  deep frying

225g/8oz paneer*, diced

2.5cm/1in cinnamon

3 green cardamom pods

4 cloves

½ tsp cumin seeds

1 tsp turmeric

2 large potatoes, diced and fried

½ tsp chilli powder

2 tsp sugar

Salt to taste

250ml/8fl oz water

2 tbsp coriander leaves, chopped

Method

* Heat the oil for deep frying in a frying pan. Add the paneer and fry on a medium heat till golden brown. Drain and set aside.
* Heat the remaining oil in a saucepan. Add the remaining ingredients, except the water and coriander leaves. Fry for 2-3 minutes.
* Add the water. Simmer for 7-8 minutes. Add the paneer. Simmer for 5 more minutes. Garnish with the coriander leaves. Serve hot.

Corn with Coconut

Serves 4

Ingredients

2 tbsp ghee

600g/1lb 5oz corn kernels, cooked

1 tsp sugar

1 tsp salt

10g/¼oz coriander leaves,
  finely chopped

For the coconut paste:

50g/1¾oz fresh coconut, grated

3 tbsp poppy seeds

1 tsp coriander seeds

2.5cm/1in root ginger, julienned

3 green chillies

125g/4½oz peanuts

Method

* Coarsely grind all the ingredients for the coconut paste. Heat the ghee in a frying pan. Add the paste and fry for 4-5 minutes, stirring continuously.
* Add the corn, sugar and salt. Cook on a low heat for 4-5 minutes.
* Garnish with the coriander leaves. Serve hot.

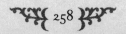

Green Pepper with Potato

Serves 4

Ingredients

2 tbsp refined vegetable oil
1 tsp cumin seeds
10 garlic cloves, finely chopped
3 large potatoes, diced
2 tsp ground coriander
1 tsp ground cumin

½ tsp turmeric
½ tsp amchoor*
½ tsp garam masala
Salt to taste
3 large green peppers, julienned
3 tbsp coriander leaves, chopped

Method

- Heat the oil in a saucepan. Add the cumin seeds and garlic. Fry for 30 seconds.
- Add the remaining ingredients, except the peppers and coriander leaves. Stir-fry on a medium heat for 5-6 minutes.
- Add the peppers. Stir-fry on a low heat for 5 more minutes. Garnish with the coriander leaves. Serve hot.

Spicy Peas with Potatoes

Serves 4

Ingredients

2 tbsp refined vegetable oil
1 tsp ginger paste
1 large onion, finely chopped
2 large potatoes, diced
500g/1lb 2oz canned peas
½ tsp turmeric

Salt to taste
½ tsp garam masala
2 large tomatoes, diced
½ tsp chilli powder
1 tsp sugar
1 tbsp coriander leaves, chopped

Method

- Heat the oil in a saucepan. Add the ginger paste and onion. Fry them till the onion is translucent.
- Add the remaining ingredients, except the coriander leaves. Mix well. Cover with a lid and cook on a low heat for 10 minutes.
- Garnish with the coriander leaves. Serve hot.

Sautéed Mushrooms

Serves 4

Ingredients

2 tbsp refined vegetable oil
4 green chillies, slit lengthways
8 garlic cloves, crushed
100g/3½oz green peppers, sliced
400g/14oz mushrooms, sliced

Salt to taste
½ tsp coarsely ground black pepper
25g/scant 1oz coriander leaves, chopped

Method

• Heat the oil in a frying pan. Add the green chillies, garlic and green peppers. Fry them on a medium heat for 1-2 minutes.
• Add the mushrooms, salt and pepper. Mix well. Sauté on a medium heat till tender.
• Garnish with the coriander leaves. Serve hot.

Spicy Mushroom with Baby Corn

Serves 4

Ingredients

2 tbsp refined vegetable oil
1 tsp cumin seeds
2 bay leaves
1 tsp ginger paste
2 green chillies, finely chopped
1 large onion, finely chopped
200g/7oz mushrooms, halved

8-10 baby corns, chopped
125g/4½oz tomato purée
½ tsp turmeric
Salt to taste
½ tsp garam masala
½ tsp sugar
10g/¼oz coriander leaves, chopped

Method

• Heat the oil in a saucepan. Add the cumin seeds and bay leaves. Let them splutter for 15 seconds.
• Add the ginger paste, green chillies and onion. Sauté for 1-2 minutes.
• Add the remaining ingredients, except the coriander leaves. Mix well. Cover with a lid and cook on a low heat for 10 minutes.
• Garnish with the coriander leaves. Serve hot.

Dry Spicy Cauliflower

Serves 4

Ingredients

750g/1lb 10oz cauliflower florets

Salt to taste

Pinch of turmeric

4 bay leaves

750ml/1¼ pints water

2 tbsp refined vegetable oil

4 cloves

4 green cardamom pods

1 large onion, sliced

1 tsp ginger paste

1 tsp garlic paste

1 tsp garam masala

½ tsp chilli powder

¼ tsp ground black pepper

10 cashew nuts, ground

2 tbsp yoghurt

3 tbsp tomato purée

3 tbsp butter

60ml/2fl oz single cream

Method

- Cook the cauliflower with the salt, turmeric, bay leaves and water in a saucepan on a medium heat for 10 minutes. Drain and arrange the florets in an ovenproof dish. Set aside.
- Heat the oil in a saucepan. Add the cloves and cardamom. Let them splutter for 15 seconds.
- Add the onion, ginger paste and garlic paste. Fry for a minute.
- Add the garam masala, chilli powder, pepper and cashew nuts. Fry for 1-2 minutes.
- Add the yoghurt and tomato purée. Mix thoroughly. Add the butter and cream. Stir for a minute. Remove from the heat.
- Pour this over the cauliflower florets. Bake at 150°C (300°F, Gas Mark 2) in a pre-heated oven for 8-10 minutes. Serve hot.

Mushroom Curry

Serves 4

Ingredients

3 tbsp refined vegetable oil

2 large onions, grated

1 tsp ginger paste

1 tsp garlic paste

½ tsp turmeric

1 tsp chilli powder

1 tsp ground coriander

400g/14oz mushrooms, quartered

200g/7oz peas

2 tomatoes, finely chopped

½ tsp garam masala

Salt to taste

20 cashew nuts, ground

240ml/6fl oz water

Method

- Heat the oil in a saucepan. Add the onions. Fry them till they are brown.
- Add the ginger paste, garlic paste, turmeric, chilli powder and ground coriander. Sauté on a medium heat for a minute.
- Add the remaining ingredients. Mix well. Cover with a lid and simmer for 8-10 minutes. Serve hot.

Baingan Bharta

(Roasted Aubergine)

Serves 4

Ingredients

1 large aubergine

3 tbsp refined vegetable oil

1 large onion, finely chopped

3 green chillies, slit lengthways

¼ tsp turmeric

Salt to taste

½ tsp garam masala

1 tomato, finely chopped

Method

- Pierce the aubergine all over with a fork and grill it for 25 minutes. Once it has cooled, discard the roasted skin and mash the flesh. Set aside.
- Heat the oil in a saucepan. Add the onion and green chillies. Fry on a medium heat for 2 minutes.
- Add the turmeric, salt, garam masala and tomato. Mix well. Fry for 5 minutes. Add the mashed aubergine. Mix well.
- Cook on a low heat for 8 minutes, stirring occasionally. Serve hot.

Vegetable Hyderabadi

Serves 4

Ingredients
2 tbsp refined vegetable oil
½ tsp mustard seeds
1 large onion, finely chopped
400g/14oz frozen, mixed vegetables
½ tsp turmeric
Salt to taste

For the spice mixture:
2.5cm/1in root ginger
8 garlic cloves
2 cloves
2.5cm/1in cinnamon
1 tsp fenugreek seeds
3 green chillies
4 tbsp fresh coconut, grated
10 cashew nuts

Method
- Grind all the ingredients of the spice mixture together. Set aside.
- Heat the oil in a saucepan. Add the mustard seeds. Let them splutter for 15 seconds. Add the onion and fry till brown.
- Add the remaining ingredients and the ground spice mixture. Mix well. Cook on a low heat for 8-10 minutes. Serve hot.

Kaddu Bhaji*
(Dry Red Pumpkin)

Serves 4

Ingredients
3 tbsp refined vegetable oil
½ tsp cumin seeds
¼ tsp fenugreek seeds
600g/1lb 5oz pumpkin, thinly sliced
Salt to taste
½ tsp roasted ground cumin
½ tsp chilli powder
¼ tsp turmeric
1 tsp amchoor*
1 tsp sugar

Method
- Heat the oil in a saucepan. Add the cumin and fenugreek seeds. Let them splutter for 15 seconds. Add the pumpkin and salt. Mix well. Cover with a lid and cook on a medium heat for 8 minutes.
- Uncover and lightly crush with the back of a spoon. Add the remaining ingredients. Mix well. Cook for 5 minutes. Serve hot.

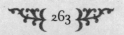

Muthia nu Shak

(Fenugreek Dumplings in Sauce)

Serves 4

Ingredients

200g/7oz fresh fenugreek leaves,
  finely chopped

Salt to taste

125g/4½oz wholemeal flour

125g/4½oz besan*

2 green chillies, finely chopped

1 tsp ginger paste

3 tsp sugar

Juice of 1 lemon

½ tsp garam masala

½ tsp turmeric

Pinch of bicarbonate of soda

3 tbsp refined vegetable oil

½ tsp ajowan seeds

½ tsp mustard seeds

Pinch of asafoetida

250ml/8fl oz water

Method

* Mix the fenugreek leaves with the salt. Set aside for 10 minutes. Squeeze out the moisture.
* Mix the fenugreek leaves with the flour, besan, green chillies, ginger paste, sugar, lemon juice, garam masala, turmeric and bicarbonate of soda. Knead into a soft dough.
* Divide the dough into 30 walnut-sized balls. Flatten slightly to form the muthias. Set aside.
* Heat the oil in a saucepan. Add the ajowan seeds, mustard seeds and asafoetida. Let them splutter for 15 seconds.
* Add the muthias and water.
* Cover with a lid and simmer for 10-15 minutes. Serve hot.

Pumpkin Koot
(Pumpkin in Lentil Curry)

Serves 4

Ingredients
50g/1¾oz fresh coconut, grated

1 tsp cumin seeds

2 red chillies

150g/5½oz mung dhal*, soaked for 30 minutes and drained

2 tbsp chana dhal*

Salt to taste

500ml/16fl oz water

2 tbsp refined vegetable oil

250g/9oz pumpkin, diced

¼ tsp turmeric

Method
* Grind the coconut, cumin seeds and red chillies to a paste. Set aside.
* Mix the dhals with the salt and water. Cook this mixture in a saucepan on a medium heat for 40 minutes. Set aside.
* Heat the oil in a saucepan. Add the pumpkin, turmeric, boiled dhals and the coconut paste. Mix well. Simmer for 10 minutes. Serve hot.

Rassa
(Cauliflower and Peas in Sauce)

Serves 4

Ingredients
2 tbsp refined vegetable oil plus extra for deep frying

250g/9oz cauliflower florets

2 tbsp fresh coconut, grated

1cm/½in root ginger, crushed

4-5 green chillies, slit lengthways

2-3 tomatoes, finely chopped

400g/14oz frozen peas

1 tsp sugar

Salt to taste

Method
* Heat the oil for deep frying in a saucepan. Add the cauliflower. Deep fry on a medium heat till golden brown. Drain and set aside.
* Grind the coconut, ginger, green chillies and tomatoes. Heat 2 tbsp oil in a saucepan. Add this paste and fry for 1-2 minutes.
* Add the cauliflower and the remaining ingredients. Mix well. Cook on a low heat for 4-5 minutes. Serve hot.

Doodhi Manpasand
(Bottle Gourd in Sauce)

Serves 4

Ingredients

3 tbsp refined vegetable oil
3 dried red chillies
1 large onion, finely chopped
500g/1lb 2oz bottle gourd*, chopped
¼ tsp turmeric
2 tsp ground coriander
1 tsp ground cumin
½ tsp chilli powder

½ tsp garam masala
2.5cm/1in root ginger, finely chopped
2 tomatoes, finely chopped
1 green pepper, cored, deseeded
   and finely chopped
Salt to taste
2 tsp coriander leaves, finely chopped

Method

- Heat the oil in a saucepan. Fry the red chillies and onion for 2 minutes.
- Add the remaining ingredients, except the coriander leaves. Mix well.
  Cook on a low heat for 5-7 minutes. Garnish with the coriander leaves.
  Serve hot.

Tomato Chokha
(Tomato Compote)

Serves 4

Ingredients

6 large tomatoes
2 tbsp refined vegetable oil
1 big onion, finely chopped
8 garlic cloves, finely chopped
1 green chilli, finely chopped

½ tsp chilli powder
10g/¼oz coriander leaves,
   finely chopped
Salt to taste

Method

- Grill the tomatoes for 10 minutes. Peel and crush to a pulp. Set aside.
- Heat the oil in a saucepan. Add the onion, garlic and green chilli. Fry for
  2-3 minutes. Add the remaining ingredients and the tomato pulp. Mix
  well. Cover with a lid and cook for 5-6 minutes. Serve hot.

Baingan Chokha
(Aubergine Compote)

Serves 4

Ingredients

1 large aubergine

2 tbsp refined vegetable oil

1 small onion, chopped

8 garlic cloves, finely chopped

1 green chilli, finely chopped

1 tomato, finely chopped

60g/2oz corn kernels, boiled

10g/¼oz coriander leaves, finely chopped

Salt to taste

Method

- Pierce the aubergine all over with a fork. Grill for 10-15 minutes. Peel and crush to a pulp. Set aside.
- Heat the oil in a saucepan. Add the onion, garlic and green chilli. Fry them on a medium heat for 5 minutes.
- Add the remaining ingredients and the aubergine pulp. Mix well. Cook for 3-4 minutes. Serve hot.

Cauliflower & Peas Curry

Serves 4

Ingredients

3 tbsp refined vegetable oil

¼ tsp turmeric

3 green chillies, slit lengthways

1 tsp ground coriander

2.5cm/1in root ginger, grated

250g/9oz cauliflower florets

400g/14oz fresh green peas

60ml/2fl oz water

Salt to taste

1 tbsp coriander leaves, finely chopped

Method

- Heat the oil in a saucepan. Add the turmeric, green chillies, ground coriander and ginger. Fry on a medium heat for a minute.
- Add the remaining ingredients, except the coriander leaves. Mix well. Simmer for 10 minutes.
- Garnish with the coriander leaves. Serve hot.

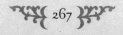

Aloo Methi ki Sabzi

(Potato and Fenugreek Curry)

Serves 4

Ingredients

100g/3½oz fenugreek leaves, chopped

Salt to taste

4 tbsp refined vegetable oil

1 tsp cumin seeds

5-6 green chillies

¼ tsp turmeric

Pinch of asafoetida

6 large potatoes, boiled and chopped

Method
- Mix the fenugreek leaves with the salt. Set aside for 10 minutes.
- Heat the oil in a saucepan. Add the cumin seeds, chillies and turmeric. Let them splutter for 15 seconds.
- Add the remaining ingredients and the fenugreek leaves. Mix well. Cook for 8-10 minutes on a low heat. Serve hot.

Sweet & Sour Karela

Serves 4

Ingredients

500g/1lb 2oz bitter gourds*

Salt to taste

750ml/1¼ pints water

1cm/½in root ginger

10 garlic cloves

4 large onions, chopped

4 tbsp refined vegetable oil

Pinch of asafoetida

½ tsp turmeric

1 tsp ground coriander

1 tsp ground cumin

1 tsp tamarind paste

2 tbsp jaggery*, grated

Method
- Peel the bitter gourds. Slice and soak them in salty water for 1 hour. Rinse and squeeze out the excess water. Wash and set aside.
- Grind the ginger, garlic and onions to a paste. Set aside.
- Heat the oil in a saucepan. Add the asafoetida. Let it splutter for 15 seconds. Add the ginger-onion paste and the remaining ingredients. Mix well. Fry for 3-4 minutes. Add the bitter gourds. Mix well. Cover with a lid and cook on a low heat for 8-10 minutes. Serve hot.

Karela Koshimbir
(Crispy Crushed Bitter Gourd)

Serves 4

Ingredients

500g/1lb 2oz bitter gourds*, peeled	50g/1¾oz coriander leaves, chopped
Salt to taste	3 green chillies, finely chopped
Refined vegetable oil for frying	½ fresh coconut, grated
2 medium-sized onions, chopped	1 tbsp lemon juice

Method

- Slice the bitter gourds. Rub the salt on them and set aside for 2-3 hours.
- Heat the oil in a saucepan. Add the bitter gourds and fry on a medium heat till brown and crispy. Drain, cool a little and crush with your fingers.
- Mix the remaining ingredients in a bowl. Add the gourds and serve while they are still warm.

Karela Curry
(Bitter Gourd Curry)

Serves 4

Ingredients

½ coconut	2 green chillies, finely chopped
2 red chillies	Salt to taste
1 tsp cumin seeds	½ tsp turmeric
3 tbsp refined vegetable oil	500g/1lb 2oz bitter gourds*, peeled and chopped
1 pinch of asafoetida	2 tomatoes, finely chopped
2 large onions, finely chopped	

Method

- Grate half of the coconut and chop the rest. Set aside.
- Dry roast (see cooking techniques) the grated coconut, red chillies and cumin seeds. Cool and grind together to a fine paste. Set aside.
- Heat the oil in a frying pan. Add the asafoetida, onions, green chillies, salt, turmeric and chopped coconut. Fry for 3 minutes, stirring frequently.
- Add the bitter gourds and tomatoes. Cook for 3-4 minutes.
- Add the ground coconut paste. Cook for 5-7 minutes and serve hot.

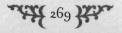

Chilli Cauliflower

Serves 4

Ingredients

3 tbsp refined vegetable oil

5cm/2in root ginger, finely chopped

12 garlic cloves, finely chopped

1 cauliflower, chopped into florets

5 red chillies, quartered and deseeded

6 spring onions, halved

3 tomatoes, blanched and chopped

Salt to taste

Method

- Heat the oil in a saucepan. Add the ginger and garlic. Fry on a medium heat for a minute.
- Add the cauliflower and red chillies. Stir-fry for 5 minutes.
- Add the remaining ingredients. Mix well. Cook on a low heat for 7-8 minutes. Serve hot.

Nutty Curry

Serves 4

Ingredients

4 tbsp ghee

10g/¼oz cashew nuts

10g/¼oz almonds, blanched

10-12 peanuts

5-6 raisins

10 pistachios

10 walnuts, chopped

2.5cm/1in root ginger, grated

6 garlic cloves, crushed

4 small onions, finely chopped

4 tomatoes, finely chopped

4 dates, de-seeded and sliced

½ tsp turmeric

125g/4½oz khoya*

1 tsp garam masala

Salt to taste

75g/2½ Cheddar cheese, grated

1 tbsp coriander leaves, chopped

Method

- Heat the ghee in a frying pan. Add all the nuts and fry them on a medium heat till they turn golden brown. Drain and set aside.
- In the same ghee, fry the ginger, garlic and onion till brown.
- Add the fried nuts and all the remaining ingredients, except the cheese and coriander leaves. Cover with a lid. Cook on a low heat for 5 minutes.
- Garnish with the cheese and coriander leaves. Serve hot.

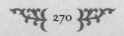

Daikon Leaves Bhaaji

Serves 4

Ingredients

2 tbsp refined vegetable oil

¼ tsp ground cumin

2 red chillies, broken into bits

Pinch of asafoetida

400g/14oz daikon leaves*, chopped

300g/10oz chana dhal*, soaked for 1 hour

1 tsp jaggery*, grated

¼ tsp turmeric

Salt to taste

Method

- Heat the oil in a saucepan. Add the cumin, red chillies and asafoetida.
- Let them splutter for 15 seconds. Add the remaining ingredients. Mix well. Cook on a low heat for 10-15 minutes. Serve hot.

Chhole Aloo

(Chickpea and Potato Curry)

Serves 4

Ingredients

500g/1lb 2oz chickpeas, soaked overnight

Pinch of bicarbonate of soda

Salt to taste

1 litre/1¾ pints water

3 tbsp ghee

2.5cm/1in root ginger, julienned

2 large onions, grated, plus 1 small onion, sliced

2 tomatoes, diced

1 tsp garam masala

1 tsp ground cumin, dry roasted (see cooking techniques)

½ tsp ground green cardamom

½ tsp turmeric

2 large potatoes, boiled and diced

2 tsp tamarind paste

1 tbsp coriander leaves, chopped

Method

- Cook the chickpeas with the bicarbonate of soda, salt and water in a saucepan on a medium heat for 45 minutes. Drain and set aside.
- Heat the ghee in a saucepan. Add the ginger and grated onions. Fry till translucent. Add the remaining ingredients, except the coriander leaves and sliced onion. Mix well. Add the chickpeas and cook for 7-8 minutes.
- Garnish with the coriander leaves and sliced onion. Serve hot.

Peanut Curry

Serves 4

Ingredients

1 tsp poppy seeds	1 tsp amchoor*
1 tsp coriander seeds	½ tsp turmeric
1 tsp cumin seeds	1 big tomato, blanched and chopped
2 red chillies	2 tsp jaggery*, grated
25g/scant 1oz fresh coconut, grated	500ml/16fl oz water
3 tbsp ghee	Salt to taste
2 small onions, grated	15g/½oz coriander leaves, chopped
900g/2lb peanuts, pounded	

Method

* Grind the poppy seeds, coriander seeds, cumin seeds, red chillies and coconut to a fine paste. Set aside.
* Heat the ghee in a saucepan. Add the onions. Fry till translucent.
* Add the ground paste and the remaining ingredients, except the coriander leaves. Mix well. Simmer for 7-8 minutes.
* Garnish with the coriander leaves. Serve hot.

French Beans Upkari

(French Beans with Coconut)

Serves 4

Ingredients

1 tbsp refined vegetable oil	500g/1lb 2oz French beans, chopped
½ tsp mustard seeds	1 tsp jaggery*, grated
½ tsp urad dhal*	Salt to taste
2-3 red chillies, broken	25g/scant 1oz fresh coconut, grated

Method

* Heat the oil in a saucepan. Add the mustard seeds. Let them splutter for 15 seconds.
* Add the dhal. Fry till golden brown. Add the remaining ingredients, except the coconut. Mix well. Cook on a low heat for 8-10 minutes.
* Garnish with the coconut. Serve hot.

Karatey Ambadey
(Bitter Gourd and Unripe Mango Curry)

Serves 4

Ingredients

250g/9oz bitter gourd*, sliced

Salt to taste

60g/2oz jaggery*, grated

1 tsp refined vegetable oil

4 dry red chillies

1 tsp urad dhal*

1 tsp fenugreek seeds

2 tsp coriander seeds

50g/1¾oz fresh coconut, grated

¼ tsp turmeric

4 small unripe mangoes

Method

- Rub the bitter gourd pieces with the salt. Set aside for an hour.
- Squeeze out the water from the gourd pieces. Cook them in a saucepan with the jaggery on a medium heat for 4-5 minutes. Set aside.
- Heat the oil in a saucepan. Add the red chillies, dhal, fenugreek and coriander seeds. Fry for a minute. Add the bitter gourd and the remaining ingredients. Mix well. Cook on a low heat for 4-5 minutes. Serve hot.

Kadhai Paneer
(Spicy Paneer)

Serves 4

Ingredients

2 tbsp refined vegetable oil

1 large onion, sliced

3 large green peppers, finely chopped

500g/1lb 2oz paneer*, chopped into 2.5cm/1in pieces

1 tomato, finely chopped

¼ tsp ground coriander, dry roasted (see cooking techniques)

Salt to taste

10g/¼oz coriander leaves, chopped

Method

- Heat the oil in a saucepan. Add the onion and peppers. Fry on a medium heat for 2-3 minutes.
- Add the remaining ingredients, except the coriander leaves. Mix well. Cook on a low heat for 5 minutes. Garnish with the coriander leaves. Serve hot.

Kathirikkai Vangi
(South Indian Aubergine Curry)

Serves 4

Ingredients

150g/5½oz masoor dhal*	1 tsp refined vegetable oil
Salt to taste	¼ tsp mustard seeds
¼ tsp turmeric	1 tsp tamarind paste
500ml/16fl oz water	8-10 curry leaves
250g/9oz thin aubergines, sliced	1 tsp sambhar powder*

Method

- Mix the masoor dhal with salt, a pinch of turmeric and half the water. Cook in a saucepan on a medium heat for 40 minutes. Set aside.
- Cook the aubergines with salt and the remaining turmeric and water in another saucepan on a medium heat for 20 minutes. Set aside.
- Heat the oil in a saucepan. Add the mustard seeds. Let them splutter for 15 seconds. Add the remaining ingredients, the dhal and the aubergine. Mix well. Simmer for 6-7 minutes. Serve hot.

Pitla
(Spicy Gram Flour Curry)

Serves 4

Ingredients

250g/9oz besan*	6 garlic cloves, crushed
500ml/16fl oz water	2 tbsp tamarind paste
2 tbsp refined vegetable oil	1 tsp garam masala
¼ tsp mustard seeds	Salt to taste
2 large onions, finely chopped	1 tbsp coriander leaves, chopped

Method

- Mix the besan and the water. Set aside.
- Heat the oil in a saucepan. Add the mustard seeds. Let them splutter for 15 seconds. Add the onions and garlic. Fry till the onions are brown.
- Add the besan paste. Cook on a low heat till it starts to boil.
- Add the remaining ingredients. Simmer for 5 minutes. Serve hot.

Cauliflower Masala

Serves 4

Ingredients

1 large cauliflower, parboiled (see
  cooking techniques) in salted water

3 tbsp refined vegetable oil

2 tbsp coriander leaves,
  finely chopped

1 tsp ground coriander

½ tsp ground cumin

¼ tsp ground ginger

Salt to taste

120ml/4fl oz water

For the sauce:

200g/7oz yoghurt

1 tbsp besan*, dry roasted
  (see cooking techniques)

¾ tsp chilli powder

Method

- Drain the cauliflower and chop into florets.
- Heat 2 tbsp oil in a frying pan. Add the cauliflower and fry it on a medium heat till golden brown. Set aside.
- Mix all the sauce ingredients together.
- Heat 1 tbsp oil in a saucepan and add this mixture. Fry for a minute.
- Cover with a lid and simmer for 8-10 minutes.
- Add the cauliflower. Mix well. Simmer for 5 minutes.
- Garnish with the coriander leaves. Serve hot.

Shukna Kacha Pepe

(Green Papaya Curry)

Serves 4

Ingredients

150g/5½oz chana dhal*, soaked overnight, drained and ground to a paste

3 tbsp refined vegetable oil plus for deep frying

2 whole dry red chillies

½ tsp fenugreek seeds

½ tsp mustard seeds

1 unripe papaya, peeled and grated

1 tsp turmeric

1 tbsp sugar

Salt to taste

Method

- Divide the dhal paste into walnut-sized balls. Flatten into thin discs.
- Heat the oil for deep frying in a frying pan. Add the discs. Deep fry on a medium heat till golden brown. Drain and break into small pieces. Set aside.
- Heat the remaining oil in a saucepan. Add the chillies, fenugreek and mustard seeds. Let them splutter for 15 seconds.
- Add the remaining ingredients. Mix well. Cover with a lid and cook on a low heat for 8-10 minutes. Add the dhal pieces. Mix well and serve.

Dry Okra

Serves 4

Ingredients

3 tbsp mustard oil

½ tsp kalonji seeds*

750g/1lb 10oz okra, slit lengthways

Salt to taste

½ tsp chilli powder

½ tsp turmeric

2 tsp sugar

3 tsp ground mustard

1 tbsp tamarind paste

Method

- Heat the oil in a saucepan. Fry the onion seeds and okra for 5 minutes.
- Add the salt, chilli powder, turmeric and sugar. Cover with a lid. Cook on a low heat for 10 minutes.
- Add the remaining ingredients. Mix well. Cook for 2-3 minutes. Serve hot.

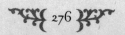

Moghlai Cauliflower

Serves 4

Ingredients

5cm/2in root ginger	2 tbsp ghee
2 tsp cumin seeds	2 bay leaves
6-7 black peppercorns	200g/7oz yoghurt
500g/1lb 2oz cauliflower florets	500ml/16fl oz coconut milk
Salt to taste	1 tsp sugar

Method

- Grind the ginger, cumin seeds and peppercorns to a fine paste.
- Marinate the cauliflower florets with this paste and salt for 20 minutes.
- Heat the ghee in a frying pan. Add the florets. Fry till golden brown. Add the remaining ingredients. Mix well. Cover with a lid and simmer for 7-8 minutes. Serve hot.

Bhapa Shorshe Baingan
(Aubergine in Mustard Sauce)

Serves 4

Ingredients

2 long aubergines	2–3 tbsp ready-made mustard
Salt to taste	1 tbsp coriander leaves, finely chopped
¼ tsp turmeric	1-2 green chillies, finely chopped
3 tbsp refined vegetable oil	
3 tbsp mustard oil	

Method

- Slice each aubergine lengthways into 8-12 pieces. Marinate with the salt and turmeric for 5 minutes.
- Heat the oil in a saucepan. Add the aubergine slices and cover with a lid. Cook on a medium heat for 3-4 minutes, turning occasionally.
- Whisk the mustard oil with the ready-made mustard and add to the aubergines. Mix well. Cook on a medium heat for a minute.
- Garnish with the coriander leaves and green chillies. Serve hot.

Baked Vegetables in Spicy Sauce

Serves 4

Ingredients

2 tbsp butter

4 garlic cloves, finely chopped

1 large onion, finely chopped

1 tbsp plain white flour

200g/7oz frozen mixed vegetables

Salt to taste

1 tsp chilli powder

1 tsp mustard paste

250ml/8fl oz ketchup

4 large potatoes, boiled and sliced

250ml/8fl oz white sauce

4 tbsp grated Cheddar cheese

Method

- Heat the butter in a saucepan. Add the garlic and onion. Fry till translucent. Add the flour and fry for a minute.
- Add the vegetables, salt, chilli powder, mustard paste and ketchup. Cook on a medium heat for 4-5 minutes. Set aside.
- Grease a baking dish. Arrange the vegetable mixture and the potatoes in alternate layers. Pour the white sauce and cheese on top.
- Bake in an oven at 200°C (400°F, Gas Mark 6) for 20 minutes. Serve hot.

Tasty Tofu

Serves 4

Ingredients

2 tbsp refined vegetable oil

3 small onions, grated

1 tsp ginger paste

1 tsp garlic paste

3 tomatoes, puréed

50g/1¾oz Greek yoghurt, whisked

400g/14oz tofu, chopped into 2.5cm/1in pieces

25g/scant 1oz coriander leaves, finely chopped

Salt to taste

Method

- Heat the oil in a saucepan. Add the onions, ginger paste and garlic paste. Stir-fry for 5 minutes on a medium heat.
- Add the remaining ingredients. Mix well. Simmer for 3-4 minutes. Serve hot.

Aloo Baingan
(Potato and Aubergine Curry)

Serves 4

Ingredients

3 tbsp refined vegetable oil	6 curry leaves
1 tsp mustard seeds	½ tsp turmeric
½ tsp asafoetida	3 large potatoes, boiled and diced
1cm/½in root ginger, finely chopped	250g/9oz aubergines, chopped
4 green chillies, slit lengthways	½ tsp amchoor*
10 garlic cloves, finely chopped	Salt to taste

Method
- Heat the oil in a saucepan. Add the mustard seeds and asafoetida. Let them splutter for 15 seconds.
- Add the ginger, green chillies, garlic and curry leaves. Fry for 1 minute, stirring continuously.
- Add the remaining ingredients. Mix well. Cover with a lid and simmer for 10-12 minutes. Serve hot.

Sugar Snap Pea Curry

Serves 4

Ingredients

500g/1lb 2oz sugar snap peas	½ tsp garam masala
2 tbsp refined vegetable oil	½ tsp chilli powder
1 tsp ginger paste	1 tsp sugar
1 large onion, finely chopped	2 large tomatoes, diced
2 large potatoes, peeled and diced	Salt to taste
½ tsp turmeric	

Method
- Peel the strings from the edges of the pea pods. Chop the pods. Set aside.
- Heat the oil in a saucepan. Add the ginger paste and onion. Fry till translucent. Add the remaining ingredients and the pods. Mix well. Cover with a lid and cook on a low heat for 7-8 minutes. Serve hot.

Potato Pumpkin Curry

Serves 4

Ingredients

2 tbsp refined vegetable oil

1 tsp panch phoron*

Pinch of asafoetida

1 dried red chilli, broken into bits

1 bay leaf

4 large potatoes, diced

200g/7oz pumpkin, diced

½ tsp ginger paste

½ tsp garlic paste

1 tsp ground cumin

1 tsp ground coriander

¼ tsp turmeric

½ tsp garam masala

1 tsp amchoor*

500ml/16fl oz water

Salt to taste

Method

- Heat the oil in a saucepan. Add the panch phoron. Let them splutter for 15 seconds.
- Add the asafoetida, red chilli pieces and the bay leaf. Fry for a minute.
- Add the remaining ingredients. Mix well. Simmer for 10-12 minutes. Serve hot.

Egg Thoran
(Spicy Scrambled Egg)

Serves 4

Ingredients

60ml/2fl oz refined vegetable oil

¼ tsp mustard seeds

2 onions, finely chopped

1 large tomato, finely chopped

1 tsp freshly ground black pepper

Salt to taste

4 eggs, whisked

25g/scant 1oz fresh coconut, grated

50g/1¾oz coriander leaves, chopped

Method

- Heat the oil in a saucepan and fry the mustard seeds. Let them splutter for 15 seconds. Add the onions and fry till brown. Add the tomato, pepper and salt. Fry for 2-3 minutes.
- Add the eggs. Cook on a low heat, scrambling continuously.
- Garnish with the coconut and coriander leaves. Serve hot.

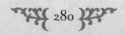

Baingan Lajawab
(Aubergine with Cauliflower)

Serves 4

Ingredients

4 large aubergines

2 tbsp refined vegetable oil plus extra for deep frying

1 tsp cumin seeds

½ tsp turmeric

2.5cm/1in root ginger, ground

2 green chillies, finely chopped

1 tsp amchoor*

Salt to taste

100g/3½oz frozen peas

Method

- Slit each aubergine lengthways and scoop out the flesh.
- Heat the oil. Add the aubergine shells. Deep fry for 2 minutes. Set aside.
- Heat 2 tbsp oil in a saucepan. Add the cumin seeds and turmeric. Let them splutter for 15 seconds. Add the remaining ingredients and the aubergine flesh. Mash lightly and cook on a low heat for 5 minutes.
- Carefully stuff the aubergine shells with this mixture. Grill for 3-4 minutes. Serve hot.

Veggie Bahar
(Vegetables in a Nutty Sauce)

Serves 4

Ingredients

3 tbsp refined vegetable oil

1 large onion, finely chopped

2 large tomatoes, finely chopped

1 tsp ginger paste

1 tsp garlic paste

20 cashew nuts, ground

2 tbsp walnuts, ground

2 tbsp poppy seeds

200g/7oz yoghurt

100g/3½oz frozen mixed vegetables

1 tsp garam masala

Salt to taste

Method

- Heat the oil in a saucepan. Add the onion. Fry on a medium heat till brown. Add the tomatoes, ginger paste, garlic paste, cashew nuts, walnuts and poppy seeds. Fry for 3-4 minutes.
- Add the remaining ingredients. Cook for 7-8 minutes. Serve hot.

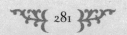

Stuffed Vegetables

Serves 4

Ingredients
4 small potatoes
100g/3½oz okra
4 small aubergines
4 tbsp refined vegetable oil
½ tsp mustard seeds
Pinch of asafoetida

For the filling:
250g/9oz besan*
1 tsp ground coriander
1 tsp ground cumin
½ tsp turmeric
1 tsp chilli powder
1 tsp garam masala
Salt to taste

Method
• Mix all the filling ingredients together. Set aside.
• Slit the potatoes, okra and aubergines. Stuff with the filling. Set aside.
• Heat the oil in a saucepan. Add the mustard seeds and asafoetida. Let them splutter for 15 seconds. Add the stuffed vegetables. Cover with a lid and cook on a low heat for 8-10 minutes. Serve hot.

Singhi Aloo
(Drumsticks with Potatoes)

Serves 4

Ingredients
5 tbsp refined vegetable oil
3 small onions, finely chopped
3 green chillies, finely chopped
2 large tomatoes, finely chopped
2 tsp ground coriander

Salt to taste
5 Indian drumsticks*, chopped into 7.5cm/3in pieces
2 large potatoes, chopped
360ml/12fl oz water

Method
• Heat the oil in a saucepan. Add the onions and chillies. Fry them on a low heat for a minute.
• Add the tomatoes, ground coriander and salt. Fry for 2-3 minutes.
• Add the drumsticks, potatoes and water. Mix well. Simmer for 10-12 minutes. Serve hot.

Sindhi Curry

Serves 4

Ingredients

150g/5½oz masoor dhal*
Salt to taste
1 litre/1¾ pints water
4 tomatoes, finely chopped
5 tbsp refined vegetable oil
½ tsp cumin seeds
¼ tsp fenugreek seeds
8 curry leaves
3 green chillies, slit lengthways

¼ tsp asafoetida
4 tbsp besan*
½ tsp chilli powder
½ tsp turmeric
8 okras, slit lengthways
10 French beans, diced
6-7 kokum*
1 large carrot, julienned
1 large potato, diced

Method

- Mix the dhal with the salt and water. Cook this mixture in a saucepan on a medium heat for 45 minutes, stirring occasionally.
- Add the tomatoes and simmer for 7-8 minutes. Set aside.
- Heat the oil in a saucepan. Add the cumin and fenugreek seeds, curry leaves, green chillies and asafoetida. Let them splutter for 30 seconds.
- Add the besan. Fry for a minute, stirring constantly.
- Add the remaining ingredients and the dhal mixture. Mix thoroughly. Simmer for 10 minutes. Serve hot.

Gulnar Kofta
(Paneer Balls In Spinach)

Serves 4

Ingredients
150g/5½oz mixed dry fruits
200g/7oz khoya*
4 large potatoes, boiled
  and mashed
150g/5½oz paneer*,
  crumbled
100g/3½oz Cheddar cheese
2 tsp cornflour
Refined vegetable oil for
  deep frying
2 tsp butter
100g/3½oz spinach, finely
  chopped
1 tsp single cream
Salt to taste

For the spice mixture:
2 cloves
1cm/½in cinnamon
3 black peppercorns

Method
- Mix the dry fruits with the khoya. Set aside.
- Grind together all the ingredients of the spice mixture. Set aside.
- Mix the potatoes, paneer, cheese and cornflour into a dough. Divide the dough into walnut-sized balls and flatten into discs. Place a portion of the dry fruit-khoya mixture on each disc and seal like a pouch.
- Smooth into walnut-sized balls to make the koftas. Set aside.
- Heat the oil in a frying pan. Add the koftas and deep fry them on a medium heat till they turn golden brown. Drain and set aside in a serving dish.
- Heat the butter in a saucepan. Add the ground spice mixture. Fry for a minute.
- Add the spinach and cook for 2-3 minutes.
- Add the cream and salt. Mix well. Pour this mixture over the koftas. Serve hot.

Paneer Korma

(Rich Paneer Curry)

Serves 4

Ingredients

500g/1lb 2oz paneer*

3 tbsp refined vegetable oil

1 large onion, chopped

2.5cm/1in root ginger, julienned

8 garlic cloves, crushed

2 green chillies, finely chopped

1 large tomato, finely chopped

¼ tsp turmeric

½ tsp ground coriander

½ tsp ground cumin

1 tsp chilli powder

½ tsp garam masala

125g/4½oz yoghurt

Salt to taste

250ml/8fl oz water

2 tbsp coriander leaves, finely chopped

Method

- Grate half of the paneer and chop the remainder into 2.5cm/1in pieces.
- Heat the oil in a frying pan. Add the paneer pieces. Fry them on a medium heat till they turn golden brown. Drain and set aside.
- In the same oil, fry the onion, ginger, garlic and green chillies on a medium heat for 2-3 minutes.
- Add the tomato. Fry for 2 minutes.
- Add the turmeric, ground coriander, ground cumin, chilli powder and garam masala. Mix well. Fry for 2-3 minutes.
- Add the yoghurt, salt and water. Mix well. Simmer for 8-10 minutes.
- Add the fried paneer pieces. Mix well. Simmer for 5 minutes.
- Garnish with the grated paneer and coriander leaves. Serve hot.

Chutney Potatoes

Serves 4

Ingredients

100g/3½oz coriander leaves, finely chopped

4 green chillies

2.5cm/1in root ginger

7 garlic cloves

25g/scant 1oz fresh coconut, grated

1 tbsp lemon juice

1 tsp cumin seeds

1 tsp coriander seeds

½ tsp turmeric

½ tsp chilli powder

Salt to taste

750g/1lb 10oz large potatoes, peeled and chopped into discs

4 tbsp refined vegetable oil

¼ tsp mustard seeds

Method

• Mix the coriander leaves, green chillies, ginger, garlic, coconut, lemon juice, cumin and coriander seeds. Grind this mixture to a fine paste.

• Mix this paste with the turmeric, chilli powder and salt.

• Marinate the potatoes with this mixture for 30 minutes.

• Heat the oil in a saucepan. Add the mustard seeds. Let them splutter for 15 seconds.

• Add the potatoes. Cook them on a low heat for 8-10 minutes, stirring occasionally. Serve hot.

Lobia

(Black Eyed Peas Curry)

Serves 4

Ingredients

400g/14oz black eyed peas, soaked
  overnight

Pinch of bicarbonate of soda

Salt to taste

1.4 litres/2½ pints water

1 large onion

4 garlic cloves

3 tbsp ghee

2 tsp ground coriander

1 tsp ground cumin

1 tsp amchoor*

½ tsp garam masala

½ tsp chilli powder

¼ tsp turmeric

2 tomatoes, diced

3 green chillies, finely chopped

2 tbsp coriander leaves,
  finely chopped

Method

• Mix the black eyed peas with the bicarbonate of soda, salt and 1.2 litres/
  2 pints of water. Cook this mixture in a saucepan on a medium heat for
  45 minutes. Drain and set aside.

• Grind the onion and garlic to a paste.

• Heat the ghee in a saucepan. Add the paste and fry it on a medium heat
  till it turns brown.

• Add the cooked black eyed peas, the remaining water and all the
  remaining ingredients, except the coriander leaves. Simmer for 8-10
  minutes.

• Garnish with the coriander leaves. Serve hot.

Khatta Meetha Vegetable

(Sweet and Sour Vegetables)

Serves 4

Ingredients

1 tbsp flour

1 tbsp malt vinegar

2 tbsp sugar

50g/1¾oz cabbage, finely chopped into long strips

1 large green pepper, chopped into strips

1 large carrot, chopped into strips

50g/1¾oz French beans, slit and chopped

100g/3½oz baby corn

1 tbsp refined vegetable oil

½ tsp ginger paste

½ tsp garlic paste

2-3 green chillies, finely chopped

4-5 spring onions, finely chopped

125g/4½oz tomato purée

120ml/8fl oz ketchup

Salt to taste

10g/¼oz coriander leaves, finely chopped

Method

- Mix the flour with the vinegar and sugar. Set aside.
- Mix together the cabbage, green pepper, carrot, French beans and baby corn. Steam (see cooking techniques) this mixture in a steamer for 10 minutes. Set aside.
- Heat the oil in a saucepan. Add the ginger paste, garlic paste and chillies. Fry for 30 seconds.
- Add the spring onions. Fry for 1-2 minutes.
- Add the steamed vegetables and the tomato purée, ketchup and salt. Cook on a low heat for 5-6 minutes.
- Add the flour paste. Cook for 3-4 minutes.
- Garnish with the coriander leaves. Serve hot.

Dahiwale Chhole

(Chickpea in Yoghurt Sauce)

Serves 4

Ingredients

500g/1lb 2oz chickpeas, soaked overnight

Pinch of bicarbonate of soda

Salt to taste

1 litre/1¾ pints water

3 tbsp ghee

2 large onions, grated

1 tsp ginger, grated

150g/5½oz yoghurt

1 tsp garam masala

1 tsp ground cumin, dry roasted (see cooking techniques)

½ tsp chilli powder

¼ tsp turmeric

1 tsp amchoor*

½ tbsp cashew nuts

½ tbsp raisins

Method

- Mix the chickpeas with the bicarbonate of soda, salt and water. Cook this mixture in a saucepan on a medium heat for 45 minutes. Drain and set aside.
- Heat the ghee in a saucepan. Add the onions and ginger. Fry them on a medium heat till the onions are translucent.
- Add the chickpeas and the remaining ingredients, except the cashew nuts and raisins. Mix well. Cook on a low heat for 7-8 minutes.
- Garnish with the cashew nuts and raisins. Serve hot.

Teekha Papad Bhaji*
(Spicy Poppadam Dish)

Serves 4

Ingredients

1 tbsp refined vegetable oil

¼ tsp mustard seeds

¼ tsp cumin seeds

¼ tsp fenugreek seeds

2 tsp ground coriander

3 tsp sugar

Salt to taste

250ml/8fl oz water

6 poppadams, broken into bits

1 tbsp coriander leaves, chopped

Method

- Heat the oil in a saucepan. Add the mustard, cumin and fenugreek seeds, ground coriander, sugar and salt. Let them splutter for 30 seconds. Add the water and simmer for 3-4 minutes.
- Add the poppadam pieces. Simmer for 5-7 minutes. Garnish with the coriander leaves. Serve hot.

Vegetable Jhalfrezie
(Spicy Mixed Vegetables)

Serves 4

Ingredients

3 tbsp ghee

2 large onions, finely chopped

2 tomatoes, finely chopped

4 green chillies, finely chopped

1cm/½in root ginger, finely chopped

1 tbsp coriander leaves, chopped

120ml/4fl oz ketchup

3 spring onions, finely chopped

1 tsp chilli powder

1 tsp sugar

300g/10oz mixed frozen vegetables

Salt to taste

Method

- Heat the ghee. Add the onions. Fry on a medium heat till they turn brown.
- Add the tomatoes, chillies, ginger and coriander leaves. Fry for 2 minutes.
- Add the remaining ingredients. Mix well. Simmer for 5-10 minutes. Serve hot.

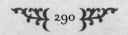

Kele ki Bhaji*

(Unripe Banana Curry)

Serves 4

Ingredients

6 unripe bananas, peeled and sliced into 2.5cm/1in thick pieces

Salt to taste

3 tbsp refined vegetable oil

1 large onion, finely sliced

2 garlic cloves, crushed

2-3 green chillies, slit lengthways

1cm/½in root ginger

1 tsp turmeric

½ tsp cumin seeds

½ fresh coconut, grated

Method

* Soak the bananas in cold water and salt for an hour. Drain and set aside.
* Heat the oil in a saucepan. Add the onion, garlic, green chillies and ginger. Fry them on a medium heat till the onion turns brown.
* Add the bananas and the turmeric, cumin and salt.
  Mix well. Cover with a lid and cook on a low heat for 5-6 minutes.
* Add the coconut, toss lightly and cook for 2-3 minutes. Serve hot.

Coconut Kathal
(Green Jackfruit with Coconut)

Serves 4

Ingredients
500g/1lb 2oz unripe jackfruit*, peeled
  and chopped
500ml/16fl oz water
Salt to taste
100ml/3½fl oz mustard oil
2 bay leaves
1 tsp cumin seeds
1 tsp ginger paste
250ml/8fl oz coconut milk
Sugar to taste

For the seasoning:
75g/2½oz ghee
1cm/½in cinnamon
4 green cardamom pods
1 tsp chilli powder
2 green chillies, slit lengthways

Method
- Mix the jackfruit pieces with the water and salt. Cook this mixture in a saucepan on a medium heat for 30 minutes. Drain and set aside.
- Heat the mustard oil in a saucepan. Add the bay leaves and cumin seeds. Let them splutter for 15 seconds.
- Add the jackfruit and the ginger paste, coconut milk and sugar. Cook for 3-4 minutes, stirring continuously. Set aside.
- Heat the ghee in a frying pan. Add the seasoning ingredients. Fry for 30 seconds.
- Pour this mixture over the jackfruit mixture. Serve hot.

Spicy Yam Slices

Serves 4

Ingredients

500g/1lb 2oz yam
1 medium-sized onion
1 tsp ginger paste
1 tsp garlic paste
1 tsp chilli powder
1 tsp ground coriander
4 cloves

1cm/½in cinnamon
4 green cardamom pods
½ tsp pepper
50g/1¾oz coriander leaves
50g/1¾oz mint leaves
Salt to taste
Refined vegetable oil for frying

Method

- Peel the yams and chop into 1cm/½in thick slices. Steam (see cooking techniques) for 5 minutes. Set aside.
- Grind the rest of the ingredients, except the oil, to a smooth paste.
- Apply the paste to both the sides of the yam slices.
- Heat the oil a non-stick pan. Add the yam slices. Fry on both sides till crisp, adding a little oil along the edges. Serve hot.

Yam Masala

Serves 4

Ingredients

400g/14oz yam, peeled and diced
750ml/1¼ pints water
Salt to taste
3 tbsp refined vegetable oil
¼ mustard seeds

2 whole red chillies, roughly chopped
¼ tsp turmeric
¼ tsp ground cumin
1 tsp ground coriander
3 tbsp peanuts, coarsely pounded

Method

- Boil the yam with the water and salt in a saucepan for 30 minutes. Drain and set aside.
- Heat the oil in a saucepan. Add the mustard seeds and red chilli pieces. Let them splutter for 15 seconds.
- Add the remaining ingredients and the boiled yam. Mix well. Cook on a low heat for 7-8 minutes. Serve hot.

Beetroot Masala

Serves 4

Ingredients

2 tbsp refined vegetable oil

3 small onions, finely chopped

½ tsp ginger paste

½ tsp garlic paste

3 green chillies, slit lengthways

3 beetroots, peeled and chopped

¼ tsp turmeric

1 tsp ground coriander

¼ tsp garam masala

Salt to taste

125g/4½oz tomato purée

1 tbsp coriander leaves, chopped

Method

- Heat the oil in a saucepan. Add the onions. Fry them on a medium heat till they turn translucent.
- Add the ginger paste, garlic paste and green chillies. Stir-fry on a low heat for 2-3 minutes.
- Add the beetroots, turmeric, ground coriander, garam masala, salt and tomato purée. Mix well. Cook for 7-8 minutes. Garnish with the coriander leaves. Serve hot.

Bean Sprouts Masala

Serves 4

Ingredients

2 tbsp refined vegetable oil

3 small onions, finely chopped

4 green chillies, finely chopped

1cm/½in root ginger, julienned

8 garlic cloves, crushed

¼ tsp turmeric

1 tsp ground coriander

2 tomatoes, finely chopped

200g/7oz sprouted mung beans, steamed

Salt to taste

1 tbsp coriander leaves, chopped

Method

- Heat the oil in a saucepan. Add the onions, green chillies, ginger and garlic. Fry the mixture on a medium heat till the onions turn brown.
- Add the remaining ingredients, except the coriander leaves. Mix well. Cook the mixture on a low heat for 8-10 minutes, stirring occasionally.
- Garnish with the coriander leaves. Serve hot.

Mirch Masala

(Spicy Green Pepper)

Serves 4

Ingredients

100g/3½oz spinach, finely chopped

10g/¼oz fenugreek leaves, finely chopped

25g/scant 1oz coriander leaves, finely chopped

3 green chillies, slit lengthways

60ml/2fl oz water

3½ tbsp refined vegetable oil

2 tbsp besan*

1 large potato, boiled and mashed

¼ tsp turmeric

2 tsp ground coriander

½ tsp chilli powder

Salt to taste

8 small green peppers, cored and deseeded

1 large onion, finely chopped

2 tomatoes, finely chopped

Method

• Mix the spinach, fenugreek, coriander leaves and chillies with the water. Steam (see cooking techniques) the mixture for 15 minutes. Drain and grind this mixture to a paste.

• Heat half the oil in a saucepan. Add the besan, potato, turmeric, ground coriander, chilli powder, salt and the spinach paste. Mix well. Fry this mixture on a medium heat for 3-4 minutes. Remove from the heat.

• Stuff this mixture into the green peppers.

• Heat ½ tbsp of oil in a frying pan. Add the stuffed peppers. Fry them on a medium heat for 7-8 minutes, turning them occasionally. Set aside.

• Heat the remaining oil in a saucepan. Add the onion. Fry it on a medium heat till it turns brown. Add the tomatoes and the fried stuffed peppers. Mix well. Cover with a lid and cook on a low heat for 4-5 minutes. Serve hot.

Tomato Kadhi
(Tomato in Gram Flour Sauce)

Serves 4

Ingredients

2 tbsp besan*
120ml/4fl oz water
3 tbsp refined vegetable oil
½ tsp mustard seeds
½ tsp fenugreek seeds
½ tsp cumin seeds
2 green chillies slit lengthways
8 curry leaves
1 tsp chilli powder
2 tsp sugar
150g/5½oz mixed frozen vegetables
Salt to taste
8 tomatoes, blanched (see cooking techniques) and puréed
2 tbsp coriander leaves, finely chopped

Method

- Mix the besan with the water to form a smooth paste. Set aside.
- Heat the oil in a saucepan. Add the mustard, fenugreek and cumin seeds, green chillies, curry leaves, chilli powder and sugar. Let them splutter for 30 seconds.
- Add the vegetables and salt. Fry the mixture on a medium heat for a minute.
- Add the tomato purée. Mix well. Cook the mixture on a low heat for 5 minutes.
- Add the besan paste. Cook for another 3-4 minutes.
- Garnish the kadhi with the coriander leaves. Serve hot.

Vegetable Kolhapuri
(Spicy Mixed Vegetable)

Serves 4

Ingredients

200g/7oz mixed frozen
  vegetables

125g/4½oz frozen peas

500ml/16fl oz water

2 red chillies

2.5cm/1in root ginger

8 garlic cloves

2 green chillies

50g/1¾oz coriander leaves,
  finely chopped

3 tbsp refined vegetable oil

3 small onions,
  finely chopped

3 tomatoes,
  finely chopped

¼ tsp turmeric

¼ tsp ground coriander

Salt to taste

Method

- Mix the vegetables and peas with the water. Cook the mixture in a saucepan on a medium heat for 10 minutes. Set aside.
- Grind together the red chillies, ginger, garlic, green chillies and coriander leaves to a fine paste.
- Heat the oil in a frying pan. Add the ground red chillies-ginger paste and the onions. Fry the mixture on a medium heat for 2 minutes.
- Add the tomatoes, turmeric, ground coriander and salt. Fry this mixture for 2-3 minutes, stirring occasionally.
- Add the cooked vegetables. Mix well. Cover with a lid and cook the mixture on a low heat for 5-6 minutes, stirring at regular intervals.
- Serve hot.

Undhiyu
(Gujarati Mixed Vegetable with Dumplings)

Serves 4

Ingredients

2 large potatoes, peeled

250g/9oz broad beans in their pods

1 unripe banana, peeled

20g/¾oz yam, peeled

2 small aubergines

60g/2oz fresh coconut, grated

8 garlic cloves

2 green chillies

2.5cm/1in root ginger

100g/3½oz coriander leaves, finely chopped

Salt to taste

60ml/2fl oz refined vegetable oil plus extra for deep frying

Pinch of asafoetida

½ tsp mustard seeds

250ml/8fl oz water

For the muthias:

60g/2oz besan*

25g/scant 1oz fresh fenugreek leaves, finely chopped

½ tsp ginger paste

2 green chillies, finely chopped

Method

- Dice the potatoes, beans, banana, yam and aubergines. Set aside.
- Grind together the coconut, garlic, green chillies, ginger and coriander leaves to a paste. Mix this paste with the diced vegetables and salt. Set aside.
- Mix all the muthia ingredients together. Knead the mixture to a firm dough. Divide the dough into walnut-sized balls.
- Heat the oil for deep frying in a frying pan. Add the muthias. Deep fry them on a medium heat till golden brown. Drain and set aside.
- Heat the remaining oil in a saucepan. Add the asafoetida and mustard seeds. Let them splutter for 15 seconds.
- Add the water, muthias and the vegetable mixture. Mix well. Cover with a lid and simmer for 20 minutes, stirring at regular intervals. Serve hot.

Banana Kofta Curry

Serves 4

Ingredients
For the koftas:

2 unripe bananas, boiled
and peeled

2 large potatoes, boiled
and peeled

3 green chillies,
finely chopped

1 large onion,
finely chopped

1 tbsp coriander leaves,
finely chopped

1 tbsp besan*

½ tsp chilli powder

Salt to taste

Ghee for deep frying

For the curry:

75g/2½oz ghee

1 large onion,
finely chopped

10 garlic cloves, crushed

1 tbsp ground coriander

1 tsp garam masala

2 tomatoes,
finely chopped

3 curry leaves

Salt to taste

250ml/8fl oz water

½ tbsp coriander leaves,
finely chopped

Method

- Mash the bananas and potatoes together.
- Mix with the remaining kofta ingredients, except the ghee. Knead this mixture to a firm dough. Divide the dough into walnut-sized balls to make the koftas.
- Heat the ghee for deep frying in a frying pan. Add the koftas. Fry them on a medium heat till they turn golden brown. Drain and set aside.
- For the curry, heat the ghee in a saucepan. Add the onion and garlic. Fry on a medium heat till the onion turns translucent. Add the ground coriander and garam masala. Fry for 2-3 minutes.
- Add the tomatoes, curry leaves, salt and water. Mix well. Simmer the mixture for 15 minutes, stirring occasionally.
- Add the fried koftas. Cover with a lid and continue to simmer for 2-3 minutes.
- Garnish with the coriander leaves. Serve hot.

Bitter Gourd with Onion

Serves 4

Ingredients

500g/1lb 2oz bitter gourds*
Salt to taste
750ml/1¼ pints water
4 tbsp refined vegetable oil
½ tsp cumin seeds
½ tsp mustard seeds
Pinch of asafoetida
½ tsp ginger paste
½ tsp garlic paste
2 large onions,
  finely chopped
½ tsp turmeric
1 tsp chilli powder
1 tsp ground cumin
1 tsp ground coriander
1 tsp sugar
Juice of 1 lemon
1 tbsp coriander leaves,
  finely chopped

Method

- Peel the bitter gourds and slice them into thin rings. Discard the seeds.
- Cook them with the salt and water in a saucepan on a medium heat for 5-7 minutes. Remove from the heat, drain and squeeze out the water, set aside.
- Heat the oil in a saucepan. Add the cumin and mustard seeds. Let them splutter for 15 seconds.
- Add the asafoetida, ginger paste and garlic paste. Fry the mixture on a medium heat for a minute.
- Add the onions. Fry them for 2-3 minutes.
- Add the turmeric, chilli powder, ground cumin and ground coriander. Mix well.
- Add the bitter gourd, sugar and lemon juice. Mix thoroughly. Cover with a lid and cook the mixture on a low heat for 6-7 minutes, stirring at regular intervals.
- Garnish with the coriander leaves. Serve hot.

Sukha Khatta Chana
(Dry Sour Chickpeas)

Serves 4

Ingredients
4 black peppercorns

2 cloves

2.5cm/1in cinnamon

½ tsp coriander seeds

½ tsp black cumin seeds

½ tsp cumin seeds

500g/1lb 2oz chickpeas, soaked overnight

Salt to taste

1 litre/1¾ pints water

1 tbsp dried pomegranate seeds

Salt to taste

1cm/½in root ginger, finely chopped

1 green chilli, chopped

2 tsp tamarind paste

2 tbsp ghee

1 small potato, diced

1 tomato, finely chopped

Method
• For the spice mixture, grind together the peppercorns, cloves, cinnamon, coriander, black cumin seeds and cumin seeds to a fine powder. Set aside.

• Mix the chickpeas with the salt and water. Cook this mixture in a saucepan on a medium heat for 45 minutes. Set aside.

• Dry roast (see cooking techniques) the pomegranate seeds in a frying pan on a medium heat for 2-3 minutes. Remove from the heat and grind to a powder. Mix with the salt and dry roast the mixture again for 5 minutes. Transfer to a saucepan.

• Add the ginger, green chilli and tamarind paste. Cook this mixture on a medium heat for 4-5 minutes. Add the ground spice mixture. Mix thoroughly and set aside.

• Heat the ghee in another pan. Add the potatoes. Fry them on a medium heat till golden brown.

• Add the fried potatoes to the cooked chickpeas. Also add the tamarind-ground spice mixture.

• Mix thoroughly and cook on a low heat for 5-6 minutes.

Bharwan Karela
(Stuffed Bitter Gourd)

Serves 4

Ingredients
500g/1lb 2oz small bitter
  gourds*

Salt to taste

1 tsp turmeric

Refined vegetable oil for
  deep frying

For the stuffing:
5-6 green chillies

2.5cm/1in root ginger

12 garlic cloves

3 small onions

1 tbsp refined vegetable oil

4 large potatoes, boiled
  and mashed

½ tsp turmeric

½ tsp chilli powder

1 tsp ground cumin

1 tsp ground coriander

Pinch of asafoetida

Salt to taste

Method
- Peel the bitter gourds. Slit them lengthways carefully, keeping the bases intact. Remove the seeds and the pulp and discard them. Rub the salt and turmeric on the outer shells. Set them aside for 4-5 hours.
- For the stuffing, grind together the chillies, ginger, garlic and onions to a paste. Set aside.
- Heat 1 tbsp oil in a frying pan. Add the onion-ginger-garlic paste. Fry it on a medium heat for 2-3 minutes.
- Add the remaining stuffing ingredients. Mix well. Fry the mixture on a medium heat for 3-4 minutes.
- Remove from the heat and cool the mixture. Stuff this mixture into the gourds. Tie each gourd with a thread so the stuffing does not fall out while cooking.
- Heat the oil for deep frying in a pan. Add the stuffed gourds. Fry them on a medium heat till they turn brown and crispy, turning them frequently.
- Untie the bitter gourds and discard the threads. Serve hot.

Cabbage Kofta Curry

(Cabbage Dumplings in Sauce)

Serves 4

Ingredients

1 large cabbage, grated

250g/9oz besan*

Salt to taste

Refined vegetable oil for
  deep frying

2 tbsp coriander
  leaves, to garnish

For the sauce:

3 tbsp refined vegetable oil

3 bay leaves

1 black cardamom

1cm/½in cinnamon

1 clove

1 large onion,
  finely chopped

2.5cm/1in root ginger,
  julienned

3 tomatoes,
  finely chopped

1 tsp ground coriander

1 tsp ground cumin

Salt to taste

250ml/8fl oz water

Method

- Knead together the cabbage, besan and salt to a soft dough. Divide the dough into walnut-sized balls.
- Heat the oil in a frying pan. Add the balls. Deep fry them on a medium heat till they turn golden brown. Drain and set aside.
- For the sauce, heat the oil in a saucepan. Add the bay leaves, cardamom, cinnamon and clove. Let them splutter for 30 seconds.
- Add the onion and ginger. Fry this mixture on a medium heat till the onion turns translucent.
- Add the tomatoes, ground coriander and ground cumin. Mix well. Fry for 2-3 minutes.
- Add the salt and water. Stir for a minute. Cover with a lid and simmer for 5 minutes.
- Uncover the pan and add the kofta balls. Simmer for 5 more minutes, stirring occasionally.
- Garnish with the coriander leaves. Serve hot.

Pineapple Gojju
(Spicy Pineapple Compote)

Serves 4

Ingredients
3 tbsp refined vegetable oil
250ml/8fl oz water
1 tsp mustard seeds
6 curry leaves, crushed
Pinch of asafoetida
½ tsp turmeric
Salt to taste
400g/14oz pineapple, chopped

For the spice mixture:
4 tbsp fresh coconut, grated
3 green chillies
2 red chillies
½ tsp fennel seeds
½ tsp fenugreek seeds
1 tsp cumin seeds
2 tsp coriander seeds
1 small bunch coriander leaves
1 clove
2-3 peppercorns

Method
- Mix all the spice mixture ingredients together.
- Heat 1 tbsp of the oil in a saucepan. Add the spice mixture. Fry it on a medium heat for 1-2 minutes, stirring frequently. Remove from the heat and grind with half the water to a smooth paste. Set aside.
- Heat the remaining oil in a saucepan. Add the mustard seeds and curry leaves. Let them splutter for 15 seconds.
- Add the asafoetida, turmeric and salt. Fry for a minute.
- Add the pineapple, the spice mixture paste and the remaining water. Mix well. Cover with a lid and simmer for 8-12 minutes. Serve hot.

Bitter Gourd Gojju

(Spicy Bitter Gourd Compote)

Serves 4

Ingredients

Salt to taste

4 large bitter gourds*, peeled, slit lengthways, deseeded and sliced

6 tbsp refined vegetable oil

1 tsp mustard seeds

8-10 curry leaves

1 large onion, grated

3-4 garlic cloves, crushed

2 tsp chilli powder

1 tsp ground cumin

½ tsp turmeric

1 tsp ground coriander

2 tsp sambhar powder*

2 tsp fresh coconut, shredded

1 tsp fenugreek seeds, dry roasted (see cooking techniques) and ground

2 tsp white sesame seeds, dry roasted (see cooking techniques) and ground

2 tbsp jaggery*, melted

½ tsp tamarind paste

250ml/8fl oz water

Pinch of asafoetida

Method

- Rub the salt on the bitter gourd slices. Place them in a bowl and seal it with foil. Set aside for 30 minutes. Squeeze out any excess moisture.
- Heat half the oil in a saucepan. Add the bitter gourds. Fry them on a medium heat till they turn golden brown. Set aside.
- Heat the remaining oil in another saucepan. Add the mustard seeds and curry leaves. Let them splutter for 15 seconds.
- Add the onion and garlic. Fry this mixture on a medium heat till the onion turns brown.
- Add the chilli powder, ground cumin, turmeric, ground coriander, sambhar powder and coconut. Fry for 2-3 minutes.
- Add the remaining ingredients, except the water and asafoetida. Fry for another minute.
- Add the fried bitter gourds, some salt and the water. Mix well. Cover with a lid and simmer for 12-15 minutes.
- Add the asafoetida. Mix well. Serve hot.

Baingan Mirchi ka Salan

(Aubergine and Chilli)

Serves 4

Ingredients

6 whole green peppers
4 tbsp refined vegetable oil
600g/1lb 5oz small aubergines, quartered
4 green chillies
1 tsp sesame seeds
10 cashew nuts
20-25 peanuts
5 black peppercorns
¼ tsp fenugreek seeds
¼ tsp mustard seeds
1 tsp ginger paste
1 tsp garlic paste
1 tsp ground coriander
1 tsp ground cumin
½ tsp turmeric
125g/4½oz yoghurt
2 tsp tamarind paste
3 whole red chillies
Salt to taste
1 litre/1¾ pints water

Method

- Deseed and chop the green peppers into long strips.
- Heat 1 tbsp oil in a saucepan. Add the green peppers and sauté them on a medium heat for 1-2 minutes. Set aside.
- Heat 2 tbsp oil in another saucepan. Add the aubergines and green chillies. Sauté on a medium heat for 2-3 minutes. Set aside.
- Heat a frying pan and dry roast (see cooking techniques) the sesame seeds, cashew nuts, peanuts and peppercorns on a medium heat for 1-2 minutes. Remove from the heat and grind the mixture coarsely.
- Heat the remaining oil in a saucepan. Add the fenugreek seeds, mustard seeds, ginger paste, garlic paste, ground coriander, ground cumin, turmeric and the sesame seeds-cashew nuts mixture. Fry on a medium heat for 2-3 minutes.
- Add the sautéed green peppers, the sautéed aubergines and all the remaining ingredients. Simmer for 10-12 minutes.
- Serve hot.

POULTRY

Poultry is very popular in Indian cuisine, especially in the northern parts, and in Mughlai cooking. In this chapter you will find not only recipes of famous Indian chicken dishes such as Butter Chicken, Chicken Tikka Masala and Tandoori Chicken, but many not-so-famous ones too, which are equally delicious. Duck dishes too are great cooked in Indian style.

Chicken with Greens

Serves 4

Ingredients

750g/1lb 10oz chicken, chopped into 8 pieces

50g/1¾oz spinach, finely chopped

25g/scant 1oz fresh fenugreek leaves, finely chopped

100g/3½oz coriander leaves, finely chopped

50g/1¾oz mint leaves, finely chopped

6 green chillies, finely chopped

120ml/4fl oz refined vegetable oil

2-3 large onions, finely sliced

Salt to taste

For the marinade:

1 tsp garam masala

1 tsp ground coriander

1 tsp ground cumin

200g/7oz yoghurt

¼ tsp turmeric

1 tsp chilli powder

1 tsp ginger paste

1 tsp garlic paste

Method

- Mix all the marinade ingredients together. Marinate the chicken with this mixture for an hour.
- Grind together the spinach, fenugreek leaves, coriander leaves and mint leaves with the green chillies to a smooth paste. Mix this paste with the marinated chicken. Set aside.
- Heat the oil in a saucepan. Add the onions. Fry them on a medium heat till they turn brown.
- Add the chicken mixture and the salt. Mix well. Cover with a lid and cook on a low heat for 40 minutes, stirring occasionally. Serve hot.

Chicken Tikka Masala

Serves 4

Ingredients

200g/7oz yoghurt

½ tbsp ginger paste

½ tbsp garlic paste

Dash of orange
food colour

2 tbsp refined vegetable oil

500g/1lb 2oz boneless
chicken, chopped into
bite-sized pieces

1 tbsp butter

6 tomatoes,
finely chopped

2 large onions

½ tsp ginger paste

½ tsp garlic paste

½ tsp turmeric

1 tbsp garam masala

1 tsp chilli powder

Salt to taste

1 tbsp coriander leaves,
finely chopped

Method

- For the tikka, mix together the yoghurt, ginger paste, garlic paste, food colour and 1 tbsp oil. Marinate the chicken with this mixture for 5 hours.
- Grill the marinated chicken for 10 minutes. Set aside.
- Heat the butter in a saucepan. Add the tomatoes. Fry them on a medium heat for 3-4 minutes. Remove from the heat and blend to a smooth paste. Set aside.
- Grind the onion into a smooth paste.
- Heat the remaining oil in a saucepan. Add the onion paste. Fry it on a medium heat till it turns brown.
- Add the ginger paste and garlic paste. Fry for a minute.
- Add the turmeric, garam masala, chilli powder and the tomato paste. Mix well. Stir-fry the mixture for 3-4 minutes.
- Add the salt and the grilled chicken. Mix gently till the sauce coats the chicken.
- Garnish with the coriander leaves. Serve hot.

Spicy Stuffed Chicken in Rich Sauce

Serves 4

Ingredients

½ tsp chilli powder

½ tsp garam masala

4 tsp ginger paste

4 tsp garlic paste

Salt to taste

8 chicken breasts, flattened

4 large onions, finely chopped

5cm/1in root ginger, finely chopped

5 green chillies, finely chopped

200g/7oz khoya*

2 tbsp lemon juice

50g/1¾oz coriander leaves, finely chopped

15 cashew nuts

5 tsp desiccated coconut

30g/1oz flaked almonds

1 tsp saffron, soaked in 1 tbsp milk

150g/5½oz ghee

200g/7oz yoghurt, whisked

Method

- Mix the chilli powder, garam masala, half the ginger paste, half the garlic paste and some salt. Marinate the chicken breasts with this mixture for 2 hours.
- Mix together half the onions with the chopped ginger, green chillies, khoya, lemon juice, salt and half the coriander leaves. Divide this mixture into 8 equal portions.
- Place each portion at the narrower end of each chicken breast and roll inwards to seal the breast. Set aside.
- Preheat the oven to 200°C (400°F, Gas Mark 6). Place the stuffed chicken breasts in a greased tray and roast them for 15-20 minutes till they turn golden brown. Set aside.
- Grind together the cashew nuts and coconut to a smooth paste. Set aside.
- Soak the almonds in the saffron milk mixture. Set aside.
- Heat the ghee in a saucepan. Add the remaining onions. Fry them on a medium heat till they turn translucent. Add the remaining ginger paste and garlic paste. Fry the mixture for a minute.
- Add the cashew nuts-coconut paste. Fry for a minute. Add the yoghurt and the roasted chicken breasts. Mix well. Cook on a low heat for 5-6 minutes, stirring frequently. Add the almond-saffron mixture. Mix gently. Simmer for 5 minutes.
- Garnish with the coriander leaves. Serve hot.

Spicy Chicken Masala

Serves 4

Ingredients

6 whole dry red chillies

2 tbsp coriander seeds

6 green cardamom pods

6 cloves

5cm/2in cinnamon

2 tsp fennel seeds

½ tsp black peppercorns

120ml/4fl oz refined
  vegetable oil

2 large onions, sliced

1cm/½in root ginger,
  grated

8 garlic cloves, crushed

2 large tomatoes,
  finely chopped

3-4 bay leaves

1kg/2¼lb chicken, chopped
  into 12 pieces

½ tsp turmeric

Salt to taste

500ml/16fl oz water

100g/3½oz coriander
  leaves, finely chopped

Method

- Mix the red chillies, coriander seeds, cardamom, cloves, cinnamon, fennel seeds and peppercorns together.
- Dry roast (see cooking techniques) the mixture and grind to a powder. Set aside.
- Heat the oil in a saucepan. Add the onions. Fry them on a medium heat till they turn brown.
- Add the ginger and garlic. Fry for a minute.
- Add the tomatoes, bay leaves and the ground red chillies-coriander seeds powder. Continue to fry for 2-3 minutes.
- Add the chicken, turmeric, salt and water. Mix well. Cover with a lid and simmer for 40 minutes, stirring at regular intervals.
- Garnish the chicken with the coriander leaves. Serve hot.

Kashmiri Chicken

Serves 4

Ingredients

2 tbsp malt vinegar

2 tsp chilli flakes

2 tsp mustard seeds

2 tsp cumin seeds

½ tsp black peppercorns

7.5cm/3in cinnamon

10 cloves

75g/2½oz ghee

1kg/2¼lb chicken, chopped
into 12 pieces

1 tbsp refined vegetable oil

4 bay leaves

4 medium-sized onions,
finely chopped

1 tbsp ginger paste

1 tbsp garlic paste

3 tomatoes,
finely chopped

1 tsp turmeric

500ml/16fl oz water

Salt to taste

20 cashew nuts, ground

6 strands saffron soaked in
the juice of 1 lemon

Method

- Mix the malt vinegar with the chilli flakes, mustard seeds, cumin seeds, peppercorns, cinnamon and cloves. Grind this mixture to a smooth paste. Set aside.
- Heat the ghee in a saucepan. Add the chicken pieces and fry them on a medium heat till they turn golden brown. Drain and set aside.
- Heat the oil in a saucepan. Add the bay leaves and onions. Fry this mixture on a medium heat till the onions turn brown.
- Add the vinegar paste. Mix well and cook this on a low heat for 7-8 minutes.
- Add the ginger paste and garlic paste. Fry this mixture for a minute.
- Add the tomatoes and turmeric. Mix thoroughly and cook on a medium heat for 2-3 minutes.
- Add the fried chicken, water and salt. Mix well to coat the chicken. Cover with a lid and simmer for 30 minutes, stirring occasionally.
- Add the cashew nuts and saffron. Continue to simmer for 5 minutes. Serve hot.

Rum 'n' Chicken

Serves 4

Ingredients

1 tsp garam masala

1 tsp chilli powder

1kg/2¼lb chicken, chopped
   into 8 pieces

6 garlic cloves

4 black peppercorns

4 cloves

½ tsp cumin seeds

2.5cm/1in cinnamon

50g/1¾oz fresh coconut,
   grated

4 almonds

1 green cardamom pod

1 tbsp coriander seeds

300ml/10fl oz water

75g/2½oz ghee

3 large onions,
   finely chopped

Salt to taste

½ tsp saffron

120ml/4fl oz dark rum

1 tbsp coriander leaves,
   finely chopped

Method

- Mix together the garam masala and the chilli powder. Marinate the chicken with this mixture for 2 hours.
- Dry roast (see cooking techniques) the garlic, peppercorns, cloves, cumin seeds, cinnamon, coconut, almonds, cardamom and coriander seeds.
- Grind with 60ml/2fl oz water to a smooth paste. Set aside.
- Heat the ghee in a saucepan. Add the onions and fry them on a medium heat till they turn translucent.
- Add the garlic-peppercorn paste. Mix well. Fry the mixture for 3-4 minutes.
- Add the marinated chicken and the salt. Mix well. Continue to fry for 3-4 minutes, stirring occasionally.
- Add 240ml/8fl oz water. Stir gently. Cover with a lid and cook on a low heat for 40 minutes, stirring at regular intervals.
- Add the saffron and rum. Mix well and continue to simmer for 10 minutes.
- Garnish with the coriander leaves. Serve hot.

Chicken Shahjahani
(Chicken in Spicy Gravy)

Serves 4

Ingredients

5 tbsp refined vegetable oil

2 bay leaves

5cm/2in cinnamon

6 green cardamom pods

½ tsp cumin seeds

8 cloves

3 large onions, finely chopped

1 tsp turmeric

1 tsp chilli powder

1 tsp ginger paste

1 tsp garlic paste

Salt to taste

75g/2½oz cashew nuts, ground

150g/5½oz yoghurt, whisked

1kg/2¼lb chicken, chopped into 8 pieces

2 tbsp single cream

¼ tsp ground black cardamom

10g/¼oz coriander leaves, finely chopped

Method

- Heat the oil in a saucepan. Add the bay leaves, cinnamon, cardamom, cumin seeds and cloves. Let them splutter for 15 seconds.
- Add the onions, turmeric and chilli powder. Sauté the mixture on a medium heat for 1-2 minutes.
- Add the ginger paste and garlic paste. Fry for 2-3 minutes, stirring constantly.
- Add the salt and ground cashew nuts. Mix well and fry for another minute.
- Add the yoghurt and the chicken. Stir gently till the mixture coats the chicken pieces.
- Cover with a lid and cook the mixture on a low heat for 40 minutes, stirring at frequent intervals.
- Uncover the pan and add the cream and ground cardamom. Stir gently for 5 minutes.
- Garnish the chicken with the coriander leaves. Serve hot.

Easter Chicken

Serves 4

Ingredients

1 tsp lemon juice

1 tsp ginger paste

1 tsp garlic paste

Salt to taste

1kg/2¼lb chicken, chopped
  into 8 pieces

2 tbsp coriander seeds

12 garlic cloves

2.5cm/1in root ginger

1 tsp cumin seeds

8 red chillies

4 cloves

2.5cm/1in cinnamon

1 tsp turmeric

1 litre/1¾ pints water

4 tbsp refined vegetable oil

3 large onions,
  finely chopped

4 green chillies, slit
  lengthways

3 tomatoes,
  finely chopped

1 tsp tamarind paste

2 large potatoes, quartered

Method

- Mix the lemon juice, ginger paste, garlic paste and salt together. Marinate the chicken pieces with this mixture for 2 hours.
- Mix the coriander seeds, garlic, ginger, cumin seeds, red chillies, cloves, cinnamon and turmeric together.
- Grind this mixture with half the water to a smooth paste. Set aside.
- Heat the oil in a saucepan. Add the onions. Fry them on a medium heat till they turn translucent.
- Add the green chillies and the coriander seeds-garlic paste. Fry this mixture for 3-4 minutes.
- Add the tomatoes and the tamarind paste. Continue to fry for 2-3 minutes.
- Add the marinated chicken, potatoes and the remaining water. Mix thoroughly. Cover with a lid and simmer for 40 minutes, stirring at regular intervals.
- Serve hot.

Spicy Duck with Potatoes

Serves 4

Ingredients

1 tsp ground coriander

2 tsp chilli powder

¼ tsp turmeric

5cm/2in cinnamon

6 cloves

4 green cardamom pods

1 tsp fennel seeds

60ml/2fl oz refined vegetable oil

4 large onions, thinly sliced

5cm/2in root ginger, shredded

8 garlic cloves

6 green chillies, slit lengthways

3 large potatoes, quartered

1kg/2¼lb duck, chopped into 8-10 pieces

2 tsp malt vinegar

750ml/1¼ pints coconut milk

Salt to taste

1 tsp ghee

1 tsp mustard seeds

2 shallots, sliced

8 curry leaves

Method

- Mix the coriander, chilli powder, turmeric, cinnamon, cloves, cardamom and fennel seeds together. Grind this mixture to a powder. Set aside.
- Heat the oil in a saucepan. Add the onions, ginger, garlic and green chillies. Fry on a medium heat for 2-3 minutes.
- Add the spice mixture powder. Sauté for 2 minutes.
- Add the potatoes. Continue to fry for 3-4 minutes.
- Add the duck, malt vinegar, coconut milk and salt. Stir for 5 minutes. Cover with a lid and cook the mixture on a low heat for 40 minutes, stirring at frequent intervals. Once the duck is cooked, remove from the heat and set aside.
- Heat the ghee in a small saucepan. Add the mustard seeds, shallots and curry leaves. Stir-fry on a high heat for 30 seconds.
- Pour this over the duck. Mix well. Serve hot.

Duck Moile
(Simple Duck Curry)

Serves 4

Ingredients

1kg/2¼lb duck, chopped into 12 pieces

Salt to taste

1 tbsp ground coriander

1 tsp ground cumin

6 black peppercorns

4 cloves

2 green cardamom pods

2.5cm/1in cinnamon

120ml/4fl oz refined vegetable oil

3 large onions, finely chopped

5cm/2in root ginger, finely sliced

3 green chillies, finely chopped

½ tsp sugar

2 tbsp malt vinegar

360ml/12fl oz water

Method

- Marinate the duck pieces with the salt for an hour.
- Mix the ground coriander, ground cumin, peppercorns, cloves, cardamom and cinnamon together. Dry roast (see cooking techniques) this mixture in a frying pan on a medium heat for 1-2 minutes.
- Remove from the heat and grind to a fine powder. Set aside.
- Heat the oil in a saucepan. Add the marinated duck pieces. Fry them on a medium heat till they turn brown. Turn occasionally to make sure that they do not burn. Drain and set aside.
- Heat the same oil and add the onions. Fry them on a medium heat till they turn brown.
- Add the ginger and green chillies. Continue to fry for 1-2 minutes.
- Add the sugar, malt vinegar and the coriander-cumin powder. Stir for 2-3 minutes.
- Add the fried duck pieces along with the water. Mix well. Cover with a lid and simmer for 40 minutes, stirring occasionally.
- Serve hot.

Bharwa Murgh Kaju

(Chicken Stuffed with Cashew Nuts)

Serves 4

Ingredients

3 tsp ginger paste
3 tsp garlic paste
10 cashew nuts, ground
1 tsp chilli powder
1 tsp garam masala
Salt to taste
8 chicken breasts, flattened
4 large onions,
   finely chopped
200g/7oz khoya*
6 green chillies,
   finely chopped
25g/scant 1oz mint leaves,
   finely chopped
25g/scant 1oz coriander
   leaves, finely chopped
2 tbsp lemon juice
75g/2½oz ghee
75g/2½oz cashew nuts,
   ground
400g/14oz yoghurt,
   whisked
2 tsp garam masala
2 tsp saffron, soaked in 2
   tbsp warm milk
Salt to taste

Method

- Mix together half the ginger paste and half the garlic paste with the ground cashew nuts, chilli powder, garam masala and some salt.
- Marinate the chicken breasts with this mixture for 30 minutes.
- Mix half the onions with the khoya, green chillies, mint leaves, coriander leaves and lemon juice. Divide this mixture into 8 equal portions.
- Spread out a marinated chicken breast. Place a portion of the onion-khoya mixture on it. Roll like a wrap.
- Repeat this for the rest of the chicken breasts.
- Grease a baking dish and place the stuffed chicken breasts inside, with the loose ends face-down.
- Roast the chicken in an oven at 200°C (400°F, Gas Mark 6) for 20 minutes. Set aside.
- Heat the ghee in a saucepan. Add the remaining onions. Fry them on a medium heat till they turn translucent.
- Add the remaining ginger paste and garlic paste. Fry the mixture for 1-2 minutes.
- Add the ground cashew nuts, yoghurt and garam masala. Stir for 1-2 minutes.
- Add the roasted chicken rolls, saffron mixture and some salt. Mix well. Cover with a lid and cook on a low heat for 15-20 minutes. Serve hot.

Yoghurt Chicken Masala

Serves 4

Ingredients

1kg/2¼lb chicken, chopped into 12 pieces

7.5cm/3in root ginger, grated

10 garlic cloves, crushed

½ tsp chilli powder

½ tsp garam masala

½ tsp turmeric

2 green chillies

Salt to taste

200g/7oz yoghurt

½ tsp cumin seeds

1 tsp coriander seeds

4 cloves

4 black peppercorns

2.5cm/1in cinnamon

4 green cardamom pods

6-8 almonds

5 tbsp ghee

4 medium-sized onions, finely chopped

250ml/8fl oz water

1 tbsp coriander leaves, finely chopped

Method

- Pierce the chicken pieces with a fork. Set aside.
- Mix half the ginger and garlic with the chilli powder, garam masala, turmeric, green chillies and salt. Grind this mixture to a smooth paste. Whisk the paste with the yoghurt.
- Marinate the chicken with this mixture for 4-5 hours. Set aside.
- Heat a saucepan. Dry roast (see cooking techniques) the cumin seeds, coriander seeds, cloves, peppercorns, cinnamon, cardamom and almonds. Set aside.
- Heat 4 tbsp of the ghee in a heavy saucepan. Add the onions. Fry them on a medium heat till they turn translucent.
- Add the remaining ginger and garlic. Fry for 1-2 minutes.
- Remove from the heat and grind this mixture with the dry roasted cumin-coriander mixture to a smooth paste.
- Heat the remaining ghee in a saucepan. Add the paste and fry it on a medium heat for 2-3 minutes.
- Add the marinated chicken and fry for another 3-4 minutes.
- Add the water. Stir gently for a minute. Cover with a lid and simmer for 30 minutes, stirring at regular intervals.
- Garnish with the coriander leaves and serve hot.

Chicken Dhansak

(Chicken cooked the Parsi Way)

Serves 4

Ingredients

75g/2½oz toor dhal*

75g/2½oz mung dhal*

75g/2½oz masoor dhal*

75g/2½oz chana dhal*

1 small aubergine,
finely chopped

25g/scant 1oz pumpkin,
finely chopped

Salt to taste

1 litre/1¾ pints water

8 black peppercorns

6 cloves

2.5cm/1in cinnamon

Pinch of mace

2 bay leaves

1 star anise

3 dry red chillies

2 tbsp refined vegetable oil

50g/1¾oz coriander leaves,
finely chopped

50g/1¾oz fresh fenugreek
leaves, finely chopped

50g/1¾oz mint leaves,
finely chopped

750g/1lb 10oz boneless
chicken, chopped into
12 pieces

1 tsp turmeric

¼ tsp grated nutmeg

1 tbsp garlic paste

1 tbsp ginger paste

1 tbsp tamarind paste

Method

- Mix the dhals with the aubergine, pumpkin, salt and half the water. Cook this mixture in a saucepan on a medium heat for 45 minutes.
- Remove from the heat and blend this mixture to a smooth paste. Set aside.
- Mix the peppercorns, cloves, cinnamon, mace, bay leaves, star anise and red chillies together. Dry roast (see cooking techniques) the mixture on a medium heat for 2-3 minutes. Remove from the heat and grind to a fine powder. Set aside.
- Heat the oil in a saucepan. Add the coriander, fenugreek and mint leaves. Fry them on a medium heat for 1-2 minutes. Remove from the heat and grind to a paste. Set aside.
- Mix the chicken with the turmeric, nutmeg, garlic paste, ginger paste, the dhal paste and the remaining water. Cook this mixture in a saucepan on a medium heat for 30 minutes, stirring occasionally.
- Add the coriander-fenugreek-mint leaves paste. Cook for 2-3 minutes.
- Add the peppercorn-clove powder and the tamarind paste. Mix well. Stir the mixture on a low heat for 8-10 minutes.
- Serve hot.

Chatpata Chicken
(Tangy Chicken)

Serves 4

Ingredients

500g/1lb 2oz boneless chicken, chopped into small pieces

2 tbsp refined vegetable oil

150g/5½oz cauliflower florets

200g/7oz mushrooms, sliced

1 large carrot, sliced

1 large green pepper, deseeded and chopped

Salt to taste

½ tsp ground black pepper

10-15 curry leaves

5 green chillies, finely chopped

5cm/2in root ginger, finely chopped

10 garlic cloves, finely chopped

4 tbsp tomato purée

4 tbsp coriander leaves, finely chopped

For the marinade:
125g/4½oz yoghurt

1½ tbsp ginger paste

1½ tbsp garlic paste

1 tsp chilli powder

1 tsp garam masala

Salt to taste

Method

- Mix all the marinade ingredients together.
- Marinate the chicken with this mixture for 1 hour.
- Heat half a tbsp of the oil in a saucepan. Add the cauliflower, mushrooms, carrot, green pepper, salt and ground black pepper. Mix well. Fry the mixture on a medium heat for 3-4 minutes. Set aside.
- Heat the remaining oil in another saucepan. Add the curry leaves and green chillies. Fry them on a medium heat for a minute.
- Add the ginger and garlic. Fry for another minute.
- Add the marinated chicken and the fried vegetables. Fry for 4-5 minutes.
- Add the tomato purée. Mix well. Cover with a lid and cook the mixture on a low heat for 40 minutes, stirring occasionally.
- Garnish with the coriander leaves. Serve hot.

Masala Duck in Coconut Milk

Serves 4

Ingredients

1kg/2¼lb duck, chopped into 12 pieces

Refined vegetable oil for deep frying

3 large potatoes, chopped

750ml/1¼ pints water

4 tsp coconut oil

1 large onion, finely sliced

100g/3½oz coconut milk

For the spice mixture:

2 tsp ground coriander

½ tsp turmeric

1 tsp ground black pepper

¼ tsp cumin seeds

¼ tsp black cumin seeds

2.5cm/1in cinnamon

9 cloves

2 green cardamom pods

8 garlic cloves

2.5cm/1in root ginger

1 tsp malt vinegar

Salt to taste

Method

- Mix the ingredients of the spice mixture together and grind to a smooth paste.
- Marinate the duck with this paste for 2-3 hours.
- Heat the oil in a saucepan. Add the potatoes and fry them on a medium heat till they turn golden brown. Drain and set aside.
- Heat the water in a saucepan. Add the marinated duck pieces and simmer for 40 minutes, stirring occasionally. Set aside.
- Heat the coconut oil in a frying pan. Add the onion and fry on a medium heat till brown.
- Add the coconut milk. Cook the mixture for 2 minutes, stirring frequently.
- Remove from the heat and add this mixture to the boiled duck. Mix well and simmer for 5-10 minutes.
- Garnish with the fried potatoes. Serve hot.

Chicken Dil Bahar

(Creamy Chicken)

Serves 4

Ingredients

4-5 tbsp refined vegetable oil

2 bay leaves

5cm/2in cinnamon

3 green cardamom pods

4 cloves

2 large onions, finely chopped

1 tsp ginger paste

1 tsp garlic paste

2 tsp ground cumin

2 tsp ground coriander

½ tsp turmeric

4 green chillies, slit lengthways

750g/1lb 10oz boneless chicken, chopped into 16 pieces

50g/1¾oz spring onions, finely chopped

1 large green pepper, finely chopped

1 tsp garam masala

Salt to taste

150g/5½oz tomato purée

125g/4½oz yoghurt

250ml/8fl oz water

2 tbsp butter

85g/3oz cashew nuts

500ml/16fl oz condensed milk

250ml/8fl oz single cream

1 tbsp coriander leaves, finely chopped

Method

- Heat the oil in a saucepan. Add the bay leaves, cinnamon, cardamom and cloves. Let them splutter for 30 seconds.
- Add the onions, ginger paste and garlic paste. Fry this mixture on a medium heat till the onions are brown.
- Add the ground cumin, ground coriander, turmeric and green chillies. Fry the mixture for 2-3 minutes.
- Add the chicken pieces. Mix well. Fry them for 5 minutes.
- Add the spring onions, green pepper, garam masala and salt. Continue to fry for 3-4 minutes.
- Add the tomato purée, yoghurt and water. Mix well and cover with a lid. Cook the mixture on a low heat for 30 minutes, stirring occasionally.
- While the chicken mixture is cooking, heat the butter in another saucepan. Add the cashew nuts and fry them on a medium heat till they turn golden brown. Set aside.
- Add the condensed milk and cream to the chicken mixture. Mix well and continue to simmer for 5 minutes.
- Add the butter with the fried cashew nuts and mix thoroughly for 2 minutes.
- Garnish with the coriander leaves. Serve hot.

Dum ka Murgh

(Slow-cooked Chicken)

Serves 4

Ingredients

4 tbsp refined vegetable oil plus extra for deep frying

3 large onions, sliced

10 almonds

10 cashew nuts

1 tbsp desiccated coconut

1 tsp ginger paste

1 tsp garlic paste

½ tsp turmeric

1 tsp chilli powder

Salt to taste

200g/7oz yoghurt

1kg/2¼lb chicken, finely chopped

1 tbsp coriander leaves, roughly chopped

1 tbsp mint leaves, roughly chopped

½ tsp saffron

Method

- Heat the oil for deep frying. Add the onions and deep fry them on a medium heat till they turn golden brown. Drain and set aside.
- Mix together the almonds, cashew nuts and coconut. Dry roast (see cooking techniques) the mixture. Grind with enough water to form a smooth paste.
- Heat 4 tbsp of the oil in a saucepan. Add the ginger paste, garlic paste, turmeric and chilli powder. Fry on a medium heat for 1-2 minutes.
- Add the almonds-cashew nut paste, the fried onions, the salt and yoghurt. Cook for 4-5 minutes.
- Transfer to an ovenproof dish. Add the chicken, coriander and mint leaves. Mix thoroughly.
- Sprinkle the saffron on top. Seal with foil and cover tightly with a lid. Bake in an oven at 180°C (350°F, Gas Mark 4) for 40 minutes.
- Serve hot.

Murgh Kheema Masala

(Spicy Minced Chicken)

Serves 4

Ingredients

60ml/2fl oz refined
  vegetable oil

5cm/2in cinnamon

4 cloves

2 green cardamom pods

½ tsp cumin seeds

2 large onions,
  finely chopped

1 tsp ground coriander

½ tsp ground cumin

½ tsp turmeric

1 tsp chilli powder

2 tsp ginger paste

3 tsp garlic paste

3 tomatoes,
  finely chopped

200g/7oz frozen peas

1kg/2¼lb chicken mince

75g/2½oz cashew nuts,
  ground

125g/4½oz yoghurt

250ml/8fl oz water

Salt to taste

4 tbsp single cream

25g/scant 1oz coriander
  leaves, finely chopped

Method

- Heat the oil in a saucepan. Add the cinnamon, cloves, cardamom and cumin seeds. Let them splutter for 15 seconds.
- Add the onions, ground coriander, ground cumin, turmeric and chilli powder. Fry on a medium heat for 1-2 minutes.
- Add the ginger paste and garlic paste. Continue to fry for a minute.
- Add the tomatoes, peas and chicken mince. Mix well. Cook this mixture on a low heat for 10-15 minutes, stirring occasionally.
- Add the yoghurt, water and salt. Mix well. Cover with a lid and simmer for 20-25 minutes.
- Garnish with the cream and coriander leaves. Serve hot.

Stuffed Chicken Nawabi

Serves 4

Ingredients

200g/7oz yoghurt
2 tbsp lemon juice
½ tsp turmeric
Salt to taste
1kg/2¼lb chicken
100g/3½oz breadcrumbs

For the stuffing:

120ml/4fl oz refined
 vegetable oil
1½ tsp ginger paste
1½ tsp garlic paste
2 large onions,
 finely chopped
2 green chillies,
 finely chopped
½ tsp chilli powder
1 chicken gizzard, chopped
1 chicken liver, chopped
200g/7oz peas
2 carrots, diced
50g/1¾oz coriander leaves,
 finely chopped
2 tbsp mint leaves, finely
 chopped
½ tsp ground
 black pepper
½ tsp garam masala
20 cashew nuts, chopped
20 raisins

Method

- Whisk the yoghurt with the lemon juice, turmeric and salt. Marinate the chicken with this mixture for 1-2 hours.
- For the stuffing, heat the oil in a saucepan. Add the ginger paste, garlic paste and onions and fry them on a medium heat for 1-2 minutes.
- Add the green chillies, chilli powder, chicken gizzard and chicken liver. Mix well. Fry for 3-4 minutes.
- Add the peas, carrots, coriander leaves, mint leaves, pepper, garam masala, cashew nuts and raisins. Stir for 2 minutes. Cover with a lid and cook on a low heat for 20 minutes, stirring occasionally.
- Remove from the heat and set aside to cool.
- Stuff this mixture into the marinated chicken.
- Roll the stuffed chicken in the breadcrumbs and roast in a preheated oven at 200°C (400°F, Gas Mark 6) for 50 minutes.
- Serve hot.

Murgh ke Nazare

(Chicken with Cheddar Cheese and Paneer)

Serves 4

Ingredients

Salt to taste

½ tbsp ginger paste

½ tbsp garlic paste

Juice of 1 lemon

750g/1lb 10oz boneless chicken pieces, flattened

75g/2½oz paneer*, grated

250g/9oz chicken mince

75g/2½oz Cheddar cheese, grated

1 tsp ground coriander

½ tsp garam masala

½ tsp turmeric

125g/4½oz khoya*

1 tsp chilli powder

2 eggs, boiled and finely chopped

3 tomatoes, finely chopped

2 green chillies, finely chopped

2 large onions, finely chopped

2 tbsp coriander leaves, chopped

½ tsp ginger powder

For the sauce:

4 tbsp refined vegetable oil

½ tbsp ginger paste

½ tbsp garlic paste

2 large onions, ground

2 green chillies, finely chopped

½ tsp turmeric

1 tsp ground coriander

½ tsp ground white pepper

½ tsp ground cumin

½ tsp dry ginger powder

200g/7oz yoghurt

4 cashew nuts, ground

4 almonds, ground

125g/4½oz khoya*

Method

• Mix the salt, ginger paste, garlic paste and lemon juice together. Marinate the chicken with this mixture for 1 hour. Set aside.

• Mix the paneer with the chicken mince, cheese, ground coriander, garam masala, turmeric and khoya.

• Spread this mixture over the marinated chicken. Sprinkle the chilli powder, eggs, tomatoes, green chillies, onions, coriander leaves and ginger powder on top of it. Roll the chicken like a wrap and seal by tying it tightly with a string.

• Bake in an oven at 200°C (400°F, Gas Mark 6) for 30 minutes. Set aside.

• For the sauce, heat the oil in a saucepan. Add the ginger paste, garlic paste, onions and green chillies. Fry them on a medium heat for 2-3 minutes. Add the remaining sauce ingredients. Cook for 7-8 minutes.

• Slice the chicken roll into bite-sized pieces and arrange in a serving dish. Pour the sauce over them. Serve hot.

Murgh Pasanda
(Spicy Chicken Bites)

Serves 4

Ingredients
1 tsp turmeric

30g/1oz coriander leaves, chopped

1 tsp chilli powder

10g/¼oz mint leaves, finely chopped

1 tsp garam masala

5cm/2in piece of raw papaya, ground

1 tsp ginger paste

1 tsp garlic paste

Salt to taste

750g/1lb 10oz chicken breast, chopped into thin slices

6 tbsp refined vegetable oil

Method
- Mix all the ingredients, except the chicken and oil. Marinate the chicken slices with this mixture for 3 hours.
- Heat the oil in a frying pan. Add the marinated chicken slices and fry on a medium heat till golden brown, turning occasionally. Serve hot.

Murgh Masala
(Chicken Masala)

Serves 4

Ingredients
4 tbsp refined vegetable oil

2 large onions, grated

1 tomato, finely chopped

Salt to taste

1kg/2¼lb chicken, chopped into 8 pieces

360ml/12fl oz water

360ml/12fl oz coconut milk

For the spice mixture:
2 tbsp garam masala

1 tsp cumin seeds

1½ tsp poppy seeds

4 red chillies

½ tsp turmeric

8 garlic cloves

2.5cm/1in root ginger

Method
- Grind the spice mixture with enough water to form a smooth paste. Set aside.
- Heat the oil in a saucepan. Add the onions and fry on a medium heat till brown. Add the spice mixture paste and fry for 5-6 minutes.
- Add the tomato, salt, chicken and water. Cover with a lid and simmer for 20 minutes. Add the coconut milk, mix well and serve hot.

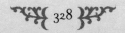

Bohri Chicken Cream
(Chicken in Creamy Gravy)

Serves 4

Ingredients

3 large onions

2.5cm/1in root ginger

8 garlic cloves

6 green chillies

100g/3½oz coriander leaves, finely chopped

3 tbsp mint leaves, finely chopped

120ml/4fl oz water

1kg/2¼lb chicken, chopped into 8 pieces

2 tbsp lemon juice

1 tsp ground black pepper

250ml/8fl oz single cream

30g/1oz ghee

Salt to taste

Method

- Mix the onions, ginger, garlic, green chillies, coriander leaves and mint leaves together. Grind this mixture with the water to make a fine paste.
- Marinate the chicken with half this paste and the lemon juice for 1 hour.
- Place the marinated chicken in a saucepan and pour the remaining paste over it. Sprinkle the remaining ingredients on top of this mixture.
- Seal with foil, cover tightly with a lid and cook on a low heat for 45 minutes. Serve hot.

Jhatpat Murgh
(Quick Chicken)

Serves 4

Ingredients

4 tbsp refined vegetable oil

2 large onions, finely sliced

2 tsp ginger paste

Salt to taste

1kg/2¼lb chicken, chopped into 12 pieces

¼ tsp saffron, dissolved in 2 tbsp milk

Method

- Heat the oil in a saucepan. Add the onions and ginger paste. Fry them on a medium heat for 2 minutes.
- Add the salt and chicken. Cook on a low heat for 30 minutes, stirring frequently. Sprinkle with the saffron mixture. Serve hot.

Green Chicken Curry

Serves 4

Ingredients

Salt to taste

A pinch of turmeric

Juice of 1 lemon

1kg/2¼lb chicken, chopped into 12 pieces

3.5cm/1½in root ginger

8 garlic cloves

100g/3½oz coriander leaves, chopped

3 green chillies

4 tbsp refined vegetable oil

2 large onions, grated

½ tsp garam masala

250ml/8fl oz water

Method

• Mix the salt, turmeric and lemon juice. Marinate the chicken with this mixture for 30 minutes.

• Grind the ginger, garlic, coriander leaves and chillies to a smooth paste.

• Heat the oil in a saucepan. Add the paste along with the grated onions and fry on a medium heat for 2-3 minutes.

• Add the marinated chicken, garam masala and water. Mix well and simmer for 40 minutes, stirring frequently. Serve hot.

Murgh Bharta
(Stewed Chicken with Eggs)

Serves 4

Ingredients

4 tbsp refined vegetable oil

2 large onions, finely sliced

500g/1lb 2oz boneless chicken, diced

1 tsp garam masala

½ tsp turmeric

Salt to taste

3 tomatoes, finely sliced

30g/1oz coriander leaves, chopped

4 hard-boiled eggs, halved

Method

• Heat the oil in a saucepan. Fry the onions on a medium heat till brown. Add the chicken, garam masala, turmeric and salt. Fry for 5 minutes.

• Add the tomatoes. Mix well and cook on a low heat for 30-40 minutes. Garnish with the coriander leaves and eggs. Serve hot.

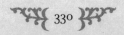

Chicken with Ajowan Seeds

Serves 4

Ingredients

3 tbsp refined vegetable oil

1½ tsp ajowan seeds

2 large onions, finely chopped

1 tsp ginger paste

1 tsp garlic paste

4 tomatoes, finely chopped

2 tsp ground coriander

1 tsp chilli powder

1 tsp turmeric

1kg/2¼lb chicken, chopped into 8 pieces

250ml/8fl oz water

Juice of 1 lemon

1 tsp garam masala

Salt to taste

Method

- Heat the oil in a saucepan. Add the ajowan seeds. Let them splutter for 15 seconds.
- Add the onions and fry on a medium heat till brown. Add the ginger paste, garlic paste and tomatoes. Fry for 3 minutes, stirring occasionally.
- Add all the remaining ingredients. Mix well and cover with a lid. Simmer for 40 minutes and serve hot.

Spinach Chicken Tikka

Serves 4

Ingredients

1kg/2¼lb boneless chicken, chopped into 16 pieces

2 tbsp ghee

1 tsp chaat masala*

2 tbsp lemon juice

For the marinade:

100g/3½oz spinach, ground

50g/1¾oz coriander leaves, ground

1 tsp ginger paste

1 tsp garlic paste

200g/7oz yoghurt

1½ tsp garam masala

Method

- Mix all the ingredients for the marinade. Marinate the chicken with this mixture for 2 hours.
- Baste the chicken with the ghee and roast in an oven at 200°C (400°F, Gas Mark 6) for 45 minutes. Sprinkle the chaat masala and lemon juice on top. Serve hot.

Yakhni Chicken
(Kashmiri-style Chicken)

Serves 4

Ingredients

3 tbsp refined vegetable oil

1kg/2¼lb chicken, chopped into 8 pieces

400g/14oz yoghurt

125g/4½oz besan*

2 cloves

2.5cm/1in cinnamon

6 peppercorns

1 tsp ground ginger

2 tsp ground fennel

Salt to taste

250ml/8fl oz water

50g/1¾oz coriander leaves, chopped

Method

- Heat half the oil in a frying pan. Add the chicken pieces and fry them on a medium heat till they turn golden brown. Set aside.
- Whisk the yoghurt with the besan to form a thick paste. Set aside.
- Heat the remaining oil in a saucepan. Add the cloves, cinnamon, peppercorns, ground ginger, ground fennel and salt. Fry for 4-5 minutes.
- Add the fried chicken, water and the yoghurt paste. Mix well and simmer for 40 minutes. Garnish with the coriander leaves. Serve hot.

Chilli Chicken

Serves 4

Ingredients

3 tbsp refined vegetable oil

4 green chillies, finely chopped

1 tsp ginger paste

1 tsp garlic paste

3 large onions, sliced

250ml/8fl oz water

750g/1lb 10oz boneless chicken, chopped

2 large green peppers, julienned

2 tbsp soy sauce

30g/1oz coriander leaves, chopped

Salt to taste

Method

- Heat the oil in a saucepan. Add the green chillies, ginger paste, garlic paste and onions. Fry on a medium heat for 3-4 minutes.
- Add the water and chicken. Simmer for 20 minutes.
- Add all the remaining ingredients and cook for 20 minutes. Serve hot.

Pepper Chicken

Serves 4

Ingredients

4 tbsp refined vegetable oil

3 large onions, finely chopped

6 garlic cloves, finely chopped

1kg/2¼lb chicken, chopped into
   12 pieces

3 tsp ground coriander

2½ tsp freshly ground black pepper

½ tsp turmeric

Salt to taste

250ml/8fl oz water

Juice of 1 lemon

50g/1¾oz coriander leaves,
   chopped

Method

- Heat the oil in a saucepan. Add the onions and garlic and fry on a medium heat till brown.
- Add the chicken. Fry for 5 minutes, stirring frequently.
- Add the ground coriander, pepper, turmeric and salt. Fry for 3-4 minutes.
- Pour in the water, mix well and cover with a lid. Simmer for 40 minutes.
- Garnish with the lemon juice and coriander leaves. Serve hot.

Chicken with Figs

Serves 4

Ingredients

4 tbsp refined vegetable oil

2 large onions, finely chopped

1 tsp ginger paste

1 tsp garlic paste

1kg/2¼lb chicken, chopped into
   12 pieces

250ml/8fl oz warm water

200g/7oz tomato purée

Salt to taste

2 tsp malt vinegar

12 dry figs, soaked for 2 hours

Method

- Heat the oil in a frying pan. Add the onions. Fry them on a medium heat till translucent. Add the ginger paste and garlic paste. Fry for 2-3 minutes.
- Add the chicken and water. Cover with a lid and simmer for 30 minutes.
- Add the tomato purée, salt and vinegar. Mix well. Drain the figs and add them to the chicken mixture. Simmer for 8-10 minutes. Serve hot.

No-Oil Chicken

Serves 4

Ingredients

400g/14oz yoghurt
1 tsp chilli powder
1 tsp ginger paste
1 tsp garlic paste
2 green chillies, finely chopped

50g/1¾oz coriander leaves, ground
1 tsp garam masala
Salt to taste
750g/1lb 10oz boneless chicken,
  chopped into 8 pieces

Method
- Mix together all the ingredients, except the chicken. Marinate the chicken with this mixture overnight.
- Cook the marinated chicken in a saucepan on a medium heat for 40 minutes, stirring frequently. Serve hot.

Kozi Varatha Curry
(Kairali Chicken Curry from Kerala)

Serves 4

Ingredients

60ml/2fl oz refined vegetable oil
7.5cm/3in root ginger, finely chopped
15 garlic cloves, finely chopped
8 shallots, sliced
3 green chillies, slit lengthways
1kg/2¼lb chicken, chopped into
  12 pieces

¾ tsp turmeric
Salt to taste
2 tbsp ground coriander
1 tbsp garam masala
½ tsp cumin seeds
750ml/1¼ pints coconut milk
5-6 curry leaves

Method
- Heat the oil in a saucepan. Add the ginger and garlic. Fry on a medium heat for 30 seconds.
- Add the shallots and green chillies. Stir-fry for a minute.
- Add the chicken, turmeric, salt, ground coriander, garam masala and cumin seeds. Mix well. Cover with a lid and cook on a low heat for 20 minutes. Add the coconut milk. Simmer for 20 minutes.
- Garnish with the curry leaves and serve hot.

Chicken Stew

Serves 4

Ingredients

1 tbsp refined vegetable oil

2 cloves

2.5cm/1in cinnamon

6 black peppercorns

3 bay leaves

2 large onions, chopped into 8 pieces

1 tsp ginger paste

1 tsp garlic paste

8 chicken drumsticks

200g/7oz frozen mixed vegetables

250ml/8fl oz water

Salt to taste

2 tsp plain white flour,
  dissolved in 360ml/12fl oz milk

Method

- Heat the oil in a saucepan. Add the cloves, cinnamon, peppercorns and bay leaves. Let them splutter for 30 seconds.
- Add the onions, ginger paste and garlic paste. Fry for 2 minutes.
- Add the remaining ingredients, except the flour mixture. Cover with a lid and simmer for 30 minutes. Add the flour mixture. Mix well.
- Simmer for 10 minutes, stirring frequently. Serve hot.

Chicken Himani

(Cardamom Chicken)

Serves 4

Ingredients

1kg/2¼lb chicken, chopped into 10
  pieces

3 tbsp refined vegetable oil

¼ tsp ground green cardamom

Salt to taste

For the marinade:

1 tsp ginger paste

1 tsp garlic paste

200g/7oz yoghurt

2 tbsp mint leaves, ground

Method

- Mix all the marinade ingredients together. Marinate the chicken with this mixture for 4 hours.
- Heat the oil in a saucepan. Add the marinated chicken and fry on a low heat for 10 minutes. Add the cardamom and salt. Mix well and cook for 30 minutes, stirring frequently. Serve hot.

White Chicken

Serves 4

Ingredients

750g/1lb 10oz boneless chicken, chopped
1 tsp ginger paste
1 tsp garlic paste
1 tbsp ghee
2 cloves
2.5cm/1in cinnamon

8 black peppercorns
2 bay leaves
Salt to taste
250ml/8fl oz water
30g/1oz cashew nuts, ground
10-12 almonds, ground
1 tbsp single cream

Method

• Marinate the chicken with the ginger paste and garlic paste for 30 minutes.
• Heat the ghee in a saucepan. Add the cloves, cinnamon, peppercorns, bay leaves and salt. Let them splutter for 15 seconds.
• Add the marinated chicken and water. Simmer for 30 minutes. Add the cashew nuts, almonds and cream. Cook for 5 minutes and serve hot.

Chicken in Red Masala

Serves 4

Ingredients

3 tbsp refined vegetable oil
2 large onions, finely sliced
1 tbsp poppy seeds
5 dry red chillies
50g/1¾oz fresh coconut, grated
2.5cm/1in cinnamon
2 tsp tamarind paste

6 garlic cloves
500g/1lb 2oz chicken, chopped
2 tomatoes, finely sliced
1 tbsp ground coriander
1 tsp ground cumin
500ml/16fl oz water
Salt to taste

Method

• Heat the oil in a saucepan. Fry the onions on a medium heat till brown. Add the poppy seeds, chillies, coconut and cinnamon. Fry for 3 minutes.
• Add the tamarind paste and garlic. Mix well and grind into a paste.
• Mix this paste with all the remaining ingredients. Cook the mixture in a saucepan on a low heat for 40 minutes. Serve hot.

Chicken Jhalfrezie
(Chicken in Thick Tomato Gravy)

Serves 4

Ingredients

3 tbsp refined vegetable oil

3 large onions, finely chopped

2.5cm/1in root ginger, finely sliced

1 tsp garlic paste

1kg/2¼lb chicken, chopped into 8 pieces

½ tsp turmeric

3 tsp ground coriander

1 tsp ground cumin

4 tomatoes, blanched and puréed

Salt to taste

Method

- Heat the oil in a saucepan. Add the onions, ginger and garlic paste. Fry on a medium heat till the onions are brown.
- Add the chicken, turmeric, ground coriander and ground cumin. Fry for 5 minutes.
- Add the tomato purée and salt. Mix well and cook on a low heat for 40 minutes, stirring occasionally. Serve hot.

Simple Chicken Curry

Serves 4

Ingredients

2 tbsp refined vegetable oil

2 large onions, sliced

½ tsp turmeric

1 tsp ginger paste

1 tsp garlic paste

6 green chillies, sliced

750g/1lb 10oz chicken, chopped into 8 pieces

125g/4½oz yoghurt

125g/4½oz khoya*

Salt to taste

50g/1¾oz coriander leaves, finely chopped

Method

- Heat the oil in a saucepan. Add the onions. Fry till they turn translucent.
- Add the turmeric, ginger paste, garlic paste and green chillies. Fry on a medium heat for 2 minutes. Add the chicken and fry for 5 minutes.
- Add the yoghurt, khoya and salt. Mix thoroughly. Cover with a lid and cook on a low heat for 30 minutes, stirring occasionally.
- Garnish with the coriander leaves. Serve hot.

Sour Chicken Curry

Serves 4

Ingredients

1kg/2¼lb chicken, chopped into 8 pieces
Salt to taste
½ tsp turmeric
4 tbsp refined vegetable oil
3 onions, finely chopped
8 curry leaves
3 tomatoes, finely chopped

1 tsp ginger paste
1 tsp garlic paste
1 tbsp ground coriander
1 tsp garam masala
1 tbsp tamarind paste
½ tbsp ground black pepper
250ml/8fl oz water

Method

- Marinate the chicken pieces with the salt and turmeric for 30 minutes.
- Heat the oil in a saucepan. Add the onions and curry leaves. Fry on a low heat till the onions are translucent.
- Add all the remaining ingredients and the marinated chicken. Mix well, cover with a lid and simmer for 40 minutes. Serve hot.

Anjeer Dry Chicken
(Dry Chicken with Figs)

Serves 4

Ingredients

750g/1lb 10oz chicken, chopped into 12 pieces
4 tbsp ghee
2 large onions, finely chopped
250ml/8fl oz water
Salt to taste

For the marinade:

10 dry figs, soaked for 1 hour
1 tsp ginger paste
1 tsp garlic paste
200g/7oz yoghurt
1½ tsp garam masala
2 tbsp single cream

Method

- Mix all the marinade ingredients together. Marinate the chicken with this mixture for an hour.
- Heat the ghee in a saucepan. Fry the onions on a medium heat till brown.
- Add the marinated chicken, water and salt. Mix well, cover with a lid and simmer for 40 minutes. Serve hot.

Chicken Yoghurt

Serves 4

Ingredients

30g/1oz mint leaves, finely chopped
30g/1oz coriander leaves, chopped
2 tsp ginger paste
2 tsp garlic paste
400g/14oz yoghurt
200g/7oz tomato purée

Juice of 1 lemon
1kg/2¼lb chicken, chopped into 12 pieces
2 tbsp refined vegetable oil
4 large onions, finely chopped
Salt to taste

Method

* Grind the mint leaves and coriander leaves to a fine paste. Mix this with the ginger paste, garlic paste, yoghurt, tomato purée and lemon juice. Marinate the chicken with this mixture for 3 hours.
* Heat the oil in a saucepan. Fry the onions on a medium heat till brown.
* Add the marinated chicken. Cover with a lid and simmer for 40 minutes, stirring occasionally. Serve hot.

Spicy Fried Chicken

Serves 4

Ingredients

1 tsp ginger paste
2 tsp garlic paste
2 green chillies, finely chopped
1 tsp chilli powder
1 tsp garam masala
2 tsp lemon juice

½ tsp turmeric
Salt to taste
1kg/2¼lb chicken, chopped into 8 pieces
Refined vegetable oil for deep-frying
Breadcrumbs, to coat

Method

* Mix the ginger paste, garlic paste, green chillies, chilli powder, garam masala, lemon juice, turmeric and salt together. Marinate the chicken with this mixture for 3 hours.
* Heat the oil in a frying pan. Coat each marinated chicken piece with the breadcrumbs and deep fry on a medium heat till golden brown.
* Drain on absorbent paper and serve hot.

Chicken Supreme

Serves 4

Ingredients

1 tsp ginger paste

1 tsp garlic paste

1kg/2¼lb chicken, chopped into 8 pieces

200g/7oz yoghurt

Salt to taste

250ml/8fl oz water

2 tbsp refined vegetable oil

2 large onions, sliced

4 red chillies

5cm/2in cinnamon

2 black cardamom pods

4 cloves

1 tbsp chana dhal*, dry roasted
  (see cooking techniques)

Method

- Mix the ginger paste and garlic paste together. Marinate the chicken with this mixture for 30 minutes. Add the yoghurt, salt and water. Set aside.
- Heat the oil in a saucepan. Add the onions, chillies, cinnamon, cardamom, cloves and chana dhal. Fry for 3-4 minutes on a low heat.
- Grind to a paste and add to the chicken mixture. Mix well.
- Cook on a low heat for 30 minutes. Serve hot.

Chicken Vindaloo

(Spicy Goan-style Chicken Curry)

Serves 4

Ingredients

60ml/2fl oz malt vinegar

1 tbsp cumin seeds

1 tsp peppercorns

6 red chillies

1 tsp turmeric

Salt to taste

4 tbsp refined vegetable oil

3 large onions, finely chopped

1kg/2¼lb chicken, chopped into 8 pieces

Method

- Grind the vinegar with the cumin seeds, peppercorns, chillies, turmeric and salt to a smooth paste. Set aside.
- Heat the oil in a saucepan. Add the onions and fry till translucent. Add the vinegar-cumin seeds paste. Mix well and fry for 4-5 minutes.
- Add the chicken and cook on a low heat for 30 minutes. Serve hot.

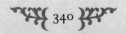

Caramelized Chicken

Serves 4

Ingredients
200g/7oz yoghurt

1 tsp ginger paste

1 tsp garlic paste

2 tbsp ground coriander

1 tsp ground cumin

1½ tsp garam masala

Salt to taste

1kg/2¼lb chicken, chopped into 8 pieces

3 tbsp refined vegetable oil

2 tsp sugar

3 cloves

2.5cm/1in cinnamon

6 black peppercorns

Method
- Mix together the yoghurt, ginger paste, garlic paste, ground coriander, ground cumin, garam masala and salt. Marinate the chicken with this mixture overnight.
- Heat the oil in a saucepan. Add the sugar, cloves, cinnamon and peppercorns. Fry for a minute. Add the marinated chicken and cook on a low heat for 40 minutes. Serve hot.

Cashew Chicken

Serves 4

Ingredients
1kg/2¼lb chicken, chopped into 12 pieces

Salt to taste

1 tsp ginger paste

1 tsp garlic paste

4 tbsp refined vegetable oil

4 large onions, sliced

15 cashew nuts, ground to a paste

6 red chillies, soaked for 15 minutes

2 tsp ground cumin

60ml/2fl oz ketchup

500ml/16fl oz water

Method
- Marinate the chicken with the salt and ginger and garlic pastes for 1 hour.
- Heat the oil in a saucepan. Fry the onions on a medium heat till brown.
- Add the cashew nuts, chillies, cumin and ketchup. Cook for 5 minutes.
- Add the chicken and the water. Simmer for 40 minutes and serve hot.

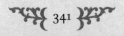 341

Quick Chicken

Serves 4

Ingredients

4 tbsp refined vegetable oil

6 red chillies

6 black peppercorns

1 tsp coriander seeds

1 tsp cumin seeds

2.5cm/1in cinnamon

4 cloves

1 tsp turmeric

8 garlic cloves

1 tsp tamarind paste

4 medium-sized onions, finely sliced

2 large tomatoes, finely chopped

1kg/2¼lb chicken, chopped into 12 pieces

250ml/8fl oz water

Salt to taste

Method

● Heat half a tbsp of oil in a saucepan. Add the red chillies, peppercorns, coriander seeds, cumin seeds, cinnamon and cloves. Fry them on a medium heat for 2-3 minutes.

● Add the turmeric, garlic and tamarind paste. Grind the mixture to a smooth paste. Set aside.

● Heat the remaining oil in a saucepan. Add the onions and fry them on a medium heat till they are brown. Add the tomatoes and sauté for 3-4 minutes.

● Add the chicken and sauté for 4-5 minutes.

● Add the water and salt. Mix well and cover with a lid. Simmer for 40 minutes, stirring occasionally.

● Serve hot.

Coorgi Chicken Curry

Serves 4

Ingredients

1kg/2¼lb chicken, chopped into 12
   pieces
Salt to taste
1 tsp turmeric
50g/1¾oz grated coconut
3 tbsp refined vegetable oil

1 tsp garlic paste
2 large onions, finely sliced
1 tsp ground cumin
1 tsp ground coriander
360ml/12fl oz water

Method
- Marinate the chicken with the salt and turmeric for an hour. Set aside.
- Grind the coconut with enough water to form a smooth paste.
- Heat the oil in a saucepan. Add the coconut paste with the garlic paste, onions, ground cumin and coriander. Fry on a low heat for 4-5 minutes.
- Add the marinated chicken. Mix well and fry for 4-5 minutes. Add the water, cover with a lid and simmer for 40 minutes. Serve hot.

Pan Chicken

Serves 4

Ingredients

4 tbsp refined vegetable oil
1 tsp ginger paste
1 tsp garlic paste
2 large onions, finely chopped
1 tsp garam masala
1½ tbsp cashew nuts, ground
1½ tbsp melon seeds*, ground

1 tsp ground coriander
500g/1lb 2oz boneless chicken
200g/7oz tomato purée
2 chicken stock cubes
250ml/8fl oz water
Salt to taste

Method
- Heat the oil in a saucepan. Add the ginger paste, garlic paste, onions and garam masala. Fry for 2-3 minutes on a low heat. Add the cashew nuts, melon seeds and ground coriander. Fry for 2 minutes.
- Add the chicken and fry for 5 minutes. Add the tomato purée, stock cubes, water and salt. Cover and simmer for 40 minutes. Serve hot.

Spinach Chicken

Serves 4

Ingredients

3 tbsp refined vegetable oil
6 cloves
5cm/2in cinnamon
2 bay leaves
2 large onions, finely chopped
12 garlic cloves, finely chopped

400g/14oz spinach, coarsely chopped
200g/7oz yoghurt
250ml/8fl oz water
750g/1lb 10oz chicken, chopped into 8 pieces
Salt to taste

Method

* Heat 2 tbsp oil in a saucepan. Add the cloves, cinnamon and bay leaves. Let them splutter for 15 seconds.
* Add the onions and fry them on a medium heat till they turn translucent.
* Add the garlic and spinach. Mix well. Cook for 5-6 minutes. Cool and grind with enough water to make a smooth paste.
* Heat the remaining oil in a saucepan. Add the spinach paste and fry for 3-4 minutes. Add the yoghurt and water. Cook for 5-6 minutes. Add the chicken and salt. Cook on a low heat for 40 minutes. Serve hot.

Chicken Indienne

Serves 4

Ingredients

4-5 tbsp refined vegetable oil
4 large onions, minced
1kg/2¼lb chicken, chopped into 10 pieces
Salt to taste
500ml/16fl oz water

For the spice mixture:

2.5cm/1in root ginger
10 garlic cloves
1 tbsp garam masala
2 tsp fennel seeds
1½ tbsp coriander seeds
60ml/2fl oz water

Method

* Grind the spice mixture ingredients into a smooth paste. Set aside.
* Heat the oil in a saucepan. Fry the onions on a medium heat till brown.
* Add the spice mixture paste, the chicken and salt. Fry for 5-6 minutes. Add the water. Cover and cook for 40 minutes. Serve hot.

Kori Gassi
(Mangalorean Chicken with Curry)

Serves 4

Ingredients

4 tbsp refined vegetable oil
6 whole red chillies
1 tsp black peppercorns
4 tsp coriander seeds
2 tsp cumin seeds
150g/5½oz fresh coconut, grated
8 garlic cloves

500ml/16fl oz water
3 large onions, finely chopped
1 tsp turmeric
1kg/2¼lb chicken, chopped into 8 pieces
2 tsp tamarind paste
Salt to taste

Method

- Heat 1 tsp oil in a saucepan. Add the red chillies, peppercorns, coriander seeds and cumin seeds. Let them splutter for 15 seconds.
- Grind this mixture to a paste with the coconut, garlic and half the water.
- Heat the remaining oil in a saucepan. Add the onions, turmeric and the coconut paste. Fry on a medium heat for 5-6 minutes.
- Add the chicken, tamarind paste, salt and the remaining water. Mix well. Cover with a lid and simmer for 40 minutes. Serve hot.

Chicken Ghezado
(Goan-style Chicken)

Serves 4

Ingredients

3 tbsp refined vegetable oil
2 large onions, finely chopped
1 tsp ginger paste
1 tsp garlic paste
2 tomatoes, finely chopped

1kg/2¼lb chicken, chopped into 8 pieces
1 tbsp ground coriander
2 tbsp garam masala
Salt to taste
250ml/8fl oz water

Method

- Heat the oil in a saucepan. Add the onions, ginger paste and garlic paste. Fry for 2 minutes. Add the tomatoes and chicken. Fry for 5 minutes.
- Add all the remaining ingredients. Simmer for 40 minutes and serve hot.

Chicken in Tomato Gravy

Serves 4

Ingredients

1 tbsp ghee
2.5cm/1in root ginger, finely chopped
10 garlic cloves, finely chopped
2 large onions, finely chopped
4 red chillies
1 tsp garam masala

1 tsp turmeric
800g/1¾lb tomato purée
1kg/2¼lb chicken, chopped into 8 pieces
Salt to taste
200g/7oz yoghurt

Method

- Heat the ghee in a saucepan. Add the ginger, garlic, onions, red chillies, garam masala and turmeric. Fry on a medium heat for 3 minutes.
- Add the tomato purée and fry for 4 minutes on a low heat.
- Add the chicken, salt and yoghurt. Mix thoroughly.
- Cover and simmer for 40 minutes, stirring occasionally. Serve hot.

Shahenshah Murgh
(Chicken cooked in Special Gravy)

Serves 4

Ingredients

250g/9oz peanuts, soaked for 4 hours
60g/2oz raisins
4 green chillies, slit lengthways
1 tbsp cumin seeds
4 tbsp ghee

1 tbsp ground cinnamon
3 large onions, finely chopped
1kg/2¼lb chicken, chopped in 12 pieces
Salt to taste

Method

- Drain the peanuts and grind them with the raisins, green chillies, cumin seeds and enough water to form a smooth paste. Set aside.
- Heat the ghee in a saucepan. Add the ground cinnamon. Let it splutter for 30 seconds.
- Add the onions and the ground peanut-raisin paste. Fry for 2-3 minutes.
- Add the chicken and salt. Mix well. Cook on a low heat for 40 minutes, stirring occasionally. Serve hot.

Chicken do Pyaaza
(Chicken with Onions)

Serves 4

Ingredients

4 tbsp ghee plus extra for deep frying
4 cloves
½ tsp fennel seeds
1 tsp ground coriander
1 tsp ground black pepper
2.5cm/1in root ginger, finely chopped
8 garlic cloves, finely chopped

4 large onions, sliced
1kg/2¼lb chicken, chopped into 12 pieces
½ tsp turmeric
4 tomatoes, finely chopped
Salt to taste

Method
- Heat 4 tbsp ghee in a saucepan. Add the cloves, fennel seeds, ground coriander and pepper. Let them splutter for 15 seconds.
- Add the ginger, garlic and onions. Fry on a medium heat for 1-2 minutes.
- Add the chicken, turmeric, tomatoes and salt. Mix well. Cook on a low heat for 30 minutes, stirring frequently. Serve hot.

Bengali Chicken

Serves 4

Ingredients

300g/10oz yoghurt
1 tsp ginger paste
1 tsp garlic paste
3 large onions, 1 grated plus 2 finely chopped
1 tsp turmeric

2 tsp chilli powder
Salt to taste
1kg/2¼lb chicken, chopped into 12 pieces
4 tbsp mustard oil
500ml/16fl oz water

Method
- Mix the yoghurt, ginger paste, garlic paste, onion, turmeric, chilli powder and salt together. Marinate the chicken with this mixture for 30 minutes.
- Heat the oil in a saucepan. Add the chopped onions and fry till brown.
- Add the marinated chicken, water and salt. Mix well. Cover with a lid and simmer for 40 minutes. Serve hot.

Lasooni Murgh

(Chicken cooked with Garlic)

Serves 4

Ingredients

200g/7oz yoghurt

2 tbsp garlic paste

1 tsp garam masala

2 tbsp lemon juice

1 tsp ground black pepper

5 saffron strands

Salt to taste

750g/1lb 10oz boneless chicken, chopped into 8 pieces

2 tbsp refined vegetable oil

60ml/2fl oz double cream

Method

• Mix together the yoghurt, garlic paste, garam masala, lemon juice, pepper, saffron, salt and chicken. Refrigerate the mixture overnight.

• Heat the oil in a saucepan. Add the chicken mixture, cover with a lid and cook on a low heat for 40 minutes, stirring occasionally.

• Add the cream and stir for a minute. Serve hot.

Chicken Cafreal

(Goan Chicken in a Coriander Sauce)

Serves 4

Ingredients

1kg/2¼lb chicken, chopped into 8 pieces

5 tbsp refined vegetable oil

250ml/8fl oz water

Salt to taste

4 lemons, quartered

For the marinade:

50g/1¾oz coriander leaves, chopped

2.5cm/1in root ginger

10 garlic cloves

120ml/4fl oz malt vinegar

1 tbsp garam masala

Method

• Mix all the marinade ingredients together and grind with enough water to form a smooth paste. Marinate the chicken with this mixture for an hour.

• Heat the oil in a saucepan. Add the marinated chicken and fry on a medium heat for 5 minutes. Add the water and salt. Cover with a lid and simmer for 40 minutes, stirring occasionally. Serve hot with the lemons.

Chicken with Apricots

Serves 4

Ingredients

4 tbsp refined vegetable oil
3 large onions, finely sliced
1 tsp ginger paste
1 tsp garlic paste
1kg/2¼lb chicken, chopped into 8 pieces
1 tsp chilli powder
1 tsp turmeric

2 tsp ground cumin
2 tbsp sugar
300g/10oz dried apricots, soaked for 10 minutes
60ml/2fl oz water
1 tbsp malt vinegar
Salt to taste

Method

- Heat the oil in a saucepan. Add the onions, ginger paste and garlic paste. Fry on a medium heat till the onions are brown.
- Add the chicken, chilli powder, turmeric, ground cumin and sugar. Mix well and fry for 5-6 minutes.
- Add the remaining ingredients. Simmer for 40 minutes and serve hot.

Grilled Chicken

Serves 4

Ingredients

Salt to taste
1 tbsp malt vinegar
1 tsp ground black pepper
1 tsp ginger paste
1 tsp garlic paste

2 tsp garam masala
1kg/2¼lb chicken, chopped into 8 pieces
2 tbsp ghee
2 large onions, sliced
2 tomatoes, finely chopped

Method

- Mix the salt, vinegar, pepper, ginger paste, garlic paste and garam masala together. Marinate the chicken with this mixture for an hour.
- Heat the ghee in a saucepan. Add the onions and fry on a medium heat till they turn brown.
- Add the tomatoes and marinated chicken. Mix thoroughly and fry for 4-5 minutes.
- Remove from the heat and grill the mixture for 40 minutes. Serve hot.

Pepper Duck Roast

Serves 4

Ingredients

2 tbsp malt vinegar

1½ tsp ginger paste

1 tsp garlic paste

Salt to taste

1 tsp ground black pepper

1kg/2¼lb duck

2 tbsp butter

2 tbsp refined vegetable oil

3 large onions, finely sliced

4 tomatoes, finely chopped

1 tsp sugar

500ml/16fl oz water

Method

- Mix the vinegar, ginger paste, garlic paste, salt and pepper. Pierce the duck with a fork and marinate with this mixture for 1 hour.
- Heat the butter and oil together in a saucepan. Add the onions and tomatoes. Fry on a medium heat for 3-4 minutes. Add the duck, sugar and water. Mix well and simmer for 45 minutes. Serve hot.

Bhuna Chicken

(Chicken cooked in Yoghurt)

Serves 4

Ingredients

4 tbsp refined vegetable oil

1kg/2¼lb chicken, chopped into 12 pieces

1 tsp ginger paste

1 tsp garlic paste

½ tsp turmeric

2 large onions, finely chopped

1½ tsp garam masala

1 tsp freshly ground black pepper

150g/5½oz yoghurt, whisked

Salt to taste

Method

- Heat the oil in a saucepan. Add the chicken and fry on a medium heat for 6-7 minutes. Drain and set aside.
- To the same oil, add the ginger paste, garlic paste, turmeric and onions. Fry on a medium heat for 2 minutes, stirring frequently.
- Add the fried chicken and all the remaining ingredients. Cook for 40 minutes on a low heat. Serve hot.

Chicken Curry with Eggs

Serves 4

Ingredients

6 garlic cloves

2.5cm/1in root ginger

25g/scant 1oz grated fresh coconut

2 tsp poppy seeds

1 tsp garam masala

1 tsp cumin seeds

1 tbsp coriander seeds

1 tsp turmeric

Salt to taste

4 tbsp refined vegetable oil

2 large onions, finely chopped

1kg/2¼lb chicken, chopped into 8 pieces

4 eggs, hard-boiled and halved

Method

• Grind together the garlic, ginger, coconut, poppy seeds, garam masala, cumin seeds, coriander seeds, turmeric and salt. Set aside.

• Heat the oil in a saucepan. Add the onions and the ground paste. Fry on a medium heat for 3-4 minutes. Add the chicken and mix well to coat.

• Simmer for 40 minutes. Garnish with the eggs and serve hot.

Chicken Fried with Spices

Serves 4

Ingredients

1kg/2¼lb chicken, chopped into 8 pieces

250ml/8fl oz refined vegetable oil

For the marinade:

1½ tsp ground coriander

4 green cardamom pods

7.5cm/3in cinnamon

½ tsp fennel seeds

1 tbsp garam masala

4-6 garlic cloves

2.5cm/1in root ginger

1 large onion, grated

1 large tomato, puréed

Salt to taste

Method

• Grind all the marinade ingredients together. Marinate the chicken with this mixture for 30 minutes.

• Cook the marinated chicken in a saucepan on a medium heat for 30 minutes, stirring occasionally.

• Heat the oil and fry the cooked chicken for 5-6 minutes. Serve hot.

Goan Kombdi
(Goan Chicken Curry)

Serves 4

Ingredients

1kg/2¼lb chicken, chopped into 8 pieces
Salt to taste
½ tsp turmeric
6 red chillies
5 cloves
5cm/2in cinnamon

1 tbsp coriander seeds
½ tsp fenugreek seeds
½ tsp mustard seeds
4 tbsp oil
1 tbsp tamarind paste
500ml/16fl oz coconut milk

Method

- Marinate the chicken with the salt and turmeric for 1 hour. Set aside.
- Grind together the chillies, cloves, cinnamon, coriander seeds, fenugreek seeds and mustard seeds with enough water to form a paste.
- Heat the oil in a saucepan. Fry the paste for 4 minutes. Add the chicken, tamarind paste and coconut milk. Simmer for 40 minutes and serve hot.

South Chicken Curry

Serves 4

Ingredients

16 cashew nuts
6 red chillies
2 tbsp coriander seeds
½ tsp cumin seeds
1 tbsp lemon juice
5 tbsp ghee
3 large onions, finely chopped

10 garlic cloves, finely chopped
2.5cm/1in root ginger, finely chopped
1kg/2¼lb chicken, chopped into 12 pieces
1 tsp turmeric
Salt to taste
500ml/16fl oz coconut milk

Method

- Grind the cashew nuts, red chillies, coriander seeds, cumin seeds and lemon juice with enough water to form a smooth paste. Set aside.
- Heat the ghee. Add the onions, garlic and ginger. Fry for 2 minutes.
- Add the chicken, turmeric, salt and the cashew nut paste. Fry for 5 minutes. Add the coconut milk and simmer for 40 minutes. Serve hot.

Nizami Chicken

(Chicken cooked with Saffron and Almonds)

Serves 4

Ingredients

4 tbsp refined vegetable oil
1 large chicken, chopped into 8 pieces
Salt to taste
750ml/1¼ pints milk
½ tsp saffron, soaked in 2 tsp milk

For the spice mixture:

1 tbsp ginger paste
3 tbsp poppy seeds
5 red chillies
25g/scant 1oz desiccated coconut
20 almonds
6 tbsp milk

Method

- Grind the spice mixture ingredients together to form a smooth paste.
- Heat the oil in a saucepan. Fry the paste on a low heat for 4 minutes.
- Add the chicken, salt and milk. Simmer for 40 minutes, stirring frequently. Add the saffron and simmer for another 5 minutes. Serve hot.

Duck Buffad

(Duck cooked with Vegetables)

Serves 4

Ingredients

4 tbsp ghee
3 large onions, quartered
750g/1lb 10oz duck, chopped into 8 pieces
3 large potatoes, quartered
50g/1¾oz cabbage, chopped
200g/7oz frozen peas
1 tsp turmeric

4 green chillies, slit lengthways
1 tsp ground cinnamon
1 tsp ground cloves
30g/1oz mint leaves, finely chopped
Salt to taste
750ml/1¼ pints water
1 tbsp malt vinegar

Method

- Heat the ghee in a saucepan. Add the onions and fry on a medium heat till brown. Add the duck and sauté for 5-6 minutes.
- Add the remaining ingredients, except the water and vinegar. Fry for 8 minutes. Add the water and vinegar. Simmer for 40 minutes. Serve hot.

Adraki Murgh
(Ginger Chicken)

Serves 4

Ingredients

2 tbsp refined vegetable oil
2 large onions, finely chopped
2 tbsp ginger paste
½ tsp garlic paste
½ tsp turmeric

1 tbsp garam masala
1 tomato, finely chopped
1kg/2¼lb chicken, chopped into 12 pieces
Salt to taste

Method

- Heat the oil in a saucepan. Add the onions, ginger paste and garlic paste and fry on a medium heat for 1-2 minutes.
- Add all the remaining ingredients and sauté for 5-6 minutes.
- Grill the mixture for 40 minutes and serve hot.

Bharva Murgh
(Stuffed Chicken)

Serves 4

Ingredients

½ tsp ginger paste
½ tsp garlic paste
1 tsp tamarind paste
1kg/2¼lb chicken
75g/2½oz ghee
2 large onions, finely chopped
Salt to taste

3 large potatoes, chopped
2 tsp ground coriander
1 tsp ground cumin
1 tsp mustard powder
50g/1¾oz coriander leaves, chopped
2 cloves
2.5cm/1in cinnamon

Method

- Mix the ginger, garlic and tamarind pastes. Marinate the chicken with the mixture for 3 hours. Set aside.
- Heat the ghee in a saucepan and fry the onions till brown. Add all the remaining ingredients, except the marinated chicken. Fry for 6 minutes.
- Stuff this mixture into the marinated chicken. Roast in an oven at 190°C (375°F, Gas Mark 5) for 45 minutes. Serve hot.

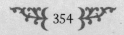

Malaidar Murgh
(Chicken cooked in Creamy Gravy)

Serves 4

Ingredients

4 tbsp refined vegetable oil

2 large onions, finely chopped

¼ tsp ground cloves

Salt to taste

1kg/2¼lb chicken, chopped into 12 pieces

250ml/8fl oz water

3 tomatoes, finely chopped

125g/4½oz yoghurt, whisked

500ml/16fl oz single cream

2 tbsp cashew nuts, ground

10g/¼oz coriander leaves, chopped

Method

- Heat the oil in a saucepan. Add the onions, cloves and salt. Fry on a medium heat for 3 minutes. Add the chicken and sauté for 7-8 minutes.
- Add the water and tomatoes. Cook for 30 minutes.
- Add the yoghurt, cream and cashew nuts. Simmer for 10 minutes.
- Garnish with the coriander leaves and serve hot.

Bombay Chicken Curry

Serves 4

Ingredients

8 tbsp refined vegetable oil

1kg/2¼lb chicken, chopped into 12 pieces

2 large onions, sliced

1 tsp ginger paste

1 tsp garlic paste

4 cloves, ground

2.5cm/1in cinnamon, ground

1 tsp ground cumin

Salt to taste

2 tomatoes, finely chopped

500ml/16fl oz water

Method

- Heat half the oil in a frying pan. Add the chicken and fry on a medium heat for 5-6 minutes. Set aside.
- Heat the remaining oil in a saucepan. Add the onions, ginger paste and garlic paste and fry on a medium heat till the onions turn brown. Add the remaining ingredients, except the water and chicken. Sauté for 5-6 minutes.
- Add the fried chicken and water. Simmer for 30 minutes and serve hot.

Durbari Chicken
(Rich Gravy Chicken)

Serves 4

Ingredients

150g/5½oz chana dhal*
Salt to taste
1 litre/1¾ pints water
2.5cm/1in root ginger
10 garlic cloves
4 red chillies
3 tbsp ghee
2 large onions, finely chopped
½ tsp turmeric

2 tbsp garam masala
½ tbsp poppy seeds
2 tomatoes, finely chopped
1kg/2¼lb chicken, chopped into
   10-12 pieces
2 tsp tamarind paste
20 cashew nuts, ground to a paste
250ml/8fl oz water
250ml/8fl oz coconut milk

Method
* Mix the dhal with salt and half the water. Cook in a saucepan on a medium heat for 45 minutes. Grind to a paste with the ginger, garlic and red chillies.
* Heat the ghee in a saucepan. Add the onions, dhal mixture and turmeric. Fry on a medium heat for 3-4 minutes. Add all the remaining ingredients.
* Mix well and simmer for 40 minutes, stirring occasionally. Serve hot.

Duck Fry

Serves 4

Ingredients

3 tbsp malt vinegar
2 tbsp ground coriander
½ tsp ground black pepper
Salt to taste

1kg/2¼lb duck, chopped into 8 pieces
60ml/2fl oz refined vegetable oil
2 small onions
1 litre/1¾ pints hot water

Method
* Mix the vinegar with the ground coriander, pepper and salt. Marinate the duck with this mixture for 1 hour.
* Heat the oil in a saucepan. Fry the onions on a medium heat till brown.
* Add the water, salt and the duck. Simmer for 45 minutes and serve hot.

Coriander Garlic Chicken

Serves 4

Ingredients

4 tbsp refined vegetable oil

5cm/2in cinnamon

3 green cardamom pods

4 cloves

2 bay leaves

3 large onions, finely chopped

10 garlic cloves, finely chopped

1 tsp ginger paste

3 tomatoes, finely chopped

1 large chicken, chopped

250ml/8fl oz water

150g/5½oz coriander leaves, chopped

Salt to taste

Method

• Heat the oil in a saucepan. Add the cinnamon, cardamom, cloves, bay leaves, onions, garlic and ginger paste. Fry for 2-3 minutes.

• Add all the remaining ingredients. Simmer for 40 minutes and serve hot.

Masala Duck

Serves 4

Ingredients

30g/1oz ghee plus 1 tbsp for frying

1 large onion, finely sliced

1 tsp ginger paste

1 tsp garlic paste

1 tsp ground coriander

½ tsp ground black pepper

1 tsp turmeric

1kg/2¼lb duck, chopped into 12 pieces

1 tbsp malt vinegar

Salt to taste

5cm/2in cinnamon

3 cloves

1 tsp mustard seeds

Method

• Heat 30g/1oz of the ghee in a saucepan. Add the onion, ginger paste, garlic paste, coriander, pepper and turmeric. Fry for 6 minutes.

• Add the duck. Fry on a medium heat for 5 minutes. Add the vinegar and salt. Mix well and simmer for 40 minutes. Set aside.

• Heat the remaining ghee in a saucepan and add the cinnamon, cloves and mustard seeds. Let them splutter for 15 seconds. Pour this over the duck mixture and serve hot.

Mustard Chicken

Serves 4

Ingredients

2 large tomatoes, finely chopped

10g/¼oz mint leaves, finely chopped

30g/1oz coriander leaves, chopped

2.5cm/1in root ginger, peeled

8 garlic cloves

3 tbsp mustard oil

2 tsp mustard seeds

½ tsp fenugreek seeds

1kg/2¼lb chicken, chopped into 12 pieces

500ml/16fl oz warm water

Salt to taste

Method

- Grind the tomatoes, mint leaves, coriander leaves, ginger and garlic to a smooth paste. Set aside.
- Heat the oil in a saucepan. Add the mustard seeds and fenugreek seeds. Let them splutter for 15 seconds.
- Add the tomato paste and fry on a medium heat for 2-3 minutes. Add the chicken, water and salt. Mix well and simmer for 40 minutes. Serve hot.

Murgh Lassanwallah
(Garlic Chicken)

Serves 4

Ingredients

400g/14oz yoghurt

3 tsp garlic paste

1½ tsp garam masala

Salt to taste

750g/1lb 10oz boneless chicken, chopped into 12 pieces

1 tbsp refined vegetable oil

1 tsp cumin seeds

25g/scant 1oz dill leaves

500ml/16fl oz milk

1 tbsp ground black pepper

Method

- Mix the yoghurt, garlic paste, garam masala and salt together. Marinate the chicken with this mixture for 10-12 hours.
- Heat the oil. Add the cumin seeds and let them splutter for 15 seconds. Add the marinated chicken and fry on a medium heat for 20 minutes.
- Add the dill leaves, milk and pepper. Simmer for 15 minutes. Serve hot.

Pepper Chicken Chettinad
(South Indian Pepper Chicken)

Serves 4

Ingredients

2½ tbsp refined vegetable oil

10 curry leaves

3 large onions, finely chopped

1 tsp ginger paste

1 tsp garlic paste

½ tsp turmeric

2 tomatoes, finely chopped

½ tsp ground fennel seeds

¼ tsp ground cloves

500ml/16fl oz water

1kg/2¼lb chicken, chopped into 12 pieces

Salt to taste

1½ tsp coarsely ground black pepper

Method

- Heat the oil in a saucepan. Add the curry leaves, onions, ginger paste and garlic paste. Fry on a medium heat for a minute.
- Add all the remaining ingredients. Simmer for 40 minutes and serve hot.

Chicken Mince with Eggs

Serves 4

Ingredients

3 tbsp refined vegetable oil

4 eggs, hard-boiled and sliced

2 large onions, finely chopped

2 tsp ginger paste

2 tsp garlic paste

2 tomatoes, finely chopped

1 tsp ground cumin

2 tsp ground coriander

½ tsp turmeric

8-10 curry leaves

1 tsp garam masala

750g/1lb 10oz chicken, minced

Salt to taste

360ml/12fl oz water

Method

- Heat the oil in a saucepan. Add the eggs. Fry for 2 minutes and set aside.
- To the same oil, add the onions, ginger paste and garlic paste. Fry on a medium heat for 2-3 minutes.
- Add all the remaining ingredients, except the water. Mix well and fry for 5 minutes. Add the water. Simmer for 30 minutes.
- Garnish with the eggs. Serve hot.

Dry Chicken

Serves 4

Ingredients

1kg/2¼lb chicken, chopped into 12 pieces
6 tbsp refined vegetable oil
3 large onions, thinly sliced

For the marinade:
8 red chillies
1 tbsp sesame seeds

1 tbsp coriander seeds
1 tsp garam masala
4 green cardamom pods
10 garlic cloves
3.5cm/1½in root ginger
6 tbsp malt vinegar
Salt to taste

Method

- Grind all the marinade ingredients together to a smooth paste. Marinate the chicken with this paste for 3 hours.
- Heat the oil in a saucepan. Fry the onions on a low heat till brown. Add the chicken and cook for 40 minutes, stirring frequently. Serve hot.

Murgh Bagan-e-Bahar
(Grilled Chicken Drumsticks)

Serves 4

Ingredients

Salt to taste
1½ tsp ginger paste
1½ tsp garlic paste
1 tsp garam masala
8 chicken drumsticks
30g/1oz mint leaves, finely chopped

2 tbsp dried pomegranate seeds
50g/1¾oz yoghurt
1 tsp ground black pepper
Juice of 1 lemon
Chaat masala* to taste

Method

- Mix the salt, ginger paste, garlic paste and garam masala. Make incisions on the drumsticks and marinate them with this mixture for 1 hour.
- Grind together the remaining ingredients, except the chaat masala.
- Mix the ground mixture with the chicken and set aside for 4 hours.
- Grill the chicken for 30 minutes. Sprinkle with the chaat masala. Serve.

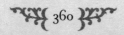

Butter Chicken

Serves 4

Ingredients

1kg/2¼lb chicken, chopped into 12
  pieces
Salt to taste
1 tsp turmeric
Juice of 1 lemon
4 tbsp butter

3 large onions, finely chopped
1 tsp ginger paste
1 tsp garlic paste
1 tbsp ground coriander
4 large tomatoes, puréed
125g/4½oz yoghurt

Method

- Marinate the chicken with the salt, turmeric and lemon juice for an hour.
- Heat the butter in a saucepan. Add the onions and fry till translucent.
- Add the ginger paste, garlic paste and ground coriander. Fry on a medium heat for 5 minutes.
- Add the marinated chicken. Fry for 5 minutes. Add the tomato purée and yoghurt. Cover with a lid and simmer for 35 minutes. Serve hot.

Chicken Sukha
(Dry Chicken)

Serves 4

Ingredients

2 tbsp refined vegetable oil
4 large onions, finely chopped
1kg/2¼lb chicken, chopped into
  12 pieces
4 tomatoes, finely chopped
1 tsp turmeric
2 green chillies, sliced

8 garlic cloves, crushed
5cm/2in root ginger, grated
2 tbsp garam masala
2 cubes chicken stock
Salt to taste
50g/1¾oz coriander leaves, chopped

Method

- Heat the oil in a saucepan. Fry the onions on a medium heat till brown. Add the remaining ingredients, except the coriander leaves.
- Mix well and cook on a low heat for 40 minutes, stirring occasionally.
- Garnish with the coriander leaves. Serve hot.

Indian Roast Chicken

Serves 4

Ingredients

1kg/2¼lb chicken

1 tbsp lemon juice

Salt to taste

2 large onions

2.5cm/1in root ginger

4 garlic cloves

3 cloves

3 green cardamom pods

5cm/2in cinnamon

4 tbsp refined vegetable oil

200g/7oz breadcrumbs

2 apples, chopped

4 hard-boiled eggs, chopped

Method

* Marinate the chicken with the lemon juice and salt for 1 hour.
* Grind together the onions, ginger, garlic, cloves, cardamom and cinnamon with enough water to form a smooth paste.
* Heat the oil in a saucepan. Add the paste and fry on a low heat for 7 minutes. Add the breadcrumbs, apples and salt. Cook for 3-4 minutes.
* Stuff the chicken with this mixture and roast in an oven at 230°C (450°F, Gas Mark 8) for 40 minutes. Garnish with the eggs. Serve hot.

Spicy Scramble

Serves 4

Ingredients

3 tbsp refined vegetable oil

750g/1lb 10oz chicken sausages, sliced

4 green peppers, julienned

1 tsp chilli powder

2 tsp ground cumin

10 garlic cloves, finely chopped

3 tomatoes, quartered

4 tbsp cold water

½ tsp freshly ground pepper

Salt to taste

4 eggs, lightly whisked

Method

* Heat the oil in a saucepan. Add the sausages and fry on a medium heat till brown. Add all the remaining ingredients, except the eggs. Mix well. Cook on a low heat for 8-10 minutes.
* Gently add the eggs and scramble till the eggs are done. Serve hot.

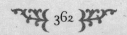

Chicken Curry with Dry Coconut

Serves 4

Ingredients

1kg/2¼lb chicken, chopped into 12
   pieces
Salt to taste
Juice of half a lemon
1 large onion, sliced
4 tbsp desiccated coconut
1 tsp turmeric

8 garlic cloves
2.5cm/1in root ginger
½ tsp fennel seeds
1 tsp garam masala
1 tsp poppy seeds
4 tbsp refined vegetable oil
500ml/16fl oz water

Method

• Marinate the chicken with the salt and lemon juice for 30 minutes.
• Dry roast (see cooking techniques) the onion and coconut for 5 minutes.
• Mix with all the remaining ingredients, except the oil and water. Grind
  with enough water to form a smooth paste.
• Heat the oil in a saucepan. Add the paste and fry on a low heat for 7-8
  minutes. Add the chicken and water. Simmer for 40 minutes. Serve hot.

Simple Chicken

Serves 4

Ingredients

1kg/2¼lb chicken, chopped into 8 pieces
Salt to taste
1 tsp chilli powder
½ tsp turmeric
3 tbsp refined vegetable oil
2 large onions, finely sliced

1 tsp ginger paste
1 tsp garlic paste
4-5 whole red chillies, deseeded
4 small tomatoes, finely chopped
1 tbsp garam masala
250ml/8fl oz water

Method

• Marinate the chicken with the salt, chilli powder and turmeric for 1 hour.
• Heat the oil in a saucepan. Add the onions and fry on a medium heat till
  brown. Add the ginger paste and garlic paste. Fry for 1 minute.
• Add the marinated chicken and the remaining ingredients. Mix well.
  Cover with a lid and simmer for 40 minutes. Serve hot.

Southern Chicken Curry

Serves 4

Ingredients

1 tsp ginger paste

1 tsp garlic paste

2 green chillies, finely chopped

1 tsp lemon juice

Salt to taste

1kg/2¼lb chicken, chopped into 10 pieces

3 tbsp refined vegetable oil

2.5cm/1in cinnamon

3 green cardamom pods

3 cloves

1 star anise

2 bay leaves

3 large onions, finely chopped

½ tsp chilli powder

½ tsp turmeric

1 tbsp ground coriander

250ml/8fl oz coconut milk

For the seasoning:

½ tsp mustard seeds

8 curry leaves

3 whole dry red chillies

Method

- Mix the ginger paste, garlic paste, green chillies, lemon juice and salt together. Marinate the chicken with this mixture for 30 minutes.
- Heat half the oil in a saucepan. Add the cinnamon, cardamom, cloves, star anise and bay leaves. Let them splutter for 30 seconds.
- Add the onions and fry them on a medium heat till they turn brown.
- Add the marinated chicken, chilli powder, turmeric and ground coriander. Mix well and cover with a lid. Cook on a low heat for 20 minutes.
- Add the coconut milk. Mix well and cook for 10 more minutes, stirring frequently. Set aside.
- Heat the remaining oil in a small saucepan. Add the seasoning ingredients. Let them splutter for 30 seconds.
- Pour this seasoning in the chicken curry. Mix well and serve hot.

Chicken Stew in Coconut Milk

Serves 4

Ingredients

2 tbsp refined vegetable oil

2 onions, chopped into 8 pieces each

1 tsp ginger paste

1 tsp garlic paste

3 green chillies, slit lengthways

2 tbsp garam masala

8 chicken drumsticks

750ml/1¼ pints coconut milk

200g/7oz frozen mixed vegetables

Salt to taste

2 tsp rice flour, dissolved in
    120ml/4fl oz water

Method

- Heat the oil in a saucepan. Add the onions, ginger paste, garlic paste, green chillies and garam masala. Fry for 5 minutes, stirring constantly.
- Add the drumsticks and coconut milk. Mix well. Simmer for 20 minutes.
- Add the vegetables and salt. Mix well and cook for 15 minutes.
- Add the rice flour mixture. Simmer for 5-10 minutes and serve hot.

Chandi Tikka

(Fried Chicken Pieces coated with Oatmeal)

Serves 4

Ingredients

1 tbsp lemon juice

1 tsp ginger paste

1 tsp garlic paste

75g/2½oz Cheddar cheese

200g/7oz yoghurt

¾ tsp ground white pepper

1 tsp black cumin seeds

Salt to taste

4 chicken breasts

1 egg, whisked

45g/1½oz oatmeal

Method

- Mix together all the ingredients, except the chicken breasts, egg and oatmeal. Marinate the chicken with this mixture for 3-4 hours.
- Dip the marinated chicken breasts in the egg, coat with the oatmeal and grill for an hour, turning occasionally. Serve hot.

Tandoori Chicken

Serves 4

Ingredients

1 tbsp lemon juice
2 tsp ginger paste
2 tsp garlic paste
2 green chillies, finely grated
1 tbsp coriander leaves, ground
1 tsp chilli powder

1 tbsp garam masala
1 tbsp ground raw papaya
½ tsp orange food colour
1½ tbsp refined vegetable oil
Salt to taste
1kg/2¼lb whole chicken

Method

• Mix together all the ingredients, except the chicken. Make incisions on the chicken and marinate it with this mixture for 6-8 hours.
• Roast the chicken in an oven at 200°C (400°F, Gas Mark 6) for 40 minutes. Serve hot.

Murgh Lajawab
(Chicken cooked with Rich Indian Spices)

Serves 4

Ingredients

1kg/2¼lb chicken, chopped into 8 pieces
1 tsp ginger paste
1 tsp garlic paste
4 tbsp ghee
2 tsp poppy seeds, ground
1 tsp melon seeds*, ground
6 almonds

3 green cardamom pods
¼ tsp ground nutmeg
1 tsp garam masala
2 pieces mace
Salt to taste
750ml/1¼ pints milk
6 strands saffron

Method

• Marinate the chicken with the ginger paste and garlic paste for an hour.
• Heat the ghee in a saucepan and fry the marinated chicken for 10 minutes on a medium heat.
• Add all the remaining ingredients except the milk and saffron. Mix well, cover with a lid and simmer for 20 minutes.
• Add the milk and saffron and simmer for 10 minutes. Serve hot.

Lahori Chicken
(North-West Frontier-style Chicken)

Serves 4

Ingredients

50g/1¾oz yoghurt

1 tsp ginger paste

1 tsp garlic paste

1 tsp chilli powder

½ tsp turmeric

1kg/2¼lb chicken, chopped into 12 pieces

4 tbsp refined vegetable oil

2 large onions, finely chopped

1 tsp sesame seeds, ground

1 tsp poppy seeds, ground

10 cashew nuts, ground

2 large green peppers, deseeded and finely chopped

500ml/16fl oz coconut milk

Salt to taste

Method
- Mix together the yoghurt, ginger paste, garlic paste, chilli powder and turmeric. Marinate the chicken with this mixture for 1 hour.
- Heat the oil in a saucepan. Fry the onions on a low heat till brown.
- Add the marinated chicken. Fry for 7-8 minutes. Add all the remaining ingredients and cook for 30 minutes, stirring occasionally. Serve hot.

Chicken Liver

Serves 4

Ingredients

3 tbsp refined vegetable oil

2 large onions, finely sliced

5 garlic cloves, minced

8 chicken livers

1 tsp ground black pepper

1 tsp lemon juice

Salt to taste

Method
- Heat the oil in a saucepan. Add the onions and garlic. Fry on a medium heat for 3-4 minutes.
- Add all the remaining ingredients. Fry for 15-20 minutes, stirring occasionally. Serve hot.

Balti Chicken

Serves 4

Ingredients

4 tbsp ghee

1 tsp turmeric

1 tbsp mustard seeds

1 tbsp cumin seeds

8 garlic cloves, finely chopped

2.5cm/1in root ginger, finely chopped

3 small onions, finely chopped

7 green chillies

750g/1lb 10oz chicken breast, chopped

1 tbsp ground coriander

1 tbsp single cream

1 tsp garam masala

Salt to taste

Method

- Heat the ghee in a saucepan. Add the turmeric, mustard seeds and cumin seeds. Let them splutter for 30 seconds. Add the garlic, ginger, onions and green chillies and fry on a medium heat for 2-3 minutes.
- Add all the remaining ingredients. Cook on a low heat for 30 minutes, stirring occasionally. Serve hot.

Tangy Chicken

Serves 4

Ingredients

8 chicken drumsticks

2 tsp green chilli sauce

2 tbsp refined vegetable oil

2 large onions, finely sliced

10 garlic cloves, finely chopped

Salt to taste

Pinch of sugar

2 tsp malt vinegar

Method

- Marinate the chicken with the chilli sauce for 30 minutes.
- Heat the oil in a saucepan. Add the onions and fry on a medium heat till translucent.
- Add the garlic, marinated chicken and salt. Mix well and cook on a low heat for 30 minutes, stirring occasionally.
- Add the sugar and vinegar. Mix thoroughly and serve hot.

Chicken Dilruba

(Chicken in Rich Gravy)

Serves 4

Ingredients

5 tbsp refined vegetable oil

20 almonds, ground

20 cashew nuts, ground

2 small onions, ground

5cm/2in root ginger, grated

1kg/2¼lb chicken, chopped into 8 pieces

200g/7oz yoghurt

240ml/6fl oz milk

1 tsp garam masala

½ tsp turmeric

1 tsp chilli powder

Salt to taste

1 pinch saffron, soaked in 1 tbsp milk

2 tbsp coriander leaves, chopped

Method

- Heat the oil in a saucepan. Add the almonds, cashew nuts, onions and ginger. Fry on a medium heat for 3 minutes.
- Add the chicken and yoghurt. Mix well and cook on a medium heat for 20 minutes.
- Add the milk, garam masala, turmeric, chilli powder and salt. Mix well. Cover with a lid and cook on a low heat for 20 minutes.
- Garnish with the saffron and coriander leaves. Serve hot.

Fried Chicken Wings

Serves 4

Ingredients

¼ tsp turmeric

1 tsp garam masala

1 tsp chaat masala*

Salt to taste

1 egg, whisked

Refined vegetable oil for deep frying

12 chicken wings

Method

- Mix together the turmeric, garam masala, chaat masala, salt and egg to make a smooth batter.
- Heat the oil in a frying pan. Dip the chicken wings in the batter and deep fry on a medium heat till golden brown.
- Drain on absorbent paper and serve hot.

Murgh Mussalam
(Stuffed Chicken)

Serves 6

Ingredients

2 tbsp ghee

2 large onions, grated

4 black cardamom pods, ground

1 tsp poppy seeds

50g/1¾oz desiccated coconut

1 tsp mace

1kg/2¼lb chicken

4-5 tbsp besan*

2-3 bay leaves

6-7 green cardamom pods

3 tsp garlic paste

200g/7oz yoghurt

Salt to taste

Method

• Heat ½ tbsp ghee in a saucepan. Add the onions and fry till brown.

• Add the cardamom, poppy seeds, coconut and mace. Fry for 3 minutes.

• Stuff the chicken with this mixture and sew up the opening. Set aside.

• Heat the remaining ghee in a saucepan. Add all the remaining ingredients and the chicken. Simmer for 1½ hours, stirring occasionally. Serve hot.

Chicken Delight

Serves 4

Ingredients

4 tbsp refined vegetable oil

5cm/2in ground cinnamon

1 tbsp cardamom powder

8 ground cloves

½ tsp grated nutmeg

2 large onions, ground

10 garlic cloves, crushed

2.5cm/1in root ginger, grated

Salt to taste

1kg/2¼lb chicken, chopped into 8 pieces

200g/7oz yoghurt

300g/10oz tomato purée

Method

• Heat the oil in a saucepan. Add the cinnamon, cardamom, cloves, nutmeg, onions, garlic and ginger. Fry on a medium heat for 5 minutes.

• Add the salt, chicken, yoghurt and tomato purée. Mix well and simmer for 40 minutes, stirring frequently. Serve hot.

Salli Chicken

(Chicken with Potato Crisps)

Serves 4

Ingredients

Salt to taste	2 large onions, finely chopped
1 tsp ginger paste	1 tsp sugar
1 tsp garlic paste	4 tomatoes, puréed
1kg/2¼lb chicken, chopped	1 tsp turmeric
3 tbsp refined vegetable oil	250g/9oz plain salted potato crisps

Method
- Mix together the salt, ginger paste and garlic paste. Marinate the chicken with this mixture for 1 hour. Set aside.
- Heat the oil in a saucepan. Fry the onions on a low heat till brown.
- Add the marinated chicken and the sugar, tomato purée and turmeric. Cover with a lid and simmer for 40 minutes, stirring frequently.
- Sprinkle the potato crisps on top and serve hot.

Fried Chicken Tikka

Serves 4

Ingredients

1kg/2¼lb boneless chicken, chopped	2 bay leaves
1 litre/1¾ pints milk	250g/9oz Basmati rice
1 tsp saffron	4 tsp fennel seeds
8 green cardamom pods	Salt to taste
5 cloves	150g/5½oz yoghurt
2.5cm/1in cinnamon	Refined vegetable oil for deep-frying

Method
- Mix the chicken with the milk, saffron, cardamom, cloves, cinnamon and bay leaves. Cook in a saucepan on a low heat for 50 minutes. Set aside.
- Grind the rice with the fennel seeds, salt and enough water to form a fine paste. Add this paste to the yoghurt and whisk thoroughly.
- Heat the oil in a frying pan. Dip the chicken pieces in the yoghurt mixture and fry on a medium heat till golden brown. Serve hot.

Chicken Seekh

Serves 4

Ingredients

500g/1lb 2oz chicken, minced
10 garlic cloves, ground
5cm/2in root ginger, julienned

2 green chillies, finely chopped
½ tsp black cumin seeds
Salt to taste

Method

- Mix the mince with all the ingredients and knead into a smooth dough. Divide this mixture into 8 equal portions.
- Skewer and grill for 10 minutes.
- Serve hot with mint chutney (see page 15).

Nadan Kozhikari
(Chicken with Fennel and Coconut Milk)

Serves 4

Ingredients

½ tsp turmeric
2 tsp ginger paste
Salt to taste
1kg/2¼lb chicken, chopped into 8 pieces
1 tbsp coriander seeds
3 red chillies
1 tsp fennel seeds

1 tsp mustard seeds
3 large onions
3 tbsp refined vegetable oil
750ml/1¼ pints coconut milk
250ml/8fl oz water
10 curry leaves

Method

- Mix the turmeric, ginger paste and salt for 1 hour. Marinate the chicken with this mixture for 1 hour.
- Dry roast (see cooking techniques) the coriander seeds, red chillies, fennel seeds and mustard seeds. Mix with the onions and grind to a smooth paste.
- Heat the oil in a saucepan. Add the onion paste and fry on a low heat for 7 minutes. Add the marinated chicken, coconut milk and water. Simmer for 40 minutes. Serve garnished with the curry leaves.

Mum's Chicken

Serves 4

Ingredients

3 tbsp refined vegetable oil

5cm/2in cinnamon

2 green cardamom pods

4 cloves

4 large onions, finely chopped

2.5cm/1in root ginger, grated

8 garlic cloves, crushed

3 large tomatoes, finely chopped

2 tsp ground coriander

1 tsp turmeric

Salt to taste

1kg/2¼lb chicken, chopped into 12 pieces

500ml/16fl oz water

Method

• Heat the oil in a saucepan. Add the cinnamon, cardamom and cloves. Let them splutter for 15 seconds.

• Add the onions, ginger and garlic. Fry on a medium heat for 2 minutes.

• Add the remaining ingredients, except the water. Fry for 5 minutes.

• Pour in the water. Mix well and simmer for 40 minutes. Serve hot.

Methi Chicken

(Chicken cooked with Fenugreek Leaves)

Serves 4

Ingredients

1 tsp ginger paste

2 tsp garlic paste

2 tsp ground coriander

½ tsp ground cloves

Juice of 1 lemon

1kg/2¼lb chicken, chopped into 8 pieces

4 tsp butter

1 tsp dry ginger powder

2 tbsp dried fenugreek leaves

50g/1¾oz coriander leaves, chopped

10g/¼oz mint leaves, finely chopped

Salt to taste

Method

• Mix the ginger paste, garlic paste, ground coriander, cloves and half the lemon juice. Marinate the chicken with this mixture for 2 hours.

• Bake in an oven at 200°C (400°F, Gas Mark 6) for 50 minutes. Set aside.

• Heat the butter in a saucepan. Add the roasted chicken and all the remaining ingredients. Toss well. Cook for 5-6 minutes and serve hot.

Spicy Chicken Drumsticks

Serves 4

Ingredients
8-10 chicken drumsticks, pricked all over
  with a fork
2 eggs, whisked
100g/3½oz semolina
Refined vegetable oil for deep-frying

For the spice mixture:
6 red chillies
6 garlic cloves
2.5cm/1in root ginger
1 tbsp coriander leaves, chopped
6 cloves
15 black peppercorns
Salt to taste
4 tbsp malt vinegar

Method
- Grind the ingredients for the spice mixture to a smooth paste. Marinate the drumsticks with this paste for an hour.
- Heat the oil in a frying pan. Dip the drumsticks in the egg, roll in the semolina and fry on a medium heat till golden brown. Serve hot.

Dieter's Chicken Curry

Serves 4

Ingredients
1 tsp ginger paste
1 tsp garlic paste
200g/7oz yoghurt
1 tsp chilli powder
½ tsp turmeric
2 tomatoes, finely chopped
1 tsp ground coriander

1 tsp ground cumin
1 tsp dried fenugreek leaves, crushed
2 tsp garam masala
1 tsp mango pickle
Salt to taste
750g/1lb 10oz chicken, chopped

Method
- Mix together all the ingredients, except the chicken. Marinate the chicken with this mixture for 3 hours.
- Cook the mixture in an earthenware pot or a saucepan on a low heat for 40 minutes. Add water if required. Serve hot.

Heavenly Chicken

Serves 4

Ingredients

4 tbsp refined vegetable oil
1kg/2¼lb chicken, chopped into 8 pieces
Salt to taste
1 tsp pepper
1 tsp turmeric
6 spring onions, finely chopped
250ml/8fl oz water

For the spice mixture:

1½ tsp ginger paste
1½ tsp garlic paste
3 green peppers, deseeded and sliced
2 green chillies
½ fresh coconut, grated
2 tomatoes, finely chopped

Method
• Grind together the spice mixture ingredients into a smooth paste.
• Heat the oil in a saucepan. Add the paste and fry on a low heat for 7 minutes. Add the remaining ingredients, except the water. Fry for 5 minutes. Add the water. Mix well and simmer for 40 minutes. Serve hot.

Chicken Rizala

Serves 4

Ingredients

6 tbsp refined vegetable oil
2 large onions, sliced lengthways
1 tsp ginger paste
1 tsp garlic paste
2 tbsp poppy seeds, ground
1 tbsp ground coriander
2 large green peppers, julienned
360ml/12fl oz water

1kg/2¼lb chicken, chopped into 8 pieces
6 green cardamom pods
5 cloves
200g/7oz yoghurt
1 tsp garam masala
Juice of 1 lemon
Salt to taste

Method
• Heat the oil in a saucepan. Add the onions, ginger paste, garlic paste, poppy seeds and ground coriander. Fry on a low heat for 2 minutes.
• Add all the remaining ingredients and mix well. Cover with a lid and simmer for 40 minutes, stirring occasionally. Serve hot.

Chicken Surprise

Serves 4

Ingredients

150g/5½oz coriander leaves, chopped
10 garlic cloves
2.5cm/1in root ginger
1 tsp garam masala
1 tbsp tamarind paste
2 tsp cumin seeds

1 tsp turmeric
4 tbsp water
Salt to taste
1kg/2¼lb chicken, chopped into 8 pieces
Refined vegetable oil for deep-frying
2 eggs, whisked

Method
- Grind all the ingredients, except the chicken, oil and eggs, into a smooth paste. Marinate the chicken with this paste for 2 hours.
- Heat the oil in a frying pan. Dip each chicken piece in the eggs and deep fry on a medium heat till brown. Serve hot.

Cheesy Chicken

Serves 4

Ingredients

12 chicken drumsticks
4 tbsp butter
1 tsp ginger paste
1 tsp garlic paste
2 large onions, finely chopped
1 tsp garam masala
Salt to taste
200g/7oz yoghurt

For the marinade:

1 tsp ginger paste
1 tsp garlic paste
1 tbsp lemon juice
¼ tsp garam masala
4 tbsp single cream
4 tbsp Cheddar cheese, grated
Salt to taste

Method
- Pierce the drumsticks all over with a fork. Mix together all the marinade ingredients. Marinate the drumsticks with this mixture for 8-10 hours.
- Heat the butter in a saucepan. Add the ginger paste and garlic paste. Fry on a medium heat for 1-2 minutes. Add all the remaining ingredients, except the yoghurt. Fry for 5 minutes.
- Add the drumsticks and the yoghurt. Simmer for 40 minutes. Serve hot.

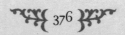

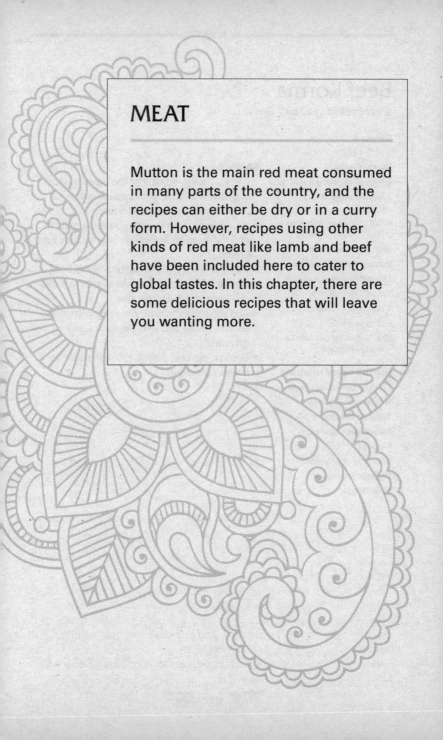

MEAT

Mutton is the main red meat consumed in many parts of the country, and the recipes can either be dry or in a curry form. However, recipes using other kinds of red meat like lamb and beef have been included here to cater to global tastes. In this chapter, there are some delicious recipes that will leave you wanting more.

Beef Korma

(Beef cooked in a Spicy Gravy)

Serves 4

Ingredients

4 tbsp refined vegetable oil

2 large onions, finely chopped

675g/1½lb beef, chopped into 2.5cm/1in pieces

360ml/12fl oz water

½ tsp ground cinnamon

120ml/4fl oz single cream

125g/4½oz yoghurt

1 tsp garam masala

Salt to taste

10g/¼oz coriander leaves, finely chopped

For the spice mixture:

1½ tbsp coriander seeds

¾ tbsp cumin seeds

3 green cardamom pods

4 black peppercorns

6 cloves

2.5cm/1in root ginger

10 garlic cloves

15 almonds

Method

- Mix all the ingredients of the spice mixture together and grind with enough water to form a smooth paste. Set aside.
- Heat the oil in a saucepan. Add the onions and fry them on a medium heat till they turn brown.
- Add the spice mixture paste and the beef. Fry for 2-3 minutes. Add the water. Mix well and simmer for 45 minutes.
- Add the ground cinnamon, cream, yoghurt, garam masala and salt. Stir thoroughly for 3-4 minutes.
- Garnish the beef korma with the coriander leaves. Serve hot.

Dhal Kheema
(Mince with Lentils)

Serves 4

Ingredients

675g/1½lb lamb, minced
1 tsp ginger paste
1 tsp garlic paste
3 large onions,
  finely chopped
360ml/12fl oz water
Salt to taste
600g/1lb 5oz chana dhal*,
  soaked in 250ml/8fl oz
  water for 30 minutes
½ tsp tamarind paste
60ml/2fl oz refined
  vegetable oil
4 cloves
2.5cm/1in cinnamon
2 green cardamom pods
4 black peppercorns
10g/¼oz coriander leaves,
  finely chopped

For the spice mixture:

2 tsp coriander seeds
3 red chillies
½ tsp turmeric
¼ tsp cumin seeds
25g/scant 1oz fresh
  coconut, grated
1 tsp poppy seeds

Method

- Dry roast (see cooking techniques) all the ingredients of the spice mixture together. Grind this mixture with enough water to form a smooth paste. Set aside.
- Mix the minced lamb with the ginger paste, garlic paste, half the onions, the remaining water and the salt. Cook in a saucepan on a medium heat for 40 minutes.
- Add the chana dhal along with the water in which it was soaked. Mix well. Simmer for 10 minutes.
- Add the spice mixture paste and the tamarind paste. Cover with a lid and simmer for 10 minutes, stirring occasionally. Set aside.
- Heat the oil in a frying pan. Add the remaining onions and fry them on a medium heat till they turn brown.
- Add the cloves, cinnamon, cardamom and peppercorns. Fry for a minute.
- Remove from the heat and pour this directly over the mince-dhal mixture. Stir thoroughly for a minute.
- Garnish the dhal kheema with the coriander leaves. Serve hot.

Pork Curry

Serves 4

Ingredients

500g/1lb 2oz pork, chopped
   into 2.5cm/1in pieces
1 tbsp malt vinegar
6 curry leaves
2.5cm/1in cinnamon
3 cloves
500ml/16fl oz water
Salt to taste
2 large potatoes, diced
3 tbsp refined vegetable oil
1 tsp garam masala

For the spice mixture:

1 tbsp coriander seeds
1 tsp cumin seeds
6 black peppercorns
½ tsp turmeric
4 red chillies
2 large onions, finely
   chopped
2.5cm/1in root ginger,
   sliced
10 garlic cloves, sliced
½ tsp tamarind paste

Method

- Mix all the ingredients for the spice mixture together. Grind with enough water to form a smooth paste. Set aside.
- Mix the pork with the vinegar, curry leaves, cinnamon, cloves, water and the salt. Cook this mixture in a saucepan on a medium heat for 40 minutes.
- Add the potatoes. Mix well and simmer for 10 minutes. Set aside.
- Heat the oil in a saucepan. Add the spice mixture paste and fry it on a medium heat for 3-4 minutes.
- Add the pork mixture and the garam masala. Mix well. Cover with a lid and simmer for 10 minutes, stirring occasionally.
- Serve hot.

Shikampoore Kebab

(Lamb Kebab)

Serves 4

Ingredients

3 large onions

8 garlic cloves

2.5cm/1in root ginger

6 dry red chillies

4 tbsp ghee plus extra for frying

1 tsp turmeric

1 tsp ground coriander

½ tsp ground cumin

10 almonds, ground

10 pistachios, ground

1 tsp garam masala

Pinch of ground cinnamon

1 tbsp ground cloves

1 tbsp ground green cardamom

2 tbsp coconut milk

Salt to taste

1 tbsp besan*

750g/1lb 10oz lamb, minced

200g/7oz Greek yoghurt

1 tbsp mint leaves, finely chopped

Method

- Mix together the onions, garlic, ginger and chillies.
- Grind this mixture with enough water to form a smooth paste.
- Heat the ghee in a saucepan. Add this paste and fry it on a medium heat for 1-2 minutes.
- Add the turmeric, ground coriander and ground cumin. Fry for a minute.
- Add the ground almonds, ground pistachios, garam masala, ground cinnamon, ground cloves and cardamom. Continue to fry for 2-3 minutes.
- Add the coconut milk and salt. Mix well. Stir for 5 minutes.
- Add the besan and the mince. Mix well. Simmer for 30 minutes, stirring occasionally. Remove from the heat and set aside to cool for 10 minutes.
- Once the mince mixture is cool, divide it into 8 balls and flatten each into a cutlet. Set aside.
- Whisk the yoghurt thoroughly with the mint leaves. Place a large spoonful of this mixture in the centre of each flattened cutlet. Seal like a pouch, roll into a ball and flatten again.
- Heat the ghee in a frying pan. Add the cutlets and deep fry them on a medium heat till golden brown. Serve hot.

Special Mutton

Serves 4

Ingredients
5 tbsp ghee
4 large onions, sliced
2 tomatoes, sliced
675g/1½lb mutton,
  chopped into 3.5cm/1½in
  pieces
1 litre/1¾ pints water
Salt to taste

For the spice mixture:
10 garlic cloves
3 green chillies
3.5cm/1½in root ginger
4 cloves
2.5cm/1in cinnamon
1 tbsp poppy seeds
1 tsp black cumin seeds
1 tsp cumin seeds
2 green cardamom pods
2 tbsp coriander seeds
7 peppercorns
5 dry red chillies
1 tsp turmeric
1 tbsp chana dhal*
25g/scant 1oz mint leaves
25g/scant 1oz coriander
  leaves
100g/3½oz fresh coconut,
  grated

Method
- Mix all the spice mixture ingredients together and grind with enough water to form a smooth paste. Set aside.
- Heat the ghee in a saucepan. Add the onions and fry them on a medium heat till they turn brown.
- Add the spice mixture paste. Fry for 3-4 minutes, stirring occasionally.
- Add the tomatoes and mutton. Fry for 8-10 minutes. Add the water and salt. Mix well, cover with a lid and simmer for 45 minutes, stirring occasionally. Serve hot.

Green Masala Chops

Serves 4

Ingredients

750g/1lb 10oz mutton chops

Salt to taste

360ml/12fl oz refined vegetable oil

3 large potatoes, sliced

5cm/2in cinnamon

2 green cardamom pods

4 cloves

3 tomatoes, finely chopped

¼ tsp turmeric

120ml/4fl oz vinegar

250ml/8fl oz water

For the spice mixture:

3 large onions

2.5cm/1in root ginger

10-12 garlic cloves

¼ tsp cumin seeds

6 green chillies, slit lengthways

1 tsp coriander seeds

1 tsp cumin seeds

50g/1¾oz coriander leaves, finely chopped

Method

- Marinate the mutton with the salt for an hour.
- Mix all the spice mixture ingredients together. Grind with enough water to form a smooth paste. Set aside.
- Heat half the oil in a frying pan. Add the potatoes and fry them on a medium heat till they turn golden brown. Drain and set aside.
- Heat the remaining oil in a saucepan. Add the cinnamon, cardamom and cloves. Let them splutter for 20 seconds.
- Add the spice mixture paste. Fry it on a medium heat for 3-4 minutes.
- Add the tomatoes and turmeric. Continue to fry for 1-2 minutes.
- Add the vinegar and the marinated mutton. Fry for 6-7 minutes.
- Add the water and mix well. Cover with a lid and simmer for 45 minutes, stirring occasionally.
- Add the fried potatoes. Cook for 5 minutes, stirring continuously. Serve hot.

Layered Kebab

Serves 4

Ingredients

120ml/4fl oz refined vegetable oil
100g/3½oz breadcrumbs

250ml/8fl oz water
2 tbsp besan*

For the white layer:

450g/1lb goat's cheese, drained
1 large potato, boiled
½ tsp salt
½ tsp ground black pepper
½ tsp chilli powder
Juice of half a lemon
50g/1¾oz coriander leaves, chopped

For the green layer:

200g/7oz spinach
2 tbsp mung dhal*
1 large onion, finely chopped
2.5cm/1in root ginger
4 cloves
¼ tsp turmeric
1 tsp garam masala
Salt to taste

For the orange layer:

1 egg, whisked
1 large onion, finely chopped
1 tbsp lemon juice
¼ tsp orange food colouring

For the meat layer:

500g/1lb 2oz meat, minced
150g/5½oz mung dhal*, soaked for 1 hour
5cm/2in root ginger
6 garlic cloves
6 cloves
1 tbsp ground cumin
1 tbsp chilli powder
10 black peppercorns
600ml/1 pint water

Method

- Mix and knead the white layer ingredients with some salt. Set aside.
- Mix together all the green layer ingredients, except the besan. Cook in a saucepan on a low heat for 45 minutes. Mash with the besan and set aside.
- Mix all the ingredients for the orange layer with some salt. Set aside.
- For the meat layer, mix all the ingredients with some salt and cook in a saucepan on a medium heat for 40 minutes. Cool and mash.
- Divide each layer mixture into 8 portions. Roll into balls and pat lightly to form cutlets. Place 1 cutlet of each layer over the other, so you have eight 4-layer patties. Press lightly into oblong-shaped kebabs.
- Heat the oil in a frying pan. Roll the kebabs in the breadcrumbs and deep fry them on a medium heat till they turn golden brown. Serve hot.

Barrah Champ
(Roasted Lamb Chops)

Serves 4

Ingredients

1 tsp ginger paste
1 tsp garlic paste
3 tbsp malt vinegar
675g/1½lb lamb chops
400g/14oz Greek yoghurt
1 tsp turmeric
4 green chillies, finely chopped
½ tsp chilli powder

1 tsp ground coriander
1 tsp ground cumin
1 tsp ground cinnamon
¾ tsp ground cloves
Salt to taste
1 tbsp chaat masala*

Method

- Mix the ginger paste and garlic paste with the vinegar. Marinate the lamb with this mixture for 2 hours.
- Mix together all the remaining ingredients, except the chaat masala. Marinate the lamb chops with this mixture for 4 hours.
- Skewer the chops and roast in an oven at 200°C (400°F, Gas Mark 6) for 40 minutes.
- Garnish with the chaat masala and serve hot.

Lamb Pickle

Serves 4

Ingredients

10 red dry chillies

10 garlic cloves

3.5cm/1½in root ginger

Salt to taste

750ml/1¼ pints water

2 tbsp yoghurt

675g/1½lb lamb, chopped into 2.5cm/1in pieces

250ml/8fl oz refined vegetable oil

1½ tsp turmeric

1 tbsp coriander seeds

10 black peppercorns

3 black cardamom pods

4 cloves

3 bay leaves

1 tsp grated mace

¼ tsp grated nutmeg

1 tsp cumin seeds

½ tsp mustard seeds

100g/3½oz desiccated coconut

½ tsp asafoetida

Juice of 1 lemon

Method

- Mix together the red chillies, garlic, ginger and salt together. Grind with enough water to form a smooth paste.
- Mix this paste with the yoghurt. Marinate the meat with this mixture for 1 hour.
- Heat half the oil in a saucepan. Add the turmeric, coriander seeds, peppercorns, cardamom, cloves, bay leaves, mace, nutmeg, cumin seeds, mustards seeds and coconut. Fry on a medium heat for 2-3 minutes.
- Grind the mixture with enough water to form a thick paste.
- Add the remaining oil in a saucepan. Add the asafoetida. Let it splutter for 10 seconds.
- Add the ground turmeric-coriander seeds paste. Fry on a medium heat for 3-4 minutes.
- Add the marinated lamb and the remaining water. Mix well. Cover with a lid and simmer for 45 minutes. Set aside to cool.
- Add the lemon juice and mix thoroughly. Store the lamb pickle in an airtight container.

NOTE: *This can be stored for a week.*

Goan Lamb Curry

Serves 4

Ingredients
240ml/6fl oz refined
  vegetable oil
4 large onions,
  finely chopped
1 tsp turmeric
4 tomatoes, puréed
675g/1½lb lamb, chopped
  into 2.5cm/1in pieces
4 large potatoes, diced
600ml/1 pint coconut milk
120ml/4fl oz water
Salt to taste

For the spice mixture:
4 green cardamom pods
5cm/2in cinnamon
6 black peppercorns
1 tsp cumin seeds
2 cloves
6 red chillies
1 star anise
50g/1¾oz coriander leaves,
  finely chopped
3 green chillies
1 tsp ginger paste
1 tsp garlic paste

Method
- To prepare the spice mixture, dry roast (see cooking techniques) the cardamom, cinnamon, peppercorns, cumin seeds, cloves, red chillies and star anise for 3-4 minutes.
- Grind this mixture with the remaining spice mixture ingredients and enough water to form a smooth paste. Set aside.
- Heat the oil in a saucepan. Add the onions and fry them on a medium heat till they turn translucent.
- Add the turmeric and tomato purée. Fry for 2 minutes.
- Add the spice mixture paste. Continue to fry for 4-5 minutes.
- Add the lamb and potatoes. Fry for 5-6 minutes.
- Add the coconut milk, water and salt. Mix well. Cover with a lid and cook the mixture on a low heat for 45 minutes, stirring occasionally. Serve hot.

Bagara Meat

(Meat cooked in Rich Indian Gravy)

Serves 4

Ingredients

120ml/4fl oz refined
   vegetable oil

3 red chillies

1 tsp cumin seeds

10 curry leaves

2 large onions

½ tsp turmeric

1 tsp chilli powder

1 tsp ground coriander

1 tsp tamarind paste

1 tsp garam masala

500g/1lb 2oz mutton, diced

Salt to taste

500ml/16fl oz water

For the spice mixture:

2 tbsp sesame seeds

2 tbsp fresh coconut,
   grated

2 tbsp peanuts

2.5cm/1in root ginger

8 garlic cloves

Method

- Mix the ingredients for the spice mixture together. Grind this mixture with enough water to form a smooth paste. Set aside.
- Heat the oil in a saucepan. Add the red chillies, cumin seeds and curry leaves. Let them splutter for 15 seconds.
- Add the onions and the spice mixture paste. Fry on a medium heat for 4-5 minutes.
- Add the remaining ingredients, except the water. Fry for 5-6 minutes.
- Add the water. Mix well. Cover with a lid and simmer for 45 minutes. Serve hot.

Liver in Coconut Milk

Serves 4

Ingredients

750g/1lb 10oz liver, chopped into 2.5cm/1in pieces

½ tsp turmeric

Salt to taste

500ml/16fl oz water

5 tbsp refined vegetable oil

3 large onions, finely chopped

1 tbsp ginger, finely chopped

1 tbsp garlic cloves, finely chopped

6 green chillies, slit lengthways

3 large potatoes, chopped into 2.5cm/1in pieces

1 tbsp malt vinegar

500ml/16fl oz coconut milk

For the spice mixture:

3 dry red chillies

2.5cm/1in cinnamon

4 green cardamom pods

1 tsp cumin seeds

8 black peppercorns

Method

- Mix the liver with the turmeric, salt and water. Cook in a saucepan on a medium heat for 40 minutes. Set aside.
- Mix all the spice mixture ingredients together and grind with enough water to form a smooth paste. Set aside.
- Heat the oil in a saucepan. Add the onions and fry them on a medium heat till they turn translucent.
- Add the ginger, garlic and green chillies. Fry for 2 minutes.
- Add the spice mixture paste. Continue to fry for 1-2 minutes.
- Add the liver mixture, potatoes, vinegar and the coconut milk. Stir thoroughly for 2 minutes. Cover with a lid and simmer for 15 minutes, stirring occasionally. Serve hot.

Lamb Masala with Yoghurt

Serves 4

Ingredients

200g/7oz yoghurt

Salt to taste

675g/1½lb lamb, chopped into 2.5cm/1in pieces

4 tbsp refined vegetable oil

3 large onions, finely chopped

3 carrots, diced

3 tomatoes, finely chopped

120ml/4fl oz water

For the spice mixture:

25g/scant 1oz coriander leaves, finely chopped

¼ tsp turmeric

2.5cm/1in root ginger

2 green chillies

8 garlic cloves

4 cardamom pods

4 cloves

5cm/2in cinnamon

3 curry leaves

¾ tsp turmeric

2 tsp ground coriander

1 tsp chilli powder

½ tsp tamarind paste

Method

- Mix all the spice mixture ingredients together. Grind with enough water to form a smooth paste.
- Mix the paste thoroughly with the yoghurt and salt. Marinate the lamb with this mixture for 1 hour.
- Heat the oil in a saucepan. Add the onions and fry them on a medium heat till they turn translucent.
- Add the carrots and tomatoes and fry for 3-4 minutes.
- Add the marinated lamb and the water. Mix well. Cover with a lid and simmer for 45 minutes, stirring occasionally. Serve hot.

Korma in Khada Masala

(Spicy Lamb in Thick Gravy)

Serves 4

Ingredients

75g/2½oz ghee

3 black cardamom pods

6 cloves

2 bay leaves

½ tsp cumin seeds

2 large onions, sliced

3 dry red chillies

2.5cm/1in root ginger, finely chopped

20 garlic cloves

5 green chillies, slit lengthways

675g/1½lb mutton, diced

½ tsp chilli powder

2 tsp ground coriander

6-8 shallots, peeled

200g/7oz canned peas

750 ml/1¼fl oz water

Pinch of saffron, dissolved in 2 tbsp warm water

Salt to taste

1 tsp lemon juice

200g/7oz yoghurt

1 tbsp coriander leaves, finely chopped

4 hard-boiled eggs, halved

Method

* Heat the ghee in a saucepan. Add the cardamom, cloves, bay leaves and cumin seeds. Let them splutter for 30 seconds.
* Add the onions and fry them on a medium heat till they turn brown.
* Add the dry red chillies, ginger, garlic and green chillies. Fry for a minute.
* Add the mutton. Fry for 5-6 minutes.
* Add the chilli powder, ground coriander, shallots and peas. Continue to fry for 3-4 minutes.
* Add the water, saffron mixture, salt and lemon juice. Stir thoroughly for 2-3 minutes. Cover with a lid and simmer for 20 minutes.
* Uncover the pan and add the yoghurt. Mix well. Cover again and continue to simmer for 20-25 minutes, stirring occasionally.
* Garnish with the coriander leaves and eggs. Serve hot.

Lamb & Kidney Curry

Serves 4

Ingredients

5 tbsp refined vegetable oil plus extra for deep frying

4 large potatoes, chopped into long strips

3 large onions, finely chopped

3 large tomatoes, finely chopped

¼ tsp turmeric

1 tsp chilli powder

2 tsp ground coriander

1 tsp ground cumin

25 cashew nuts, coarsely crushed

4 kidneys, diced

500g/1lb 2oz lamb, chopped into 5cm/2in pieces

Juice of 1 lemon

1 tsp ground black pepper

Salt to taste

500ml/16fl oz water

4 hard-boiled eggs, quartered

10g/¼oz coriander leaves, finely chopped

For the spice mixture:

1½ tsp ginger paste

1½ tsp garlic paste

4-5 green chillies

4 cardamom pods

6 cloves

1 tsp black cumin

1½ tbsp malt vinegar

Method

- Mix all the ingredients for the spice mixture together and grind with enough water to form a smooth paste. Set aside.
- Heat the oil for deep frying in a frying pan. Add the potatoes and deep fry on a medium heat for 3-4 minutes. Drain and set aside.
- Heat 5 tbsp oil in a saucepan. Add the onions and fry them on a medium heat till they turn translucent.
- Add the spice mixture paste. Fry for 2-3 minutes, stirring frequently.
- Add the tomatoes, turmeric, chilli powder, ground coriander and ground cumin. Continue to fry for 2-3 minutes.
- Add the cashew nuts, kidneys and the lamb. Fry for 6-7 minutes.
- Add the lemon juice, pepper, salt and water. Mix well. Cover with a lid and simmer for 45 minutes, stirring occasionally.
- Garnish with the eggs and coriander leaves. Serve hot.

Gosht Gulfaam

(Mutton with Goat's Cheese)

Serves 4

Ingredients

675g/1½lb boneless mutton

300g/10oz goat's cheese, drained

200g/7oz khoya*

150g/5½oz mixed dry fruit, finely chopped

6 green chillies, finely chopped

25g/scant 1 oz coriander leaves, finely chopped

2 hard-boiled eggs

For the sauce:

¾ tbsp refined vegetable oil

3 large onions, finely chopped

5cm/2in root ginger, finely chopped

10 garlic cloves, finely chopped

3 tomatoes, finely chopped

1 tsp chilli powder

120ml/4fl oz lamb stock

Salt to taste

Method

- Pat the mutton flat till it resembles a steak.
- Mix the goat's cheese, khoya, dry fruits, green chillies and coriander leaves together. Knead this mixture to a soft dough:
- Spread the dough out over the flattened mutton and place the eggs in the centre.
- Roll the mutton tightly so that the dough and eggs remain inside. Wrap in foil and bake in an oven at 180°C (350°F, Gas Mark 4) for 1 hour. Set aside.
- To prepare the sauce, heat the oil in a saucepan. Add the onions and fry on a medium heat till they turn translucent.
- Add the ginger and garlic. Fry for a minute.
- Add the tomatoes and chilli powder. Continue to fry for 2 minutes, stirring frequently.
- Add the stock and salt. Mix well. Simmer for 10 minutes, stirring occasionally. Set aside.
- Slice the baked meat roll and arrange the slices in a serving dish. Pour the sauce over them and serve hot.

Lamb Do Pyaaza
(Lamb with Onions)

Serves 4

Ingredients

120ml/4fl oz refined vegetable oil

1 tsp turmeric

3 bay leaves

4 cloves

5cm/2in cinnamon

6 dry red chillies

4 green cardamom pods

6 large onions, 2 chopped, 4 sliced

3 tbsp ginger paste

3 tbsp garlic paste

2 tomatoes, finely chopped

8 shallots, halved

2 tsp garam masala

2 tsp ground coriander

4 tsp ground cumin

1½ tsp grated mace

½ grated nutmeg

2 tsp ground black pepper

Salt to taste

675g/1½lb lamb, diced

250ml/8fl oz water

10g/¼oz coriander leaves, finely chopped

2.5cm/1in root ginger, julienned

Method

- Heat the oil in a saucepan. Add the turmeric, bay leaves, cloves, cinnamon, red chillies and cardamom. Let them splutter for 30 seconds.
- Add the chopped onions. Fry them on a medium heat till they turn translucent.
- Add the ginger paste and garlic paste. Fry for a minute.
- Add the tomatoes, shallots, garam masala, ground coriander, ground cumin, mace, nutmeg, pepper and salt. Continue to fry for 2-3 minutes.
- Add the lamb and the sliced onions. Mix well and fry for 6-7 minutes.
- Add the water and stir for a minute. Cover with a lid and simmer for 30 minutes, stirring occasionally.
- Garnish with the coriander leaves and the ginger. Serve hot.

Spicy Lamb in Yoghurt & Saffron

Serves 4

Ingredients

5 tbsp ghee

1 tsp ginger paste

1 tsp garlic paste

675g/1½lb boneless lamb, chopped into 3.5cm/1½in pieces

Salt to taste

750ml/1¼ pints water

4 large onions, sliced

1 tsp chilli powder

1 tsp garam masala

1 tbsp brown sugar, dissolved in 2 tbsp water

3 green chillies, slit lengthways

30g/1oz ground almonds

400g/14oz Greek yoghurt, whisked

10g/¼oz coriander leaves, finely chopped

½ tsp saffron, dissolved in 2 tbsp of milk

Method

- Heat half the ghee in a saucepan. Add the ginger paste and garlic paste. Fry on a medium heat for 1-2 minutes.
- Add the lamb and salt. Fry for 5-6 minutes.
- Add the water and mix well. Cover with a lid and simmer for 40 minutes, stirring occasionally. Set aside.
- Heat the remaining ghee in another saucepan. Add the onions and fry them on a medium heat till they turn translucent.
- Add the chilli powder, garam masala, sugar water, green chillies and ground almonds. Continue to fry for a minute.
- Add the yoghurt and mix well. Cook the mixture for 6-7 minutes, stirring well.
- Add this mixture to the lamb mixture. Mix well. Cover with a lid and simmer for 5 minutes, stirring occasionally.
- Garnish with the coriander leaves and saffron. Serve hot.

Lamb with Vegetables

Serves 4

Ingredients

675g/1½lb lamb, chopped
   into 2.5cm/1in pieces

Salt to taste

½ tsp ground black pepper

5 tbsp refined vegetable oil

2 bay leaves

4 green cardamom pods

4 cloves

2.5cm/1in cinnamon

2 large onions,
   finely chopped

1 tsp turmeric

1 tbsp ground cumin

1 tsp chilli powder

1 tsp ginger paste

1 tsp garlic paste

2 tomatoes,
   finely chopped

200g/7oz peas

1 tsp fenugreek seeds

200g/7oz cauliflower
   florets

500ml/16fl oz water

200g/7oz yoghurt

10g/¼oz coriander leaves,
   finely chopped

Method

- Marinate the lamb with the salt and pepper for 30 minutes.
- Heat the oil in a saucepan. Add the bay leaves, cardamom, cloves and cinnamon. Let them splutter for 30 seconds.
- Add the onions, turmeric, ground cumin, chilli powder, ginger paste and garlic paste. Fry them on a medium heat for 1-2 minutes.
- Add the marinated lamb and fry for 6-7 minutes, stirring occasionally.
- Add the tomatoes, peas, fenugreek seeds and cauliflower florets. Sauté for 3-4 minutes.
- Add the water and mix well. Cover with a lid and simmer for 20 minutes.
- Uncover the pan and add the yoghurt. Stir thoroughly for a minute, cover again and simmer for 30 minutes, stirring occasionally.
- Garnish with the coriander leaves. Serve hot.

Beef Curry with Potatoes

Serves 4

Ingredients

6 black peppercorns

3 cloves

2 black cardamom pods

2.5cm/1in cinnamon

1 tsp cumin seeds

4 tbsp refined vegetable oil

3 large onions,
   finely chopped

¼ tsp turmeric

1 tsp chilli powder

1 tsp ginger paste

1 tsp garlic paste

750g/1lb 10oz beef, minced

2 tomatoes,
   finely chopped

3 large potatoes, diced

½ tsp garam masala

1 tbsp lemon juice

Salt to taste

1 litre/1¾ pints water

1 tbsp coriander leaves,
   finely chopped

Method

- Grind the peppercorns, cloves, cardamom, cinnamon and cumin seeds to a fine powder. Set aside.
- Heat the oil in a saucepan. Add the onions and fry them on a medium heat till they turn brown.
- Add the ground peppercorns-cloves powder, turmeric, chilli powder, ginger paste and garlic paste. Fry for a minute.
- Add the beef mince and sauté for 5-6 minutes.
- Add the tomatoes, potatoes and garam masala. Mix well and cook for 5-6 minutes.
- Add the lemon juice, salt and water. Cover with a lid and simmer for 45 minutes, stirring occasionally.
- Garnish with the coriander leaves. Serve hot.

Spicy Lamb Masala

Serves 4

Ingredients

675g/1½lb lamb, diced

3 large onions, sliced

750ml/1¼ pints water

Salt to taste

4 tbsp refined vegetable oil

4 bay leaves

¼ tsp cumin seeds

¼ tsp mustard seeds

1 tsp ginger paste

1 tsp garlic paste

2 green chillies,
   finely chopped

1 tbsp peanuts, ground

1 tbsp chana dhal*, dry
   roasted (see cooking
   techniques) and ground

1 tsp chilli powder

¼ tsp turmeric

1 tsp garam masala

Juice of 1 lemon

50g/1¾oz coriander leaves,
   finely chopped

Method

- Mix the lamb with the onions, water and salt.
  Cook this mixture in a saucepan on a
  medium heat for 40 minutes. Set aside.
- Heat the oil in a saucepan. Add the bay
  leaves, cumin seeds and mustard seeds. Let
  them splutter for 30 seconds.
- Add the ginger paste, garlic paste and green
  chillies. Fry them on a medium heat for a
  minute, stirring continuously.
- Add the ground peanuts, chana dhal, chilli
  powder, turmeric and garam masala.
  Continue to fry for 1-2 minutes.
- Add the lamb mixture. Mix well. Cover with a
  lid and simmer for 45 minutes, stirring
  occasionally.
- Sprinkle the lemon juice and coriander leaves
  on top and serve hot.

Rogan Josh
(Kashmiri Lamb Curry)

Serves 4

Ingredients

Juice of 1 lemon

200g/7oz yoghurt

Salt to taste

750g/1lb 10oz lamb,
chopped into 2.5cm/1in
pieces

75g/2½oz ghee plus extra
for deep frying

2 large onions,
finely sliced

2.5cm/1in cinnamon

3 cloves

4 green cardamom pods

1 tsp ginger paste

1 tsp garlic paste

1 tsp ground coriander

1 tsp ground cumin

3 large tomatoes,
finely chopped

750ml/1¼ pints water

10g/¼oz coriander leaves,
finely chopped

Method

- Mix together the lemon juice, yoghurt and salt. Marinate the lamb with this mixture for an hour.
- Heat the ghee for deep frying in a frying pan. Add the onions and deep fry them on a medium heat till they turn golden brown. Drain and set aside.
- Heat the remaining ghee in a saucepan. Add the cinnamon, cloves and cardamom. Let them splutter for 15 seconds.
- Add the marinated lamb and fry on a medium heat for 6-7 minutes.
- Add the ginger paste and garlic paste. Sauté for 2 minutes.
- Add the ground coriander, ground cumin and tomatoes, mix well and cook for another minute.
- Add the water. Cover with a lid and simmer for 40 minutes, stirring occasionally.
- Garnish with the coriander leaves and the fried onions. Serve hot.

Grilled Pork Spare Ribs

Serves 4

Ingredients

6 green chillies

5cm/2in root ginger

15 garlic cloves

¼ small raw papaya, ground

200g/7oz yoghurt

2 tbsp refined vegetable oil

2 tbsp lemon juice

Salt to taste

750g/1lb 10oz spare ribs, chopped into
4 pieces

Method

- Grind the green chillies, ginger, garlic and raw papaya with enough water to form a thick paste.
- Mix this paste with the remaining ingredients, except the ribs. Marinate the ribs with this mixture for 4 hours.
- Grill the marinated ribs for 40 minutes, turning occasionally. Serve hot.

Beef with Coconut Milk

Serves 4

Ingredients

5 tbsp refined vegetable oil

675g/1½lb beef, chopped into
5cm/2in strips

3 large onions, finely chopped

8 garlic cloves, finely chopped

2.5cm/1in root ginger, finely chopped

2 green chillies, slit lengthways

2 tsp ground coriander

2 tsp ground cumin

2.5cm/1in cinnamon

Salt to taste

500ml/16fl oz water

500ml/16fl oz coconut milk

Method

- Heat 3 tbsp oil in a frying pan. Add the beef strips in batches and fry on a low heat for 12-15 minutes, turning occasionally. Drain and set aside.
- Heat the remaining oil in a saucepan. Add the onions, garlic, ginger and green chillies. Fry on a medium heat for 2-3 minutes.
- Add the fried beef strips, the ground coriander, ground cumin, cinnamon, salt and water. Simmer for 40 minutes.
- Add the coconut milk. Cook for 20 minutes, stirring frequently. Serve hot.

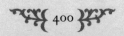

Pork Kebab

Serves 4

Ingredients

100ml/3½fl oz mustard oil

3 tbsp lemon juice

1 small onion, ground

2 tsp garlic paste

1 tsp mustard powder

1 tsp ground black pepper

Salt to taste

600g/1lb 5oz boneless pork, chopped
into 3.5cm/1½in pieces

Method

- Mix all the ingredients, except the pork, together. Marinate the pork with this mixture overnight.
- Skewer the marinated pork and grill for 30 minutes. Serve hot.

Beef Chilli Fry

Serves 4

Ingredients

750g/1lb 10oz beef, chopped into
2.5cm/1in pieces

6 black peppercorns

3 large onions, sliced

1 litre/1¾ pints water

Salt to taste

4 tbsp refined vegetable oil

2.5cm/1in root ginger, finely chopped

8 garlic cloves, finely chopped

4 green chillies

1 tbsp lemon juice

50g/1¾oz coriander leaves

Method

- Mix the beef with the peppercorns, 1 onion, water and salt. Cook this mixture in a saucepan on a medium heat for 40 minutes. Drain and set aside. Reserve the stock.
- Heat the oil in a saucepan. Fry the remaining onions on a medium heat till brown. Add the ginger, garlic and green chillies. Fry for 4-5 minutes.
- Add the lemon juice and the beef mixture. Continue to cook for 7-8 minutes. Add the reserved stock.
- Cover with a lid and simmer for 40 minutes, stirring occasionally. Add the coriander leaves and mix thoroughly. Serve hot.

Beef Scotch Eggs

Serves 4

Ingredients

500g/1lb 2oz beef, minced
Salt to taste
1 litre/1¾ pints water
3 tbsp besan*
1 egg, whisked

25g/scant 1oz mint leaves, finely
  chopped
25g/scant 1oz coriander leaves, chopped
8 hard-boiled eggs
Refined vegetable oil for deep frying

Method

* Mix the beef with the salt and water. Cook in a saucepan on a low heat
  for 45 minutes. Grind to a paste and mix with the besan, whisked egg,
  mint and coriander leaves. Wrap this mixture around the boiled eggs.
* Heat the oil in a frying pan. Add the wrapped eggs and fry them on a
  medium heat till they turn golden brown. Serve hot.

Malabar Style Dry Beef

Serves 4

Ingredients

675g/1½lb beef, diced
4 tbsp refined vegetable oil
3 large onions, sliced
1 tomato, finely chopped
100g/3½oz desiccated coconut
1 tsp chilli powder
1 tsp garam masala
1 tsp ground coriander
1 tsp ground cumin

Salt to taste
1 litre/1¾ pints water

For the spice mixture:

3.5cm/1½in root ginger
6 green chillies
1 tbsp ground coriander
10 curry leaves
1 tbsp garlic paste

Method

* Grind all the spice mixture ingredients together to form a thick paste.
  Marinate the beef with this mixture for an hour.
* Heat the oil in a saucepan. Fry the onions on a medium heat till brown.
  Add the meat and fry for 6-7 minutes.
* Add the remaining ingredients. Simmer for 40 minutes and serve hot.

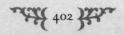

Moghlai Lamb Chops

Serves 4

Ingredients

5cm/2in root ginger
8 garlic cloves
6 dry red chillies
2 tsp lemon juice
Salt to taste

8 lamb chops, pounded and flattened
150g/5½oz ghee
2 large potatoes, sliced and deep fried
2 large onions

Method

- Grind the ginger, garlic and red chillies with the lemon juice, salt and enough water to form a smooth paste. Marinate the chops with this mixture for 4-5 hours.
- Heat the ghee in a frying pan. Add the marinated chops and fry on a medium heat for 8-10 minutes.
- Add the onions and the fried potatoes. Cook for 15 minutes. Serve hot.

Beef with Okra

Serves 4

Ingredients

4½ tbsp refined vegetable oil
200g/7oz okra
2 large onions, finely chopped
2.5cm/1in root ginger, finely chopped
4 garlic cloves, finely chopped
750g/1lb 10oz beef, chopped into
    2.5cm/1in pieces

4 dried red chillies
1 tbsp ground coriander
½ tbsp ground cumin
1 tsp garam masala
2 tomatoes, finely chopped
Salt to taste
1 litre/1¾ pints water

Method

- Heat 2 tbsp oil in a frying pan. Add the okra and fry on a medium heat till crisp and brown. Drain and set aside.
- Heat the remaining oil in a saucepan. Fry the onions on a medium heat till translucent. Add the ginger and garlic. Fry for a minute.
- Add the beef. Fry for 5-6 minutes. Add all the remaining ingredients and the okra. Simmer for 40 minutes, stirring frequently. Serve hot.

Beef Baffad
(Beef cooked with Coconut and Vinegar)

Serves 4

Ingredients

675g/1½lb beef, diced
Salt to taste
1 litre/1¾ pints water
1 tsp turmeric
½ tsp black peppercorns
½ tsp cumin seeds
5-6 cloves

2.5cm/1in cinnamon
12 garlic cloves, finely chopped
2.5cm/1in root ginger, finely chopped
100g/3½oz fresh coconut, grated
6 tbsp malt vinegar
5 tbsp refined vegetable oil
2 large onions, finely chopped

Method

- Mix the beef with the salt and water and cook in a saucepan on a medium heat for 45 minutes, stirring occasionally. Set aside.
- Grind together the remaining ingredients, except the oil and onions.
- Heat the oil in a saucepan. Add the ground mixture and the onions.
- Fry on a medium heat for 3-4 minutes. Add the beef mixture. Simmer for 20 minutes, stirring occasionally. Serve hot.

Badami Gosht
(Lamb with Almonds)

Serves 4

Ingredients

5 tbsp ghee
3 large onions, finely chopped
12 garlic cloves, crushed
3.5cm/1½in root ginger, finely chopped
750g/1lb 10oz lamb, chopped
75g/2½oz ground almonds

1 tbsp garam masala
Salt to taste
250g/9oz yoghurt
360ml/12fl oz coconut milk
500ml/16fl oz water

Method

- Heat the ghee in a saucepan. Add all the ingredients, except the yoghurt, coconut milk and water. Mix well. Sauté on a low heat for 10 minutes.
- Add the remaining ingredients. Simmer for 40 minutes. Serve hot.

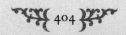

Indian Roast Beef

Serves 4

Ingredients

30g/1oz Cheddar cheese, grated
½ tsp ground black pepper
1 tsp chilli powder
10g/¼oz coriander leaves, chopped
10g/¼oz mint leaves, finely chopped
1 tsp ginger paste
1 tsp garlic paste

25g/scant 1oz breadcrumbs
1 egg, whisked
Salt to taste
675g/1½lb boneless beef, flattened and chopped into 8 pieces
5 tbsp refined vegetable oil
500ml/16fl oz water

Method

- Mix together all the ingredients, except the meat, oil and water.
- Apply this mixture on one side of each piece of beef. Roll each one up and tie with a string to seal.
- Heat the oil in a saucepan. Add the rolls and fry on a medium heat for 8 minutes. Add the water and mix well. Simmer for 30 minutes. Serve hot.

Khatta Pudina Chops

(Tangy Mint Chops)

Serves 4

Ingredients

1 tsp ground cumin
1 tbsp ground white pepper
2 tsp garam masala
5 tsp lemon juice
4 tbsp single cream
150g/5½oz yoghurt
250ml/8fl oz mint chutney (see page 15)
2 tbsp cornflour

¼ small papaya, ground
1 tbsp garlic paste
1 tbsp ginger paste
1 tsp ground fenugreek
Salt to taste
675g/1½lb lamb chops
Refined vegetable oil for basting

Method

- Mix together all the ingredients, except the lamb chops and oil. Marinate the chops with this mixture for 5 hours.
- Baste the chops with the oil and grill for 15 minutes. Serve hot.

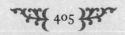

Indian Beef Steak

Serves 4

Ingredients

675g/1½lb beef, sliced for steaks

3.5cm/1½in root ginger, finely chopped

12 garlic cloves, finely chopped

2 tbsp ground black pepper

4 medium-sized onions,
  finely chopped

4 green chillies, finely chopped

3 tbsp vinegar

750ml/1¼ pints water

Salt to taste

5 tbsp refined vegetable oil plus
  extra for frying

Method

- Mix together all the ingredients, except the oil for frying, in a saucepan.
- Cover with a tight lid and simmer for 45 minutes, stirring occasionally.
- Heat the remaining oil in a frying pan. Add the cooked steaks mixture and sauté on a medium heat for 5-7 minutes, turning occasionally. Serve hot.

Lamb in Green Gravy

Serves 4

Ingredients

4 tbsp refined vegetable oil

3 large onions, grated

1½ tsp ginger paste

1 tsp garlic paste

675g/1½lb lamb, chopped into
  2.5cm/1in pieces

½ tsp ground cinnamon

½ tsp ground cloves

½ tsp ground black cardamom

6 dry red chillies, ground

2 tsp ground coriander

½ tsp ground cumin

10g/¼oz coriander leaves,
  finely chopped

4 tomatoes, puréed

Salt to taste

500ml/16fl oz water

Method

- Heat the oil in a saucepan. Add the onions, ginger paste and garlic paste. Fry on a medium heat for 2-3 minutes.
- Add all the remaining ingredients, except the water. Mix well and fry for 8-10 minutes. Add the water. Cover with a lid and simmer for 40 minutes, stirring occasionally. Serve hot.

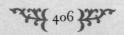

Easy Lamb Mince

Serves 4

Ingredients
3 tbsp mustard oil

2 large onions, finely chopped

7.5cm/3in root ginger, finely chopped

2 tsp coarsely ground black pepper

2 tsp ground cumin

Salt to taste

1 tsp turmeric

750g/1lb 10oz lamb mince

500ml/16fl oz water

Method
- Heat the oil in a saucepan. Add the onions, ginger, pepper, ground cumin, salt and turmeric. Fry for 2 minutes. Add the mince. Fry for 8-10 minutes.
- Add the water. Mix well and simmer for 30 minutes. Serve hot.

Pork Sorpotel
(Pork Liver cooked in Goan Gravy)

Serves 4

Ingredients
250ml/8fl oz malt vinegar

8 dry red chillies

10 black peppercorns

1 tsp cumin seeds

1 tbsp coriander seeds

1 tsp turmeric

500g/1lb 2oz pork

250g/9oz liver

Salt to taste

1 litre/1¾ pints water

120ml/4fl oz refined vegetable oil

5cm/2in root ginger, finely sliced

20 garlic cloves, finely chopped

6 green chillies, slit lengthways

Method
- Grind half the vinegar with the red chillies, peppercorns, cumin seeds, coriander seeds and turmeric to a fine paste. Set aside.
- Mix the pork and liver with the salt and water. Cook in a saucepan for 30 minutes. Drain and reserve the stock. Dice the pork and liver. Set aside.
- Heat the oil in a saucepan. Add the diced meat and fry on a low heat for 12 minutes. Add the paste and all the remaining ingredients. Mix well.
- Fry for 15 minutes. Add the stock. Simmer for 15 minutes. Serve hot.

Pickled Lamb

Serves 4

Ingredients

750g/1lb 10oz lamb, chopped into thin
   strips

Salt to taste

1 litre/1¾ pints water

6 tbsp refined vegetable oil

1 tsp turmeric

4 tbsp lemon juice

2 tbsp ground cumin, dry roasted (see
   cooking techniques)

4 tbsp ground sesame seeds

7.5cm/3in root ginger, finely chopped

12 garlic cloves, finely chopped

Method

- Mix the lamb with the salt and water, and cook in a saucepan on a medium heat for 40 minutes. Drain and set aside.
- Heat the oil in a frying pan. Add the lamb and deep fry on a medium heat for 10 minutes. Drain and mix with the remaining ingredients. Serve cold.

Haleem

(Mutton cooked Persian-style)

Serves 4

Ingredients

500g/1lb 2oz wheat, soaked for 2-3
   hours and drained

1.5 litres/2¾ pints water

Salt to taste

500g/1lb 2oz mutton, diced

4-5 tbsp ghee

3 large onions, sliced

1 tsp ginger paste

1 tsp garlic paste

1 tsp turmeric

1 tsp garam masala

Method

- Mix the wheat with 250ml/8fl oz water and some salt. Cook in a saucepan on a medium heat for 30 minutes. Mash well and set aside.
- Cook the mutton with the remaining water and salt in a saucepan for 45 minutes. Drain and grind to a fine paste. Reserve the stock.
- Heat the ghee. Fry the onions on a low heat till brown. Add the ginger paste, garlic paste, turmeric and ground meat. Fry for 8 minutes. Add the wheat, the stock and the garam masala. Cook for 20 minutes. Serve hot.

Green Masala Mutton Chops

Serves 4

Ingredients
675g/1½lb mutton chops
Salt to taste
1 tsp turmeric
500ml/16fl oz water
2 tbsp ground coriander
1 tsp ground cumin
1 tbsp ginger paste
1 tbsp garlic paste

100g/3½oz coriander leaves, ground
1 tsp lemon juice
1 tsp ground black pepper
1 tsp garam masala
60g/2oz plain white flour
Refined vegetable oil for frying
2 eggs, whisked
50g/1¾oz breadcrumbs

Method
* Mix the mutton with the salt, turmeric and water. Cook in a saucepan on a medium heat for 30 minutes. Drain and set aside.
* Mix the remaining ingredients, except the flour, oil, eggs and breadcrumbs.
* Coat the chops with this mixture and dust with the flour.
* Heat the oil in a frying pan. Dip the chops in the egg, roll in the breadcrumbs and shallow fry till golden brown. Flip and repeat. Serve hot.

Fenugreek Lamb Liver

Serves 4

Ingredients
4 tbsp refined vegetable oil
2 large onions, finely chopped
¾ tsp ginger paste
¾ tsp garlic paste
50g/1¾oz fenugreek leaves, chopped
600g/1lb 5oz lamb liver, diced

3 tomatoes, finely chopped
1 tsp garam masala
120ml/4fl oz hot water
1 tbsp lemon juice
Salt to taste

Method
* Heat the oil in a saucepan. Fry the onions on a medium heat till translucent. Add the ginger paste and garlic paste. Fry for 1-2 minutes.
* Add the fenugreek leaves and liver. Sauté for 5 minutes.
* Add the remaining ingredients. Simmer for 40 minutes and serve hot.

Hussaini Beef

(Beef cooked in North Indian-style Gravy)

Serves 4

Ingredients

4 tbsp refined vegetable oil
675g/1½lb beef, finely chopped
125g/4½oz yoghurt
Salt to taste
750ml/1¼ pints water

For the spice mixture:

4 large onions
8 garlic cloves
2.5cm/1in root ginger
2 tsp garam masala
1 tsp turmeric
2 tsp ground coriander
1 tsp ground cumin

Method
- Grind together the spice mixture ingredients to a thick paste.
- Heat the oil in a saucepan. Add the paste and fry it on a medium heat for 4-5 minutes. Add the beef. Mix well and fry for 8-10 minutes.
- Add the yoghurt, salt and water. Mix well. Cover with a lid and simmer for 40 minutes, stirring occasionally. Serve hot.

Methi Lamb

(Lamb with Fenugreek)

Serves 4

Ingredients

120ml/4fl oz refined vegetable oil
1 large onion, finely sliced
6 garlic cloves, finely chopped
600g/1lb 5oz lamb, diced
50g/1¾oz fresh fenugreek leaves, finely chopped
½ tsp turmeric
1 tsp ground coriander
125g/4½oz yoghurt
600ml/1 pint water
½ tsp ground green cardamom
Salt to taste

Method
- Heat the oil in a saucepan. Add the onion and garlic and fry on a medium heat for 4 minutes.
- Add the lamb. Fry for 7-8 minutes. Add the remaining ingredients. Mix well and simmer for 45 minutes. Serve hot.

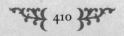

Beef Indad
(Beef cooked in East-Indian-style Gravy)

Serves 4

Ingredients
675g/1½lb beef, chopped
2.5cm/1in cinnamon
6 cloves
Salt to taste
1 litre/1¾ pints water
5 tbsp refined vegetable oil
3 large potatoes, sliced

For the spice mixture:
60ml/2fl oz malt vinegar
3 large onions
2.5cm/1in root ginger
8 garlic cloves
½ tsp turmeric
2 dry red chillies
2 tsp cumin seeds

Method
- Mix the beef with the cinnamon, cloves, salt and water. Cook in a saucepan on a medium heat for 45 minutes. Set aside.
- Grind the spice mixture ingredients to a thick paste.
- Heat the oil in a saucepan. Add the spice mixture paste and fry on a low heat for 5-6 minutes. Add the beef and the potatoes. Mix well. Simmer for 15 minutes and serve hot.

Lamb Casserole

Serves 4

Ingredients
3 tbsp refined vegetable oil
2 large onions, finely chopped
4 garlic cloves, finely chopped
500g/1lb 2oz lamb, minced
2 tsp ground cumin

6 tbsp tomato purée
150g/5½oz canned kidney beans
250ml/8fl oz meat stock
Ground black pepper to taste
Salt to taste

Method
- Heat the oil in a saucepan. Add the onions and garlic and fry on a medium heat for 2-3 minutes. Add the mince and sauté for 10 minutes. Add the remaining ingredients. Mix well and simmer for 30 minutes.
- Transfer to an ovenproof dish. Bake in an oven at 180°C (350°F, Gas Mark 4) for 25 minutes. Serve hot.

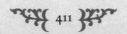

Cardamom-flavoured Lamb

Serves 4

Ingredients

Salt to taste
200g/7oz yoghurt
1½ tbsp ginger paste
2½ tsp garlic paste
2 tbsp ground green cardamom
675g/1½lb lamb, chopped into
  3.5cm/1½in pieces

6 tbsp ghee
6 cloves
7.5cm/3in cinnamon, coarsely ground
4 large onions, finely sliced
½ tsp saffron, soaked in 2 tbsp milk
1 litre/1¾ pints water
125g/4½oz roasted walnuts

Method

- Mix together the salt, yoghurt, ginger paste, garlic paste and cardamom. Marinate the meat with this mixture for 2 hours.
- Heat the ghee in a saucepan. Add the cloves and cinnamon. Let them splutter for 15 seconds.
- Add the onions. Fry for 3-4 minutes. Add the marinated meat, saffron and water. Mix well. Cover with a lid and simmer for 40 minutes.
- Serve hot, garnished with the walnuts.

Kheema
(Minced Beef)

Serves 4

Ingredients

5 tbsp refined vegetable oil
4 large onions, finely chopped
1 tsp ginger paste
1 tsp garlic paste
3 tomatoes, finely chopped

2 tsp garam masala
200g/7oz frozen peas
Salt to taste
675g/1½lb beef, minced
500ml/16fl oz water

Method

- Heat the oil in a saucepan. Add the onions and fry on a medium heat till brown. Add the ginger paste, garlic paste, tomatoes, garam masala, peas and salt. Mix well. Fry for 3-4 minutes.
- Add the beef and water. Mix well. Simmer for 40 minutes and serve hot.

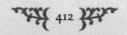

Spicy Pork Fry

Serves 4

Ingredients
675g/1½lb pork, diced
2 large onions, finely chopped
1 tsp refined vegetable oil
1 litre/1¾ pints water
Salt to taste

For the spice mixture:
250ml/8fl oz vinegar
2 large onions

1 tbsp ginger paste
1 tbsp garlic paste
1 tbsp ground black pepper
1 tbsp green chillies
1 tbsp turmeric
1 tbsp chilli powder
1 tbsp cloves
5cm/2in cinnamon
1 tbsp green cardamom pods

Method
- Grind the spice mixture ingredients to a thick paste.
- Mix with the remaining ingredients in a saucepan. Cover with a tight lid and simmer for 50 minutes. Serve hot.

Tandoori Raan
(Spicy Leg of Lamb cooked in a Tandoor)

Serves 4

Ingredients
675g/1½lb lamb leg
400g/14oz yoghurt
2 tbsp lemon juice
2 tsp ginger paste
2 tsp garlic paste
1 tsp ground cloves

1 tsp ground cinnamon
2 tsp chilli powder
1 tsp nutmeg, grated
Pinch of mace
Salt to taste
Refined vegetable oil for basting

Method
- Pierce the lamb all over with a fork.
- Mix the remaining ingredients thoroughly, except the oil. Marinate the lamb with this mixture for 4-6 hours.
- Roast the lamb in an oven at 180°C (350°F, Gas Mark 4) for 1½-2 hours, basting occasionally. Serve hot.

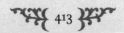

Talaa Lamb
(Fried Lamb)

Serves 4

Ingredients

675g/1½lb lamb, chopped into
   5cm/2in pieces
Salt to taste
1 litre/1¾ pints water
4 tbsp ghee
2 large onions, sliced

For the spice mixture:

8 dry chillies
1 tsp turmeric
1½ tbsp garam masala
2 tsp poppy seeds
3 large onions, finely chopped
1 tsp tamarind paste

Method

- Grind the spice mixture ingredients with water to make a thick paste.
- Mix this paste with the meat, salt and water. Cook in a saucepan on a medium heat for 40 minutes. Set aside.
- Heat the ghee in a saucepan. Add the onions and fry on a medium heat till brown. Add the meat mixture. Simmer for 6-7 minutes and serve hot.

Braised Tongue

Serves 4

Ingredients

900g/2lb beef tongue
Salt to taste
1 litre/1¾ pints water
1 tsp ghee
3 large onions, finely chopped
5cm/2in root ginger, julienned
4 tomatoes, finely chopped
125g/4½oz frozen peas
10g/¼oz mint leaves, finely chopped
1 tsp malt vinegar
1 tsp ground black pepper
½ tbsp garam masala

Method

- Place the tongue in a saucepan with the salt and water and cook on a medium heat for 45 minutes. Drain and cool for a while. Peel the skin and chop into strips. Set aside.
- Heat the ghee in a saucepan. Add the onions and ginger and fry on a medium heat for 2-3 minutes. Add the cooked tongue and all the remaining ingredients. Simmer for 20 minutes. Serve hot.

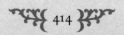

Fried Mutton Rolls

Serves 4

Ingredients

75g/2½oz Cheddar cheese, grated
½ tsp ground black pepper
1 tsp ginger paste
1 tsp garlic paste
3 eggs, whisked
50g/1¾oz coriander leaves, chopped

100g/3½oz breadcrumbs
Salt to taste
675g/1½lb boneless mutton, chopped into 10cm/4in pieces and flattened
4 tbsp ghee
250ml/8fl oz water

Method

* Mix together all the ingredients, except the meat, ghee and water. Apply the mixture on one side of the meat pieces. Roll each piece tightly and bind with a string.
* Heat the ghee in a frying pan. Add the mutton rolls and fry on a medium heat till golden brown. Add the water. Simmer for 15 minutes and serve hot.

Masala Liver Fry

Serves 4

Ingredients

4 tbsp refined vegetable oil
675g/1½lb lambs' liver, cut into 5cm/2in strips
2 tbsp ginger, julienned
15 garlic cloves, finely chopped
8 green chillies, slit lengthways

2 tsp ground cumin
1 tsp turmeric
125g/4½oz yoghurt
1 tsp ground black pepper
Salt to taste
50g/1¾oz coriander leaves, chopped
Juice of 1 lemon

Method

* Heat the oil in a saucepan. Add the liver strips and fry them on a medium heat for 10-12 minutes.
* Add the ginger, garlic, green chillies, cumin and turmeric. Fry for 3-4 minutes. Add the yoghurt, pepper and salt. Sauté for 6-7 minutes.
* Add the coriander leaves and lemon juice. Sauté on a low heat for 5-6 minutes. Serve hot.

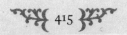

Spicy Beef Tongue

Serves 4

Ingredients

900g/2lb beef tongue	6 dry red chillies
Salt to taste	8 black peppercorns
1.5 litres/2¾ pints water	6 tbsp malt vinegar
2 tsp cumin seeds	3 tbsp refined vegetable oil
12 garlic cloves	2 large onions, finely chopped
5cm/2in cinnamon	3 tomatoes, finely chopped
4 cloves	1 tsp turmeric

Method

- Cook the tongue with the salt and 1.2 litres/2 pints water in a saucepan on a low heat for 45 minutes. Peel the skin. Dice the tongues and set aside.
- Grind the cumin seeds, garlic, cinnamon, cloves, dry red chillies and peppercorns with the vinegar to make a smooth paste. Set aside.
- Heat the oil in a saucepan. Fry the onions on a medium heat till translucent. Add the ground paste, diced tongue, tomatoes, turmeric and the remaining water. Simmer for 20 minutes and serve hot.

Lamb Pasandas

(Lamb Kebab in Yoghurt Gravy)

Serves 4

Ingredients

½ tbsp refined vegetable oil	2 tsp garam masala
3 large onions, sliced lengthways	Salt to taste
¼ small unripe papaya, ground	750g/1lb 10oz boneless lamb, chopped
200g/7oz yoghurt	into 5cm/2in pieces

Method

- Heat the oil in a saucepan. Fry the onions on a low heat till brown.
- Drain and grind the onions to a paste. Mix with the remaining ingredients, except the lamb. Marinate the lamb with this mixture for 5 hours.
- Arrange in a pie dish and bake in an oven at 180°C (350°F, Gas Mark 4) for 30 minutes. Serve hot.

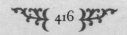

Lamb & Apple Curry

Serves 4

Ingredients

5 tbsp refined vegetable oil

4 large onions, sliced

4 large tomatoes, blanched (see cooking techniques)

½ tsp garlic paste

2 tsp ground coriander

2 tsp ground cumin

1 tsp chilli powder

30g/1oz cashew nuts, ground

750g/1lb 10oz boneless lamb, chopped into 2.5cm/1in pieces

200g/7oz yoghurt

1 tsp ground black pepper

Salt to taste

750ml/1¼ pints water

4 apples, chopped into 3.5cm/1½in pieces

120ml/4fl oz fresh single cream

Method

● Heat the oil in a frying pan. Fry the onions on a low heat till brown.

● Add the tomatoes, garlic paste, coriander and cumin. Fry for 5 minutes.

● Add the remaining ingredients, except the water, apples and cream. Mix well and sauté for 8-10 minutes.

● Pour in the water. Simmer for 40 minutes. Add the apples and stir for 10 minutes. Add the cream and stir for another 5 minutes. Serve hot.

Andhra-style Dry Mutton

Serves 4

Ingredients

675g/1½lb mutton, chopped

4 large onions, finely sliced

6 tomatoes, finely chopped

1½ tsp ginger paste

1½ tsp garlic paste

50g/1¾oz fresh coconut, grated

2½ tbsp garam masala

½ tsp ground black pepper

1 tsp turmeric

Salt to taste

500ml/16fl oz water

6 tbsp refined vegetable oil

Method

● Mix all the ingredients, except the oil, together. Cook in a saucepan on a medium heat for 40 minutes. Drain the meat and discard the stock.

● Heat the oil in another saucepan. Add the cooked meat and fry on a medium heat for 10 minutes. Serve hot.

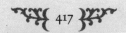

Simple Beef Curry

Serves 4

Ingredients

3 tbsp refined vegetable oil

2 large onions, finely chopped

750g/1lb 10oz beef, chopped into 2.5cm/1in pieces

1 tsp ginger paste

1 tsp garlic paste

1 tsp chilli powder

½ tsp turmeric

Salt to taste

300g/10oz yoghurt

1.2 litres/2 pints water

Method

* Heat the oil in a saucepan. Fry the onions on a low heat till brown.
* Add the remaining ingredients, except the yoghurt and water. Fry for 6-7 minutes. Add the yoghurt and water. Simmer for 40 minutes. Serve hot.

Gosht Korma

(Rich Mutton in Gravy)

Serves 4

Ingredients

3 tbsp poppy seeds

75g/2½oz cashew nuts

50g/1¾oz desiccated coconut

3 tbsp refined vegetable oil

1 large onion, finely sliced

2 tbsp ginger paste

2 tbsp garlic paste

675g/1½lb boneless mutton, diced

200g/7oz yoghurt

10g/¼oz coriander leaves, chopped

10g/¼oz mint leaves, chopped

½ tsp garam masala

Salt to taste

1 litre/1¾ pints water

Method

* Dry roast (see cooking techniques) the poppy seeds, cashew nuts and coconut. Grind with enough water to form a thick paste. Set aside.
* Heat the oil in a saucepan. Fry the onion, ginger paste and garlic paste on a medium heat for 1-2 minutes.
* Add the poppy seeds-cashew nuts paste and the remaining ingredients, except the water. Mix well and fry for 5-6 minutes.
* Add the water. Simmer for 40 minutes, stirring frequently. Serve hot.

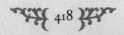

Erachi Chops
(Tender Mutton Chops)

Serves 4

Ingredients

750g/1lb 10oz mutton chops
Salt to taste
1 tsp turmeric
1 litre/1¾ pints water
2 tbsp refined vegetable oil
1 tsp ginger paste
1 tsp garlic paste

3 large onions, sliced
5 green chillies, slit lengthways
2 large tomatoes, finely chopped
½ tsp ground coriander
1 tbsp ground black pepper
1 tbsp lemon juice
2 tbsp coriander leaves, chopped

Method

- Marinate the mutton chops with the salt and turmeric for 2-3 hours.
- Cook the meat with the water on a low heat for 40 minutes. Set aside.
- Heat the oil in a saucepan. Add the ginger paste, garlic paste, onions and green chillies and fry them on a medium heat for 3-4 minutes.
- Add the tomatoes, ground coriander and pepper. Mix well. Fry for 5-6 minutes. Add the mutton and sauté for 10 minutes.
- Garnish with the lemon juice and coriander leaves. Serve hot.

Baked Mince

Serves 4

Ingredients

3 tbsp refined vegetable oil
2 large onions, finely chopped
6 garlic cloves, finely chopped
600g/1lb 5oz mutton, minced
2 tsp ground cumin

125g/4½oz tomato purée
600g/1lb 5oz canned kidney beans
500ml/16fl oz mutton stock
½ tsp ground black pepper
Salt to taste

Method

- Heat the oil in a saucepan. Add the onions and garlic. Fry on a low heat for 2-3 minutes. Add the remaining ingredients. Simmer for 30 minutes.
- Transfer to an ovenproof dish and bake in an oven at 200°C (400°F, Gas Mark 6) for 25 minutes. Serve hot.

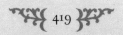

Kaleji Do Pyaaza
(Liver with Onions)

Serves 4

Ingredients

4 tbsp ghee
3 large onions, finely chopped
2.5cm/1in root ginger, finely chopped
10 garlic cloves, finely chopped
4 green chillies, slit lengthways
1 tsp turmeric

3 tomatoes, finely chopped
750g/1lb 10oz lambs' liver, diced
2 tsp garam masala
200g/7oz yoghurt
Salt to taste
250ml/8fl oz water

Method
- Heat the ghee in a saucepan. Add the onions, ginger, garlic, green chillies and turmeric and fry on a medium heat for 3-4 minutes. Add all the remaining ingredients, except the water. Mix well. Fry for 7-8 minutes.
- Add the water. Simmer for 30 minutes, stirring occasionally. Serve hot.

Lamb on the Bone

Serves 4

Ingredients

30g/1oz mint leaves, finely chopped
3 green chillies, finely chopped
12 garlic cloves, finely chopped
Juice of 1 lemon
675g/1½lb leg of lamb, chopped into 4 pieces
5 tbsp refined vegetable oil

Salt to taste
500ml/16fl oz water
1 large onion, finely chopped
4 large potatoes, diced
5 small aubergines, halved
3 tomatoes, finely chopped

Method
- Grind the mint leaves, green chillies and garlic with enough water to a form a smooth paste. Add the lemon juice and mix well.
- Marinate the meat with this mixture for 30 minutes.
- Heat the oil in a saucepan. Add the marinated meat and fry on a low heat for 8-10 minutes. Add the salt and water and simmer for 30 minutes.
- Add all the remaining ingredients. Simmer for 15 minutes and serve hot.

Beef Vindaloo
(Goan Beef Curry)

Serves 4

Ingredients

3 large onions, finely chopped
5cm/2in root ginger
10 garlic cloves
1 tbsp cumin seeds
½ tbsp ground coriander
2 tsp red chilli
½ tsp fenugreek seeds

½ tsp mustard seeds
60ml/2fl oz malt vinegar
Salt to taste
675g/1½lb boneless beef, chopped into 2.5cm/1in pieces
3 tbsp refined vegetable oil
1 litre/1¾ pints water

Method
- Grind together all the ingredients, except the meat, oil and water, to form a thick paste. Marinate the meat with this paste for 2 hours.
- Heat the oil in a saucepan. Add the marinated meat and sauté on a low heat for 7-8 minutes. Add the water. Simmer for 40 minutes, stirring occasionally. Serve hot.

Beef Curry

Serves 4

Ingredients

4 tbsp refined vegetable oil
3 large onions, grated
1½ tbsp ground cumin
1 tsp turmeric
1 tsp chilli powder
½ tbsp ground black pepper

4 medium-sized tomatoes, puréed
675g/1½lb lean beef, chopped into 2.5cm/1in pieces
Salt to taste
1½ tsp dry fenugreek leaves
250ml/8fl oz single cream

Method
- Heat the oil in a saucepan. Add the onions and fry them on a medium heat till they turn brown.
- Add the remaining ingredients, except the fenugreek leaves and cream.
- Mix well and simmer for 40 minutes. Add the fenugreek leaves and cream. Cook for 5 minutes and serve hot.

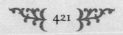

Mutton with Pumpkin

Serves 4

Ingredients

750g/1lb 10oz mutton, chopped

200g/7oz yoghurt

Salt to taste

2 large onions

2.5cm/1in root ginger

7 garlic cloves

5 tbsp ghee

¾ tsp turmeric

1 tsp garam masala

2 bay leaves

750ml/1¼ pints water

400g/14oz pumpkin, boiled and mashed

Method

- Marinate the mutton with the yoghurt and salt for 1 hour.
- Grind the onions, ginger and garlic with enough water to form a thick paste. Heat the ghee in a saucepan. Add the paste along with the turmeric and fry for 3-4 minutes.
- Add the garam masala, bay leaves and the mutton. Fry for 10 minutes.
- Add the water and pumpkin. Simmer for 40 minutes and serve hot.

Gushtaba
(Kashmiri-style Mutton)

Serves 4

Ingredients

675g/1½lb boneless mutton

6 black cardamom pods

Salt to taste

4 tbsp ghee

4 large onions, sliced into rings

600g/1lb 5oz yoghurt

1 tsp ground fennel seeds

1 tbsp ground cinnamon

1 tbsp ground cloves

1 tbsp mint leaves, crushed

Method

- Pound the mutton with the cardamom and salt till soft. Divide into 12 balls and set aside.
- Heat the ghee in a saucepan. Fry the onions on a low heat till brown. Add the yoghurt and simmer for 8-10 minutes, stirring continuously.
- Add the meat balls and all the remaining ingredients, except the mint leaves. Simmer for 40 minutes. Serve garnished with the mint leaves.

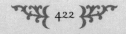

Mutton with Mixed Greens & Herbs

Serves 4

Ingredients

5 tbsp refined vegetable oil

3 large onions, finely chopped

750g/1lb 10oz mutton, diced

50g/1¾oz amaranth leaves*, finely chopped

100g/3½oz spinach leaves, finely chopped

50g/1¾oz fenugreek leaves, chopped

50g/1¾oz dill leaves, finely chopped

50g/1¾oz coriander leaves, chopped

1 tsp ginger paste

1 tsp garlic paste

3 green chillies, finely chopped

1 tsp turmeric

2 tsp ground coriander

1 tsp ground cumin

Salt to taste

1 litre/1¾ pints water

Method

- Heat the oil in a saucepan. Fry the onions on a medium heat till brown. Add the remaining ingredients, except the water. Sauté for 12 minutes.
- Add the water. Simmer for 40 minutes and serve hot.

Lemony Lamb

Serves 4

Ingredients

750g/1lb 10oz lamb, chopped into 2.5cm/1in pieces

2 tomatoes, finely chopped

4 green chillies, finely chopped

1 tsp ginger paste

1 tsp garlic paste

2 tsp garam masala

125g/4½oz yoghurt

500ml/16fl oz water

Salt to taste

1 tbsp refined vegetable oil

10 shallots

3 tbsp lemon juice

Method

- Mix the lamb with all the remaining ingredients, except the oil, shallots and lemon juice. Cook in a saucepan on a medium heat for 45 minutes. Set aside.
- Heat the oil in a saucepan. Fry the shallots on a low heat for 5 minutes.
- Mix with the lamb curry and sprinkle the lemon juice on top. Serve hot.

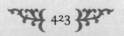

Lamb Pasanda with Almonds

(Lamb Pieces with Almonds in Yoghurt Gravy)

Serves 4

Ingredients

120ml/4fl oz refined vegetable oil

4 large onions, finely chopped

750g/1lb 10oz boneless lamb, chopped
  into 5cm/2in pieces

3 tomatoes, finely chopped

1 tsp ginger paste

1 tsp garlic paste

2 tsp ground cumin

1½ tsp garam masala

Salt to taste

200g/7oz Greek yoghurt

750ml/1¼ pints water

25 almonds, coarsely pounded

Method

• Heat the oil in a saucepan. Add the onions and fry on a low heat for 6 minutes. Add the lamb and fry for 8-10 minutes. Add the remaining ingredients, except the yoghurt, water and almonds. Sauté for 5-6 minutes.

• Add the yoghurt, water and half the almonds. Simmer for 40 minutes, stirring frequently. Serve sprinkled with the remaining almonds.

Pork Sausage Chilli Fry

Serves 4

Ingredients

2 tbsp oil

1 large onion, sliced

400g/14oz pork sausages

1 green pepper, julienned

1 potato, boiled and chopped

½ tsp ginger paste

½ tsp garlic paste

½ tsp chilli powder

¼ tsp turmeric

10g/¼oz coriander leaves, chopped

Salt to taste

4 tbsp water

Method

• Heat the oil in a saucepan. Add the onion and fry for a minute. Lower the heat and add all the other ingredients, except the water. Fry gently for 10-15 minutes until the sausages are cooked through.

• Add the water and cook on a low heat for 5 minutes. Serve hot.

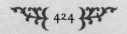

Mutton Shah Jahan
(Mutton cooked in Rich Moghlai Gravy)

Serves 4

Ingredients
5-6 tbsp ghee
4 large onions, sliced
675g/1½lb mutton, chopped
1 litre/1¾ pints water
Salt to taste
8-10 almonds, pounded

For the spice mixture:
8 garlic cloves
2.5cm/1in root ginger
2 tsp poppy seeds
50g/1¾oz coriander leaves, chopped
5cm/2in cinnamon
4 cloves

Method
- Grind the spice mixture ingredients to a paste. Set aside.
- Heat the ghee in a saucepan. Fry the onions on a low heat till brown.
- Add the spice mixture paste. Fry for 5-6 minutes. Add the mutton and sauté for 18-20 minutes. Add the water and salt. Simmer for 30 minutes.
- Garnish with the almonds and serve hot.

Gosht Chaamp Achari
(Pickled Lamb Chops)

Serves 4

Ingredients
1 tsp ginger paste
1 tsp garlic paste
2 tbsp besan*
2 tbsp yoghurt, whisked
1 small unripe papaya, peeled, deseeded and ground
½ tsp onion seeds
½ tsp fennel seeds
½ tsp ground black pepper
1 tbsp garam masala
Salt to taste
8 lamb chops
60ml/2fl oz mustard oil
½ tsp chaat masala*

Method
- Mix together all the ingredients, except the lamb chops, oil and chaat masala. Marinate the chops with this mixture for 3 hours.
- Baste generously with the oil and grill for 40 minutes. Sprinkle the chaat masala over the grilled chops and serve hot.

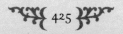

Kashmiri Mutton Chop

Serves 4

Ingredients

4 tbsp refined vegetable oil plus extra
   for deep frying

675g/1½lb mutton chops

2 tsp ginger paste

2 tsp garlic paste

6 green cardamom pods

1 tbsp garam masala

½ tsp saffron strands

250ml/8fl oz water

1 litre/1¾ pints milk

Salt to taste

250g/9oz plain white flour

3 eggs, whisked

Method

- Heat 4 tbsp oil in a saucepan. Add all the ingredients, except the flour and eggs. Simmer for 1 hour, stirring occasionally. Set aside.
- Heat the remaining oil in a frying pan. Roll the chops in the flour, dip them in the egg and deep fry on a low heat till golden brown. Serve hot.

Shahi Lamb Curry

(Meat cooked in Rich Moghlai Curry)

Serves 4

Ingredients

120ml/4fl oz refined vegetable oil

675g/1½lb lamb, chopped into
   2.5cm/1in pieces

2 tsp garam masala

1 tsp ginger paste

Salt to taste

360ml/12fl oz water

For the curry:

6 tbsp refined vegetable oil

1 tsp cumin seeds

¼ tsp asafoetida

2 bay leaves

250g/9oz besan*

1 tsp tamarind paste

1 tsp garlic paste

Method

- Heat the oil in a saucepan. Add the meat, garam masala and ginger paste. Fry for 8-10 minutes. Add the salt and water. Simmer for 40 minutes and set aside.
- For the curry, heat the oil. Fry the remaining curry ingredients for 4 minutes. Add the meat and simmer for 15 minutes. Serve hot.

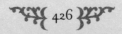

Tassa Kebab
(Lamb Kebab with Vegetables)

Serves 4

Ingredients
600g/1lb 5oz lamb, chopped
Salt to taste
½ tsp ground black pepper
1 tsp ginger paste
1 tsp garlic paste
3 green chillies, finely chopped
¼ unripe papaya, peeled and ground

6 tbsp refined vegetable oil
4 large onions, thickly sliced
4 large potatoes, thickly sliced
1 aubergine, thickly sliced
4 large tomatoes, thickly sliced
1 tbsp tamarind paste

Method
- Marinate the lamb with the salt, pepper, ginger paste, garlic paste, green chillies and ground papaya for 1 hour.
- Heat the oil in a saucepan. Arrange the onions in a layer over the oil followed by a layer each of the lamb, potatoes, aubergine and tomatoes.
- Spread the tamarind paste on top. Cover and cook on a low heat for 45 minutes. Serve hot.

Lamb Gular Kebab
(Lamb Kebab cooked with Dhal)

Serves 4

Ingredients
750g/1lb 10oz lamb, minced
225g/8oz mung dhal*
2 large onions, finely chopped
1 tsp ginger paste
2 litres/3½ pints water

50g/1¾oz yoghurt
½ tsp garam masala
2 tbsp mint leaves, finely chopped
Salt to taste
Ghee for deep frying

Method
- Mix the meat with all the ingredients, except the ghee. Cook in a saucepan on a low heat for 1 hour. Grind to a paste. Divide into 12 balls.
- Heat the ghee in a frying pan. Add the balls and deep fry on a low heat till golden brown. Serve hot.

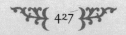

Achari Mutton
(Mutton Pieces cooked with Pickle)

Serves 4

Ingredients

120ml/4fl oz refined vegetable oil

3 large onions, finely chopped

750g/1lb 10oz mutton, chopped

1 tsp ginger paste

1 tsp garlic paste

4 green cardamom pods

2 bay leaves

Salt to taste

3 tomatoes, finely chopped

1 litre/1¾ pints water

3 tbsp hot mango pickle
  (see page 24)

Method

- Heat the oil in a saucepan. Fry the onions till brown. Add the remaining ingredients, except the tomatoes, water and pickle. Cook for 10 minutes.
- Add the tomatoes and water. Simmer for 40 minutes. Add the pickle. Mix well and simmer for 10 minutes, stirring frequently. Serve hot.

Mutton Xacutti
(Mutton cooked in Goan Gravy)

Serves 4

Ingredients

4 tbsp refined vegetable oil

1 large onion, finely sliced

675g/1½lb mutton, chopped

250ml/8fl oz coconut milk

250ml/8fl oz water

½ tsp tamarind paste

Salt to taste

1 tsp turmeric

For the spice mixture:

2 tbsp coriander leaves

1 tsp cumin seeds

100g/3½oz fresh coconut

2 large onions

1 tbsp garam masala

4 green cardamom pods

2.5cm/1in root ginger

6 garlic cloves

Method

- Grind together all the spice mixture ingredients to a paste. Set aside.
- Heat the oil in a saucepan. Fry the onion on a low heat till brown.
- Add the remaining ingredients and the spice mixture paste. Mix well and simmer for 40 minutes. Serve hot.

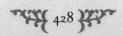

Liver Curry

Serves 4

Ingredients

750g/1lb 10oz liver, diced

Salt to taste

1 litre/1¾ pints water

500ml/16fl oz coconut milk

1 tsp ground fennel seeds

8 curry leaves

5cm/2in root ginger, finely chopped

10 garlic cloves, finely chopped

1 tsp turmeric

3 large onions, finely sliced

½ tsp ground cardamom

2 tbsp malt vinegar

5 tbsp ghee

Method

- Mix the liver with salt and half the water. Cook in a saucepan on a medium heat for 40 minutes. Drain the liver and discard the stock.
- Add the remaining ingredients, except the ghee, to the liver and cook in a saucepan on a medium heat for 10 minutes, stirring occasionally. Drain the liver mixture. Reserve the remaining stock in the saucepan.
- Heat the ghee in a frying pan. Fry the liver mixture on a low heat for 5 minutes. Add to the reserved stock. Simmer for 5 minutes. Serve hot.

Laziz Chops

(Lamb Chops in Yoghurt)

Serves 4

Ingredients

12 mutton chops

Salt to taste

1 litre/1¾ pints water

2 tbsp refined vegetable oil

3 large onions, finely chopped

4 cashew nuts, ground

200g/7oz yoghurt

1 tsp ground cumin

½ tsp dry ginger powder

2 tomatoes, finely sliced

2 green peppers, finely sliced

2.5cm/1in root ginger, julienned

Method

- Cook the chops with the salt and water on a low heat for 45 minutes.
- Heat the oil. Fry the onions on a low heat till brown. Add the remaining ingredients and the cooked chops. Cook for 20 minutes. Serve hot.

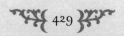

Kandahari Lamb
(Tender Lamb Curry)

Serves 4

Ingredients

675g/1½lb lamb, chopped into
   2.5cm/1in pieces

200g/7oz yoghurt

1 tbsp cumin seeds

Salt to taste

75g/2½oz ghee

4 large onions, finely chopped

1 tbsp garam masala

2.5cm/1in root ginger, finely chopped

3 green chillies, finely chopped

1 litre/1¾ pints water

¼ tsp saffron strands

250ml/8fl oz single cream

Method
- Marinate the meat with the yoghurt, cumin seeds and salt for an hour.
- Heat the ghee in a saucepan. Add the onions and garam masala and fry for 3 minutes. Add the ginger, chillies, the marinated meat and the water. Simmer for 40 minutes, stirring occasionally.
- Add the saffron and cream. Simmer for 5 minutes and serve hot.

Lamb Curry

Serves 4

Ingredients

4 tbsp refined vegetable oil

2 large onions, sliced

675g/1½lb shoulder of lamb, diced

1 tsp turmeric

2 tbsp dry mango powder*

1 tsp garam masala

360ml/12fl oz lamb stock

1 tbsp tomato purée

125g/4½oz Greek yoghurt

120ml/4fl oz water

Salt to taste

2 tbsp slivered almonds

Method
- Heat the oil in a saucepan. Fry the onions on a medium heat till translucent. Add the lamb. Sauté for 7-8 minutes. Add the turmeric, mango powder and garam masala. Sauté for 2-3 minutes.
- Add the remaining ingredients, except the almonds. Simmer for 45 minutes, stirring occasionally. Garnish with the almonds. Serve hot.

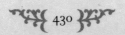

Stuffed Lamb Leg

Serves 4

Ingredients

675g/1½lb leg of lamb
400g/14oz yoghurt
2 tsp ginger paste
2 tsp garlic paste
3 green chillies, finely chopped

2 tsp garam masala
Salt to taste
100g/3½oz steamed rice (see page 519)
5 tbsp dark rum
150g/5½oz mixed dry fruits

Method

* Remove the bone from the lamb. Marinate the lamb with all the ingredients, except the rice, rum and dry fruits, for 3 hours.
* Mix the rice, rum and dry fruits. Spread this mixture on one side of the lamb, roll tightly and tie with a string. Roast in an oven at 200°C (400°F, Gas Mark 6) for an hour. Untie the string, slice the roll and serve hot.

Achar Gosht

(Spiced Mutton)

Serves 4

Ingredients

100ml/3½fl oz mustard oil
2 large onions, grated
1 tsp ginger paste
1 tsp garlic paste
500g/1lb 2oz boneless mutton, chopped
1 tsp turmeric
2 tsp ground coriander

600g/1lb 5oz yoghurt
Salt to taste
250ml/8fl oz water
1 tsp mustard seeds
1 tsp cumin seeds
1 tsp fenugreek seeds
1 tsp onion seeds

Method

* Heat 2 tbsp oil in a saucepan. Fry the onions on a low heat till brown. Add the ginger paste, garlic paste and meat. Fry for 5-6 minutes.
* Add the turmeric, coriander, yoghurt, salt and water. Mix well and simmer for 40 minutes, stirring occasionally. Set aside.
* Heat the remaining oil in a saucepan and add the remaining ingredients. Let them splutter for 20 seconds. Pour over the mutton and serve hot.

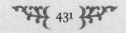

Lamb with Black Eyed Peas

Serves 4

Ingredients

500g/1lb 2oz lamb, chopped
600g/1lb 5oz canned black eyed peas
Salt to taste
1 litre/1¾ pints water
3 onions, finely chopped
4 tbsp refined vegetable oil
1 tsp ginger paste

1 tsp garlic paste
½ tsp turmeric
1 tsp ground coriander
1 tsp ground cumin
30g/1oz coriander leaves, chopped
2 tomatoes, finely chopped
1 tbsp malt vinegar

Method

- Mix the lamb and black eyed peas with the salt, water and half the onions. Cook in a saucepan on a medium heat for 45 minutes. Set aside.
- Heat the oil in a saucepan. Add the remaining onions. Fry on a low heat.
- When the onions turn brown, add the remaining ingredients, except the vinegar. Mix well. Fry for 4-5 minutes. Add the lamb mixture. Simmer for 10 minutes. Add the vinegar and simmer for 5 more minutes. Serve hot.

Masala Liver

Serves 4

Ingredients

2 tbsp refined vegetable oil
1 tsp cumin seeds
750g/1lb 10oz mutton liver, diced
Salt to taste
125g/4½oz yoghurt, whisked

For the spice mixture:

3 large onions
5cm/2in root ginger
6 garlic cloves
1 tbsp garam masala
2 green cardamom pods
1 tsp coriander seeds

Method

- Grind the spice mixture ingredients to a fine paste. Set aside.
- Heat the oil in a saucepan. Add the cumin seeds and the spice paste. Fry on a medium heat for 4-5 minutes. Add the liver and salt. Fry for 8-10 minutes. Add the yoghurt and mix well.
- Simmer for 20 minutes, stirring frequently. Serve hot.

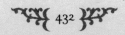

White Lamb

Serves 4

Ingredients

675g/1½lb lamb, chopped into
  2.5cm/1in pieces

400g/14oz yoghurt

3 large onions, finely chopped

10 garlic cloves, finely chopped

Salt to taste

For the spice mixture:

6 red chillies

1 tsp ground black pepper

2 tsp ground cumin

2 tsp poppy seeds

12 cashew nuts

Method

- Grind the spice mixture ingredients together finely. Mix with the remaining ingredients in a saucepan.
- Cover with a lid and simmer for 40 minutes. Serve hot.

Galouti Kebab
(Tender Kebab)

Serves 4

Ingredients

Refined vegetable oil for deep frying

2 large onions, finely sliced

675g/1½lb meat, minced

100g/3½oz unripe papaya, ground

125g/4½oz yoghurt

2 tbsp besan*

1 tsp chilli powder

2 tsp garam masala

1 tsp ground cardamom

1 tsp ginger paste

1 tsp garlic paste

4-6 saffron strands

Salt to taste

8 tbsp ghee

Method

- Heat the oil in a frying pan. Deep fry the onions on a medium heat till golden brown. Drain and grind with enough water to form a thick paste. Mix with the remaining ingredients, except the ghee. Set aside for 1 hour.
- Divide into walnut-sized balls and flatten slightly to form kebabs.
- Heat the ghee in a frying pan. Add the kebabs and shallow fry on a medium heat till golden brown. Flip and repeat. Serve hot.

Lamb Fry

Serves 4

Ingredients

675g/1½lb lamb, chopped into
  2.5cm/1in pieces
60ml/2fl oz malt vinegar
Salt to taste
750ml/1¼ pints water
1 tsp ginger paste
1 tsp garlic paste

Refined vegetable oil for deep frying
4 small potatoes, quartered
2 carrots, chopped into 2.5cm/1in pieces
2 large onions, roughly chopped
3 tomatoes, roughly chopped
2 eggs, whisked
50g/1¾oz breadcrumbs

Method

- Mix the meat with the vinegar, salt and water. Cook in a saucepan on a medium heat for 30 minutes. Add the ginger paste, garlic paste and dry red chillies. Simmer for 20 minutes. Set aside.
- Heat the oil in a frying pan. Add the potatoes and carrots and fry on a medium heat for 4-5 minutes. Drain and pierce alternately on a wooden skewer along with the meat, onions and tomatoes.
- Heat the oil in a frying pan. Dip the skewers in the egg, roll with the breadcrumbs and deep fry on a medium heat till golden. Serve hot.

Natkhat Mutton

(Spicy Mutton)

Serves 4

Ingredients

675g/1½lb mutton, diced
4 tbsp refined vegetable oil

For the marinade:
600g/1lb 5 oz tomato purée
2 tsp garlic paste

1 tsp ginger paste
3 tbsp Worcestershire sauce
3 large onions, grated
2 tbsp garam masala
Salt to taste

Method

- Mix together the marinade ingredients. Marinate the mutton with this overnight. Heat the oil. Cook the mutton for 45 minutes. Serve hot.

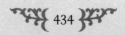

Meat Rolls

Serves 4

Ingredients

100g/3½oz breadcrumbs

200g/7oz leftover boneless chicken or mutton, finely minced

2 large potatoes, boiled and mashed

2 tbsp coriander leaves, chopped

Salt to taste

Refined vegetable oil for frying

1 egg, whisked

Method

- Mix half the breadcrumbs with the meat, potatoes, coriander leaves and salt. Divide into 8 portions and shape each into a finger-shaped roll.
- Heat the oil in a frying pan. Dip the rolls in the egg, roll in the remaining breadcrumbs and deep fry on a low heat till golden brown. Serve hot.

Anglo-Indian Pepper Steak

Serves 4

Ingredients

3 tsp ground black pepper

Salt to taste

1 tsp turmeric

3 tbsp refined vegetable oil

1 kg/1¾lb beef, sliced into 8 steaks

2 large onions, finely chopped

2 tomatoes, finely chopped

2 litres/3½ pints water

4 small potatoes, quartered

Method

- Mix the pepper, salt and turmeric with half the oil. Coat the steaks well with this mixture and leave in the refrigerator overnight.
- Heat the remaining oil in a saucepan. Add the onions and fry them on a medium heat till they turn brown.
- Add the tomatoes. Sauté for 2 minutes.
- Add the steaks. Continue to sauté for 5 minutes. Add the water, cover with a lid and simmer for 40 minutes.
- Add the potatoes and mix well. Simmer this mixture for 15 minutes. Serve hot.

Mutton in Green Gravy

Serves 4

Ingredients

500g/1lb 2oz mutton, diced

½ tsp ground coriander

½ tsp ginger paste

½ tsp garlic paste

2 tsp refined vegetable oil

1 large onion, finely chopped

50g/1¾oz spinach, finely chopped

30g/1oz coriander leaves, chopped

30g/1oz mint leaves, finely chopped

¼ tsp garam masala

Salt to taste

750ml/1¼ pints water

Method

- Marinate the meat with the ground coriander, half the ginger paste and half the garlic paste for 1 hour.
- Heat the oil in a saucepan. Add the onion and the remaining ginger paste and garlic paste. Fry on a medium heat for 1-2 minutes. Add the remaining ingredients, except the water. Sauté for 5 minutes.
- Add the marinated meat and water. Simmer for 45 minutes. Serve hot.

Crispy Fried Mutton Chops

Serves 4

Ingredients

12 mutton chops

125g/4½oz yoghurt

Salt to taste

4 tbsp refined vegetable oil plus extra for deep frying

2 large onions, finely chopped

1 tsp ginger paste

1 tsp garlic paste

2 tomatoes, finely chopped

3 eggs, whisked

60g/2oz breadcrumbs

Method

- Marinate the chops with the yoghurt and salt for 2 hours.
- Heat 4 tbsp oil in a saucepan. Add the onions, ginger paste and garlic paste. Fry on a low heat for 2-3 minutes. Add the tomatoes and the chops. Cook for 30 minutes, stirring occasionally.
- Heat the oil in a frying pan. Dip each chop in the egg, roll in the breadcrumbs and deep fry on a low heat till golden brown. Serve hot.

Mangsher Ghugni
(Lamb with Bengal Gram)

Serves 4

Ingredients

600g/1lb 5oz chana dhal*
Salt to taste
1 litre/1¾ pints water
500g/1lb 2oz boneless lamb, diced
4 tbsp ghee
2 large onions, finely chopped

2 tbsp garam masala
1 tbsp ground green cardamom
1½ tsp ground cumin
8 garlic cloves, crushed
2.5cm/1in root ginger, grated
2 bay leaves

Method

- Mix the chana dhal with some salt and half the water. Cook in a saucepan on a medium heat for 1 hour. Set aside.
- At the same time, cook the lamb in a saucepan with some salt and the remaining water on a medium heat for 40 minutes. Set aside.
- Heat the ghee in a saucepan. Fry the onions on a low heat till brown.
- Add the remaining ingredients. Mix well and fry for 2-3 minutes.
- Add the cooked dhal and meat. Simmer for 5 minutes and serve hot.

Peppers Stuffed with Beef Mince

Serves 4

Ingredients

1 tbsp refined vegetable oil
2 small onions, finely chopped
1 tsp ginger paste
1 tsp garlic paste
1 tsp ground cumin

1 tomato, finely chopped
Salt to taste
400g/14oz beef, minced
250ml/8fl oz water
8 large green peppers, hollowed

Method

- Heat the oil in a saucepan. Add the onions, ginger paste and garlic paste. Fry on a medium heat for 3 minutes. Add the remaining ingredients, except the peppers. Mix well. Simmer for 20 minutes, stirring frequently.
- Stuff this mixture into the green peppers. Bake in an oven at 200°C (400°F, Gas Mark 6) for 10 minutes. Serve hot.

Mutton Burrani
(Meat cooked in Yoghurt)

Serves 4

Ingredients

750g/1lb 10oz mutton, diced	200g/7oz yoghurt, whisked
1½ tsp ginger paste	75g/2½oz ghee
1½ tsp garlic paste	1 large onion, sliced
Salt to taste	2 tomatoes, chopped
1 tsp turmeric	2 tsp ground coriander
1 litre/1¾ pints water	1 tsp garam masala

Method
- Mix the mutton with the ginger paste, garlic paste, salt, turmeric, water and half the yoghurt. Cook in a saucepan for 40 minutes. Set aside.
- Heat half the ghee in a saucepan. Add the onion, tomatoes, ground coriander and garam masala. Fry on a low heat for 7 minutes. Set aside.
- Heat the remaining ghee. Fry the mutton for 5-6 minutes. Arrange over the onion-tomato mixture. Top with the remaining yoghurt and serve hot.

Lamb Jhalfrezie
(Spicy Lamb Curry)

Serves 4

Ingredients

4 tbsp refined vegetable oil	1 tbsp ground coriander
4 large onions, grated	Salt to taste
10 garlic cloves, finely chopped	675g/1½lb lamb, diced
2.5cm/1in root ginger, finely chopped	750ml/1¼ pints water
1 tsp garam masala	1 large green pepper, sliced
2 tbsp ground cumin	3 large tomatoes, sliced

Method
- Heat 4 tbsp oil in a saucepan. Add the onions, garlic, ginger, garam masala, cumin, ground coriander and salt. Fry on a low heat for 1 minute.
- Add the remaining ingredients. Cover with a lid and simmer for 40 minutes, stirring frequently. Serve hot.

Mutton with Cashew Nuts

Serves 4

Ingredients

150g/5½oz yoghurt

Salt to taste

1 tsp turmeric

¼ small unripe papaya, peeled, deseeded and ground

1 tsp ginger paste

1 tsp garlic paste

12 cashew nuts, ground

750g/1lb 10oz mutton, diced

75g/2½oz ghee

2 large onions, sliced

120ml/4fl oz water

125g/4½oz khoya*

1 tsp garam masala

Juice of 1 lemon

Method.

- Whisk the yoghurt with the salt, turmeric, papaya, ginger paste, garlic paste and cashew nuts. Marinate the meat with this mixture for 2 hours.
- Heat the ghee in a saucepan. Add the onions and fry on a medium heat till brown. Add the marinated meat and water. Simmer for 45 minutes.
- Add the remaining ingredients. Mix well. Cook for 5 minutes. Serve hot.

Spicy Mutton Chops

Serves 4

Ingredients

675g/1½lb mutton chops

400g/14oz yoghurt

2 tbsp soy sauce

3 tbsp refined vegetable oil

3 large onions, grated

1 tbsp malt vinegar

2 tsp ginger paste

2 tsp garlic paste

3 tsp garam masala

2 tbsp coriander leaves, ground

3 bay leaves

3 tsp salt

750ml/1¼ pints water

Method

- Marinate the chops with yoghurt and soy sauce for 1 hour.
- Heat the oil in a saucepan. Fry the onions on a low heat till brown. Add the chops and the remaining ingredients, except the water. Fry for 8 minutes. Add the water and simmer for 30 minutes. Serve hot.

Do Pyaza Lamb
(Lamb cooked with Onions)

Serves 4

Ingredients

5 tbsp refined vegetable oil

4 large onions, finely chopped

8 peppercorns

4 cloves

5cm/2in cinnamon

4 green cardamom pods

1 tsp cumin seeds

5 dry red chillies, coarsely ground

1 tsp ground coriander

5cm/2in root ginger, finely chopped

12 garlic cloves, finely chopped

2 tomatoes, finely chopped

Salt to taste

675g/1½lb lamb, chopped into 2.5cm/1in pieces

500ml/16fl oz water

Method

- Heat the oil in a saucepan. Fry the onions on a medium heat till brown. Add the remaining ingredients, except the lamb and water. Fry for 6-7 minutes. Add the lamb and sauté for 8-10 minutes.
- Add the water. Mix well and simmer for 40 minutes. Serve hot.

Khudi
(Lamb cooked in Rich Gravy)

Serves 4

Ingredients

4 tbsp ghee

1 litre/1¾ pints water

1 tbsp garam masala

675g/1½lb lamb, diced

1 tbsp tamarind paste

Salt to taste

For the spice mixture:

4 onions

50g/1¾oz fresh coconut

4 green chillies

5cm/2in root ginger

10 garlic cloves

50g/1¾oz coriander leaves, chopped

Method

- Dry roast (see cooking techniques) the spice mixture ingredients together. Grind with enough water to form a thick paste.
- Heat the ghee in a saucepan. Fry the paste on a low heat for 5 minutes.
- Add the remaining ingredients. Simmer for 40 minutes and serve hot.

Pork Fezuvad

(Pork Sausages, Kidney Beans and Meat cooked in Rich Gravy)

Serves 4

Ingredients

500g/1lb 2oz pork, chopped into
   2.5cm/1in pieces
Salt to taste
750ml/1¼ pints water
60ml/2fl oz refined vegetable oil
3 large onions, finely chopped
1 tsp ginger paste

1 tsp garlic paste
50g/1¾oz canned kidney beans
200g/7oz pork sausages, chopped
1½ tsp garam masala
¾ tsp turmeric
Sugar to taste

Method

- Mix the pork with the salt and water. Cook in a saucepan on a medium heat for 45 minutes. Set aside.
- Heat the oil in a saucepan. Add the onions and fry on a medium heat till brown. Add the cooked pork and all the remaining ingredients.
- Mix well and cook for 20 minutes. Serve hot.

Raan-e-Sikandari

(Spicy Leg of Lamb)

Serves 4

Ingredients

4 large onions
2 tsp garlic paste
2 tsp ginger paste
2 tsp ground cumin
2 tsp ground coriander
25g/scant 1oz mint leaves

25g/scant 1oz coriander leaves
1 tsp garam masala
250ml/8fl oz malt vinegar
Salt to taste
675g/1½lb leg of lamb, boneless
3 tbsp ghee

Method

- Grind together all the ingredients, except the lamb and ghee. Create deep incisions on the lamb and marinate with this mixture for 8-10 hours.
- Baste the lamb with the ghee. Roast in an oven at 200°C (400°F, Gas Mark 6) for 40 minutes, turning frequently. Serve hot.

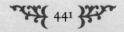

Bakar Baba Shahi

(Leg of Lamb cooked with Papaya and Yoghurt)

Serves 4

Ingredients

675g/1½lb leg of lamb, with the bone
12 black peppercorns
4 green cardamom pods
1 tsp ginger paste
1 tsp garlic paste
60ml/2fl oz rum
120ml/4fl oz malt vinegar

¼ unripe papaya, peeled, deseeded and ground
4 tomatoes, finely chopped
Salt to taste
500ml/16fl oz water
125g/4½oz yoghurt
Butter for basting

Method

- Mix the lamb with all the ingredients, except the yoghurt and butter.
- Cook in a saucepan on a low heat for 40 minutes. Drain and marinate the lamb with the yoghurt for 4 hours.
- Grill for 20 minutes, basting occasionally. Serve hot.

Mutton with Mustard Oil

Serves 4

Ingredients

400ml/14fl oz mustard oil
2 bay leaves
2 large onions, finely chopped
1 tsp ginger paste
1 tsp garlic paste
675g/1½lb mutton, chopped into 2.5cm/1in pieces

3 tomatoes, finely chopped
¾ tsp turmeric
¾ tsp chilli powder
1 tsp garam masala
500ml/16fl oz water
Salt to taste

Method

- Heat the oil in a saucepan. Add the bay leaves, onions, ginger paste and garlic paste and fry on a medium heat for 2-3 minutes.
- Add the mutton. Fry for 4-5 minutes.
- Add the remaining ingredients and mix well. Cover with a lid and simmer for 40 minutes, stirring occasionally. Serve hot.

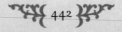

Liver & Potato Curry

Serves 4

Ingredients

5 dry red chillies

10 black peppercorns

2 tbsp coriander seeds

1 tsp cumin seeds

750g/1lb 10oz liver, diced

Salt to taste

1 tsp turmeric

500ml/16fl oz water

3 large potatoes, diced

2 tbsp malt vinegar

4 large onions, chopped and fried

10 garlic cloves, chopped

5cm/2in root ginger, julienned

250ml/8fl oz coconut milk

Method

- Dry roast (see cooking techniques) the red chillies, peppercorns, coriander seeds and cumin seeds. Grind to a powder. Set aside.
- Cook the liver with the salt, turmeric and water in a saucepan on a low heat for 40 minutes. Add the remaining ingredients and the red chillies-peppercorns powder. Mix well. Simmer for 20 minutes and serve hot.

Beef Stew

Serves 4

Ingredients

8 tbsp refined vegetable oil

500g/1lb 2oz beef, diced

2 large onions, finely chopped

6 garlic cloves, finely chopped

1 tbsp ginger paste

2 tsp ground coriander

1 tsp ground cumin

¼ tsp turmeric

2 tomatoes, blanched and chopped

300g/10oz frozen mixed vegetables

Salt to taste

1 litre/1¾ pints water

Method

- Heat 6 tbsp of the oil in a frying pan. Add the beef and fry on a medium heat for 5-6 minutes. Drain and set aside.
- Heat the remaining oil in a saucepan. Add the onions, garlic and ginger. Fry on a medium heat for 2-3 minutes. Add the remaining ingredients except the water. Fry for 5-6 minutes.
- Add the fried beef and the water. Simmer for 40 minutes and serve hot.

Hyderabadi Green Mutton

Serves 4

Ingredients

1 tsp mustard seeds

2 tsp cumin seeds

2 tsp poppy seeds

50g/1¾oz fresh coconut, grated

500ml/16fl oz water

5 tbsp refined vegetable oil

4 large onions, sliced

3 green cardamom pods

2.5cm/1in cinnamon

3 cloves

1 tsp ginger paste

1 tsp garlic paste

1 tsp turmeric

2 tomatoes, finely chopped

100g/3½oz coriander leaves, ground

60g/2oz mint leaves, ground

675g/1½lb boneless lamb, diced

Salt to taste

Method

- Dry roast (see cooking techniques) the mustard, cumin and poppy seeds. Grind with the coconut and enough water to form a thick paste. Set aside.
- Heat the oil in a saucepan. Add the onions, cardamom, cinnamon, cloves, ginger paste and garlic paste. Fry on a low heat for 5 minutes.
- Add the mustard-cumin paste and all the remaining ingredients. Mix well. Simmer for 50 minutes and serve hot.

Kashmiri Masala Lamb

Serves 4

Ingredients

75g/2½oz ghee

½ tsp asafoetida

675g/1½lb lamb, chopped into 5cm/2in pieces

125g/4½oz yoghurt

8 cloves

2 bay leaves

1½ tsp fennel seeds

1 tsp turmeric

400g/14oz frozen peas

1 litre/1¾ pints water

Salt to taste

Method

- Heat the ghee in a saucepan. Add the asafoetida and fry for 15 seconds.
- Add the lamb. Fry on a low heat for 5-6 minutes. Add all the remaining ingredients and simmer for 40 minutes, stirring occasionally. Serve hot.

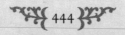

Mutton Bafat

(Mutton cooked the Parsi Way)

Serves 4

Ingredients

675g/1½lb mutton, diced
Salt to taste
250ml/8fl oz water
4 large potatoes, sliced
15 garlic cloves, sliced
1 tsp turmeric
3 large onions, sliced

For the spice mixture:

6 red chillies
1 tsp cumin seeds
1 tsp mustard seeds
1 tsp coriander seeds
10 peppercorns
5cm/2in cinnamon
2.5cm/1in root ginger, sliced

Method

• Grind the spice mixture ingredients together. Cook the mutton in a saucepan with the ground spice mixture, salt and water on a medium heat for 30 minutes, stirring occasionally.
• Add the remaining ingredients. Simmer for 15 minutes and serve hot.

Peppery Lamb

Serves 4

Ingredients

6 tbsp yoghurt
2 tsp ginger paste
2 tsp garlic paste
2 tsp ground cumin
Salt to taste
1 tbsp malt vinegar

675g/1½lb boneless lamb, chopped into 2.5cm/1in pieces
2 tbsp ground black pepper
2 tsp ground mustard seeds
4 tbsp refined vegetable oil
120ml/4fl oz fresh single cream
250ml/8fl oz water

Method

• Mix the yoghurt with the ginger paste, garlic paste, ground cumin, salt and vinegar. Marinate the meat with this mixture for 4 hours.
• Coat the meat with the pepper and ground mustard. Heat the oil in a frying pan. Fry the meat on a medium heat for 7-8 minutes. Add the cream and water. Mix well and simmer for 30 minutes. Serve hot.

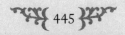

Masala Lamb in Coriander

Serves 4

Ingredients

¾ tsp salt

1 tsp ginger paste

1 tsp garlic paste

5cm/2in cinnamon, coarsely pounded

2 cardamom pods, pounded

3 bay leaves

3 cloves, coarsely pounded

200g/7oz yoghurt

675g/1½lb boneless lamb, diced

5 tbsp mustard oil

¼ tsp asafoetida

2 tsp ground coriander

2.5cm/1in root ginger, julienned

3 large onions, sliced

2 tbsp besan*

250ml/8fl oz water

Method

- Mix the salt, ginger paste, garlic paste, cinnamon, cardamom, bay leaves, cloves and yoghurt. Marinate the lamb with this mixture for 3 hours.
- Heat the oil in the saucepan. Add the asafoetida, ground coriander, ginger and onions. Fry on a medium heat for 2-3 minutes.
- Add the meat, besan and water. Simmer for 45 minutes. Serve hot.

Lamb in Mustard Oil

Serves 4

Ingredients

1 tsp turmeric

3 tbsp soy sauce

6 tbsp mustard oil

675g/1½lb lamb, chopped into 2.5cm/1in pieces

1 tbsp garlic paste

1 tbsp ginger paste

200g/7oz cooked peas

250ml/8fl oz water

Salt to taste

Method

- Mix the turmeric, soy sauce and half the oil together. Marinate the lamb with this mixture for 2 hours.
- Heat the remaining oil in a saucepan. Add the marinated lamb. Fry on a medium heat for 7-8 minutes. Add the garlic paste, ginger paste and peas. Fry for 2 minutes. Add the water and salt. Mix well. Simmer for 40 minutes, stirring occasionally. Serve hot.

Lamb Mince Kofta
(Steamed Mince Dumplings)

Serves 4

Ingredients
500g/1lb 2oz ground lamb
1 tsp ginger paste
1 tsp garlic paste
1 tsp ground coriander
½ tsp garam masala

1 tsp turmeric
½ tsp ground black pepper
1 tsp lemon juice
Salt to taste
Refined vegetable oil for frying

Method
* Knead all the ingredients, except the oil, to a soft dough. Divide into walnut-sized balls and flatten slightly.
* Steam (see cooking techniques) the meat balls for 20 minutes.
* Heat the oil in a frying pan. Add the steamed meat balls and shallow fry on a medium heat till golden brown. Flip and repeat. Serve hot.

Masoor Ma Gosh
(Lamb with Red Lentils)

Serves 4

Ingredients
12 garlic cloves
5cm/2in root ginger
1 tsp cumin seeds
4 tbsp refined vegetable oil
1.5 litres/2¾ pints water
3 onions, finely chopped
750g/1lb 10oz lamb, diced

225g/8oz whole masoor dhal*
1 tsp turmeric
2 tsp Dhansak masala*
1 tsp sugar
Salt to taste
2 tbsp malt vinegar

Method
* Grind the garlic, ginger and cumin seeds with enough water to form a thick paste. Set aside.
* Heat the oil in a saucepan. Fry the onions on a medium heat till brown.
* Add the garlic-ginger paste. Fry for 2 minutes. Add the remaining ingredients. Simmer for 45 minutes, stirring occasionally. Serve hot.

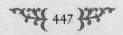

Rajasthani Pork Chops

Serves 4

Ingredients
675g/1½lb pork chops
Salt to taste
2 tbsp malt vinegar
1 tsp turmeric
4 tbsp ghee
2 large onions, sliced
500ml/16fl oz water

For the spice mixture:
10 garlic cloves
20 almonds
20 raisins
20 pistachio nuts
1½ tsp mustard seeds
2.5cm/1in root ginger
8 red chillies
1 tsp sugar

Method
* Marinate the pork chops with the salt, vinegar and turmeric for an hour.
* Grind all the ingredients for the spice mixture to a thick paste. Set aside.
* Heat the ghee in a saucepan. Add the onions. Fry on a low heat till brown.
* Add the spice mixture paste. Fry for 4-5 minutes. Add the pork chops. Fry for 8 minutes. Add the water and simmer for 40 minutes. Serve hot.

Mutton Curry

Serves 4

Ingredients
4 tbsp refined vegetable oil
3 large onions, finely chopped
675g/1½lb mutton, diced
750ml/1¼ pints water
Salt to taste
1 tsp turmeric

For the spice mixture:
2 tbsp coriander seeds
1 tbsp cumin seeds
1 tbsp garam masala
2.5cm/1in root ginger
12 garlic cloves
6 tbsp water

Method
* Grind all the spice mixture ingredients to a thick paste. Set aside.
* Heat the oil in a saucepan. Add the onions and fry on a low heat till brown. Add the spice mixture. Mix well and fry for 4-5 minutes.
* Add the remaining ingredients. Simmer for 40 minutes, stirring occasionally. Serve hot.

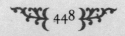

SEAFOOD

The place of honour on many an Indian dining table is the seafood dish. With their abundance of rivers, ponds and the sea, Indians are spoilt for choice. This chapter covers a gamut of such interesting recipes that are both imaginative and tasty. In the eastern region, freshwater fish like hilsa and rohu are preferred, whereas the southern and coastal regions use seawater fish, crabs, prawns and mussels.

Prawn Ball Curry

Serves 4

Ingredients

2 tbsp refined vegetable oil

2 cloves

5cm/2in cinnamon

8 black peppercorns

2 bay leaves

4 green chillies, slit
lengthways

1 large onion, minced

750ml/1¼ pints coconut
milk

Salt to taste

For the balls:

250g/9oz small prawns,
shelled and de-veined

1 large onion,
finely chopped

½ tsp garlic paste

½ tsp ginger paste

2 green chillies,
finely chopped

1 tsp ground coriander

1 tsp turmeric

3 tbsp besan*

2 tbsp rice flour

Salt to taste

Refined vegetable oil for
deep frying

Method

- For the balls, mince the prawns. Mix this mince with the remaining ingredients for the balls, except the oil. Knead the mixture to a soft dough and divide the dough into walnut-sized balls.
- Heat the oil for deep frying in a pan. Deep fry the balls on a medium heat till they turn golden brown. Drain and set aside.
- For the curry, heat 2 tbsp oil in a saucepan. Add the cloves, cinnamon, peppercorns and bay leaves. Let them splutter for 15 seconds.
- Add the green chillies and onion. Fry them on a medium heat for 1-2 minutes.
- Add the coconut milk and salt. Stir well and simmer for 10 minutes.
- Add the prawn balls to the curry and continue to simmer for 5 minutes. Serve hot.

Spicy Fish

Serves 4

Ingredients

250g/9oz plain white flour

1 tsp salt

½ tsp ground black pepper

1kg/2¼lb swordfish, skinned and filleted

60ml/2fl oz refined vegetable oil

1 green chilli, chopped

1 tsp chilli powder

2 tsp ground coriander

1 tsp ground cumin

1 tsp garam masala

1 tsp turmeric

1 tsp ginger paste

1 tsp garlic paste

250ml/8fl oz white vinegar

250ml/8fl oz water

2 bay leaves

12 peppercorns

2 large onions, sliced

Method

- Mix 180g of the flour with the salt and pepper. Roll the fish in this mixture.
- Heat half the oil in a frying pan. Add the fish and fry on a medium heat for 4-5 minutes. Flip and repeat.
- Drain the fried fish and transfer to a serving dish. Set aside.
- To prepare the sauce, mix the remaining flour with the green chilli, chilli powder, ground coriander, ground cumin, garam masala, turmeric, ginger paste and garlic paste with the vinegar and water. Grind this mixture to a smooth paste. Set aside.
- Heat the remaining oil in a saucepan. Add the bay leaves and peppercorns. Let them splutter for 15 seconds. Add the onions and fry them on a medium heat till they turn brown.
- Add the ground paste. Cook for 10 minutes. Cover with a lid and cook on a low heat for 30 minutes without water, stirring occasionally.
- Pour this sauce on top of the fish. Set aside to cool and place in the refrigerator. Serve cold.

NOTE: *This can be stored in the refrigerator for 3 days.*

Prawn Kalimiri

(Prawns with Peppercorns)

Serves 4

Ingredients

1 tbsp lemon juice

2 tsp ginger paste

2 tsp garlic paste

Salt to taste

500g/1lb 2oz medium-sized prawns, shelled and de-veined

5cm/2in cinnamon

8 cloves

1 tsp cumin seeds

1 tsp coriander seeds

1 tbsp desiccated coconut

100ml/3½fl oz refined vegetable oil

1 tsp fennel seeds

2 large onions, finely chopped

1 tsp chilli powder

1 tsp ground black pepper

¼ tsp turmeric

Method

- Mix the lemon juice, half the ginger paste, half the garlic paste and the salt and marinate the prawns with this mixture for 1 hour.
- Heat a frying pan. Dry roast (see cooking techniques) the cinnamon, cloves, cumin seeds, coriander seeds and coconut. Remove from the heat and grind coarsely. Set aside.
- Heat the oil in a saucepan. Add the fennel seeds. Let them splutter for 15 seconds.
- Add the onions. Sauté them on a medium heat till they turn translucent.
- Add the remaining ginger paste and garlic paste, the ground cinnamon-cloves mixture, chilli powder, black pepper and turmeric. Mix well. Sauté for 5 minutes.
- Add the marinated prawns. Toss well. Cook on a low heat for 10-15 minutes. Serve hot.

Spiced Bamboo & Prawn

Serves 4

Ingredients

240ml/6fl oz refined vegetable oil

2 large onions, finely sliced

150g/5½oz tinned bamboo shoots, drained

500g/1lb 2oz medium-sized prawns, shelled and de-veined

360ml/12fl oz coconut milk

Salt to taste

25g/scant 1oz coriander leaves, finely chopped

For the spice mixture:

10 garlic cloves

4 dry red chillies

4 peppercorns

2 cloves

2.5cm/1in cinnamon

2.5cm/1in root ginger

½ tsp turmeric

2 tsp coriander seeds

1 tsp cumin seeds

1 tsp poppy seeds

Method

- Grind the ingredients for the spice mixture with enough water to form a smooth paste. Set aside.
- Heat the oil in a saucepan. Add the onions and fry them on a medium heat till they turn brown.
- Add the spice mixture paste. Fry on a low heat for 4-5 minutes.
- Add the bamboo shoots and the prawns. Mix well. Stir-fry for 6-7 minutes.
- Add the coconut milk and salt. Mix well. Cover with a lid and simmer for 20 minutes, stirring occasionally.
- Garnish with the coriander leaves. Serve hot.

Coorg Meen Curry

(South Indian Fish Curry)

Serves 4

Ingredients

1kg/2¼lb sea bass, skinned and filleted

3 tbsp refined vegetable oil

250g/9oz rice flour

500ml/16fl oz water

For the marinade:

1 tsp turmeric

1 tsp chilli powder

1 tsp ginger paste

1 tsp garlic paste

2 tsp lemon juice

4 tbsp desiccated coconut

1 tsp cumin seeds

1 tsp fenugreek seeds

1 tsp coriander seeds

¼ tsp mustard seeds

For the curry:

2 tbsp refined vegetable oil

¼ tsp mustard seeds

½ tsp ginger paste

½ tsp garlic paste

2 large onions, finely sliced

2 green chillies, sliced

1 tbsp tamarind paste

Salt to taste

2 tbsp coriander leaves, finely chopped

Method

- Mix the marinade ingredients together. Dry roast the mixture in a frying pan. Remove from the heat and grind with enough water to form a smooth paste. Marinate the fish with this paste for 2 hours.
- Heat the oil for in a frying pan. Coat the marinated fish with the rice flour and fry on a medium heat till golden brown. Flip carefully and fry the other side for 2 more minutes. Drain and set aside.
- For the curry, heat the oil in a saucepan. Add the mustard seeds, ginger paste and garlic paste. Sauté on a medium heat for a minute.
- Add the onions and green chillies. Fry for 2-3 minutes.
- Add the tamarind paste and salt. Mix well and fry for 2 minutes.
- Add the fried fish and the water. Mix well. Cover with a lid and simmer for 20 minutes, stirring occasionally.
- Garnish with the coriander leaves and serve hot with steamed rice (see page 519).

Fish Kebab

Serves 4

Ingredients

1kg/2¼lb swordfish, skinned and filleted

4 tbsp refined vegetable oil plus extra for frying

75g/2½oz chana dhal*, soaked in 250ml/9oz water for 30 minutes

3 cloves

½ tsp cumin seeds

2.5cm/1in root ginger, grated

10 garlic cloves

2.5cm/1in cinnamon

2 black cardamom pods

8 black peppercorns

4 dry red chillies

¾ tsp turmeric

1 tbsp Greek yoghurt

1 tsp black cumin seeds

For the stuffing:

2 dry figs, finely chopped

4 dry apricots, finely chopped

Juice of 1 lemon

10g/¼oz mint leaves, finely chopped

10g/¼oz coriander leaves, finely chopped

Salt to taste

Method

- Steam (see cooking techniques) the fish in a steamer on a medium heat for 10 minutes. Set aside.
- Heat 2 tbsp oil in a frying pan. Drain the dhal and fry it on a medium heat till it turns golden brown.
- Mix the dhal with the cloves, cumin seeds, ginger, garlic, cinnamon, cardamom, peppercorns, red chillies, turmeric, yoghurt and black cumin seeds. Grind this mixture with enough water to form a smooth paste. Set aside.
- Heat 2 tbsp oil in a saucepan. Add this paste and fry it on a medium heat for 4-5 minutes.
- Add the steamed fish. Mix thoroughly and stir for 2 minutes.
- Divide the mixture into 8 portions and shape into patties. Set aside.
- Mix all the stuffing ingredients together. Divide into 8 portions.
- Flatten the patties and carefully place a portion of the stuffing on each patty. Seal like a pouch and roll again to form a ball. Pat the balls flat.
- Heat the oil for frying in a frying pan. Add the patties and shallow fry them on a medium heat till they turn golden brown. Flip and repeat.
- Drain on absorbent paper and serve hot.

Fish Chops

Serves 4

Ingredients

500g/1lb 2oz monkfish tail, skinned and filleted

500ml/16fl oz water

Salt to taste

1 tbsp refined vegetable oil plus extra for deep frying

1 tbsp ginger paste

1 tbsp garlic paste

1 large onion, finely grated

4 green chillies, grated

½ tsp turmeric

1 tsp garam masala

1 tsp ground cumin

1 tsp chilli powder

1 tomato, blanched and sliced

25g/scant 1oz coriander leaves, finely chopped

2 tbsp mint leaves, finely chopped

400g/14oz cooked peas

2 bread slices, soaked in water and drained

50g/1¾oz breadcrumbs

Method

● Place the fish with the water in a saucepan. Add the salt and boil on a medium heat for 20 minutes. Drain and set aside.

● For the filling, heat 1 tbsp of the oil in a saucepan. Add the ginger paste, garlic paste and onion. Sauté on a medium heat for 2-3 minutes.

● Add the green chillies, turmeric, garam masala, ground cumin and chilli powder. Fry for a minute.

● Add the tomato. Fry for 3-4 minutes.

● Add the coriander leaves, mint leaves, peas and bread slices. Mix well. Cook on a low heat for 7-8 minutes, stirring occasionally. Remove from the heat and knead the mixture well. Divide into 8 equal-sized portions and set aside.

● Mash the boiled fish and divide into 8 portions.

● Shape each fish portion like a cup and stuff it with a portion of the filling mixture. Seal like a pouch, roll into a ball and shape like a cutlet. Repeat for the remainng fish portions and the filling mixture.

● Heat the oil for deep frying in a pan. Roll the cutlets in the breadcrumbs and deep fry them on a medium heat till they turn golden brown. Serve hot.

Fish Sookha

(Dry Fish in Spices)

Serves 4

Ingredients

1cm/½in root ginger

10 garlic cloves

1 tbsp coriander leaves, finely chopped

3 green chillies

1 tsp turmeric

3 tsp chilli powder

Salt to taste

1kg/2¼lb swordfish, skinned and filleted

50g/1¾oz desiccated coconut

6-7 kokum*, soaked for 1 hour in 120ml/4fl oz water

4 tbsp refined vegetable oil

60ml/2fl oz water

Method

- Mix the ginger, garlic, coriander leaves, green chillies, turmeric, chilli powder and salt together. Grind this mixture to a smooth paste.
- Marinate the fish with the paste for 1 hour.
- Heat a saucepan. Add the coconut. Dry roast (see cooking techniques) on a medium heat for a minute.
- Discard the kokum berries and add the kokum water. Mix well. Remove from the heat and add this mixture to the marinated fish.
- Heat the oil in a saucepan. Add the fish mixture and cook on a medium heat for 4-5 minutes.
- Add the water. Mix well. Cover with a lid and simmer for 20 minutes, stirring occasionally.
- Serve hot.

Mahya Kalia
(Fish with Coconut, Sesame Seeds and Peanuts)

Serves 4

Ingredients

100g/3½oz fresh coconut, grated	1 tsp ground coriander
1 tsp sesame seeds	Salt to taste
1 tbsp peanuts	250ml/8fl oz water
1 tbsp tamarind paste	500g/1lb 2oz swordfish fillets
1 tsp turmeric	1 tbsp coriander leaves, chopped

Method

- Dry roast (see cooking techniques) the coconut, sesame seeds and peanuts together. Mix with the tamarind paste, turmeric, ground coriander and salt. Grind with enough water to form a smooth paste.
- Cook this mixture with the remaining water in a saucepan on a medium heat for 10 minutes, stirring frequently. Add the fish fillets and simmer for 10-12 minutes. Garnish with the coriander leaves and serve hot.

Prawn Curry Rosachi
(Prawns cooked with Coconut)

Serves 4

Ingredients

200g/7oz fresh coconut, grated	6 garlic cloves
5 red chillies	120ml/4fl oz refined vegetable oil
1½ tsp coriander seeds	2 large onions, finely chopped
1½ tsp poppy seeds	2 tomatoes, finely chopped
1 tsp cumin seeds	250g/9oz prawns, shelled and de-veined
½ tsp turmeric	Salt to taste

Method

- Grind the coconut, red chillies, coriander, poppy seeds, cumin seeds, turmeric and garlic with enough water to form a smooth paste. Set aside.
- Heat the oil in a saucepan. Fry the onions on a low heat till brown.
- Add the ground coconut-red chillies paste, tomatoes, prawns and salt. Mix well. Cook for 15 minutes, stirring occasionally. Serve hot.

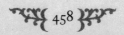

Fish Stuffed with Dates & Almonds

Serves 4

Ingredients

4 trout, 250g/9oz each, slit vertically

½ tsp chilli powder

1 tsp ginger paste

250g/9oz fresh seedless dates, blanched and finely chopped

75g/2½oz almonds, blanched and finely chopped

2-3 tbsp steamed rice (see page 519)

1 tsp sugar

¼ tsp ground cinnamon

½ tsp ground black pepper

Salt to taste

1 large onion, finely sliced

Method

• Marinate the fish with the chilli powder and ginger paste for 1 hour.

• Mix the dates, almonds, rice, sugar, cinnamon, pepper and salt together. Knead to form a soft dough. Set aside.

• Stuff the date-almond dough in the slits of the marinated fish. Place the stuffed fish on a sheet of aluminium foil and sprinkle the onion on top.

• Wrap the fish and onion inside the foil and seal the edges firmly.

• Bake in an oven at 200°C (400°F, Gas Mark 6) for 15-20 minutes. Unwrap the foil and bake the fish for 5 more minutes. Serve hot.

Tandoori Fish

Serves 4

Ingredients

1 tsp ginger paste

1 tsp garlic paste

½ tsp garam masala

1 tsp chilli powder

1 tbsp lemon juice

Salt to taste

500g/1lb 2oz monkfish tail fillets

1 tbsp chaat masala*

Method

• Mix together the ginger paste, garlic paste, garam masala, chilli powder, lemon juice and salt.

• Make incisions on the fish. Marinate with the ginger-garlic mixture for 2 hours.

• Grill the fish for 15 minutes. Sprinkle with the chaat masala. Serve hot.

Fish with Vegetables

Serves 4

Ingredients

750g/1lb 10oz salmon fillets, skinned

½ tsp turmeric

Salt to taste

2 tbsp mustard oil

¼ tsp mustard seeds

¼ tsp fennel seeds

¼ tsp onion seeds

¼ tsp fenugreek seeds

¼ tsp cumin seeds

2 bay leaves

2 dry red chillies, halved

1 large onion, finely sliced

2 large green chillies, slit lengthways

½ tsp sugar

125g/4½oz canned peas

1 large potato, chopped into strips

2-3 small aubergines, julienned

250ml/8fl oz water

Method

- Marinate the fish with the turmeric and salt for 30 minutes.
- Heat the oil in a saucepan. Add the marinated fish and fry on a medium heat for 4-5 minutes, turning occasionally. Drain and set aside.
- To the same oil, add the mustard, fennel, onion, fenugreek and cumin seeds. Let them splutter for 15 seconds.
- Add the bay leaves and red chillies. Fry for 30 seconds.
- Add the onion and green chillies. Fry on a medium heat till the onion turns brown.
- Add the sugar, peas, potato and aubergines. Mix well. Stir-fry the mixture for 7-8 minutes.
- Add the fried fish and the water. Mix well. Cover with a lid and simmer for 12-15 minutes, stirring occasionally.
- Serve hot.

Tandoor Gulnar

(Trout cooked in a Tandoor)

Serves 4

Ingredients
4 trout, 250g/9oz each
Butter for basting

For the first marinade:
120ml/4fl oz malt vinegar
2 tbsp lemon juice
2 tsp garlic paste
½ tsp chilli powder
Salt to taste

For the second marinade:
400g/14oz yoghurt
1 egg
1 tsp garlic paste
2 tsp ginger paste
120ml/4fl oz fresh single cream
180g/6½oz besan*
1 tsp ajowan seeds
1 tsp ground black pepper
1 tsp chilli powder
1 tsp turmeric

Method
- Mix all the ingredients for the first marinade together. Marinate the fish with this mixture for 1 hour.
- Whisk all the ingredients for the second marinade together. Marinate the fish with this mixture for another 2 hours.
- Skewer the marinated fish from mouth to tail. Place a tray under the fish to collect the dripping juices. Roast in an oven at 200°C (400°F, Gas Mark 6) for 10 minutes.
- Baste the fish with the butter and roast again for 3 minutes. Serve hot.

Prawns in Green Masala

Serves 4

Ingredients

1cm/½in root ginger

8 garlic cloves

3 green chillies, slit lengthways

50g/1¾oz coriander leaves, chopped

1½ tbsp refined vegetable oil

2 large onions, finely chopped

2 tomatoes, finely chopped

500g/1lb 2oz large prawns, shelled and de-veined

1 tsp tamarind paste

Salt to taste

½ tsp turmeric

Method

- Grind together the ginger, garlic, chillies and coriander leaves. Set aside.
- Heat the oil in a saucepan. Fry the onions on a low heat till brown.
- Add the ginger-garlic paste and the tomatoes. Fry for 4-5 minutes.
- Add the prawns, tamarind paste, salt and turmeric. Mix well. Cook for 15 minutes, stirring occasionally. Serve hot.

Fish Cutlet

Serves 4

Ingredients

2 eggs

1 tbsp plain white flour

Salt to taste

400g/14oz John Dory, skinned and filleted

500ml/16fl oz water

2 large potatoes, boiled and mashed

1½ tsp garam masala

1 large onion, grated

1 tsp ginger paste

Refined vegetable oil for deep frying

200g/7oz breadcrumbs

Method

- Whisk the eggs with the flour and salt. Set aside.
- Cook the fish in salted water in a saucepan on a medium heat for 15-20 minutes. Drain and knead with the potatoes, garam masala, onion, ginger paste and salt to a soft dough.
- Divide into 16 portions, roll into balls and flatten lightly to form cutlets.
- Heat the oil in a pan. Dip the cutlets in the whisked egg, roll in the breadcrumbs and deep fry on a low heat till golden brown. Serve hot.

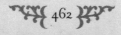

Parsi Fish Sas
(Fish cooked in White Sauce)

Serves 4

Ingredients

1 tbsp rice flour
1 tbsp sugar
60ml/2fl oz malt vinegar
2 tbsp refined vegetable oil
2 large onions, finely sliced
½ tsp ginger paste
½ tsp garlic paste

1 tsp ground cumin
Salt to taste
250ml/8fl oz water
8 fillets lemon sole
2 eggs, whisked

Method

- Grind the rice flour with the sugar and vinegar to a paste. Set aside.
- Heat the oil in a saucepan. Fry the onions on a low heat till brown.
- Add the ginger paste, garlic paste, ground cumin, salt, water and fish. Cook on a low heat for 25 minutes, stirring occasionally.
- Add the flour mixture and cook for a minute.
- Gently add the eggs. Stir for a minute. Garnish and serve hot.

Peshawari Machhi

Serves 4

Ingredients

3 tbsp refined vegetable oil
1kg/2¼lb salmon, sliced into steaks
2.5cm/1in root ginger, grated
8 garlic cloves, crushed
2 large onions, ground
3 tomatoes, blanched and chopped

1 tsp garam masala
400g/14oz yoghurt
¾ tsp turmeric
1 tsp amchoor*
Salt to taste

Method

- Heat the oil. Fry the fish on a low heat till golden. Drain and set aside.
- To the same oil, add the ginger, garlic and onions. Fry on a low heat for 6 minutes. Add the fried fish and all the remaining ingredients. Mix well.
- Simmer for 20 minutes and serve hot.

Crab Curry

Serves 4

Ingredients

4 medium-sized crabs, cleaned (see
cooking techniques)

Salt to taste

1 tsp turmeric

½ coconut, grated

6 garlic cloves

4-5 red chillies

1 tbsp coriander seeds

1 tbsp cumin seeds

1 tsp tamarind paste

3-4 green chillies, slit lengthways

1 tbsp refined vegetable oil

1 large onion, finely chopped

Method

- Marinate the crabs with the salt and turmeric for 30 minutes.
- Grind all the remaining ingredients, except the oil and onion, with enough water to form a smooth paste.
- Heat the oil in a saucepan. Fry the ground paste and the onion on a low heat till the onion are brown. Add some water. Simmer for 7-8 minutes, stirring occasionally. Add the marinated crabs. Mix well and simmer for 5 minutes. Serve hot.

Mustard Fish

Serves 4

Ingredients

8 tbsp mustard oil

4 trout, 250g/9oz each

2 tsp ground cumin

2 tsp ground mustard

1 tsp ground coriander

½ tsp turmeric

120ml/4fl oz water

Salt to taste

Method

- Heat the oil in a saucepan. Add the fish and fry it on a medium heat for 1-2 minutes. Flip the fish and repeat. Drain and set aside.
- To the same oil, add the ground cumin, mustard and coriander. Let them splutter for 15 seconds.
- Add the turmeric, water, salt and the fried fish. Mix well and simmer for 10-12 minutes. Serve hot.

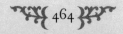

Meen Vattichathu

(Red Fish cooked with Spices)

Serves 4

Ingredients

600g/1lb 5oz swordfish, skinned and
   filleted

½ tsp turmeric

Salt to taste

3 tbsp refined vegetable oil

½ tsp mustard seeds

½ tsp fenugreek seeds

8 curry leaves

2 large onions, finely sliced

8 garlic cloves, finely chopped

5cm/2in ginger, finely sliced

6 kokum*

Method

• Marinate the fish with the turmeric and salt for 2 hours.

• Heat the oil in a saucepan. Add the mustard and fenugreek seeds. Let
   them splutter for 15 seconds. Add all the remaining ingredients and the
   marinated fish. Stir-fry on a low heat for 15 minutes. Serve hot.

Doi Maach

(Fish cooked in Yoghurt)

Serves 4

Ingredients

4 trout, skinned and filleted

2 tbsp refined vegetable oil

2 bay leaves

1 large onion, finely chopped

2 tsp sugar

Salt to taste

200g/7oz yoghurt

For the marinade:

3 cloves

5cm/2in piece cinnamon

3 green cardamom pods

5cm/2in root ginger

1 large onion, finely sliced

1 tsp turmeric

Salt to taste

Method

• Grind all the marinade ingredients together. Marinate the fish with this
   mixture for 30 minutes.

• Heat the oil in a saucepan. Add the bay leaves and onion. Fry on a low
   heat for 3 minutes. Add the sugar, salt and the marinated fish. Mix well.

• Sauté for 10 minutes. Add the yoghurt and cook for 8 minutes. Serve hot.

Fish Fry

Serves 4

Ingredients

6 tbsp besan*
2 tsp garam masala
1 tsp amchoor*
1 tsp ajowan seeds
1 tsp ginger paste

1 tsp garlic paste
Salt to taste
675g/1½lb monkfish tail, skinned and filleted
Refined vegetable oil for deep frying

Method

- Mix together all the ingredients, except the fish and the oil, with enough water to form a thick batter. Marinate the fish with this batter for 4 hours.
- Heat the oil in a frying pan. Add the fish and deep fry on a medium heat for 4-5 minutes. Flip and fry again for 2-3 minutes. Serve hot.

Machher Chop

Serves 4

Ingredients

500g/1lb 2oz salmon, skinned and filleted
Salt to taste
500ml/16fl oz water
250g/9oz potatoes, boiled and mashed
200ml/7fl oz mustard oil
2 large onions, finely chopped

½ tsp ginger paste
½ tsp garlic paste
1½ tsp garam masala
1 egg, whisked
200g/7oz breadcrumbs
Refined vegetable oil for deep frying

Method

- Place the fish with the salt and water in a saucepan. Cook on a medium heat for 15 minutes. Drain and mash with the potatoes. Set aside.
- Heat the oil in a frying pan. Add the onions and fry on a medium heat till brown. Add the fish mixture and all the remaining ingredients, except the egg and breadcrumbs. Mix well and cook on a low heat for 10 minutes.
- Cool and divide into lemon-sized balls. Flatten and shape into cutlets.
- Heat the oil for deep frying in a pan. Dip the cutlets in the egg, roll in the breadcrumbs and deep fry on a medium heat till golden. Serve hot.

Goa Swordfish
(Swordfish cooked in Goan Style)

Serves 4

Ingredients

50g/1¾oz fresh coconut, grated
1 tsp coriander seeds
1 tsp cumin seeds
1 tsp poppy seeds
4 garlic cloves
1 tbsp tamarind paste
250ml/8fl oz water

Refined vegetable oil for frying
1 large onion, finely chopped
1 tbsp kokum*
Salt to taste
½ tsp turmeric
4 swordfish steaks

Method
- Grind together the coconut, coriander seeds, cumin seeds, poppy seeds, garlic and tamarind paste with enough water to form a smooth paste. Set aside.
- Heat the oil in a saucepan. Add the onion and fry it on a medium heat till it turns brown.
- Add the ground paste and fry for 2 minutes. Add the remaining ingredients. Mix well and simmer for 15 minutes. Serve hot.

Dry Fish Masala

Serves 4

Ingredients
6 salmon fillets
¼ fresh coconut, grated
7 red chillies

1 tbsp turmeric
Salt to taste

Method
- Grill the fish fillets for 20 minutes. Set aside.
- Grind together the remaining ingredients to form a smooth paste.
- Mix with the fish. Cook the mixture in a saucepan on a low heat for 15 minutes. Serve hot.

Madras Prawn Curry

Serves 4

Ingredients

3 tbsp refined vegetable oil

3 large onions, finely chopped

12 garlic cloves, minced

3 tomatoes, blanched and chopped

½ tsp turmeric

Salt to taste

1 tsp chilli powder

2 tbsp tamarind paste

750g/1lb 10oz medium-sized prawns, shelled and de-veined

4 tbsp coconut milk

Method

- Heat the oil in a saucepan. Add the onions and garlic and fry on a medium heat for a minute. Add the tomatoes, turmeric, salt, chilli powder, tamarind paste and prawns. Mix well and fry for 7-8 minutes.
- Add the coconut milk. Simmer for 10 minutes and serve hot.

Fish in Fenugreek

Serves 4

Ingredients

8 tbsp refined vegetable oil

500g/1lb 2oz salmon, filleted

1 tbsp garlic paste

75g/2½oz fresh fenugreek leaves, finely chopped

4 tomatoes, finely chopped

2 tsp ground coriander

1 tsp ground cumin

1 tsp lemon juice

Salt to taste

1 tsp turmeric

75g/2½oz hot water

Method

- Heat 4 tbsp oil in a frying pan. Add the fish and shallow fry on a medium heat till golden brown on both sides. Drain and set aside.
- Heat 4 tbsp oil in a saucepan. Add the garlic paste. Fry on a low heat for a minute. Add the remaining ingredients, except the water. Stir-fry for 4-5 minutes.
- Add the water and the fried fish. Mix well. Cover with a lid and simmer for 10-15 minutes, stirring occasionally. Serve hot.

Karimeen Porichathu
(Fish Fillet in Masala)

Serves 4

Ingredients

1 tsp chilli powder
1 tbsp ground coriander
1 tsp turmeric
1 tsp ginger paste
2 green chillies, finely chopped

Juice of 1 lemon
8 curry leaves
Salt to taste
8 salmon fillets
Refined vegetable oil for frying

Method
- Mix together all the ingredients, except the fish and oil.
- Marinate the fish with this mixture and refrigerate for 2 hours.
- Heat the oil in a frying pan. Add the fish pieces and shallow fry them on a medium heat till golden brown.
- Serve hot.

Jumbo Prawns

Serves 4

Ingredients

500g/1lb 2oz large prawns, shelled and de-veined
1 tsp turmeric
½ tsp chilli powder
Salt to taste
3 tbsp refined vegetable oil
1 large onion, finely chopped

1cm/½in root ginger, finely chopped
10 garlic cloves, finely chopped
2-3 green chillies, slit lengthways
½ tsp sugar
250ml/8fl oz coconut milk
1 tbsp coriander leaves, finely chopped

Method
- Marinate the prawns with the turmeric, chilli powder and salt for 1 hour.
- Heat the oil in a saucepan. Add the onion, ginger, garlic and green chillies and fry on a medium heat for 2-3 minutes.
- Add the sugar, salt and the marinated prawns. Mix well and sauté for 10 minutes. Add the coconut milk. Simmer for 15 minutes.
- Garnish with the coriander leaves and serve hot.

Pickled Fish

Serves 4

Ingredients

Refined vegetable oil for frying
1kg/2¼lb swordfish, skinned and filleted
1 tsp turmeric
12 dry red chillies
1 tbsp cumin seeds

5cm/2in root ginger
15 garlic cloves
250ml/8fl oz malt vinegar
Salt to taste

Method

- Heat the oil in a frying pan. Add the fish and shallow fry on a medium heat for 2-3 minutes. Flip and fry for 1-2 minutes. Set aside.
- Grind the remaining ingredients together to form a smooth paste.
- Cook the paste in a pan on a low heat for 10 minutes. Add the fish, cook for 3-4 minutes, then cool and store in a jar, refrigerated, for up to 1 week.

Fish Ball Curry

Serves 4

Ingredients

500g/1lb 2oz salmon, skinned and filleted
Salt to taste
750ml/1¼ pints water
1 large onion
3 tsp garam masala
½ tsp turmeric

3 tbsp refined vegetable oil plus extra for deep frying
5cm/2in root ginger, grated
5 garlic cloves, crushed
250g/9oz tomatoes, blanched and diced
2 tbsp yoghurt, whisked

Method

- Cook the fish with some salt and 500ml/16fl oz water on a medium heat for 20 minutes. Drain and grind with the onion, salt, 1 tsp garam masala and the turmeric to a smooth mixture. Divide into 12 balls.
- Heat the oil for deep frying. Add the balls and deep fry on a medium heat till golden brown. Drain and set aside.
- Heat 3 tbsp oil in a saucepan. Add all the remaining ingredients, the remaining water and the fish balls. Simmer for 10 minutes and serve hot.

Fish Amritsari

(Hot Spicy Fish)

Serves 4

Ingredients

200g/7oz yoghurt
½ tsp ginger paste
½ tsp garlic paste
Juice of 1 lemon

½ tsp garam masala
Salt to taste
675g/1½lb monkfish tail, skinned and
  filleted

Method

- Mix together all the ingredients, except the fish. Marinate the fish with this mixture for 1 hour.
- Grill the marinated fish for 7-8 minutes. Serve hot.

Masala Fried Prawns

Serves 4

Ingredients

4 garlic cloves
5cm/2in ginger
2 tbsp fresh coconut, grated
2 dry red chillies
1 tbsp coriander seeds
1 tsp turmeric
Salt to taste
120ml/4fl oz water

750g/1lb 10oz prawns, shelled and
  de-veined
3 tbsp refined vegetable oil
3 large onions, finely chopped
2 tomatoes, finely chopped
2 tbsp coriander leaves, chopped
1 tsp garam masala

Method

- Grind together the garlic, ginger, coconut, red chillies, coriander seeds, turmeric and salt with enough water to form a smooth paste.
- Marinate the prawns with this paste for an hour.
- Heat the oil in a saucepan. Add the onions and fry them on a medium heat till translucent.
- Add the tomatoes and the marinated prawns. Mix well. Add the water, cover with a lid and simmer for 20 minutes.
- Garnish with the coriander leaves and garam masala. Serve hot.

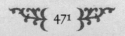

Savoury Topped Fish

Serves 4

Ingredients

2 tbsp lemon juice

Salt to taste

Ground black pepper to taste

4 swordfish steaks

2 tbsp butter

1 large onion, finely chopped

1 green pepper, cored and chopped

3 tomatoes, skinned and chopped

50g/1¾oz breadcrumbs

85g/3oz Cheddar cheese, grated

Method

* Sprinkle the lemon juice, salt and pepper on top of the fish. Set aside.
* Heat the butter in a saucepan. Add the onion and green pepper. Fry on a medium heat for 2-3 minutes. Add the tomatoes, breadcrumbs and cheese. Fry for 4-5 minutes.
* Spread this mixture evenly over the fish. Wrap in aluminium foil and bake in an oven at 200°C (400°F, Gas Mark 6) for 30 minutes. Serve hot.

Prawn Pasanda

(Prawn cooked with Yoghurt and Vinegar)

Serves 4

Ingredients

250g/9oz prawns, shelled and de-veined

Salt to taste

1 tsp ground black pepper

2 tsp malt vinegar

2 tsp refined vegetable oil

1 tbsp garlic paste

2 large onions, finely chopped

2 tomatoes, finely chopped

2 spring onions, finely chopped

1 tsp garam masala

250ml/8fl oz water

4 tbsp Greek yoghurt

Method

* Marinate the prawns with the salt, pepper and vinegar for 30 minutes.
* Grill the prawns for 5 minutes. Set aside.
* Heat the oil in a saucepan. Add the garlic paste and onions. Fry on a medium heat for a minute. Add the tomatoes, spring onions and garam masala. Sauté for 4 minutes. Add the grilled prawns and water. Cook on a low heat for 15 minutes. Add the yoghurt. Stir for 5 minutes. Serve hot.

Swordfish Rechaido
(Swordfish cooked in Goan Gravy)

Serves 4

Ingredients

4 red chillies
6 garlic cloves
2.5cm/1in root ginger
½ tsp turmeric
1 large onion
1 tsp tamarind paste

1 tsp cumin seeds
1 tbsp sugar
Salt to taste
120ml/4fl oz malt vinegar
1kg/2¼lb swordfish, cleaned
Refined vegetable oil for frying

Method
- Grind together all the ingredients, except the fish and oil.
- Make slits on the swordfish and marinate with the ground mixture, stuffing ample amounts of the mixture in the slits. Set aside for 1 hour.
- Heat the oil in a frying pan. Add the marinated fish and shallow fry on a low heat for 2-3 minutes. Flip and repeat. Serve hot.

Teekha Jhinga
(Hot Prawns)

Serves 4

Ingredients

4 tbsp refined vegetable oil
1 tsp fennel seeds
2 large onions, finely chopped
2 tsp ginger paste
2 tsp garlic paste
Salt to taste

½ tsp turmeric
3 tbsp garam masala
25g/scant 1oz desiccated coconut
60ml/2fl oz water
1 tbsp lemon juice
500g/1lb 2oz prawns, shelled and
de-veined

Method
- Heat the oil in a saucepan. Add the fennel seeds. Let them splutter for 15 seconds. Add the onions, ginger paste and garlic paste. Fry on a medium heat for a minute.
- Add the remaining ingredients, except the prawns. Sauté for 7 minutes.
- Add the prawns and cook for 15 minutes, stirring frequently. Serve hot.

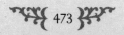

Prawns Balchow
(Prawns cooked the Goan Way)

Serves 4

Ingredients

750g/1lb 10oz prawns, shelled and de-veined

250ml/8fl oz malt vinegar

8 garlic cloves

2 large onions, finely chopped

1 tbsp ground cumin

¼ tsp turmeric

Salt to taste

120ml/4fl oz refined vegetable oil

50g/1¾oz coriander leaves, chopped

Method

- Marinate the prawns with 4 tbsp of the vinegar for 2 hours.
- Grind the remaining vinegar with the garlic, onions, ground cumin, turmeric and salt to form a smooth paste. Set aside.
- Heat the oil in a saucepan. Fry the prawns on a low heat for 12 minutes.
- Add the paste. Mix well and sauté on a low heat for 15 minutes.
- Garnish with the coriander leaves. Serve hot.

Prawns Bhujna
(Dry Prawns in Coconut and Onion)

Serves 4

Ingredients

50g/1¾oz fresh coconut, grated

2 large onions

6 red chillies

5cm/2in root ginger, grated

1 tsp garlic paste

4 tbsp refined vegetable oil

5 dry kokum*

¼ tsp turmeric

750g/1lb 10oz prawns, shelled and de-veined

250ml/8fl oz water

Salt to taste

Method

- Grind together the coconut, onions, red chillies, ginger and garlic paste.
- Heat the oil in a saucepan. Add the paste with the kokum and turmeric. Fry on a low heat for 5 minutes.
- Add the prawns, the water and salt. Simmer for 20 minutes, stirring frequently. Serve hot.

Chingdi Macher Malai
(Prawns in Coconut)

Serves 4

Ingredients

2 large onions, grated

2 tbsp ginger paste

100g/3½oz fresh coconut, grated

4 tbsp refined vegetable oil

500g/1lb 2oz prawns, shelled and de-veined

1 tsp turmeric

1 tsp ground cumin

4 tomatoes, finely chopped

1 tsp sugar

1 tsp ghee

2 cloves

2.5cm/1in cinnamon

2 green cardamom pods

3 bay leaves

Salt to taste

4 large potatoes, diced and fried

250ml/8fl oz water

Method

- Grind the onions, ginger paste and coconut to a smooth paste. Set aside.
- Heat the oil in a frying pan. Add the prawns and fry them on a medium heat for 5 minutes. Drain and set aside.
- To the same oil, add the ground paste and all the remaining ingredients, except the water. Stir-fry for 6-7 minutes. Add the fried prawns and the water. Mix well and simmer for 10 minutes. Serve hot.

Fish Sorse Bata
(Fish in Mustard Paste)

Serves 4

Ingredients

4 tbsp mustard seeds

7 green chillies

2 tbsp water

½ tsp turmeric

5 tbsp mustard oil

Salt to taste

1kg/2¼lb lemon sole, skinned and filleted

Method

- Grind together all the ingredients, except the fish, with enough water to form a smooth paste. Marinate the fish with this mixture for 1 hour.
- Steam (see cooking techniques) for 25 minutes. Serve hot.

Fish Stew

Serves 4

Ingredients

1 tbsp refined vegetable oil

2 cloves

2.5cm/1in cinnamon

3 bay leaves

5 black peppercorns

1 tsp garlic paste

1 tsp ginger paste

2 large onions, finely chopped

400g/14oz frozen mixed vegetables

Salt to taste

250ml/8fl oz warm water

500g/1lb 2oz monkfish fillets

1 tbsp plain white flour, dissolved
   in 60ml/2fl oz milk

Method

- Heat the oil in a saucepan. Add the cloves, cinnamon, bay leaves and peppercorns. Let them splutter for 15 seconds. Add the garlic paste, ginger paste and onions. Fry on a medium heat for 2-3 minutes.
- Add the vegetables, salt and water. Mix well and simmer for 10 minutes.
- Carefully add the fish and the flour mixture. Mix well. Cook on a medium heat for 10 minutes. Serve hot.

Jhinga Nissa
(Prawns with Yoghurt)

Serves 4

Ingredients

1 tbsp lemon juice

1 tsp ginger paste

1 tsp garlic paste

1 tsp sesame seeds

200g/7oz yoghurt

2 green chillies, finely chopped

½ tsp dry fenugreek leaves

½ tsp ground cloves

½ tsp ground cinnamon

½ tsp ground black pepper

Salt to taste

12 large prawns, shelled and de-veined

Method

- Mix together all the ingredients, except the prawns. Marinate the prawns with this mixture for an hour.
- Arrange the marinated prawns on skewers and grill for 15 minutes. Serve hot.

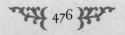

Squid Vindaloo
(Squid cooked in Spicy Goan Gravy)

Serves 4

Ingredients

8 tbsp malt vinegar
8 red chillies
3.5cm/1½in root ginger
20 garlic cloves
1 tsp mustard seeds
1 tsp cumin seeds

1 tsp turmeric
Salt to taste
6 tbsp refined vegetable oil
3 large onions, finely chopped
500g/1lb 2oz squid, sliced

Method

- Grind half the vinegar with the red chillies, ginger, garlic, mustard seeds, cumin seeds, turmeric and salt to a smooth paste. Set aside.
- Heat the oil in a saucepan. Fry the onions on a low heat till brown.
- Add the ground paste. Mix well and sauté for 5-6 minutes.
- Add the squid and the remaining vinegar. Cook on a low heat for 15-20 minutes, stirring occasionally. Serve hot.

Lobster Balchow
(Spicy Lobsters cooked in Goan Curry)

Serves 4

Ingredients

400g/14oz lobster meat, chopped
Salt to taste
½ tsp turmeric
60ml/2fl oz malt vinegar
1 tsp sugar

120ml/4fl oz refined vegetable oil
2 large onions, finely chopped
12 garlic cloves, finely chopped
1 tsp garam masala
1 tbsp coriander leaves, chopped

Method

- Marinate the lobster with the salt, turmeric, vinegar and sugar for 1 hour.
- Heat the oil in a saucepan. Add the onions and garlic. Fry on a low heat for 2-3 minutes. Add the marinated lobster and the garam masala. Cook on a low heat for 15 minutes, stirring occasionally.
- Garnish with the coriander leaves. Serve hot.

Prawns with Aubergine

Serves 4

Ingredients

4 tbsp refined vegetable oil

6 black peppercorns

3 green chillies

4 cloves

6 garlic cloves

1cm/½in root ginger

2 tbsp coriander leaves, chopped

1½ tbsp desiccated coconut

2 large onions, finely chopped

500g/1lb 2oz aubergines, chopped

250g/9oz prawns, shelled and de-veined

½ tsp turmeric

1 tsp tamarind paste

Salt to taste

10 cashew nuts

120ml/4fl oz water

Method

- Heat 1 tbsp of the oil in a saucepan. Add the peppercorns, green chillies, cloves, garlic, ginger, coriander leaves and coconut on a medium heat for 2-3 minutes. Grind the mixture to a smooth paste. Set aside.
- Heat the remaining oil in a saucepan. Add the onions and fry on a medium heat for a minute. Add the aubergines, prawns and turmeric. Stir-fry for 5 minutes.
- Add the ground paste and all the remaining ingredients. Mix well and simmer for 10-15 minutes. Serve hot.

Green Prawns

Serves 4

Ingredients

Juice of 1 lemon

50g/1¾oz mint leaves

50g/1¾oz coriander leaves

4 green chillies

2.5cm/1in root ginger

8 garlic cloves

Pinch of garam masala

Salt to taste

20 medium-sized prawns,
   shelled and de-veined

Method

- Grind together all the ingredients, except the prawns, to a smooth paste. Marinate the prawns with this mixture for 1 hour.
- Skewer the prawns. Grill for 10 minutes, turning occasionally. Serve hot.

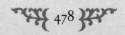

Fish with Coriander

Serves 4

Ingredients

3 tbsp refined vegetable oil
1 large onion, finely chopped
4 green chillies, finely chopped
1 tbsp ginger paste
1 tbsp garlic paste

1 tsp turmeric
Salt to taste
100g/3½oz coriander leaves, chopped
1kg/2¼lb salmon, skinned and filleted
250ml/8fl oz water

Method

- Heat the oil in a saucepan. Fry the onion on a low heat till brown.
- Add all the remaining ingredients, except the fish and water. Fry for 3-4 minutes. Add the fish and sauté for 3-4 minutes.
- Add the water. Mix well and simmer for 10-12 minutes. Serve hot.

Fish Malai
(Fish cooked in Creamy Gravy)

Serves 4

Ingredients

250ml/8fl oz refined vegetable oil
1kg/2¼lb sea bass fillets
1 tbsp plain white flour
1 large onion, grated
½ tsp turmeric
250ml/8fl oz coconut milk
Salt to taste

For the spice mixture:

1 tsp coriander seeds
1 tsp cumin seeds
4 green chillies
6 garlic cloves
6 tbsp water

Method

- Grind the spice mixture ingredients together. Squeeze the mixture to extract its juice in a small bowl. Set the juice aside. Discard the husk.
- Heat the oil in a frying pan. Coat the fish with the flour and deep fry on a medium heat till golden brown. Drain and set aside.
- To the same oil, add the onion and fry on a medium heat till brown.
- Add the spice mixture juice and all the remaining ingredients. Mix well.
- Simmer for 10 minutes. Add the fish and cook for 5 minutes. Serve hot.

Konkani Fish Curry

Serves 4

Ingredients

1kg/2¼lb salmon, skinned and filleted
Salt to taste
1 tsp turmeric
1 tsp chilli powder
2 tbsp refined vegetable oil

1 large onion, finely chopped
½ tsp ginger paste
750ml/1¼ pints coconut milk
3 green chillies, slit lengthways

Method

- Marinate the fish with the salt, turmeric and chilli powder for 30 minutes.
- Heat the oil in a saucepan. Add the onion and ginger paste. Fry on a medium heat till the onions turn translucent.
- Add the coconut milk, green chillies and the marinated fish. Mix well. Simmer for 15 minutes. Serve hot.

Spicy Prawns with Garlic

Serves 4

Ingredients

4 tbsp refined vegetable oil
2 large onions, finely chopped
1 tbsp garlic paste
12 garlic cloves, chopped
1 tsp chilli powder
1 tsp ground coriander
½ tsp ground cumin

2 tomatoes, finely chopped
Salt to taste
1 tsp turmeric
750g/1lb 10oz prawns, shelled and de-veined
250ml/8fl oz water

Method

- Heat the oil in a saucepan. Add the onions, garlic paste and chopped garlic. Fry on a medium heat till the onions turn translucent.
- Add the remaining ingredients, except the prawns and water. Fry for 3-4 minutes. Add the prawns and sauté for 3-4 minutes.
- Add the water. Mix well and simmer for 12-15 minutes. Serve hot.

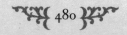

Simple Fish Curry

Serves 4

Ingredients

2 large onions, quartered
3 cloves
2.5cm/1in cinnamon
4 black peppercorns
2 tsp coriander seeds
1 tsp cumin seeds

1 tomato, quartered
Salt to taste
2 tbsp refined vegetable oil
750g/1lb 10oz salmon, skinned and filleted
250ml/8fl oz water

Method

* Grind together all the ingredients, except the oil, fish and water. Heat the oil in a saucepan. Add the paste and fry on a low heat for 7 minutes.
* Add the fish and water. Cook for 25 minutes, stirring frequently. Serve hot.

Goan Fish Curry

Serves 4

Ingredients

100g/3½oz fresh coconut, grated
4 dry red chillies
1 tsp cumin seeds
1 tsp coriander seeds
360ml/12fl oz water
3 tbsp refined vegetable oil
1 large onion, grated

1 tsp turmeric
8 curry leaves
2 tomatoes, blanched and chopped
2 green chillies, slit lengthways
1 tbsp tamarind paste
Salt to taste
1kg/2¼lb salmon, sliced

Method

* Grind the coconut, red chillies, cumin seeds and coriander seeds with 4 tbsp water into a thick paste. Set aside.
* Heat the oil in a saucepan. Fry the onion on a low heat till translucent.
* Add the coconut paste. Fry for 3-4 minutes.
* Add all the remaining ingredients, except the fish and remaining water. Sauté for 6-7 minutes. Add the fish and water. Mix well and simmer for 20 minutes, stirring occasionally. Serve hot.

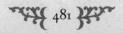

Prawn Vindaloo

(Prawns cooked in Spicy Goan Curry)

Serves 4

Ingredients

3 tbsp refined vegetable oil

1 large onion, grated

4 tomatoes, finely chopped

1½ tsp chilli powder

½ tsp turmeric

2 tsp ground cumin

750g/1lb 10oz prawns, shelled and de-veined

3 tbsp white vinegar

1 tsp sugar

Salt to taste

Method

- Heat the oil in a saucepan. Add the onion and fry on a medium heat for 1-2 minutes. Add the tomatoes, chilli powder, turmeric and cumin. Mix well and cook for 6-7 minutes, stirring occasionally.
- Add the prawns and mix well. Cook on a low heat for 10 minutes.
- Add the vinegar, sugar and salt. Simmer for 5-7 minutes. Serve hot.

Fish in Green Masala

Serves 4

Ingredients

750g/1lb 10oz swordfish, skinned and filleted

Salt to taste

1 tsp turmeric

50g/1¾oz mint leaves

100g/3½oz coriander leaves

12 garlic cloves

5cm/2in root ginger

2 large onions, sliced

5cm/2in cinnamon

1 tbsp poppy seeds

3 cloves

500ml/16fl oz water

3 tbsp refined vegetable oil

Method

- Marinate the fish with the salt and turmeric for 30 minutes.
- Grind together the remaining ingredients, except the oil, with enough water to form a thick paste.
- Heat the oil in a saucepan. Add the paste and fry on a medium heat for 4-5 minutes. Add the marinated fish and the remaining water. Mix well and simmer for 20 minutes, stirring occasionally. Serve hot.

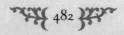

Clams Masala

Serves 4

Ingredients

500g/1lb 2oz clams, cleaned
  (see cooking techniques)

Salt to taste

¾ tsp turmeric

1 tbsp coriander seeds

3 cloves

2.5cm/1in cinnamon

4 black peppercorns

2.5cm/1in root ginger

8 garlic cloves

60g/2oz fresh coconut, grated

2 tbsp refined vegetable oil

1 large onion, finely chopped

500ml/16fl oz water

Method

- Steam (see cooking techniques) the clams in a steamer for 20 minutes. Sprinkle salt and turmeric on top of them. Set aside.
- Grind together the remaining ingredients, except the oil, onion and water.
- Heat the oil in a saucepan. Add the ground paste and onion. Fry on a medium heat for 4-5 minutes. Add the steamed clams and fry for 5 minutes. Add the water. Cook for 10 minutes and serve hot.

Fish Tikka

Serves 4

Ingredients

2 tsp ginger paste

2 tsp garlic paste

1 tsp garam masala

1 tsp chilli powder

2 tsp ground cumin

2 tbsp lemon juice

Salt to taste

1kg/2¼lb monkfish, skinned and filleted

Refined vegetable oil for
  shallow frying

2 eggs, whisked

3 tbsp semolina

Method

- Mix the ginger paste, garlic paste, garam masala, chilli powder, cumin, lemon juice and salt. Marinate the fish with this mixture for 2 hours.
- Heat the oil in a frying pan. Dip the marinated fish in the egg, roll in the semolina and shallow fry on a medium heat for 4-5 minutes.
- Flip and fry for 2-3 minutes. Drain on absorbent paper and serve hot.

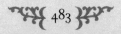

Aubergine Stuffed with Prawns

Serves 4

Ingredients

4 tbsp refined vegetable oil

1 large onion, finely grated

2 tsp ginger paste

2 tsp garlic paste

1 tsp turmeric

½ tsp garam masala

Salt to taste

1 tsp tamarind paste

180g/6½oz prawns, shelled and de-veined

60ml/2fl oz water

8 small aubergines

10g/¼oz coriander leaves, chopped, to garnish

Method

• For the stuffing, heat half the oil in a saucepan. Add the onion and fry on a low heat till brown. Add the ginger paste, garlic paste, turmeric and garam masala. Sauté for 2-3 minutes.

• Add the salt, tamarind paste, prawns and water. Mix well and simmer for 15 minutes. Set aside to cool.

• With a knife, make a cross at one end of an aubergine. Cut deeper along the cross, leaving the other end unsevered. Stuff the prawn mixture into this cavity. Repeat for all the aubergines.

• Heat the remaining oil in a frying pan. Add the stuffed aubergines. Fry on a low heat for 12-15 minutes, turning occasionally. Garnish and serve hot.

Prawns with Garlic & Cinnamon

Serves 4

Ingredients

250ml/8fl oz refined vegetable oil

1 tsp turmeric

2 tsp garlic paste

Salt to taste

500g/1lb 2oz prawns, shelled and de-veined

2 tsp ground cinnamon

Method

• Heat the oil in a saucepan. Add the turmeric, garlic paste and salt. Fry on a medium heat for 2 minutes. Add the prawns and cook for 15 minutes.

• Add the cinnamon. Cook for 2 minutes and serve hot.

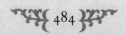

Sole Steamed in Mustard

Serves 4

Ingredients

1 tsp ginger paste

1 tsp garlic paste

¼ tsp red chilli paste

2 tsp English mustard

2 tsp lemon juice

1 tsp mustard oil

Salt to taste

1kg/2¼lb lemon sole, skinned and filleted

25g/scant 1oz coriander leaves,
  finely chopped

Method

- Mix together all the ingredients, except the fish and the coriander leaves. Marinate the fish with this mixture for 30 minutes.
- Place the fish in a shallow dish. Steam (see cooking techniques) in a steamer for 15 minutes. Garnish with the coriander leaves and serve hot.

Yellow Fish Curry

Serves 4

Ingredients

100ml/3½fl oz mustard oil

1kg/2¼lb salmon, skinned and filleted

4 tsp English mustard

1 tsp ground coriander

1 tsp chilli powder

2 tsp garlic paste

125g/4½oz tomato purée

120ml/4fl oz water

Salt to taste

1 tsp turmeric

2 tbsp coriander leaves,
  finely chopped, to garnish

Method

- Heat the oil in a frying pan. Add the fish and fry on a low heat till golden brown. Flip and repeat. Drain the fish and set aside. Reserve the oil.
- Mix the mustard with the ground coriander, chilli powder and garlic.
- Heat the oil used for frying the fish. Fry the mustard mixture for a minute.
- Add the tomato purée. Fry on a medium heat for 4-5 minutes.
- Add the fried fish, water, salt and turmeric. Mix well and simmer for 15-20 minutes, stirring occasionally.
- Garnish with the coriander leaves. Serve hot.

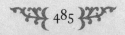

Batter Fried Fish

Serves 4

Ingredients

1kg/2¼lb monkfish, skinned and filleted
½ tsp turmeric
Salt to taste
125g/4½oz besan*
3 tbsp breadcrumbs
½ tsp chilli powder
½ tsp ground black pepper
1 green chilli, chopped
1 tsp ajowan seeds
3 tbsp chopped coriander leaves
500ml/16fl oz water
Refined vegetable oil for deep frying

Method

- Marinate the fish with the turmeric and salt for 30 minutes.
- Mix together the remaining ingredients, except the oil, to form a batter.
- Heat the oil in a pan. Dip the marinated fish in the batter and deep fry on a medium heat till golden brown.
- Drain on absorbent paper and serve hot.

Fish Caldine
(Goan-style Fish)

Serves 4

Ingredients

3 tbsp refined vegetable oil
3 large onions, finely sliced
6 green chillies, slit lengthways
750g/1lb 10oz filleted sea bass, chopped
1 tsp ground cumin
1 tsp turmeric
1 tsp ginger paste
1 tsp garlic paste
360ml/12fl oz coconut milk
2 tsp tamarind paste
Salt to taste

Method

- Heat the oil in a saucepan. Add the onions and fry on a low heat till brown.
- Add the green chillies, fish, ground cumin, turmeric, ginger paste, garlic paste and the coconut milk. Mix well and simmer for 10 minutes.
- Add the tamarind paste and salt. Mix well and simmer for 15 minutes. Serve hot.

Prawn and Egg Curry

Serves 4

Ingredients

3 tbsp refined vegetable oil

2 cloves

2.5cm/1in cinnamon

6 black peppercorns

2 bay leaves

1 large onion, finely chopped

½ tsp turmeric

1 tsp ginger paste

1 tsp garlic paste

1 tsp garam masala

12 large prawns, shelled and de-veined

Salt to taste

200g/7oz tomato purée

120ml/4fl oz water

4 hard-boiled eggs, halved lengthways

Method

- Heat the oil in a saucepan. Add the cloves, cinnamon, peppercorns and bay leaves. Let them splutter for 15 seconds.
- Add the remaining ingredients, except the tomato purée, water and eggs. Sauté on a medium heat for 6-7 minutes. Add the tomato purée and water. Simmer for 10-12 minutes.
- Add the eggs carefully. Simmer for 4-5 minutes. Serve hot.

Fish Molee

(Fish cooked in Basic Simple Curry)

Serves 4

Ingredients

2 tbsp ghee

1 small onion, finely chopped

4 garlic cloves, finely sliced

2.5cm/1in root ginger, finely sliced

6 green chillies, slit lengthways

1 tsp turmeric

Salt to taste

750ml/1¼ pints coconut milk

1kg/2¼lb sea bass, skinned and filleted

Method

- Heat the ghee in a saucepan. Add the onion, garlic, ginger and chillies. Fry on a low heat for 2 minutes. Add the turmeric. Cook for 3-4 minutes.
- Add the salt, coconut milk and fish. Mix well and simmer for 15-20 minutes. Serve hot.

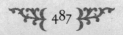

Prawns Bharta

(Prawns cooked in Classic Indian Gravy)

Serves 4

Ingredients

100ml/3½fl oz mustard oil

1 tsp cumin seeds

1 large onion, grated

1 tsp turmeric

1 tsp garam masala

2 tsp ginger paste

2 tsp garlic paste

2 tomatoes, finely chopped

3 green chillies, slit lengthways

750g/1lb 10oz prawns, shelled and de-veined

250ml/8fl oz water

Salt to taste

Method

- Heat the oil in a saucepan. Add the cumin seeds. Let them splutter for 15 seconds. Add the onion and fry on a medium heat till brown.
- Add all the remaining ingredients. Simmer for 15 minutes and serve hot.

Spicy Fish & Vegetables

Serves 4

Ingredients

2 tbsp mustard oil

500g/1lb 2oz lemon sole, skinned and filleted

¼ tsp mustard seeds

¼ tsp fennel seeds

¼ tsp fenugreek seeds

¼ tsp cumin seeds

2 bay leaves

½ tsp turmeric

2 dry red chillies, halved

1 large onion, finely sliced

200g/7oz frozen mixed vegetables

360ml/12fl oz water

Salt to taste

Method

- Heat the oil in a saucepan. Add the fish and shallow fry on a medium heat till golden brown. Flip and repeat. Drain and set aside.
- To the same oil, add the mustard, fennel, fenugreek and cumin seeds, bay leaves, turmeric and red chillies. Fry for 30 seconds.
- Add the onion. Fry on a medium heat for 1 minute. Add the remaining ingredients and the fried fish. Simmer for 30 minutes and serve hot.

Mackerel Cutlet

Serves 4

Ingredients

4 large mackerel, cleaned

Salt to taste

½ tsp turmeric

2 tsp malt vinegar

250ml/8fl oz water

1 tbsp refined vegetable oil plus extra
for shallow frying

2 big onions, finely chopped

1 tsp ginger paste

1 tsp garlic paste

1 tomato, finely chopped

1 tsp ground black pepper

1 egg, whisked

10g/¼oz coriander leaves, chopped

3 bread slices, soaked and squeezed

60g/2oz rice flour

Method

- Cook the mackerel in a saucepan with the salt, turmeric, vinegar and
  water on a medium heat for 15 minutes. De-bone and mash. Set aside.
- Heat 1 tbsp oil in a saucepan. Fry the onions on a low heat till brown.
- Add the ginger paste, garlic paste and tomato. Sauté for 4-5 minutes.
- Add the pepper and salt and remove from the heat. Mix with the mashed
  fish, egg, coriander leaves and bread. Knead and shape into 8 cutlets.
- Heat the oil in a frying pan. Roll the cutlets in the rice flour and shallow
  fry on a medium heat for 4-5 minutes. Flip and repeat. Serve hot.

Tandoori Crab

Serves 4

Ingredients

2 tsp ginger paste

2 tsp garlic paste

2 tsp garam masala

1 tbsp lemon juice

125g/4½oz Greek yoghurt

Salt to taste

4 crabs, cleaned (see cooking
techniques)

1 tbsp refined vegetable oil

Method

- Mix all ingredients together except the crabs and oil. Marinate the crabs
  with this mixture for 3-4 hours.
- Brush the marinated crab with the oil. Grill for 10-15 minutes. Serve hot.

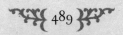

Stuffed Fish

Serves 4

Ingredients

2 tbsp refined vegetable oil plus extra
  for shallow frying
1 large onion, finely minced
1 large tomato, finely chopped
1 tsp ginger paste
1 tsp garlic paste
1 tsp ground coriander

1 tsp ground cumin
Salt to taste
1 tsp turmeric
2 tbsp malt vinegar
1kg/2¼lb salmon, slit
  at the belly
25g/scant 1oz breadcrumbs

Method
- Heat 2 tbsp of the oil in a saucepan. Add the onion and fry on a low heat till brown. Add the remaining ingredients, except the vinegar, fish and breadcrumbs. Sauté for 5 minutes.
- Add the vinegar. Simmer for 5 minutes. Stuff the fish with the mixture.
- Heat the remaining oil in a frying pan. Roll the fish in the breadcrumbs and shallow fry on a medium heat till golden brown. Flip and repeat. Serve hot.

Prawn & Cauliflower Curry

Serves 4

Ingredients

10 tbsp refined vegetable oil
1 large onion, finely chopped
¾ tsp turmeric
250g/9oz prawns, shelled and de-veined
200g/7oz cauliflower florets
Salt to taste

For the spice mixture:
1 tbsp coriander seeds
1 tbsp garam masala
5 red chillies
2.5cm/1in root ginger
8 garlic cloves
60g/2oz fresh coconut

Method
- Heat half the oil in a frying pan. Add the spice mixture ingredients and fry on a medium heat for 5 minutes. Grind to a thick paste. Set aside.
- Heat the remaining oil in a saucepan. Fry the onion on a medium heat till translucent. Add all the remaining ingredients and the spice paste.
- Simmer for 15-20 minutes, stirring occasionally. Serve hot.

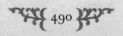

Stir-Fried Clams

Serves 4

Ingredients

500g/1lb 2oz clams, cleaned (see cooking techniques)
6 tbsp refined vegetable oil
2 large onions, finely chopped
1 tsp turmeric
1 tsp garam masala

2 tsp ginger paste
2 tsp garlic paste
10g/¼oz coriander leaves, chopped
6 kokums*
Salt to taste
250ml/8fl oz water

Method

- Steam (see cooking techniques) the clams for 25 minutes. Set aside.
- Heat the oil in a saucepan. Fry the onions on a low heat till brown.
- Add the remaining ingredients, except the water. Sauté for 5-6 minutes.
- Add the steamed clams and the water. Cover with a lid and simmer for 10 minutes. Serve hot.

Batter Fried Shrimp

Serves 4

Ingredients

250g/9oz shrimps, peeled
250g/9oz besan*
2 green chillies, finely chopped
1 tsp chilli powder
1 tsp turmeric
1 tsp ground coriander
1 tsp ground cumin

½ tsp amchoor*
1 small onion, grated
¼ tsp bicarbonate of soda
Salt to taste
Refined vegetable oil for deep frying

Method

- Mix together all the ingredients, except the oil, with enough water to form a thick batter.
- Heat the oil in a pan. Drop a few spoonfuls of the batter in it and fry on a medium heat till golden on all sides.
- Repeat for the remaining batter. Serve hot.

Mackerel in Tomato Gravy

Serves 4

Ingredients

1 tbsp refined vegetable oil

2 large onions, finely chopped

2 tomatoes, finely chopped

1 tbsp ginger paste

1 tbsp garlic paste

1 tsp chilli powder

½ tsp turmeric

8 dry kokum*

2 green chillies, sliced

Salt to taste

4 large mackerel, skinned and filleted

120ml/4fl oz water

Method

- Heat the oil in a saucepan. Fry the onions on a medium heat till brown. Add all the remaining ingredients, except the fish and water. Mix well and sauté for 5-6 minutes.
- Add the fish and water. Mix well. Simmer for 15 minutes and serve hot.

Konju Ullaruathu
(Scampi in Red Masala)

Serves 4

Ingredients

120ml/4fl oz refined vegetable oil

1 large onion, finely chopped

5cm/2in root ginger, finely sliced

12 garlic cloves, finely sliced

2 tbsp green chillies, finely chopped

8 curry leaves

2 tomatoes, finely chopped

1 tsp turmeric

2 tsp ground coriander

1 tsp ground fennel

600g/1lb 5oz scampi, shelled and de-veined

3 tsp chilli powder

Salt to taste

1 tsp garam masala

Method

- Heat the oil in a saucepan. Add the onion, ginger, garlic, green chillies and curry leaves and fry on a medium heat for 1-2 minutes.
- Add all the remaining ingredients, except the garam masala. Mix well and cook on a low heat for 15-20 minutes.
- Sprinkle with the garam masala and serve hot.

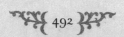

Chemeen Manga Curry
(Curried Prawns with Unripe Mango)

Serves 4

Ingredients

200g/7oz fresh coconut, grated

1 tbsp chilli powder

2 large onions, finely sliced

3 tbsp refined vegetable oil

2 green chillies, chopped

2.5cm/1in root ginger, thinly sliced

Salt to taste

1 tsp turmeric

1 small unripe mango, diced

120ml/4fl oz water

750g/1lb 10oz tiger prawns, shelled and de-veined

1 tsp mustard seeds

10 curry leaves

2 whole red chillies

4-5 shallots, sliced

Method

* Grind together the coconut, chilli powder and half the onions. Set aside.
* Heat half the oil in a saucepan. Sauté the remaining onions with the green chillies, ginger, salt and turmeric on a low heat for 3-4 minutes.
* Add the coconut paste, unripe mango and water. Simmer for 8 minutes.
* Add the prawns. Simmer for 10-12 minutes and set aside.
* Heat the remaining oil. Add the mustard seeds, curry leaves, chillies and shallots. Fry for a minute. Add this mixture to the prawns and serve hot.

Simple Machchi Fry
(Fish fried with Spices)

Serves 4

Ingredients

8 fillets of firm white fish such as cod

¾ tsp turmeric

½ tsp chilli powder

1 tsp lemon juice

250ml/8fl oz refined vegetable oil

2 tbsp plain white flour

Method

* Marinate the fish with the turmeric, chilli powder and lemon juice for 1 hour.
* Heat the oil in a frying pan. Coat the fish with the flour and shallow fry on a medium heat for 3-4 minutes. Flip and fry for 2-3 minutes. Serve hot.

Machher Kalia

(Fish in Rich Gravy)

Serves 4

Ingredients

1 tsp coriander seeds	3 bay leaves
2 tsp cumin seeds	1 large onion, finely chopped
1 tsp chilli powder	4 garlic cloves, finely chopped
2.5cm/1in root ginger, peeled	4 green chillies, sliced
250ml/8fl oz water	Salt to taste
120ml/4fl oz refined vegetable oil	1 tsp turmeric
500g/1lb 2oz trout fillets, skinned	2 tbsp yoghurt

Method

- Grind the coriander seeds, cumin seeds, chilli powder and ginger with enough water to form a thick paste. Set aside.
- Heat the oil in a saucepan. Add the fish and fry on a medium heat for 3-4 minutes. Flip and repeat. Drain and set aside.
- To the same oil, add the bay leaves, onion, garlic and green chillies. Fry for 2 minutes. Add the remaining ingredients, the fried fish and the paste. Mix well and simmer for 15 minutes. Serve hot.

Fish Fried in Egg

Serves 4

Ingredients

500g/1lb 2oz John Dory, skinned and filleted	1 tbsp plain white flour
Juice of 1 lemon	½ tsp ground black pepper
Salt to taste	1 tsp chilli powder
2 eggs	250ml/8fl oz refined vegetable oil
	100g/3½oz breadcrumbs

Method

- Marinate the fish with the lemon juice and salt for 4 hours.
- Whisk the eggs with the flour, pepper and chilli powder.
- Heat the oil in a frying pan. Dip the marinated fish in the egg mixture, roll in the breadcrumbs and fry on a low heat till golden brown. Serve hot.

Lau Chingri
(Shrimps with Pumpkin)

Serves 4

Ingredients

250g/9oz shrimps, peeled
500g/1lb 2oz pumpkin, diced
2 tbsp mustard oil
¼ tsp cumin seeds
1 bay leaf

½ tsp turmeric
1 tbsp ground coriander
¼ tsp sugar
1 tbsp milk
Salt to taste

Method
- Steam (see cooking techniques) the shrimps and pumpkin together for 15-20 minutes. Set aside.
- Heat the oil in a saucepan. Add the cumin seeds and bay leaf. Fry for 15 seconds. Add the turmeric and ground coriander. Fry on a medium heat for 2-3 minutes. Add the sugar, milk, salt and the steamed shrimps and pumpkin. Simmer for 10 minutes. Serve hot.

Tomato Fish

Serves 4

Ingredients

2 tbsp plain white flour
1 tsp ground black pepper
500g/1lb 2oz lemon sole, skinned and filleted
3 tbsp butter
2 bay leaves

1 small onion, grated
6 garlic cloves, finely chopped
2 tsp lemon juice
6 tbsp fish stock
150g/5½oz tomato purée
Salt to taste

Method
- Mix the flour and pepper together. Toss the fish in the mixture.
- Heat the butter in a frying pan. Fry the fish on a medium heat till golden. Drain and set aside.
- In the same butter, fry the bay leaves, onion and garlic on a medium heat for 2-3 minutes. Add the fried fish and all the remaining ingredients. Mix well and simmer for 20 minutes. Serve hot.

Chingri Machher Kalia
(Rich Prawn Curry)

Serves 4

Ingredients

24 large prawns, shelled
   and de-veined
½ tsp turmeric
Salt to taste
250ml/8fl oz water

3 tbsp mustard oil
2 large onions, finely grated
6 dry red chillies, ground
2 tbsp coriander leaves,
   finely chopped

Method
* Cook the prawns with the turmeric, salt and water in a saucepan on a medium heat for 20-25 minutes. Set aside. Do not discard the water.
* Heat the oil in a saucepan. Add the onions and red chillies and fry on a medium heat for 2-3 minutes.
* Add the cooked prawns and the reserved water. Mix well and simmer for 20-25 minutes. Garnish with the coriander leaves. Serve hot.

Fish Tikka Kebab

Serves 4

Ingredients

1 tbsp malt vinegar
1 tbsp yoghurt
1 tsp ginger paste
1 tsp garlic paste
2 green chillies, finely chopped
1 tsp garam masala

1 tsp ground cumin
1 tsp chilli powder
Dash of orange food colouring
Salt to taste
675g/1½lb monkfish, skinned and
   filleted

Method
* Mix together all the ingredients, except the fish. Marinate the fish with this mixture for 3 hours.
* Arrange the marinated fish on skewers and grill for 20 minutes. Serve hot.

Chingri Machher Cutlet
(Prawn Cutlets)

Serves 4

Ingredients

12 prawns, shelled and de-veined

Salt to taste

500ml/16fl oz water

4 green chillies, finely chopped

2 tbsp, garlic paste

50g/1¾oz coriander leaves, chopped

1 tsp ground cumin

Pinch of turmeric

Refined vegetable oil for deep frying

1 egg, whisked

4 tbsp breadcrumbs

Method
• Cook the prawns with the salt and water in a saucepan on a medium heat for 20 minutes. Drain and mash with all the remaining ingredients, except the oil, egg and breadcrumbs.
• Divide the mixture into 8 portions, roll into balls and flatten into cutlets.
• Heat the oil in a pan. Dip the cutlets in the egg, roll in the breadcrumbs and deep fry on a medium heat till golden. Serve hot.

Baked Fish

Serves 4

Ingredients

500g/1lb 2oz lemon sole or red snapper fillets, skinned

Salt to taste

1 tsp ground black pepper

¼ tsp dry red chillies, finely chopped

2 large green peppers, finely chopped

2 tomatoes, sliced

1 large onion, sliced

Juice of 1 lemon

3 green chillies, slit lengthways

10 garlic cloves, finely sliced

1 tbsp olive oil

Method
• Place the fish fillets in an ovenproof dish and sprinkle the salt, pepper and chillies on top of them.
• Spread the remaining ingredients over this mixture.
• Cover the dish and bake in an oven at 200°C (400°F, Gas Mark 6) for 15 minutes. Uncover and bake for 10 minutes. Serve hot.

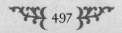

Prawns with Green Peppers

Serves 4

Ingredients

4 tbsp refined vegetable oil
2 large onions, finely sliced
5cm/2in root ginger, finely sliced
12 garlic cloves, finely sliced
4 green chillies, slit lengthways
½ tsp turmeric

2 tomatoes, finely chopped
500g/1lb 2oz prawns, shelled and de-veined
3 green peppers, cored and sliced
Salt to taste
1 tbsp coriander leaves, chopped

Method

- Heat the oil in a saucepan. Add the onions, ginger, garlic and green chillies. Fry on a low heat for 1-2 minutes. Add the remaining ingredients, except the coriander leaves. Mix well and sauté for 15 minutes.
- Garnish with the coriander leaves. Serve hot.

Machher Jhole
(Fish in Gravy)

Serves 4

Ingredients

500g/1lb 2oz trout, skinned and filleted
1 tsp turmeric
Salt to taste
4 tbsp mustard oil
3 dry red chillies
1 tsp garam masala

1 large onion, grated
2 tsp ginger paste
1 tsp ground mustard
1 tsp ground coriander
250ml/8fl oz water
1 tbsp coriander leaves, chopped

Method

- Marinate the fish with the turmeric and salt for 30 minutes.
- Heat the oil in a frying pan. Fry the marinated fish on a medium heat for 2-3 minutes. Flip and repeat. Set aside.
- In the same oil, fry the chillies and the garam masala on a medium heat for 1-2 minutes. Add the remaining ingredients, except the coriander leaves. Mix well and simmer for 10 minutes. Add the fish and mix well.
- Simmer for 10 minutes. Sprinkle with the coriander leaves and serve hot.

Machher Paturi
(Fish Steamed in Banana Leaves)

Serves 4

Ingredients

5 tbsp mustard seeds
5 green chillies
1 tsp turmeric
1 tsp chilli powder
1 tbsp mustard oil
½ tsp fennel seeds
2 tbsp coriander leaves, finely chopped

½ tsp sugar
Salt to taste
750g/1lb 10oz trout, skinned and filleted
20 x 15cm/8 x 6in banana leaves, washed

Method

- Grind together all the ingredients, except the fish and the banana leaves, to a smooth paste. Marinate the fish with this paste for 30 minutes.
- Wrap the fish in the banana leaves and steam (see cooking techniques) in a steamer for 20-25 minutes. Unwrap carefully and serve hot.

Chingri Machher Shorsher Jhole
(Prawn Mustard Curry)

Serves 4

Ingredients

6 dry red chillies
½ tsp turmeric
3 tsp cumin seeds
1 tbsp mustard seeds
12 garlic cloves

2 large onions
Salt to taste
24 prawns, shelled and de-veined
3 tbsp mustard oil
500ml/16fl oz water

Method

- Grind together all the ingredients, except the prawns, oil and water, to a smooth paste. Marinate the prawns with this paste for 1 hour.
- Heat the oil in a saucepan. Add the prawns and fry them on a medium heat for 4-5 minutes.
- Add the water. Mix well and simmer for 20 minutes. Serve hot.

Prawn & Potato Curry

Serves 4

Ingredients

3 tbsp refined vegetable oil

2 large onions, finely chopped

3 tomatoes, finely chopped

1 tsp garlic paste

1 tsp chilli powder

½ tsp turmeric

1 tsp garam masala

250g/9oz prawns, shelled and de-veined

2 large potatoes, diced

250ml/8fl oz hot water

1 tsp lemon juice

10g/¼oz coriander leaves, chopped

Salt to taste

Method

- Heat the oil in a saucepan. Fry the onions on a low heat till brown.
- Add the tomatoes, garlic paste, chilli powder, turmeric and garam masala. Sauté for 4-5 minutes. Add the remaining ingredients. Mix well.
- Simmer for 20 minutes and serve hot.

Prawn Molee

(Prawns cooked in a Simple Curry)

Serves 4

Ingredients

3 tbsp refined vegetable oil

2 large onions, finely chopped

2.5cm/1in root ginger, julienned

8 garlic cloves, chopped

4 green chillies, slit lengthways

375g/13oz prawns, shelled and de-veined

3 tomatoes, finely chopped

1 tsp turmeric

½ tsp chilli powder

Salt to taste

750ml/1¼ pints coconut milk

Method

- Heat the oil in a saucepan. Add the onions, ginger, garlic and green chillies and fry on a medium heat for 1-2 minutes.
- Add the prawns, tomatoes, turmeric, chilli powder and salt. Sauté for 5-6 minutes. Add the coconut milk. Mix well and simmer for 10-12 minutes. Serve hot.

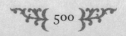

Fish Koliwada
(Spicy Fried Fish)

Serves 4

Ingredients

675g/1½lb monkfish, skinned and filleted

Salt to taste

1 tsp lemon juice

250g/9oz besan*

3 tbsp flour

1 tsp turmeric

2 tsp chaat masala*

1 tsp garam masala

2 tbsp coriander leaves, chopped

1 tbsp malt vinegar

1 tsp chilli powder

4 tbsp water

Refined vegetable oil for deep frying

Method

* Marinate the fish with the salt and lemon juice for 2 hours.
* Mix all the remaining ingredients, except the oil, to form a thick batter.
* Heat the oil in a pan. Generously coat the fish with the batter and deep fry on a medium heat till golden brown. Drain and serve hot.

Fish & Potato Roll

Serves 4

Ingredients

675g/1½lb lemon sole, skinned and filleted

Salt to taste

¼ tsp turmeric

1 large potato, boiled

2 tsp lemon juice

2 tbsp coriander, finely chopped

2 small onions, finely chopped

1 tsp garam masala

2-3 small green chillies

½ tsp chilli powder

Refined vegetable oil for deep frying

2 eggs, whisked

6-7 tbsp breadcrumbs

Method

* Steam (see cooking techniques) the fish for 15 minutes.
* Drain and mix with the remaining ingredients, except the oil, eggs and breadcrumbs. Knead and divide into 8 rolls, 6cm/2½in thick.
* Heat the oil in a frying pan. Dip the rolls in the egg, roll in the breadcrumbs and deep fry on a medium heat till golden. Drain and serve hot.

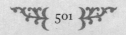

Prawn Masala

Serves 4

Ingredients

4 tbsp refined vegetable oil

3 onions, 1 sliced and 2 chopped

2 tsp coriander seeds

3 cloves

2.5cm/1in cinnamon

5 peppercorns

100g/3½oz fresh coconut, grated

6 dry red chillies

500g/1lb 2oz prawns, shelled and de-veined

½ tsp turmeric

250ml/8fl oz water

2 tsp tamarind paste

Salt to taste

Method

- Heat 1 tbsp of the oil in a saucepan. Fry the sliced onion, coriander seeds, cloves, cinnamon, peppercorns, coconut and red chillies on a medium heat for 2-3 minutes. Grind to a smooth paste. Set aside.
- Heat the remaining oil in a saucepan. Add the chopped onions and fry on a medium heat till brown. Add the prawns, turmeric and water. Mix well and simmer for 5 minutes.
- Add the ground paste, tamarind paste and salt. Stir-fry for 15 minutes. Serve hot.

Fish with Garlic

Serves 4

Ingredients

500g/1lb 2oz swordfish, skinned and filleted

Salt to taste

1 tsp turmeric

1 tbsp refined vegetable oil

2 large onions, finely grated

2 tsp garlic paste

½ tsp ginger paste

1 tsp ground coriander

125g/4½oz tomato purée

Method

- Marinate the fish with the salt and turmeric for 30 minutes.
- Heat the oil in a saucepan. Add the onions, garlic paste, ginger paste and ground coriander. Fry on a medium heat for 2 minutes.
- Add the tomato purée and fish. Simmer for 15-20 minutes. Serve hot.

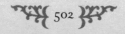

RICE

There are few Indian meals where rice doesn't figure. Indeed, in some regions of India, rice is eaten three times a day, for breakfast, lunch and dinner. Indian biryanis and pulaos are legendary and have graced many a table over the decades. This chapter contains many such famous and delicious rice dishes, along with Faada-Ni-Khichdi and Cous Cous Biryani, both classic rice dishes but here given a twist with the use of cracked wheat and cous cous respectively.

Potato Rice

Serves 4

Ingredients

150g/5½oz ghee plus extra for deep frying

1 large onion

2.5cm/1in root ginger

6 garlic cloves

125g/4½oz yoghurt, whisked

4 tbsp milk

2 green cardamom pods

2 cloves

1cm/½in cinnamon

250g/9oz basmati rice, soaked for 30 minutes and drained

Salt to taste

1 litre/1¾ pints water

15 cashew nuts, fried

For the dumplings:

3 large potatoes, boiled and mashed

125g/4½oz besan*

½ tsp chilli powder

½ tsp turmeric

1 tsp garam masala powder

1 large onion, grated

Method

* Mix all the dumpling ingredients together. Divide the mixture into small dumplings.
* Heat the ghee for deep frying in a pan. Add the dumplings and deep fry on a medium heat till golden brown. Drain and set them aside.
* Grind the onion, ginger and garlic to a paste.
* Heat 60g/2oz ghee in a saucepan. Add the paste and fry it on a medium heat till it turns translucent.
* Add the yoghurt, milk and potato dumplings. Simmer the mixture for 10-12 minutes. Set aside.
* Heat the remaining ghee in another saucepan. Add the cardamom, cloves, cinnamon, rice, salt and water. Cover with a lid and simmer for 15-20 minutes.
* Arrange the rice and potato mixture in alternate layers in an ovenproof dish. End it with a layer of rice. Garnish with cashew nuts.
* Bake the potato rice in an oven at 200°C (400°F, Gas Mark 6) for 7-8 minutes. Serve hot.

Vegetable Pulao

Serves 4

Ingredients

5 tbsp refined vegetable oil

2 cloves

2 green cardamom pods

4 black peppercorns

2.5cm/1in cinnamon

1 large onion, finely chopped

1 tsp ginger paste

1 tsp garlic paste

2 green chillies, finely chopped

1 tsp garam masala

150g/5½oz mixed vegetables (French beans, potatoes, carrots, etc.)

500g/1lb 2oz long-grained rice, soaked for 30 minutes and drained

Salt to taste

600ml/1 pint hot water

Method

- Heat the oil in a saucepan. Add the cloves, cardamom, peppercorns and cinnamon. Let them splutter for 15 seconds.
- Add the onion and fry on a medium heat for 2-3 minutes, stirring occasionally.
- Add the ginger paste, garlic paste, green chillies and garam masala. Mix well. Fry this mixture for a minute.
- Add the vegetables and rice. Stir-fry the pulao on a medium heat for 4 minutes.
- Add the salt and the water. Mix well. Cook on a medium heat for a minute.
- Cover with a lid and simmer for 10-12 minutes. Serve hot.

Kachche Gosht ki Biryani

(Lamb Biryani)

Serves 4-6

Ingredients

1kg/2¼lb lamb, chopped
  into 5cm/2in pieces

1 litre/1¾ pints water

Salt to taste

6 cloves

5cm/2in cinnamon

5 green cardamom pods

4 bay leaves

6 black peppercorns

750g/1lb 10oz basmati rice,
  soaked for 30 minutes
  and drained

150g/5½oz ghee

Pinch of saffron, dissolved
  in 1 tbsp milk

5 large onions, sliced and
  deep fried

For the marinade:

200g/7oz yoghurt

1 tsp turmeric

1 tsp chilli powder

1 tsp ginger paste

1 tsp garlic paste

1 tsp salt

25g/scant 1oz coriander
  leaves, finely chopped

25g/scant 1oz mint leaves,
  finely chopped

Method

- Mix all the marinade ingredients together and marinate the lamb pieces with this mixture for 4 hours.
- In a saucepan, mix the water with the salt, cloves, cinnamon, cardamom, bay leaves and peppercorns. Cook on a medium heat for 5-6 minutes.
- Add the drained rice. Cook for 5-7 minutes. Drain the extra water and set the rice aside.
- Pour the ghee in a large heat-proof dish and place the marinated meat over it. Place the rice in a layer over the meat.
- Sprinkle the saffron milk and some ghee on the top layer.
- Seal the pan with foil and cover with a lid.
- Simmer for 40 minutes.
- Remove from the heat and allow it to stand for another 30 minutes.
- Garnish the biryani with the onions. Serve at room temperature.

Achari Gosht ki Biryani

(Pickled Mutton Biryani)

Serves 4-6

Ingredients

4 medium-sized onions, finely chopped

400g/14oz yoghurt

2 tsp ginger paste

2 tsp garlic paste

1kg/2¼lb mutton, cut into 5cm/2in pieces

2 tsp cumin seeds

2 tsp fenugreek seeds

1 tsp onion seeds

2 tsp mustard seeds

10 green chillies

6½ tbsp ghee

50g/1¾oz mint leaves, finely chopped

100g/3½oz coriander leaves, finely chopped

2 tomatoes, quartered

750g/1lb 10oz basmati rice, soaked for 30 minutes and drained

Salt to taste

3 cloves

2 bay leaves

5cm/2in cinnamon

4 black peppercorns

Large pinch of saffron, dissolved in 1 tbsp milk

Method

- Mix the onions, yoghurt, ginger paste and garlic paste together. Marinate the mutton with this mixture for 30 minutes.
- Dry roast (see cooking techniques) the cumin, fenugreek, onion and mustard seeds together. Pound them into a coarse mixture.
- Slit the green chillies and stuff them with the pounded mixture. Set aside.
- Heat 6 tbsp ghee in a saucepan. Add the mutton. Stir-fry the mutton on a medium heat for 20 minutes. Make sure that all sides of the mutton pieces are equally browned.
- Add the stuffed green chillies. Continue to cook for another 10 minutes.
- Add the mint leaves, coriander leaves and tomatoes. Stir well for 5 minutes. Set aside.
- Mix the rice with the salt, cloves, bay leaves, cinnamon and the peppercorns. Parboil (see cooking techniques) the mixture. Set aside.
- Pour the remaining ghee in an ovenproof dish.
- Place the fried mutton pieces over the ghee. Arrange the parboiled rice in a layer over the mutton.
- Pour the saffron milk on top of the rice.
- Seal the dish with foil and cover with a lid. Bake the biryani in a preheated oven at 200°C (400°F, Gas Mark 6) for 8-10 minutes.
- Serve hot.

Yakhni Pulao

(Kashmiri Pulao)

Serves 4

Ingredients

600g/1lb 5oz mutton, cut into 2.5cm/1in pieces

2 bay leaves

10 black peppercorns

Salt to taste

1.7 litres/3 pints hot water

5 tbsp refined vegetable oil

4 cloves

3 green cardamom pods

2.5cm/1in cinnamon

1 tbsp garlic paste

1 tbsp ginger paste

3 large onions, finely chopped

500g/1lb 2oz basmati rice, soaked for 30 minutes and drained

1 tsp ground cumin

2 tsp ground coriander

200g/7oz yoghurt, whisked

1 tsp garam masala

60g/2oz onions, chopped into rings and deep fried

4-5 fried raisins

½ cucumber, sliced

1 tomato, sliced

1 egg, hard-boiled and sliced

1 green pepper, sliced

Method

- Add the mutton, bay leaves, peppercorns, and salt to the water. Cook this mixture in a saucepan on a medium heat for 20-25 minutes.
- Drain the mutton mixture and set aside. Reserve the stock.
- Heat the oil in a saucepan. Add the cloves, cardamom and cinnamon. Let them splutter for 15 seconds.
- Add the garlic paste, ginger paste and onions. Fry them on a medium heat till brown.
- Add the mutton mixture. Fry for 4-5 minutes, stirring at regular intervals.
- Add the rice, cumin, coriander, yoghurt, garam masala and salt. Stir lightly.
- Add the mutton stock, along with enough hot water to stand 2.5cm/1in above the level of the rice.
- Simmer the pulao for 10-12 minutes.
- Garnish with the onion rings, raisins, cucumber, tomato, egg and green pepper. Serve hot.

Hyderabadi Biryani

Serves 4

Ingredients

1kg/2¼lb mutton, cut into 3.5cm/1½in pieces

2 tsp ginger paste

2 tsp garlic paste

Salt to taste

6 tbsp refined vegetable oil

500g/1lb 2oz yoghurt

2 litres/3½ pints water

2 large potatoes, peeled and quartered

750g/1lb 10oz basmati rice, parboiled (see cooking techniques)

1 tbsp ghee, heated

For the spice mixture:

4 large onions, thinly sliced

3 cloves

2.5cm/1in cinnamon

3 green cardamom pods

2 bay leaves

6 peppercorns

6 green chillies

50g/1¾oz coriander leaves, crushed

2 tsp lemon juice

1 tbsp ground cumin

1 tsp turmeric

1 tbsp ground coriander

Method

- Marinate the mutton with the ginger paste, garlic paste and salt for 2 hours.
- Mix all the spice mixture ingredients together.
- Heat the oil in a saucepan. Add the spice mixture and fry it on a medium heat for 5-7 minutes.
- Add the yoghurt, the marinated mutton and 250ml/8fl oz water. Simmer for 15-20 minutes, stirring occasionally.
- Add the potatoes, rice and the remaining water. Simmer for 15 minutes.
- Pour the ghee over the rice and cover tightly with a lid.
- Simmer till the rice is done. Serve hot.

Vegetable Biryani

Serves 4

Ingredients

4 tbsp refined vegetable oil

2 big onions, thinly sliced

1 tbsp ginger paste

1 tbsp garlic paste

6 peppercorns

2 bay leaves

3 green cardamom pods

2.5cm/1in cinnamon

3 cloves

1 tsp turmeric

1 tbsp ground coriander

6 red chillies, ground

50g/1¾oz fresh coconut, grated

200g/7oz frozen mixed vegetables

2 slices pineapple, finely chopped

10-12 cashew nuts

200g/7oz yoghurt

Salt to taste

750g/1lb 10oz basmati rice, parboiled (see cooking techniques)

Dash of yellow food colour

4 tsp ghee

1 tbsp ground cumin

3 tbsp coriander leaves, finely chopped

Method

- Heat the oil in a saucepan. Add all the onions, ginger paste and garlic paste. Stir-fry the mixture on a medium heat till the onions turn translucent.
- Add the peppercorns, bay leaves, cardamom, cinnamon, cloves, turmeric, ground coriander, red chillies and the coconut. Mix well. Fry for 2-3 minutes, stirring occasionally.
- Add the vegetables, pineapple and cashew nuts. Stir-fry the mixture for 4-5 minutes.
- Add the yoghurt. Stir well for a minute.
- Spread the rice in a layer over the vegetable mixture, and sprinkle the food colour on top.
- Heat the ghee in another small saucepan. Add the ground cumin. Let it splutter for 15 seconds.
- Pour this directly over the rice.
- Cover with a lid and make sure that no steam escapes. Cook on a low heat for 10-15 minutes.
- Garnish with the coriander leaves. Serve hot.

Kale Moti ki Biryani

(Whole Black Gram Biryani)

Serves 4

Ingredients

500g/1lb 2oz basmati rice, soaked for 30 minutes and drained

500ml/16fl oz milk

1 tsp garam masala

500ml/16fl oz water

Salt to taste

75g/2½oz ghee

2 tsp ginger paste

2 tsp garlic paste

3 green chillies, slit lengthways

6 large potatoes, peeled and quartered

2 tomatoes, finely chopped

½ tsp chilli powder

⅓ tsp turmeric

200g/7oz yoghurt

300g/10oz urad beans*, cooked

1 tsp saffron, soaked in 60ml/2fl oz milk

25g/scant 1oz coriander leaves, finely chopped

10g/¼oz mint leaves, finely chopped

2 large onions, sliced and deep fried

3 green cardamom pods

5 cloves

2.5cm/1in cinnamon

1 bay leaf

Method

- Cook the rice with the milk, garam masala, water and salt in a saucepan on a medium heat for 7-8 minutes. Set aside.
- Heat the ghee in an ovenproof dish. Add the ginger paste and garlic paste. Stir-fry on a medium heat for a minute.
- Add the green chillies and potatoes. Fry the mixture for 3-4 minutes.
- Add the tomatoes, chilli powder and turmeric. Mix well. Fry for 2-3 minutes, stirring frequently.
- Add the yoghurt. Stir thoroughly for 2-3 minutes.
- Add the urad beans. Cook on a low heat for 7-10 minutes.
- Sprinkle the coriander leaves, mint leaves, onions, cardamom, cloves, cinnamon and bay leaf over the beans.
- Spread the cooked rice evenly over the beans mixture. Pour the saffron milk over the rice.
- Seal with foil and cover with a lid.
- Bake the biryani in an oven at 200°C (400°F, Gas Mark 6) for 15-20 minutes. Serve hot.

Mince & Masoor Pulao

(Mince and Whole Red Lentil with Pilau Rice)

Serves 4

Ingredients

6 tbsp refined vegetable oil

2 cloves

2 green cardamom pods

6 black peppercorns

2 bay leaves

2.5cm/1in cinnamon

1 tsp ginger paste

1 tsp garlic paste

1 large onion,
   finely chopped

2 green chillies,
   finely chopped

1 tsp chilli powder

½ tsp turmeric

2 tsp ground coriander

1 tsp ground cumin

500g/1lb 2oz lamb mince

150g/5½oz whole masoor*,
   soaked for 30 minutes
   and drained

250g/9oz long-grained rice,
   soaked for 30 minutes
   and drained

750ml/1¼ pints hot water

Salt to taste

10g/¼oz coriander leaves,
   finely chopped

Method

- Heat the oil in a saucepan. Add the cloves, cardamom, peppercorns, bay leaves, cinnamon, ginger paste and garlic paste. Fry this mixture on a medium heat for 2-3 minutes.
- Add the onion. Stir-fry till it turns translucent.
- Add the green chillies. Fry for a minute.
- Add the chilli powder, turmeric, ground coriander and cumin. Stir for 2 minutes.
- Add the mince, masoor and rice. Fry well on a medium heat for 5 minutes, stirring lightly at regular intervals.
- Add the hot water and the salt.
- Cover with a lid and simmer for 15 minutes.
- Garnish the pulao with the coriander leaves. Serve hot.

Chicken Biryani

Serves 4

Ingredients

1kg/2¼lb skinned chicken with the bones, cut into 8 pieces

6 tbsp refined vegetable oil

10 cashew nuts

10 raisins

500g/1lb 2oz basmati rice, soaked for 30 minutes and drained

3 cloves

2 bay leaves

5cm/2in cinnamon

4 black peppercorns

Salt to taste

4 large onions, finely sliced

250ml/8fl oz water

2½ tbsp ghee

A large pinch of saffron, dissolved in 1 tbsp milk

For the marinade:

1½ tsp garlic paste

1½ tsp ginger paste

3 green chillies, finely chopped

1 tsp garam masala

1 tsp ground black pepper

1 tbsp ground coriander

2 tsp ground cumin

125g/4½oz yoghurt

Method

* Mix all the marinade ingredients together. Marinate the chicken with this mixture for 3-4 hours.
* Heat 1 tbsp oil in a small saucepan. Add the cashew nuts and raisins. Fry on a medium heat till brown. Drain and set aside.
* Parboil (see cooking techniques) the drained rice with the cloves, bay leaves, cinnamon, peppercorns and salt. Set aside.
* Heat 3 tbsp oil in a saucepan. Add the chicken pieces and fry on a medium heat for 20 minutes, turning occasionally. Set aside.
* Heat the remaining oil in another saucepan. Add the onions and fry them on a medium heat till brown.
* Add the fried chicken pieces. Cook them for 5 more minutes on a medium heat.
* Add the water and simmer till the chicken is cooked. Set aside.
* Pour 2 tbsp ghee in an ovenproof dish. Add the chicken mixture. Arrange the rice in a layer over the chicken.
* Pour the saffron milk on top and add the remaining ghee.
* Seal with foil and cover tightly with a lid.
* Bake in an oven at 200°C (400°F, Gas Mark 6) for 8-10 minutes.
* Garnish with the fried cashew nuts and raisins. Serve hot.

Prawn Biryani

Serves 6

Ingredients

600g/1lb 5oz big prawns, cleaned
and de-veined

Salt to taste

1 tsp turmeric

250ml/8fl oz refined vegetable oil

4 large onions, sliced

4 tomatoes, finely chopped

2-3 potatoes, peeled and diced

50g/1¾oz coriander leaves,
finely chopped

25g/scant 1oz mint leaves,
finely chopped

200g/7oz yoghurt

2 green chillies, chopped

450g/1lb steamed basmati rice
(see page 519)

For the spice mixture:

4 cloves

2.5cm/1in cinnamon

3 green cardamom pods

4 black peppercorns

2-3 green chillies

¼ fresh coconut, grated

4 red chillies

12 garlic cloves

1 tsp cumin

1 tsp coriander

Method

- Coarsely grind together all the spice mixture ingredients. Set aside.
- Mix the prawns with the salt and turmeric. Set aside.
- Heat 2 tbsp of the oil in a saucepan. Add the onions and fry them on a medium heat till they turn brown. Set aside.
- Heat the remaining oil in a saucepan. Add half of the fried onions along with the ground spice mixture. Mix well and fry on a medium heat for a minute.
- Add the tomatoes, potatoes, salt and the prawns. Cook the mixture for 5 minutes.
- Add the coriander, mint leaves, yoghurt and green chillies. Mix well. Simmer for 10 minutes, stirring lightly at frequent intervals. Set aside.
- In a large saucepan, arrange the rice and prawn mixture in alternate layers. End with a layer of rice.
- Sprinkle the remaining onions over it, cover with a lid and simmer for 30 minutes. Serve hot.

Egg Potato Biryani

Serves 4-5

Ingredients

5 tbsp refined vegetable oil
3 cloves
2.5cm/1in cinnamon
3 green cardamom pods
2 bay leaves
6 peppercorns
3 large onions, finely sliced
3 large tomatoes, finely chopped
Salt to taste
¼ tsp turmeric
200g/7oz yoghurt
3 large potatoes, peeled, quartered and deep fried
6 eggs, boiled and halved lengthways

300g/10oz steamed basmati rice (see page 519)
2 tbsp ghee
1 tbsp cumin seeds
Dash of yellow food colour

For the paste:

1 tbsp white sesame seeds
4-5 red chillies
8 garlic cloves
5cm/2in root ginger
2-3 green chillies
50g/1¾oz coriander leaves
1 tbsp coriander seeds

Method

- Grind together all the paste ingredients with enough water to form a thick paste. Set aside.
- Heat the oil in a saucepan. Add all the cloves, cinnamon, cardamom, bay leaves and peppercorns. Let them splutter for 30 seconds.
- Add the onions. Fry them on a medium heat till they turn translucent.
- Add the paste with the tomatoes, salt and turmeric. Fry for 2-3 minutes, stirring ocasionally.
- Add the yoghurt. Cook the mixture on a medium heat, stirring frequently.
- Add the potatoes. Toss them well to coat them with the sauce.
- Gently add the egg pieces, yolk side up.
- Spread the rice over the egg pieces. Set this arrangement aside.
- Heat the ghee in a small saucepan. Add the cumin seeds. Let them splutter for 15 seconds.
- Pour this mixture directly on top of the rice arrangement.
- Sprinkle the food colour over it and cover the pan with a lid.
- Simmer for 30 minutes. Serve hot.

Mince Pulao
(Minced Lamb with Pilau Rice)

Serves 4

Ingredients

5 tbsp refined vegetable oil

2 cloves

2 green cardamom pods

6 black peppercorns

2 bay leaves

2.5cm/1in cinnamon

1 large onion, finely chopped

1 tsp ginger paste

1 tsp garlic paste

2 green chillies, finely chopped

2 tsp ground coriander

1 tsp chilli powder

½ tsp turmeric

1 tsp ground cumin

500g/1lb 2oz lamb mince

350g/12oz long-grained rice, soaked for 30 minutes in water and drained

750 ml/1¼fl oz hot water

Salt to taste

10g/¼oz coriander leaves, finely chopped

Method

* Heat the oil in a saucepan. Add the cloves, cardamom, peppercorns, bay leaves and cinnamon. Let them splutter for 15 seconds.
* Add the onion. Fry on a medium heat till translucent.
* Add the ginger paste, garlic paste, green chillies, ground coriander, chilli powder, turmeric and ground cumin.
* Fry for 2 minutes. Add the mince and rice. Stir-fry this mixture for 5 minutes.
* Add the hot water and the salt.
* Cover with a lid and simmer for 15 minutes.
* Garnish the pulao with the coriander leaves. Serve hot.

Chana Pulao
(Chickpeas with Pilau Rice)

Serves 4

Ingredients
2 tbsp refined vegetable oil

1 tsp cumin seeds

1 large onion, finely chopped

1 tsp ginger paste

1 tsp garlic paste

2 green chillies, finely chopped

300g/10oz canned chickpeas

300g/10oz long-grained rice, soaked for 30 minutes and drained

Salt to taste

250ml/8fl oz water

Method
- Heat the oil in a saucepan. Add the cumin seeds. Let them splutter for 15 seconds.
- Add the onion, ginger paste, garlic paste and green chillies. Fry this mixture on a medium heat for 2-3 minutes.
- Add the chickpeas and rice. Stir-fry for 4-5 minutes.
- Add the salt and the water. Cook the pulao on a medium heat for a minute.
- Cover with a lid and simmer for 10-12 minutes.
- Serve hot.

Simple Khichdi
(Rice and Lentil Melange)

Serves 4

Ingredients
1 tbsp ghee

1 tsp cumin seeds

2 green chillies, slit lengthways

250g/9oz long-grained rice

150g/5½oz mung dhal*

1 litre/1¾ pints hot water

Salt to taste

Method
- Heat the ghee in a saucepan. Add the cumin seeds and green chillies. Let them splutter for 15 seconds.
- Add the rice and mung dhal. Stir-fry for 5 minutes.
- Add the hot water and salt. Mix well. Cover with a lid. Simmer the khichdi for 15 minutes – it should have a porridge-like consistency.
- Serve hot.

Masala Rice
(Spicy Rice)

Serves 4

Ingredients

6 tbsp refined vegetable oil
½ tsp mustard seeds
10 curry leaves
2 green chillies, slit lengthways
¼ tsp turmeric
2 large onions, finely sliced

½ tsp chilli powder
2 tsp lemon juice
Salt to taste
300g/10oz steamed long-grained rice (see page 519)
1 tbsp coriander leaves, chopped

Method

- Heat the oil in a saucepan. Add the mustard seeds, curry leaves and green chillies. Let them splutter for 15 seconds. Add the turmeric and the onions. Fry the mixture on a medium heat till the onions are brown.
- Add the remaining ingredients, except the coriander. Stir gently over a low heat for 5 minutes. Garnish with the coriander leaves. Serve hot.

Onion Rice

Serves 4

Ingredients

5 tbsp refined vegetable oil
½ tsp mustard seeds
½ tsp cumin
4 medium-sized onions, finely sliced
3 green chillies, finely chopped
5 garlic cloves, finely chopped

300g/10oz steamed basmati rice (see page 519)
Salt to taste
60ml/2fl oz water
10g/¼oz coriander leaves, chopped

Method

- Heat the oil in a saucepan. Add the mustard seeds and cumin. Let them splutter for 15 seconds.
- Add the onions, green chillies and garlic. Fry this mixture on a medium heat till the onions are translucent.
- Add the rice, salt and water. Cook on a medium heat for 5-7 minutes.
- Garnish the onion rice with the coriander leaves. Serve hot.

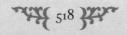

Steamed Rice

Serves 4

Ingredients

375g/13oz long-grained or
  basmati rice
750ml/1¼ pints water

Method

- Wash the rice well.
- Heat the water in a saucepan. Add the rice
  and cook on a high heat for 8-10 minutes.
- Press a grain of rice lightly between your
  thumb and your forefinger to check if it is
  cooked.
- Remove from the heat and drain in a
  colander. Serve hot.

Prawn Pulao

(Prawns Cooked with Pilau Rice)

Serves 4

Ingredients

250g/9oz prawns, shelled
  and de-veined
Salt to taste
1 tsp turmeric
8 tbsp refined vegetable oil
1 large onion, chopped
2 tomatoes, chopped
1 tsp ginger paste
2 tsp garlic paste
2 green chillies, chopped
2 tsp ground coriander
1 tsp ground cumin
½ tsp chilli powder
500g/1lb 2oz long-grained
  rice, soaked for 30
  minutes and drained
1 litre/1¾ pints hot water
25g/scant 1oz coriander
  leaves, finely chopped

Method

- Marinate the prawns with the salt and
  turmeric. Set aside for 20 minutes.
- Heat the oil in a saucepan. Fry the onions on
  a medium heat till translucent.
- Add the tomatoes, ginger paste, garlic paste,
  green chillies, ground coriander, ground
  cumin and chilli powder. Fry this mixture for
  2-3 minutes.
- Add the prawns and fry well for 4-5 minutes.
- Add the rice and continue to fry the pulao for
  5 minutes.
- Add the water and salt. Cover with a lid and
  simmer for 15 minutes.
- Garnish the pulao with the coriander leaves.
  Serve hot.

Peas Pulao

(Pilau Rice with Peas)

Serves 4

Ingredients

4 tbsp refined vegetable oil

1 tsp cumin seeds

½ tsp ginger paste

2 green chillies, chopped

200g/7oz cooked peas

Salt to taste

300g/10oz steamed rice
(see page 519)

Method

- Heat the oil in a saucepan. Add the cumin seeds. Let them splutter for 15 seconds.
- Add the ginger paste and green chillies. Fry the mixture on a low heat for a minute.
- Add the peas and salt. Stir well for 5 minutes.
- Add the rice. Mix well. Cover with a lid and simmer the pulao for 5 minutes. Serve hot.

Chicken Pulao

(Chicken Cooked with Pilau Rice)

Serves 4

Ingredients

500g/1lb 2oz long-grained rice

Salt to taste

1 tsp turmeric

1 tbsp lemon juice

50g/1¾oz coriander leaves, ground

1kg/2¼lb chicken with bones, skinned and chopped

9 tbsp refined vegetable oli

4 large onions, chopped

2 tomatoes, chopped

2 tsp ginger paste

1½ tsp garlic paste

2 tsp garam masala

1 litre/1¾ pints hot water

Method

- Soak the rice for 30 minutes. Set aside.
- Mix the salt, turmeric, lemon juice and coriander leaves together. Marinate the chicken with the mixture for 1 hour.
- Heat 8 tbsp oil in a saucepan. Add three-quarters of the onions and fry till they turn translucent.
- Add the tomatoes, ginger paste, garlic paste, garam masala and the marinated chicken. Fry for 10 minutes on a low heat, stirring occasionally.
- Add the soaked rice and the hot water. Cover with a lid and simmer for 7-10 minutes.
- Fry the remaining onions in 1 tbsp oil till golden brown. Sprinkle over the pulao.
- Serve hot.

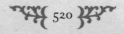

Vaangi Bhaat
(Aubergine Rice)

Serves 4

Ingredients

3 tbsp refined vegetable oil
2 large onions, finely chopped
300g/10oz aubergines, diced
1½ tsp ground coriander
1 tsp chilli powder
½ tsp ginger paste

½ tsp garlic paste
Salt to taste
500g/1lb 2oz long-grained rice, soaked and drained
1 litre/1¾ pints hot water
1 tbsp coriander leaves, chopped

Method

- Heat the oil in a saucepan. Sauté the onions till transparent. Add all the ingredients, except the rice, hot water and coriander. Fry for 4-5 minutes.
- Add the rice and water. Mix well. Cover with a lid and simmer for 10-15 minutes. Garnish with the coriander leaves. Serve hot.

Pea & Mushroom Pulao

Serves 4

Ingredients

3 tbsp refined vegetable oil
1 large onion, finely chopped
3 green chillies, slit lengthways
Pinch of turmeric
1 tomato, finely chopped
200g/7oz peas

200g/7oz mushrooms, steamed lightly (see cooking techniques) and sliced
Salt to taste
300g/10oz steamed basmati rice (see page 519)

Method

- Heat the oil in a saucepan. Add the onion, green chillies and turmeric and fry on a medium heat for 8-10 minutes, stirring occasionally.
- Add the tomato and fry for a minute.
- Add the peas, half the mushrooms and salt. Cook on a low heat till tender.
- Add the rice and toss well to mix. Cook for 5 minutes.
- Garnish the pulao with the remaining mushroom slices. Serve hot.

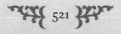

Green Pulao

Serves 4

Ingredients

150g/5½oz coriander leaves, chopped
50g/1¾oz mint leaves
4 tbsp refined vegetable oil
3 small onions, finely chopped
1 tsp garam masala
½ tsp ginger paste

½ tsp garlic paste
Salt to taste
125g/4½oz peas
2 large potatoes, sliced and deep fried
200g/7oz long-grained rice, parboiled
  (see cooking techniques)

Method

* Grind the coriander and mint leaves into a paste. Set aside.
* Heat the oil in a saucepan. Add the onions and fry them on a medium heat till translucent. Add the garam masala, ginger paste and garlic paste. Fry for 2 minutes. Add the coriander-mint paste. Cook till thick.
* Add the salt, peas and the potatoes. Mix well. Add the rice and mix gently. Cover with a lid and simmer the pulao for 5 minutes. Serve hot.

Festive Pulao

Serves 4

Ingredients

1 tbsp ghee plus extra for deep frying
4 large onions, finely sliced
2.5cm/1in cinnamon
3 cloves
2 bay leaves
3 green cardamom pods

1 litre/1¾ pints water
500g/1lb 2oz basmati rice, soaked for
  30 minutes and drained
Salt to taste
60g/2oz cashew nuts, fried
60g/2oz raisins, fried

Method

* Heat the ghee for deep frying in a pan. Add the onions and fry them on a medium heat till brown. Set the onions aside.
* Heat 1 tbsp ghee in another saucepan. Add the cinnamon, cloves, bay leaves and cardamom. Fry for 15 seconds, add the water and bring to a boil.
* Add the drained rice and salt. Cook for 10-15 minutes. Garnish the pulao with the fried onions, cashew nuts and raisins. Serve hot.

Pulihora
(Tamarind Rice)

Serves 6

Ingredients

750g/1lb 10oz long-grained rice,
  parboiled (see cooking techniques)
½ tsp turmeric
20 curry leaves
7 tbsp refined vegetable oil
½ tsp mustard seeds
2 tbsp mung dhal*
3 dried red chillies, broken into bits

8 black peppercorns
½ tsp asafoetida
125g/4½oz roasted peanuts
2 green chillies, slit lengthways
5 tbsp tamarind paste
Salt to taste
1 tbsp ground sesame seeds
50g/1¾oz coriander leaves, chopped

Method

- Mix the rice, turmeric, half the curry leaves and 2 tbsp oil. Set aside.
- In a frying pan, heat the remaining oil. Fry the mustard, mung dhal, red chillies, peppercorns, asafoetida and peanuts till the peanuts turn brown.
- Add the remaining curry leaves, the green chillies and tamarind paste. Stir the mixture lightly for 5-7 minutes. Add the salt, ground sesame seeds and coriander leaves. Serve hot.

Tadka Rice
(Rice with a Classic Indian Twist)

Serves 4

Ingredients

2 tbsp refined vegetable oil
1 tsp cumin seeds
1 green chilli, chopped
5-6 curry leaves

Pinch of turmeric
2 tbsp roasted peanuts
Salt to taste
300g/10oz steamed rice (see page 519)

Method

- Heat the oil in a saucepan. Add all the ingredients, except the salt and rice, and fry them on a medium heat for 20 seconds.
- Add the salt and rice. Stir for 3-4 minutes. Serve hot.

Cous Cous Biryani

Serves 4

Ingredients

100g/3½oz cous cous
600ml/1 pint hot water
2 tbsp refined vegetable oil
2-3 cloves
2-3 green cardamom pods
1 tsp cumin
Salt to taste

1 medium-sized onion, finely chopped
1 tomato, finely chopped
1 medium-sized potato, diced
¼ tsp turmeric
125g/4½oz thick yoghurt
10g/¼oz coriander leaves, chopped

Method

- Wash the cous cous well. Transfer to a bowl. Add 500ml/16fl oz hot water and allow it to stand for 30 minutes.
- Steam (see cooking techniques) the soaked cous cous in a steamer for 10 minutes. Remove from the heat and set aside to cool for an hour.
- Heat 1 tbsp of the oil in a saucepan. Add the cloves, cardamom, cumin, and salt. Stir-fry the mixture for 2-3 minutes on a medium heat. Set aside.
- Heat the remaining oil in a saucepan. Add the onion and sauté it on a medium heat for 2-3 minutes. Add the tomato, potato and the remaining water. Cook the mixture on a medium heat for 5-6 minutes, stirring frequently.
- Add the turmeric, yoghurt and salt. Mix well.
- Add the cous cous. Toss the mixture gently. Simmer for 10-15 minutes.
- Garnish the biryani with the coriander leaves. Serve hot.

Mushroom Rice

Serves 4

Ingredients

4 tbsp refined vegetable oil	1 tsp ground cumin
2 bay leaves	1 tsp ground coriander
4 spring onions, finely sliced	½ tsp chilli powder
2 large onions, finely chopped	150g/5½oz button mushrooms, sliced
2 tomatoes, finely chopped	Salt to taste
1 tsp garam masala	300g/10oz steamed rice (see page 519)
½ tsp ginger paste	

Method

* Heat the oil in a saucepan. Add the bay leaves and spring onions and fry them till the spring onions turn translucent. Add the onions and fry on a medium heat till they turn translucent.
* Add the tomatoes, garam masala, ginger paste, ground cumin, ground coriander and chilli powder. Fry for a minute on a medium heat.
* Add the mushrooms and salt. Cook for 5-7 minutes. Add the rice.
* Mix thoroughly and stir-fry on a low heat for 5-7 minutes. Serve hot.

Simple Coconut Rice

Serves 4

Ingredients

1 tbsp ghee	500g/1lb 2oz basmati rice
2 cloves	Salt to taste
2.5cm/1in cinnamon	250ml/8fl oz hot water
2 green cardamom pods	500ml/16fl oz coconut milk
3 black peppercorns	60g/2oz fresh coconut, grated

Method

* Heat the ghee in a saucepan. Add the cloves, cinnamon, cardamom and peppercorns. Let them splutter for 30 seconds.
* Add the rice, salt, water and coconut milk. Simmer the mixture for 12-15 minutes, stirring at frequent intervals.
* Garnish the rice with the grated coconut. Serve hot.

Mixed Pulao

Serves 4

Ingredients

250g/9oz long-grained rice
150g/5½oz masoor dhal*
60g/2oz cous cous
500ml/16fl oz water
4 tbsp refined vegetable oil
1 large onion, finely chopped
3 cloves

2.5cm/1in cinnamon
50g/1¾oz fenugreek leaves, chopped
2 carrots, grated
¼ tsp turmeric
1 tsp garam masala
Salt to taste

Method

- Mix the rice, dhal, cous cous and water in a saucepan. Cook the mixture on a medium heat for 45 minutes. Set aside to cool.
- Heat the oil in a frying pan. Fry the onion on a medium heat till translucent. Add all the remaining ingredients and cook for 2-3 minutes.
- Add the rice dhal mixture. Mix thoroughly. Serve hot.

Lemon Rice

Serves 4

Ingredients

4 tbsp refined vegetable oil
1 tsp mustard seeds
2 tsp urad dhal*
2 tsp chana dhal*
8 curry leaves
4 green chillies, slit lengthways

½ tsp turmeric
2 large onions, finely chopped
60g/2oz grated fresh coconut
2 tbsp lemon juice
Salt to taste
300g/10oz steamed rice (see page 519)

Method

- Heat the oil in a saucepan. Add the mustard seeds. Let them splutter for 15 seconds.
- Add both the dhals and fry them on a medium heat for 15 minutes, stirring frequently. Add the curry leaves, green chillies, turmeric, onions and grated coconut. Fry this mixture on a low heat for a minute.
- Add the lemon juice, salt and rice. Mix the rice well. Serve hot.

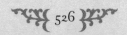

Manipuri Rice

Serves 4

Ingredients

7 garlic cloves
7 red chillies
2.5cm/1in root ginger
1 tbsp coriander seeds
4½ tbsp ghee
2 large onions, sliced
250g/9oz frozen mixed vegetables

2 large potatoes, boiled and diced
500ml/16fl oz water
Salt to taste
2 tbsp coriander leaves, chopped
1 tomato, sliced
300g/10oz steamed rice (see page 519)

Method

- Grind the garlic, chillies, ginger and coriander seeds together. Set aside.
- Heat half a tbsp ghee in a saucepan. Fry the onions on a medium heat till brown. Set aside.
- Heat the remaining ghee in a saucepan. Fry the ground garlic-chillies mixture on a medium heat for 3-5 minutes. Add the vegetables and potatoes. Sauté for 3 minutes.
- Add the remaining ingredients, except the rice. Simmer for 5-7 minutes.
- Add the rice. Stir well and cook for 3-4 minutes. Serve hot.

Sesame Pulao
(Sesame Seeds Cooked with Pilau Rice)

Serves 4

Ingredients

2 tbsp ghee
1 tbsp sesame seeds
1 large onion, finely sliced

2 chicken stock cubes, crumbled
Salt to taste
300g/10oz steamed rice (see page 519)

Method

- Heat the ghee in a saucepan. Add the sesame seeds. Let them splutter for 15 seconds.
- Add the onion and fry on a medium heat till translucent.
- Sprinkle the stock cubes and salt in and stir thoroughly for a minute.
- Add the rice. Toss well. Serve hot.

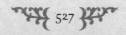

Khichuri

(Lentils and Rice Broth with Vegetables)

Serves 4-6

Ingredients

2 tbsp refined vegetable oil

½ tsp cumin seeds

2.5cm/1in cinnamon

4 green cardamom pods

6 cloves

2.5cm/1in root ginger, finely chopped

250g/9oz long-grained rice

300g/10oz mung dhal*, boiled

2 large onions, finely chopped

2 large potatoes, finely chopped

50g/1¾oz cauliflower florets

30g/1oz carrots, finely chopped

30g/1oz French beans, finely chopped

½ tsp turmeric

2 green chillies

1½ tsp sugar

Salt to taste

1.25 litres/2½ pints water

Method

• Heat the oil in a saucepan. Add the cumin seeds, cinnamon, cardamom, cloves and ginger. Fry the mixture on a medium heat till the ginger turns light brown.

• Add all the remaining ingredients, except the water. Fry the mixture for 5 minutes. Add the water. Simmer for 15-20 minutes. Serve hot.

Yellow Rice

Serves 4

Ingredients

3 tbsp refined vegetable oil

½ tsp cumin

2 bay leaves

2 cloves

4 black peppercorns

1 tsp turmeric

2 large onions, finely chopped

250g/9oz basmati rice

Salt to taste

600ml/1 pint hot water

Method

• Heat the oil in a saucepan. Add the cumin, bay leaves, cloves, peppercorns and turmeric. Let them splutter for 15 seconds. Add the onions. Fry them on a medium heat till they turn brown.

• Add the rice, salt and water. Simmer for 15 minutes. Serve hot.

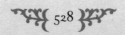

Chingri Mache Bhaat
(Steamed Prawns and Rice)

Serves 4

Ingredients
250g/9oz prawns, cleaned and de-veined
Salt to taste
1 tsp turmeric
1 tsp ready-made mustard

1½ tbsp mustard oil
300g/10oz steamed rice (see page 519)
1 tbsp coriander leaves, chopped

Method
* Marinate the prawns with the salt and turmeric for 30 minutes.
* Mix together the marinated prawns, ready-made mustard and mustard oil in a double boiler. Steam (see cooking techniques) for 17 minutes.
* Toss the rice with the prawns. Garnish with the coriander. Serve hot.

Carrot & Green Pepper Rice

Serves 4

Ingredients
4 tbsp refined vegetable oil
¼ tsp mustard seeds
¼ tsp cumin seeds
Pinch of turmeric
8 curry leaves
1 green pepper, finely chopped
1 large carrot, grated

1 tsp garam masala
Salt to taste
300g/10oz steamed rice (see page 519)
1 tbsp lemon juice
1 tbsp coriander leaves, finely chopped

Method
* Heat the oil in a deep saucepan. Add the mustard seeds, cumin seeds, turmeric and curry leaves. Let them splutter for 15 seconds.
* Add the green pepper and carrot. Stir-fry the vegetables for a minute. Cover with a lid and simmer for 5 minutes, stirring occasionally.
* Uncover and add the garam masala and salt. Mix well. Add the rice. Stir-fry the mixture for 4-5 minutes.
* Add the lemon juice and coriander leaves. Toss to mix well and cook for 2-3 minutes. Serve hot.

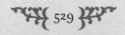

Thakkali Saadham
(Tomato Rice)

Serves 4

Ingredients

3 tbsp refined vegetable oil
½ tsp mustard seeds
½ tsp cumin seeds
8 curry leaves
½ tsp turmeric
Pinch of asafoetida

¾ tsp chilli powder
2 large onions, finely chopped
2 tomatoes, finely chopped
300g/10oz steamed rice (see page 519)
Salt to taste
1 tbsp coriander leaves, to garnish

Method
- Heat the oil in a saucepan. Add the mustard, cumin, curry leaves, turmeric, asafoetida, chilli powder, onions and tomatoes.
- Stir-fry for 5 minutes. Add the rice and salt. Garnish and serve hot.

Palak Pulao
(Spinach Pulao)

Serves 4

Ingredients

4½ tbsp refined vegetable oil
1 large onion, finely chopped
2 tomatoes, finely chopped
¾ tsp ginger paste
¾ tsp garlic paste
350g/12oz long-grained rice
750ml/1¼ pints hot water

200g/7oz spinach, steamed (see cooking techniques) and puréed
10 cashew nuts
1 tsp lemon juice
½ tsp garam masala
Salt to taste

Method
- Heat the oil in a saucepan. Add the onion and fry it on a medium heat till it turns brown.
- Add the tomatoes, ginger paste and garlic paste. Simmer for 2 minutes.
- Stir in the rice and water and cook for 12-15 minutes.
- Add the spinach, cashew nuts, lemon juice, garam masala and salt. Stir this mixture gently. Simmer for 2-3 minutes. Serve hot.

 530

Lemon Grass & Green Chilli Pulao

Serves 4

Ingredients

150g/5½oz lemon grass, diced

4 green chillies slit lengthways

2.5cm/1in root ginger, julienned

750ml/1¼ pint vegetable stock

3 tbsp refined vegetable oil

1 tsp cumin seeds

500g/1lb 2oz long-grained rice

Salt to taste

150g/5½oz mung dhal*, boiled

25g/scant 1oz coriander leaves, chopped

Method

- Mix the lemon grass, green chillies, ginger and the vegetable stock together.
- Heat the oil in a saucepan. Add the cumin seeds. Let them splutter for 15 seconds. Add the rice, salt and the stock mixture. Toss the mixture well. Cover with a lid and simmer for 12-15 minutes.
- Garnish the pulao with the mung dhal and coriander leaves. Serve hot.

Tomato & Spring Onion Rice

Serves 4

Ingredients

3 tbsp ghee

4 cloves

2.5cm/1in cinnamon

½ tsp cumin seeds

200g/7oz spring onions, finely chopped

1 tsp ground black pepper

Salt to taste

200g/7oz tomato purée

300g/10oz steamed rice (see page 519)

1 tsp lemon juice

Method

- Heat the ghee in a saucepan. Add the cloves, cinnamon and cumin seeds. Let them splutter for 15 seconds.
- Add the spring onions. Fry them for 4-5 minutes on a medium heat.
- Stir in the pepper, salt and the tomato purée. Simmer for 2-3 minutes.
- Add the rice. Toss the mixture well.
- Sprinkle the lemon juice over the rice. Serve hot.

Sofiyani Pulao
(Chicken Drumsticks Pulao)

Serves 4

Ingredients

16 chicken drumsticks
3 tbsp almonds, ground
3 tbsp khoya*
600g/1lb 5oz long-grained rice
5 green cardamom pods
5 cloves
5cm/2in cinnamon
4 black peppercorns
Salt to taste

30g/1oz ghee
250ml/8fl oz milk

For the marinade:

1 tsp ginger paste
1 tsp garlic paste
2 green chillies, slit lengthways
3 tsp lemon juice
600g/1lb 5 oz yoghurt, whisked

Method

- Mix all the marinade ingredients together and marinate the chicken drumsticks with this mixture for 30 minutes. Cook them in a saucepan on a medium heat for 20 minutes. Add the almonds and khoya. Set aside.
- Parboil (see cooking techniques) the rice with the cardamom, cloves, cinnamon, peppercorns and salt. Set the mixture aside.
- Pour the ghee in a thick-bottomed saucepan. Arrange the rice and chicken in alternate layers. Pour milk on top of the mixture, seal the pan with foil and cover with a lid. Simmer for 20 minutes. Serve hot.

Indian Fried Rice

Serves 4

Ingredients

2 tbsp refined vegetable oil
1 tsp cumin seeds
1 large onion, finely sliced

1 tomato, finely chopped
Salt to taste
300g/10oz steamed rice (see page 519)

Method

- Heat the oil in a saucepan. Add the cumin seeds. Let them splutter for 15 seconds. Add the onion and tomato. Fry on a low heat for 2-3 minutes.
- Add the salt and rice. Toss the rice well for 2-3 minutes. Serve hot.

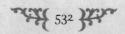

Peshawari Biryani
(North Indian Biryani)

Serves 4

Ingredients

6 tbsp ghee
3 large onions, finely chopped
1 tsp ginger paste
1 tsp garlic paste
750g/1lb 10oz boneless mutton
400g/14oz yoghurt
750g/1lb 10oz basmati rice

Salt to taste
1.4 litres/2¼ pints water
12-15 cashew nuts
12-15 raisins
12-15 prunes
2 slices canned pineapple, chopped
2 tsp garam masala

Method
- Heat the ghee in a saucepan. Add the onions, ginger paste and garlic paste. Fry this mixture on a medium heat for 3-4 minutes.
- Add the mutton. Fry for 25 minutes. Add the remaining ingredients.
- Cover with a lid and simmer the biryani for 20-25 minutes. Serve hot.

Dill Pulao

Serves 4

Ingredients

2 tbsp refined vegetable oil
2 large onions, finely chopped
1cm/½in root ginger, finely chopped
1 garlic clove, finely chopped
125g/4½oz yoghurt
½ tsp turmeric

Salt to taste
350g/12oz long-grained rice
750ml/1¼ pints hot water
Juice of 1 lemon
60g/2oz dill leaves, finely chopped

Method
- Heat the oil in a saucepan. Add the onions and fry them on a medium heat till they turn translucent.
- Add the ginger, garlic, yoghurt, turmeric, salt and rice. Fry the mixture for 5 minutes.
- Add the hot water. Simmer for 12-15 minutes, stirring frequently.
- Garnish the pulao with the lemon juice and dill. Serve hot.

Mutton Pulao

Serves 6

Ingredients

4 tbsp refined vegetable oil

3 large onions, finely chopped

675g/1½lb mutton, chopped

2 tomatoes, blanched and chopped (see cooking techniques)

1.25 litres/2½ pints hot water

500g/1lb 2oz basmati rice

1 tbsp cashew nuts

1 tbsp raisins

For the spice mixture:

4 cloves

4 green cardamom pods

2.5cm/1in cinnamon

1 tsp ginger paste

1 tsp garlic paste

2 green chillies, finely chopped

2 tsp ground coriander

½ tsp chilli powder

1 tsp turmeric

Salt to taste

Method

- Heat 3 tbsp oil in a saucepan. Add the onions and fry them on a medium heat till they turn brown. Add the spice mixture and fry for 10-12 minutes.
- Add the mutton and tomatoes. Cook till the mixture is dry. Add 250ml/8fl oz hot water and cook till the mutton is tender. Add the rice and the remaining water. Simmer for 20 minutes. Set aside.
- Heat 1 tbsp oil in a saucepan and fry the cashews and raisins till brown.
- Sprinkle the cashews and raisins over the rice. Serve hot.

Ghee Chawal

(Rice with Ghee)

Serves 4

Ingredients

75g/2½oz ghee

½ tsp ground black pepper

Salt to taste

300g/10oz steamed rice (see page 519)

10g/¼oz mint leaves, finely chopped

Method

- Heat the ghee in a saucepan. Fry the pepper and salt for 10 seconds.
- Pour this in the steamed rice. Garnish with the mint leaves. Serve hot.

Enn Pongal
(Rice with Roasted Split Green Gram)

Serves 4

Ingredients

225g/8oz mung dhal*, dry roasted
 (see cooking techniques)
500g/1lb 2oz long-grained rice
½ tsp turmeric
Salt to taste
5-6 tbsp ghee

25 cashew nuts
1½ tsp cumin seeds, pounded
½ tsp black peppercorns
15 curry leaves
2.5cm/1in root ginger, finely chopped

Method
* Boil the dhal, rice, turmeric and salt together for 30 minutes. Set aside.
* Heat the ghee in a saucepan. Add the cashew nuts and fry till they turn golden brown.
* Add the cumin, peppercorns, curry leaves and ginger. Fry for 20 seconds.
* Add this mixture to the dhal-rice mixture. Stir gently. Serve hot.

Paneer Pulao

Serves 4

Ingredients

4 tbsp refined vegetable oil
2 large onions, sliced
1 tsp ginger paste
1 tsp garlic paste
2 green chillies, finely chopped
400g/14oz paneer*, diced

400g/14oz tomato purée
375g/13oz basmati rice
Salt to taste
600ml/1 pint hot water
1 tbsp coriander leaves, chopped

Method
* Heat the oil in a saucepan. Fry the onions, ginger paste, garlic paste and green chillies on a medium heat for 2 minutes, stirring continuously.
* Add the paneer and tomato purée. Cook the mixture for 2-3 minutes.
* Add the rice, salt and water. Cook over a low heat till the rice is cooked.
* Garnish the pulao with the coriander leaves. Serve hot.

Coconut Rice

Serves 4

Ingredients
3 tbsp ghee

1 large onion, finely chopped

6 garlic cloves, finely chopped

2 green cardamom pods

2.5cm/1in cinnamon

2 cloves

4 black peppercorns

300g/10oz basmati rice, soaked for 30 minutes and drained

1.2 litres/2 pints coconut milk

Salt to taste

Method
- Heat the ghee in a saucepan. Add the onion, garlic, cardamom, cinnamon, cloves and peppercorns. Fry them on a medium heat for 3-4 minutes.
- Add the drained rice. Stir-fry on a medium heat for 2-3 minutes.
- Add the coconut milk and salt. Mix well and simmer for 7-8 minutes.
- Cover with a lid and cook for 15 more minutes.
- Serve hot.

Saffron Pulao

Serves 4

Ingredients
4 tbsp ghee

1 tsp cumin seeds

2 bay leaves

375g/13oz basmati rice, soaked for 30 minutes and drained

Salt to taste

750ml/1¼ pints hot water

1 tsp saffron

1 tbsp coriander leaves, finely chopped

Method
- Heat the ghee in a saucepan. Add the cumin seeds and bay leaves. Let them splutter for 15 seconds.
- Add the rice and salt. Fry the mixture on a medium heat for 3-4 minutes.
- Add the hot water and the saffron. Simmer for 8-10 minutes or till the rice is cooked, stirring at regular intervals.
- Garnish with the coriander leaves. Serve hot.

Dhal Rice Mix

Serves 4

Ingredients

2 tbsp masoor dhal*

2 tbsp urad dhal*

2 tbsp mung dhal*

2 tbsp chana dhal*

500ml/16fl oz water

4 tbsp ghee

1 large onion, finely sliced

1 tsp garam masala

250g/9oz basmati rice, parboiled
  (see cooking techniques)

1 tsp turmeric

1 bay leaf

Salt to taste

250ml/8fl oz milk

Method

- Mix all the dhals together. Cook them with the water in a saucepan on a medium heat for 30 minutes. Set aside.
- Heat the ghee in a saucepan. Add the onion and garam masala. Fry on a medium heat till the onion is translucent.
- Add the rice, turmeric, bay leaf and salt. Mix well. Add the milk and the dhal mixture. Cover with a lid and simmer for 7-8 minutes. Serve hot.

Kairi Bhaat
(Rice with Green Mango)

Serves 4

Ingredients

4 tbsp refined vegetable oil

½ tsp mustard seeds

Pinch of asafoetida

½ tsp turmeric

8 curry leaves

180g/6¼oz roasted peanuts

1 tsp ground coriander

2 unripe mangoes, peeled and grated

Salt to taste

300g/10oz steamed rice (see page 519)

Method

- Heat the oil in a saucepan. Add the mustard seeds, asafoetida, turmeric and curry leaves. Let them splutter for 15 seconds.
- Add the peanuts, ground coriander, mangoes and salt. Fry them on a medium heat for 5 minutes.
- Add the cooked rice and stir the bhaat gently. Serve hot.

Prawn Khichdi

Serves 4

Ingredients

5 tbsp refined vegetable oil

3 small onions, finely chopped

250g/9oz prawns, cleaned and de-veined

1 tsp ginger paste

1 tsp garlic paste

2 tsp ground coriander

1 tsp ground cumin

½ tsp turmeric

375g/13oz long-grained rice

Salt to taste

360ml/12fl oz hot water

360ml/12fl oz coconut milk

Method

- Heat the oil in a saucepan. Fry the onions till translucent.
- Add the prawns, ginger paste, garlic paste, ground coriander, ground cumin and turmeric. Sauté on a medium heat for 3-4 minutes.
- Add the remaining ingredients. Simmer for 10 minutes. Serve hot.

Curd Rice

Serves 4

Ingredients

300g/10oz steamed rice (see page 519)

400g/14oz yoghurt

8-10 curry leaves

3 green chillies, slit lengthways

Pinch of asafoetida

1 tbsp coriander leaves,
  finely chopped

Salt to taste

2 tsp refined vegetable oil

½ tsp mustard seeds

¼ tsp cumin seeds

½ tsp urad dhal*

Method

- Mash the rice with a wooden spoon. Mix with the yoghurt, curry leaves, green chillies, asafoetida, coriander leaves and salt. Set aside.
- Heat the oil in a saucepan. Add the mustard seeds, cumin seeds and urad dhal. Let them splutter for 15 seconds.
- Pour this mixture directly on top of the rice mixture. Stir thoroughly.
- Serve chilled with hot mango pickle (see page 24).

Chicken & Rice Hotpot

Serves 4

Ingredients

3 tbsp refined vegetable oil

4 cloves

5cm/2in cinnamon

2 green cardamom pods

2 bay leaves

3 large onions, finely chopped

12 chicken drumsticks

½ tsp ginger paste

½ tsp garlic paste

3 chicken stock cubes, dissolved in 1.7 litres/3 pints hot water

½ tsp freshly ground black pepper

Salt to taste

500g/1lb 2oz basmati rice

250g/9oz carrots, thinly sliced

Method

- Heat the oil in a saucepan. Add the cloves, cinnamon, cardamom and bay leaves. Let them splutter for 15 seconds.
- Add the onions. Cook for 2 minutes. Add all the remaining ingredients, except the rice and carrots. Mix well. Cook for 4-5 minutes.
- Add the rice and carrots, and stir well. Cover with a lid and simmer for 35-40 minutes. Serve hot.

Corn Pulao

Serves 4

Ingredients

5 tbsp refined vegetable oil

2 small onions, finely chopped

300g/10oz corn kernels, boiled

2 tsp ground coriander

1 tsp ground cumin

¼ tsp turmeric

125g/4½oz tomato purée

Salt to taste

375g/13oz basmati rice

500ml/16fl oz hot water

1 tsp lemon juice

1 tbsp coriander leaves, chopped

Method

- Heat the oil in a pan. Fry the onions on a medium heat till translucent. Add the remaining ingredients, except the rice, water, lemon juice and coriander. Fry for 3-4 minutes. Add the rice, water and lemon juice.
- Simmer for 10 minutes. Sprinkle coriander leaves on top and serve hot.

Dhansak Rice

(Spicy Parsi Rice)

Serves 4

Ingredients

60ml/2fl oz refined
  vegetable oil

2 bay leaves

2 green cardamom pods

4 black peppercorns

2.5cm/1in cinnamon

1 tsp sugar

1 large onion, finely
  chopped

375g/13oz long-grained
  rice, soaked for 10
  minutes and drained

Salt to taste

750ml/1¼ pints hot water

Method

- Heat the oil in a saucepan. Add the bay leaves, cardamom, peppercorns, cinnamon and sugar. Stir on a medium heat till the sugar has caramelized.
- Add the onion and fry on a medium heat till it turns brown. Add the rice and stir until the rice turns brown.
- Add the salt and the hot water. Cover with a lid and cook for 10 minutes over a low heat.
- Serve hot with Dhansak (see page 172).

Brown Rice

Serves 4

Ingredients

3 tbsp refined vegetable oil

½ tsp ginger paste

½ tsp garlic paste

2 large onions, quartered

375g/13oz long-grained
  rice, soaked for 30
  minutes and drained

1 tsp garam masala

600ml/1 pint hot water

Salt to taste

Method

- Heat the oil in a saucepan. Add the ginger paste and garlic paste. Fry for a few seconds.
- Add the onion pieces and sauté them on a medium heat for a minute.
- Add the drained rice and garam masala. Cook for 2-3 minutes, stirring well.
- Add the hot water and salt. Simmer the mixture till the rice is cooked.
- Serve hot.

Mutton Biryani

Serves 4-6

Ingredients

1kg/2¼lb mutton, cut into 5cm/2in pieces

360ml/12fl oz refined vegetable oil

2 large potatoes, quartered

4 cloves

5cm/2in cinnamon

3 bay leaves

6 peppercorns

2 black cardamom pods

Salt to taste

3 tbsp ghee

750g/1lb 10oz basmati rice, parboiled (see cooking techniques)

A large pinch of saffron, dissolved in 1 tbsp milk

For the marinade:

100g/3½oz coriander leaves, ground to a paste

50g/1¾oz mint leaves, ground to a paste

200g/7oz beaten yoghurt

1½ tsp ginger paste

1½ tsp garlic paste

3 green chillies, finely chopped

1½ tsp garam masala

1 tsp ground cumin

1 tsp ground coriander

4 large onions, chopped and deep fried

Method

- Mix all the marinade ingredients together and marinate the mutton with this mixture overnight in the refrigerator.
- Heat 250ml/8fl oz oil in a saucepan. Add the potatoes and fry them on a medium heat for 10 minutes. Drain and set aside.
- Heat the remaining oil in a large saucepan. Add the cloves, cinnamon, bay leaves, peppercorns and cardamom. Let them splutter for 30 seconds.
- Add the marinated mutton and salt. Simmer for 45 minutes, stirring occasionally. Add the fried potatoes. Stir lightly. Remove from the heat.
- Pour the ghee in a saucepan. Place the meat-potatoes mixture in the saucepan. Arrange the parboiled rice in a layer over the meat-potatoes mixture.
- Pour the saffron milk on top. Seal with foil and cover with a tight lid. Cook on a low heat for 20 minutes.
- Serve hot.

Faada-ni-Khichdi
(Cracked Wheat Porridge)

Serves 4

Ingredients

125g/4½oz cracked wheat
150g/5½oz mung dhal*
150g/5½oz masoor dhal*
2 litres/3½ pints water
2 tomatoes, puréed
100g/3½oz frozen mixed vegetables
½ tsp turmeric
½ tsp chilli powder
½ tsp ground coriander
½ tsp ground cumin
2 green chillies, finely chopped

Salt to taste
4 tbsp ghee
2 cloves
2.5cm/1in cinnamon
6 black peppercorns
2 bay leaves
8 curry leaves
3 tbsp coriander leaves, finely chopped
1 tsp cumin seeds, dry-roasted (see cooking techniques) and ground

Method

- Mix the cracked wheat, dhals and the water in a saucepan and bring to a boil on a high heat. Cook the mixture on a low heat for 30 minutes.
- Add the tomato purée, mixed vegetables, turmeric, chilli powder, ground coriander, cumin, chillies and salt. Stir well and simmer for 5 minutes.
- Heat the ghee in a small pan. Add the cloves, cinnamon, peppercorns, bay leaves and curry leaves. Let them splutter for 15 seconds.
- Pour this seasoning in the cooked wheat mixture and let it simmer for 3-5 minutes.
- Garnish the khichdi with the coriander leaves and ground cumin. Serve hot.

INDIAN BREADS

Perfect for soaking up the rich flavours of Indian dishes, these breads are an essential part of an Indian meal. Various grains such as wheat, rice and millet are steamed, fried or cooked over direct heat to make the perfect accompaniment to each dish.

Most Indian breads are cooked on a heavy flat pan (tawa) though in India naans, kulchas and tandoori rotis are baked in clay ovens called tandoors. All are straightforward to make and tasty to eat. In this chapter, choose from naan, chapatti, dosa, paratha, bhatura and many more.

Urad Dhal Roti

(Split Black Gram Bread)

Makes 15

Ingredients

600g/1lb 5oz urad dhal*, soaked overnight

2 tbsp ghee

1 tsp turmeric

1 tsp ginger powder

1 tsp ground coriander

¼ tsp chilli powder

350g/12oz plain white flour

1 tsp crushed anardana*

2 tbsp coriander leaves, finely chopped

3 green chillies, finely chopped

1 small onion, grated

Salt to taste

120ml/4fl oz water

Method

- Drain the dhal and grind to a thick paste.
- Heat the ghee in a frying pan. Add the dhal paste along with the turmeric, ginger powder, coriander and chilli powder. Fry on a medium heat for 4-5 minutes. Cool for 5 minutes and divide into 15 portions. Set aside.
- Knead all the remaining ingredients to form a stiff dough. Divide into 15 balls and roll out into discs, 10cm/4in in diameter.
- Place a portion of the dhal mixture on each disc, seal and roll out again into discs, 15cm/6in in diameter.
- Grease and heat a flat pan. Cook a roti till the underside is brown. Flip and repeat. Cook each side twice.
- Repeat for the rest of the rotis.
- Serve hot.

Murgh-Methi-Malai Paratha
(Chicken and Fenugreek Pan-fried Bread)

Makes 14

Ingredients
4 tsp refined vegetable oil

½ tsp cumin seeds

6 garlic cloves,
   finely chopped

1 large onion,
   finely chopped

4 green chillies,
   finely chopped

1cm/½in root ginger,
   finely chopped

½ tsp chilli powder

½ tsp garam masala

200g/7oz chicken, minced

60g/2oz fresh fenugreek
   leaves, finely chopped

1 tsp lemon juice

1 tbsp coriander leaves,
   finely chopped

750g/1lb 10oz wholemeal
   flour

Salt to taste

360ml/12fl oz water

Ghee for greasing

Method
- Heat half the oil in a saucepan. Add the cumin seeds, garlic, onion, green chillies, ginger, chilli powder and garam masala. Let them splutter for 30 seconds.
- Add the chicken, fenugreek, lemon juice and coriander leaves. Mix well. Cook on a medium heat for 30 minutes, stirring occasionally. Set aside.
- Knead the flour, salt and the remaining oil with the water to form a stiff dough. Divide into 14 balls and roll out into discs of 10cm/4in diameter.
- Place a spoonful of the chicken mixture on each disc, seal and roll out carefully into discs of 12.5cm/5in diameter.
- Heat a flat pan and cook a paratha on a low heat till the underside is light brown. Smear some ghee on the top, flip and repeat. Cook each side twice.
- Repeat for the remaining parathas. Serve hot.

Meethi Puri
(Sweet Puffed Bread)

Makes 20

Ingredients

250g/9oz sugar
60ml/2fl oz warm water
350g/12oz plain white flour
2 tbsp ghee

1 tbsp Greek yoghurt
Salt to taste
Refined vegetable oil for deep frying

Method
- Cook the sugar and water in a saucepan on a medium heat till it achieves a 1-thread consistency (see cooking techniques). Set aside.
- Mix all the remaining ingredients, except the oil, together. Cook in a saucepan on a medium heat for 3-4 minutes. Knead into a stiff dough.
- Divide into 20 balls. Roll out into discs, 7.5cm/3in in diameter.
- Heat the oil. Deep fry the puris on a medium heat till golden brown.
- Drain and toss the fried puris in the sugar syrup. Serve hot.

Kulcha
(Baked Flat Bread)

Makes 8

Ingredients

1 tsp dry yeast, dissolved in 120ml/4fl oz warm water
½ tsp salt
90ml/3fl oz water
350g/12oz plain white flour

1 tsp bicarbonate of soda
60ml/2fl oz warm milk
4 tbsp sour cream
1 tbsp refined vegetable oil
Ghee for greasing

Method
- Mix the yeast with the salt. Set aside for 10 minutes.
- Knead with all the remaining ingredients, except the ghee, to form a firm dough. Cover with a wet cloth. Set aside for 5 hours.
- Divide into 8 balls and roll out into teardrop shapes.
- Grease and heat a flat pan. Cook each kulcha on a low heat for a minute. Flip and repeat. Serve hot.

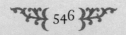

Garlic & Cheese Naan

(Garlic and Cheese Naan Bread)

Makes 8

Ingredients

15 garlic cloves, finely chopped
85g/3oz Cheddar cheese, grated
350g/12oz plain white flour
¼ tsp baking powder
1 tbsp dry yeast, dissolved in
  120ml/4fl oz warm water

2 tbsp plain yoghurt
2 tbsp sugar
Salt to taste
120ml/4fl oz water
Refined vegetable oil for greasing

Method

* Knead all the ingredients together to form a dough.
* Grease and heat a flat pan. Spread a large spoonful of the batter like a thick pancake.
* Cook till the underside is brown. Flip and repeat.
* Repeat for the remaining batter. Serve hot.

Tri-flour Roti

Makes 14

Ingredients

175g/6oz wholemeal flour
175g/6oz soy flour
175g/6oz millet flour
1 tsp ground coriander
½ tsp ground cumin
½ tsp chilli powder

½ tsp turmeric
2 tsp refined vegetable oil
Salt to taste
250ml/8fl oz water

Method

* Knead all the ingredients to form a pliable dough.
* Divide into 14 balls and roll out into discs 15cm/6in in diameter.
* Heat a flat pan and cook each roti on both sides, flipping every 30 seconds, till each side is golden brown.
* Serve hot.

Sheera Chapatti
(Sweet Semolina Flat Bread)

Makes 10

Ingredients

350g/12oz plain white flour

250ml/8fl oz water

3 tbsp ghee

150g/5½oz semolina

250g/9oz jaggery*, grated

1 tbsp ground green cardamom

Method
- Knead the flour with half the water to form a stiff dough. Divide into 10 balls. Set aside.
- Heat half a tbsp of ghee in a saucepan. Fry the semolina on a medium heat till golden brown. Add the remaining water and stir till it evaporates.
- Add the jaggery and cardamom. Mix well and cook for 3-4 minutes.
- Cool the mixture for 10 minutes, then divide into 10 portions.
- Flatten each dough ball and place a portion of semolina in the centre of each. Seal and roll out into discs 12.5cm/5in in diameter.
- Grease and heat a flat pan. Cook a chapatti on a low heat till the underside is golden brown.
- Smear some ghee on the top, flip and repeat. Cook each side twice.
- Repeat for the remaining chapattis. Serve hot.

Bhakri
(Plain Flat Bread)

Makes 8

Ingredients

350g/12oz millet flour

Salt to taste

120ml/4fl oz warm water

1 tbsp ajowan seeds

Method
- Knead all the ingredients to form a soft dough. Divide into 8 balls and pat to flatten into discs 15cm/6in in diameter.
- Heat a flat pan, place a bhakri on the pan and spread a tsp of water over it. Flip and cook till the underside is brown. Cook each side twice.
- Repeat for the remaining bhakri. Serve hot.

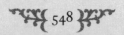

Chapatti
(Pan-baked Puffed Bread)

Makes 10

Ingredients

350g/12oz wholemeal flour
½ tsp salt

2 tsp refined vegetable oil
120ml/4fl oz water

Method
- Knead all the ingredients to form a soft, pliable dough.
- Divide into 10 balls. Roll out with a flour-coated rolling pin into thin tortilla-like discs.
- Grease and heat a flat pan. Spread out a chapatti on the pan and cook on a low heat till the underside is light brown. Flip and repeat.
- Repeat for the rest of the chapattis.
- Serve hot.

Rice & Coconut Roti
(Rice and Coconut Bread)

Makes 8

Ingredients

175g/6oz rice flour
25g/scant 1oz coriander leaves,
   finely chopped
60g/2oz fresh coconut, grated

1 tsp refined vegetable oil
1 tsp cumin seeds
Salt to taste
90ml/3fl oz warm water

Method
- Knead all the ingredients together to form a pliable dough. Divide into 8 balls. Roll out into discs 15cm/6in in diameter.
- Heat a flat pan and cook a roti on a low heat till the underside is brown.
- Smear some oil on top, flip and repeat. Cook each side twice.
- Repeat for the remaining rotis. Serve hot.

Egg Paratha
(Pan-fried Bread with Egg)

Makes 10

Ingredients

350g/12oz wholemeal flour
120ml/4fl oz water
4 eggs, whisked
1 small onion, finely chopped
4 green chillies, finely chopped

10g/¼oz coriander leaves,
  finely chopped
1 tomato, finely chopped
¾ tsp salt
150ml/5fl oz refined vegetable oil

Method

- Knead the flour with the water to form a firm dough. Divide into 10 balls. Roll out into 10 discs of 15cm/6in diameter.
- Mix the remaining ingredients, except the oil, together. Set aside.
- Heat a flat pan and cook a paratha on a low heat for 2-3 minutes. Flip over and spread 1 tbsp of the egg mixture on the cooked side of the disc. Pour 1 tbsp oil over it.
- Gently flip and cook, egg-side-down, for 30 seconds. Carefully remove from the flat pan with a spatula.
- Repeat for the remaining parathas. Serve hot.

Onion Paneer Kulcha
(Baked Bread Topped with Onion and Paneer)

Makes 8

Ingredients

300g/10oz soft goat's cheese, drained
1 small onion, finely chopped
2 green chillies, finely chopped
1 tbsp coriander leaves, chopped

½ tbsp butter
Salt to taste
8 kulchas (see page 546)

Method

- Mix all the ingredients, except the kulchas, together. Divide the mixture into 8 portions.
- Spread a portion on each kulcha and bake in an oven at 200°C (400°F, Gas Mark 6) for 3 minutes. Serve hot.

Gobi Paratha

(Pan-fried Bread Stuffed with Cabbage)

Makes 10

Ingredients

1 small cabbage, finely grated and lightly steamed

350g/12oz wholemeal flour

2 tsp refined vegetable oil

½ tsp ginger paste

½ tsp garlic paste

1 tsp ground coriander

1 tsp ground cumin

½ tsp ajowan seeds

¾ tsp salt

120ml/4fl oz water

Ghee for greasing

Method

- Knead all the ingredients, except the ghee, to form a firm dough. Divide into 10 balls. Roll out into discs of 15cm/6in diameter.
- Heat a flat pan. Cook a paratha on a low heat for 3 minutes. Smear some ghee on top. Flip and repeat. Repeat for the rest of the parathas.

Mixed Flour Roti

Makes 10

Ingredients

250g/9oz millet flour

250g/9oz wholemeal flour

85g/3oz plain white flour

1 tsp ground coriander

1 tsp ground cumin

50g/1¾oz yoghurt

1 tsp chilli powder

½ tsp turmeric

1 tsp salt

120ml/4fl oz water

Ghee for greasing

Method

- Knead all the ingredients, except the ghee, to form a stiff dough.
- Divide into 10 balls and roll out into discs 12.5cm/5in in diameter.
- Heat a flat pan and cook a roti till the underside turns brown.
- Smear some ghee on top. Flip and repeat.
- Repeat for the remaining rotis. Serve hot.

Theplas
(Fenugreek Flat Bread)

Makes 10-12

Ingredients

50g/1¾oz fresh fenugreek leaves
¾ tbsp salt
175g/6oz wholemeal flour
125g/4½oz besan*
1 tsp ground coriander
1 tsp ground cumin

1 tsp chilli powder
1 tbsp yoghurt
2 tbsp refined vegetable oil
120ml/4fl oz water
Ghee for greasing

Method

- Chop the fenugreek leaves and mix with the salt. Set aside for 10 minutes. Drain and squeeze out the excess water.
- Knead with the remaining ingredients, except the ghee, to form a firm dough. Divide into 10-12 balls. Roll out into discs 15cm/6in in diameter.
- Heat a flat pan. Cook a thepla on a low heat till golden brown. Spread some ghee on top. Flip and repeat. Repeat for the rest of the theplas. Serve hot.

Puri
(Fried Puffed Bread)

Makes 20

Ingredients

350g/12oz wholemeal flour
120ml/4fl oz water

4 tsp refined vegetable oil plus extra for deep frying

Method

- Knead the flour, water and 4 tbsp oil to form a stiff dough. Set aside for 10 minutes.
- Divide the dough into 20 balls. Roll out into discs 10cm/4in in diameter.
- Heat the oil in a saucepan and fry the puris, two at a time, on a medium heat till they puff up. Flip and fry till golden brown.
- Repeat for the remaining puris.
- Drain on absorbent paper. Serve hot.

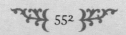

Aloo Paratha
(Pan-fried Bread Stuffed with Potatoes)

Makes 4

Ingredients

350g/12oz wholemeal flour
½ tsp salt
2 tsp refined vegetable oil
120ml/4fl oz water
2 large potatoes, boiled and mashed

25g/scant 1oz coriander leaves, chopped
1 tsp amchoor*
Salt to taste
Ghee for greasing

Method

* Knead the flour, salt and oil with the water to form a firm dough. Divide into 8 balls. Roll out into discs of 7.5cm/3in diameter. Set aside.
* Mix the remaining ingredients, except the ghee, together.
* Place 1 tbsp potato mixture on each of 4 discs and cover with another disc.
* Press the sides together. Roll out to make a paratha 15cm/6in in diameter. Repeat for the rest of the discs.
* Grease and heat a flat pan. Cook a paratha till the underside is brown. Smear ghee on top, flip and repeat. Repeat for the remaining parathas. Serve hot.

Spicy Besan Puri
(Spicy Gram Flour Puffed Bread)

Makes 12

Ingredients

175g/6oz besan*
85g/3oz wholemeal flour
250g/9oz plain white flour
¾ tsp ghee
½ tsp turmeric

½ tsp ground cumin
½ tsp ground coriander
Salt to taste
200ml/7fl oz water
Refined vegetable oil for frying

Method

* Sift all the ingredients, except the water and oil, together. Knead with the water. Divide into 12 balls. Roll out into discs 10cm/4in in diameter.
* Heat the oil in a frying pan. Fry the puris, two at a time, on a low heat till golden brown. Drain and serve hot.

Masala Puri
(Spicy Puffed Bread)

Makes 20

Ingredients

1 tsp chilli powder

¼ tsp turmeric

1 tsp ground cumin, dry roasted (see cooking techniques)

1 tsp ground coriander, dry roasted (see cooking techniques)

350g/12oz wholemeal flour

¾ tsp salt

2 tsp refined vegetable oil plus extra for frying

120ml/4fl oz water

Method
- Knead all the ingredients to form a stiff dough.
- Follow the recipe for making puris (see page 552). Serve hot.

Tilgul Chapatti
(Sesame Flat Bread)

Makes 10

Ingredients

350g/12oz rice flour

1 tbsp refined vegetable oil

¾ tsp salt

120ml/4fl oz water

500g/1lb 2oz jaggery*, grated

60g/2oz sesame seeds, dry roasted (see cooking techniques)

60g/2oz besan*, dry roasted (see cooking techniques)

Method
- Knead the flour, oil and salt with the water to form a stiff dough. Divide into 20 balls and roll out into discs of 10cm/4in diameter. Set aside.
- Mix the jaggery, sesame seeds and besan. Divide into 10 portions.
- Spread 1 portion each of the sesame mixture on 10 discs. Cover each of these with another disc. Seal the edges. Roll out into discs 15cm/6in in diameter.
- Heat a flat pan and cook a chapatti on a low heat till the underside is brown. Flip and repeat. Cook each side twice.
- Repeat for the remaining chapattis. Serve hot.

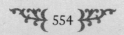

Tandoori Roti
(Flat Bread)

Makes 8

Ingredients

350g/12oz wholemeal flour

125g/4½oz plain white flour

2 tbsp refined vegetable oil

2 tbsp yoghurt

¾ tsp salt

120ml/4fl oz water

Method

* Knead all the ingredients to form a stiff dough. Divide into 8 balls. Roll out into discs of 15cm/6in diameter.
* Heat a flat pan. Wet one side of the disc and place it damp side down on the pan. Cook on a low heat till the underside is brown. Flip and repeat.
* Repeat for the remaining discs. Serve hot.

Makke ki Roti
(Flat Corn Bread)

Makes 8

Ingredients

350g/12oz maize flour

1 large onion, grated

2 green chillies, finely chopped

1 tbsp ghee

10g/¼oz coriander leaves, chopped

1 tsp salt

120ml/4fl oz water

Ghee for greasing

Method

* Knead all the ingredients, except the ghee, to form a firm dough.
* Divide into 8 balls. Roll out into discs of 10cm/4in diameter.
* Grease and heat a flat pan. Cook a roti on a low heat till the underside is golden brown. Flip and repeat. Spread some ghee on the cooked side. Flip again. Cook till done.
* Repeat for the remaining rotis. Serve hot.

Missi Roti
(Gram Flour Bread)

Makes 12

Ingredients

250g/9oz besan*
175g/6oz wholemeal flour
2 tbsp dry fenugreek leaves
1 tbsp chilli powder
½ tsp turmeric

Pinch of asafoetida
½ tsp cumin seeds
1 tsp salt
120ml/4fl oz water
Ghee for greasing

Method
- Knead all the ingredients except the ghee to form a firm dough.
- Divide into 12 balls and roll out into discs of 10cm/4in diameter.
- Smear ghee on a disc and fold it in half. Smear some more ghee on the half-moon and fold it in half to form a triangle.
- Dust with some dry flour and roll out into a disc of 15cm/6in diameter.
- Grease and heat a flat pan. Cook a roti on a low heat till the underside is golden brown. Flip and repeat.
- Repeat for the remaining rotis. Serve hot.

Besan Puri

Makes 20

Ingredients

125g/4½oz besan*
85g/3oz wholemeal flour
85g/3oz plain white flour
1 tbsp ghee

Salt to taste
100ml/3½fl oz water
Refined vegetable oil for frying

Method
- Knead all the ingredients, except the oil, to form a stiff dough.
- Divide into 20 balls and roll out into discs 7.5cm/3in in diameter.
- Heat the oil in a frying pan and fry the puris on a medium heat till golden brown.
- Repeat for the remaining dough. Drain on absorbent paper. Serve hot.

Bhatura
(Thick Fried Bread)

Makes 12

Ingredients
175g/6oz plain white flour

Pinch of baking powder

200g/7oz yoghurt

½ tsp salt

120ml/4fl oz water

Refined vegetable oil for frying

Method
- Knead all the ingredients, except the oil, to form a firm dough. Cover with a damp cloth. Set aside for 4 hours.
- Divide into 12 balls and roll out into discs of 10cm/4in diameter.
- Follow the recipe for making puris (see page 552).
- Serve hot.

Rice Puri

Makes 20

Ingredients
100g/3½oz steamed basmati rice (see page 519), mashed

175g/6oz wholemeal flour

1 tsp ground coriander

1 tsp chilli powder

1 tsp ajowan seeds

Salt to taste

100ml/3½fl oz water

Refined vegetable oil for frying

Method
- Knead all the ingredients, except the oil, to form a stiff dough.
- Divide into 20 balls and roll out into discs of 7.5cm/3in diameter.
- Heat the oil in a frying pan and fry the puris, two at a time, on a medium heat till golden brown.
- Drain on absorbent paper. Serve hot.

Palak Thalipeeth
(Multi-grain Pancake with Spinach)

Makes 10

Ingredients

85g/3oz besan*
85g/3oz millet flour
85g/3oz wholemeal flour
100g/3½oz spinach, chopped, steamed and ground
1 large onion, finely chopped
1 tbsp ground coriander

2 tbsp coriander leaves, finely chopped
4 green chillies, finely chopped
Salt to taste
150ml/5fl oz water
Refined vegetable oil for greasing

Method

- Mix all the ingredients, except the oil, to form a thick batter.
- Grease a flat pan. Spread a large spoonful of the batter, like a pancake.
- Cook on a medium heat till the underside is golden. Flip and repeat.
- Repeat for the remaining batter. Serve hot.

Khasta Puri
(Crispy Fried Bread)

Makes 20

Ingredients

175g/6oz wholemeal flour
140g/5oz self-raising flour
1 tsp butter
3 tbsp refined vegetable oil plus extra for frying

1 tsp ajowan seeds
Salt to taste
100ml/3½fl oz water

Method

- Knead all the ingredients to form a stiff dough. Cover with a damp cloth. Set aside for 15 minutes.
- Divide into 20 balls and roll out into discs 7.5cm/3in in diameter.
- Heat the oil in a frying pan and fry each puri on a medium heat till golden brown.
- Drain on absorbent paper. Serve hot.

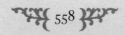

Appam
(Rice Pancake)

Makes 8

Ingredients

500g/1lb 2oz long-grained rice, soaked
  for 5 hours

300g/10oz fresh coconut, grated

100g/3½oz steamed basmati rice
  (see page 519)

¼ tsp yeast, soaked in 1 tbsp
  warm water

½ tsp sugar

Salt to taste

Refined vegetable oil for greasing

Method

- Drain the rice. Grind with the coconut and steamed rice to form a thick paste. Add the remaining ingredients, except the oil. Mix well. Allow to ferment for 8-10 hours.
- Grease and heat a frying pan. Add a large spoonful of the rice mixture. Rotate the pan so that the mixture forms a thick layer in the middle of the pan and thinner layers at the edge.
- Cover with a lid and cook on a medium heat for 4-5 minutes.
- Remove carefully with a spatula. Repeat for the remaining batter. Serve hot.

Sweet Puri
(Sweet Puffed Bread)

Makes 20

Ingredients

350g/12oz plain white flour

2 tbsp caster sugar

¼ tsp salt

1 tsp ghee plus extra for frying

120ml/4fl oz milk

Method

- Knead the flour, caster sugar, salt and 1 tbsp ghee with the milk to form a stiff dough.
- Follow the recipe for making puris (see page 552).
- Serve hot.

Seyal Dabal Hare Masale Mein
(Green Masala Sindhi Bread)

Serves 8

Ingredients

100g/3½oz coriander leaves

10 garlic cloves

2.5cm/1in root ginger

1 tbsp cumin seeds

2 small onions

4 tbsp refined vegetable oil

2 tsp ground coriander

¼ tsp turmeric

1 tbsp lemon juice

500ml/16fl oz water

Salt to taste

12 slices white bread

Method

* Grind the coriander leaves, garlic, ginger, cumin and onions together.
* Heat the oil in a saucepan. Fry the paste on a low heat for 6 minutes.
* Add the remaining ingredients, except the bread. Mix well. Cook on a low heat for 7-8 minutes. Spread spoonfuls of the mixture on the bread slices and chop into bite-sized pieces. Serve immediately.

Cheese Paratha
(Pan-fried Bread Stuffed with Cheese)

Makes 8

Ingredients

3 eggs

1 tbsp milk

2 green chillies, finely chopped

2 tbsp coriander leaves, chopped

Salt to taste

150g/5½oz Cheddar cheese, grated

8 chapattis (see page 549)

Ghee for greasing

Method

* Whisk the eggs with all the ingredients, except the chapattis and ghee. Set aside.
* Grease and heat a flat pan. Cook a chapatti on a low heat on both sides.
* Pour some egg mixture on one side to cover the chapatti. Allow to set. Carefully flip and cook for a minute. Gently remove with a spatula. Now roll the cheese paratha so that the egg is on the inside.
* Repeat for the remaining chapattis. Serve hot.

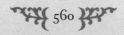

Addie Roti
(Bread with Lentils)

Makes 10

Ingredients

225g/8oz mung dhal*
75g/2½oz urad dhal*
125g/4½oz plain white flour
175g/6oz wholemeal flour
2 tbsp refined vegetable oil
1 green chilli, finely chopped
1 tsp ginger paste
1 tsp chilli powder

1 tsp ground coriander
1 tsp ground cumin
1 tsp onion seeds
½ tsp amchoor*
Salt to taste
120ml/4fl oz water
Refined vegetable oil for greasing

Method

- Soak both the dhals separately for 4 hours. Drain and grind together to form a thick paste. Divide into 10 portions. Set aside.
- Knead the remaining ingredients, except the oil, with enough water to form a soft dough.
- Divide into 10 balls and roll out into discs 10cm/4in in diameter.
- Place a portion of the dhal mixture on each disc. Seal and roll out into discs 15cm/6in in diameter.
- Grease and heat a flat pan and cook a roti on a low heat till the underside is brown. Flip and repeat. Cook each side twice.
- Repeat for the remaining rotis. Serve hot.

Thalipeeth
(Multi-grain Pancake)

Makes about 8

Ingredients

85g/3oz besan*
85g/3oz wholemeal flour
85g/3oz millet flour
1 tomato, finely chopped
1 large onion, finely chopped
1 tsp ground coriander

1 tsp ground cumin
2 tbsp coriander leaves, chopped
Salt to taste
150ml/5fl oz warm water
Refined vegetable oil for greasing

Method
* Knead all the ingredients, except the oil, to form a thick batter.
* Grease and heat a frying pan. Spread a large spoonful of the batter, like a pancake.
* Cook on a low heat till the underside is golden brown. Flip and repeat.
* Repeat for the remaining batter. Serve hot.

Khamiri Puri
(Puffed Sweet Bread)

Makes 20

Ingredients

350g/12oz plain white flour
1 tbsp yoghurt
1 tsp sugar
1 tbsp raisins
1 tbsp cashew nuts,
  coarsely pounded

½ tsp ground black pepper
½ tsp salt
120ml/4fl oz water
Refined vegetable oil for deep frying

Method
* Knead all the ingredients, except the oil, into a firm dough. Cover with a damp cloth. Set aside for 5 hours.
* Divide the dough into walnut-sized balls. Follow the recipe used for making puris (see page 552). Serve hot.

Satpura Paratha
(Layered Pan-fried Bread)

Makes 10

Ingredients

350g/12oz plain white flour

1 tsp ajowan seeds

3 tbsp ghee

Salt to taste

120ml/4fl oz water

Refined vegetable oil for greasing

Method

- Knead all the ingredients except the oil to form a stiff dough.
- Divide into 10 balls and roll out into long strips.
- Apply ghee on top of a strip. Place one edge of the strip on your palm and coil the rest around your palm. Gently remove from your palm and pat into a patty. Apply flour on both sides.
- Roll out into a disc 12.5cm/5in in diameter.
- Grease and heat a flat pan. Cook the disc till the underside is golden brown. Smear some ghee on top, flip and repeat.
- Repeat for the remaining strips.
- Serve hot.

Pyaaz Puri
(Rice Flour Puffed Bread with Onions)

Makes 20

Ingredients

60g/2oz steamed rice, mashed

175g/6oz wholemeal flour

2 large onions, finely sliced

1 tsp garam masala

¼ tsp ajowan seeds

Salt to taste

100ml/3½fl oz water

Refined vegetable oil for frying

Method

- Knead all the ingredients, except the oil, to form a stiff dough.
- Divide into 20 balls and roll out into discs 7.5cm/3in in diameter.
- Heat the oil in a frying pan and fry each puri on a medium heat till golden brown. Drain and serve hot.

Methi Puris
(Puffed Fenugreek Bread)

Makes 20

Ingredients
25g/scant 1 oz fresh
  fenugreek leaves, finely
  chopped
Salt to taste
175g/6oz wholemeal flour
125g/4½oz besan*
½ tsp ground coriander
½ tsp ground cumin
½ tsp caster sugar
120ml/4fl oz water
Refined vegetable oil for
  frying

Method
- Mix the fenugreek leaves and salt. Set aside for 1 hour. Squeeze out the excess moisture. Mix with all the remaining ingredients, except the oil, and knead into a firm dough.
- Divide into 20 balls. Roll out into discs of 10cm/4in diameter.
- Follow the recipe for making puris (see page 552).
- Serve hot.

Bajre Ki Roti
(Millet Flour Flat Bread)

Makes 8

Ingredients
350g/12oz millet flour
1 tsp refined vegetable oil
Salt to taste
120ml/4fl oz warm water
Ghee for greasing

Method
- Knead all the ingredients, except the ghee, to form a firm dough.
- Divide into 8 balls. Roll out into discs of 12.5cm/5in diameter.
- Heat a flat pan and cook a roti on a low heat till the underside is brown. Flip and repeat. Cook each side three times.
- Repeat for the remaining rotis.
- Smear one side with ghee. Serve hot.

Naan
(Baked Flour Bread)

Makes 8

Ingredients

350g/12oz refined flour

1 tbsp yoghurt

1 tsp kalonji seeds*

2 tbsp refined vegetable oil

½ tsp bicarbonate of soda

Salt to taste

120ml/4fl oz water

Method

- Knead all the ingredients together to form a pliable dough. Cover with a damp cloth. Set aside for 30 minutes.
- Divide into 8 balls and roll out into oval shapes.
- Heat a flat pan. Sprinkle water on one side of the naan and place on the pan, damp side down. Cook on a low heat till the underside is brown. Flip and cook for 3 minutes. Repeat for the remaining dough. Serve hot.

Koki
(Sindhi Bread)

Makes 8

Ingredients

350g/12oz wholemeal flour, mixed with 1 tbsp ghee

1 large onion, finely chopped

3 green chillies, finely chopped

1 tbsp coriander leaves, chopped

Salt to taste

120ml/4fl oz water

Ghee for greasing

Method

- Knead all the ingredients, except the ghee, to form a stiff dough. Divide into 8 balls. Roll out into discs of 10cm/4in diameter.
- With a knife, make diagonal, criss-crossing lines on the kokis, from one end to the other.
- Grease and heat a flat pan. Cook a koki on a low heat till the underside is light brown. Smear some ghee on top, flip and repeat. Cook each side twice.
- Repeat for the remaining kokis. Serve hot.

Kheema Paratha
(Pan-fried Bread Stuffed with Mince)

Makes 10

Ingredients

350g/12oz plain white flour

120ml/4fl oz water

2 tsp refined vegetable oil plus extrafor frying

1 large onion, finely chopped

2 green chillies, finely chopped

1 tsp garam masala

¼ tsp ginger paste

¼ tsp garlic paste

250g/9oz minced beef

Salt to taste

1 tbsp coriander leaves, finely chopped

4 eggs, whisked with salt and a pinch of turmeric

Method

- Knead the flour with half the water to make a pliable dough. Cover with a damp cloth. Set aside for 3-4 hours.
- Heat 2 tsp oil in a saucepan. Fry the onion on a medium heat till translucent.
- Add the remaining water and all the remaining ingredients, except the eggs. Mix well, cover with a lid and simmer for 30 minutes. Set aside.
- Divide the dough into 10 balls. Roll out into discs of 15cm/6in diameter.
- Spread the mince mixture over a disc and pour some egg mixture on top. Fold the disc like a pouch and seal it carefully. Pat into a patty.
- With a rolling pin, roll the patty into a square-shaped paratha.
- Repeat for the remaining dough.
- Heat the remaining oil in a frying pan and fry each paratha on a low heat till golden brown. Serve hot.

Paneer Paratha
(Pan-fried Bread Stuffed with Paneer)

Makes 10

Ingredients

350g/12oz plain white flour
Salt to taste
120ml/4fl oz water
300g/10oz paneer*

1 tbsp coriander leaves, chopped
½ tsp ground black pepper
Ghee for greasing

Method
- Knead the flour and salt to form a stiff dough. Divide into 20 balls. Roll out into discs of 7.5cm/3in diameter. Set aside.
- Grind the remaining ingredients, except the ghee, into a smooth paste.
- Spread a large spoonful of the paste on 10 discs and cover each with the remaining 10. Seal the edges. Roll out into discs 15cm/6in in diameter.
- Grease and heat a flat pan. Cook the paratha on a low heat till the underside is golden brown. Smear some ghee on top, flip and repeat.
- Repeat for the remaining discs. Serve hot.

Meetha Paratha
(Sweet Pan-fried Bread)

Makes 8

Ingredients

350g/12oz wholemeal flour
2 tbsp caster sugar
1 tsp refined vegetable oil

Salt to taste
120ml/4fl oz water
Ghee for greasing

Method
- Knead all the ingredients, except the ghee, to form a stiff dough. Divide into 8 balls and roll out into discs of 10cm/4in diameter.
- Grease and heat a flat pan. Cook a paratha on a low heat till the underside is brown. Smear some ghee on top, flip and repeat. Cook each side twice.
- Repeat for the remaining dough. Serve hot.

Dhal Paratha
(Pan-fried Bread with Lentils)

Makes 8

Ingredients
150g/5½ oz leftover varan (see page 167)   120ml/4fl oz water
350g/12oz wholemeal flour   Ghee for greasing

Method
* Cook the varan in a saucepan on a medium heat till it starts to dry. Set aside to cool.
* Knead the flour and water to form a stiff dough. Divide into 8 balls and roll out into discs of 10cm/4in diameter.
* Place a large spoonful of the varan on each disc and seal, like a pouch. Roll out carefully into discs of 15cm/6in diameter.
* Grease and heat a flat pan. Cook a paratha on a low heat till the underside is light brown. Smear some ghee on top, flip and repeat. Cook each side twice.
* Repeat for the remaining discs. Serve hot.

DESSERTS

Desserts are everybody's favourite part of a meal and in India, sweets and desserts are considered to be a symbol of good times, feasting and much rejoicing. This chapter has many such delicious recipes to choose from. Delight your taste-buds with treats such as delicious Carrot Halwa or yummy Kesar Kulfi!

Imartis

(Fried Lentil Spirals dipped in Sugar Syrup)

Serves 4

Ingredients
600g/1lb 5oz urad dhal*, soaked overnight
500ml/16fl oz water
¼ tsp yellow food colour
750g/1lb 10oz sugar
½ tsp ground green cardamom
450g/1lb ghee

Method
- Drain the dhal and grind with 60ml/2fl oz water to a thick batter.
- Add the food colour. Whisk till the mixture is fluffy. Set aside for 3 hours.
- Boil the remaining water with the sugar in a saucepan on a medium heat. Cook till it achieves 1-thread consistency (see cooking techniques). Add the ground cardamom. Stir lightly. Set aside.
- Heat the ghee in a frying pan. Fill a piping bag with the dhal mixture and form spirals in the ghee. Fry these spirals on a low heat till they turn crisp. Flip the spirals and repeat.
- Drain the spirals and soak them in the water-sugar mixture for 3-4 minutes. Drain them again. Serve hot or cold.

NOTE: *You can fry 4-5 imartis at a time, depending on the size of the frying pan.*

Boondi Laddoo

Makes 12

Ingredients
600g/1lb 5oz boondi (see page 597)
2 tsp ground green cardamom

Method
- Place the boondi in a bowl and mix with the cardamom. Divide this mixture into 12 equal-sized balls. Serve.

NOTE: *This can be stored for up to 1 month.*

Sweet Kachori
(Sweet Deep Fried Stuffed Patties)

Makes 15

Ingredients
600g/1lb 2oz sugar
250ml/8fl oz water
1 tbsp milk

For the filling:
125g/4½oz khoya*
½ tsp ground green cardamom

½ tsp ground cinnamon
¼ tsp fennel seeds

For the pastry:
500g/1lb 2oz plain white flour
1 tbsp cornflour
75g/2½oz ghee plus extra for frying
2 tbsp water

Method
• Mix the filling ingredients together. Divide this mixture into 15 balls. Set aside.
• Knead all the pastry ingredients together. Cover this mixture with a wet cloth. Set aside.
• In a saucepan, boil the sugar, water and milk on a medium heat until they achieve 1-thread consistency (see cooking techniques). Set aside.
• Knead the pastry and divide into 15 pieces. Roll out into discs of 7.5cm/3in diameter. Place one filling-ball in each disc, seal and flatten into a patty.
• Heat the ghee in a frying pan and fry the kachoris on a medium heat till golden brown. Make a hole in each kachori. Pour half a tbsp of the syrup into each kachori. Serve after half an hour.

Kulfi Delight

Serves 4

Ingredients
3 malai kulfis (see page 576)
20 lychees, deseeded

20 cherries, chopped
75g/2½oz mixed nuts, to garnish

Method
• Leave the malai kulfis to thaw outside the refrigerator for 5 minutes.
• Add the lychees and cherries. Mix well.
• Sprinkle the nuts on top. Serve chilled.

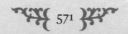

Karanji
(Deep Fried Pastries)

Makes 15

Ingredients
125g/4½oz khoya*
250g/9oz plain white flour
1 tbsp ghee plus extra for frying

For the filling:
50g/1¾oz desiccated coconut
1 tbsp poppy seeds
1 tsp ground green cardamom
4 almonds, ground
60g/2oz caster sugar
10-15 raisins

Method
- To make the dough, dry roast (see cooking techniques) the khoya in a saucepan on a medium heat for 2-3 minutes.
- Cool the khoya and crumble it. Knead with the flour, ghee and enough water to form a soft dough. Set aside.
- For the filling, dry roast the coconut for 2-3 minutes.
- Mix this with the remaining filling ingredients and divide into 15 equal portions. Set aside.
- Divide the pastry dough into 15 balls and roll each out into a disc of 10cm/4in diameter.
- Place a portion of the filling on one half of each disc and fold the other half over it. Press the edges together to seal. Set the pastries aside on a clean cloth for 30 minutes.
- Heat the ghee in a frying pan. Fry the stuffed pastries on a medium heat till they turn light brown. Drain the pastries and cool them. Store in an airtight container.

NOTE: *This can be stored for a week.*

Peanut Laddoo

Makes 10-12

Ingredients
500g/1lb 2oz peanuts, coarsely ground
250g/9oz caster sugar
150g/5½oz ghee

Method
- Heat a frying pan and dry roast (see cooking techniques) the ground peanuts on a medium heat for 1-2 minutes.
- Mix with the remaining ingredients. Divide the mixture into 10-12 lime-sized balls. Serve.

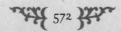

Puranpoli
(Sweet Roti Delicacy)

Makes 12

Ingredients
900g/2lb chana dhal*
1.25 litres/2½ pints water
750g/1lb 10oz jaggery*, grated
1 tsp ground green cardamom
1 tbsp refined oil
375g/13oz plain white flour
Ghee for greasing

Method
- For the filling, cook the dhal with the water on a medium heat for 45 minutes. Drain and set aside in a colander for 10-15 minutes.
- Mix this dhal with the jaggery and cardamom. Cook in a saucepan on a medium heat till it forms a soft lump. Grind to a paste.
- Divide into 12 equal portions. Set aside.
- Knead the oil and flour with enough water to make a soft, pliable dough.
- Divide into 12 balls and roll them out into discs of 10cm/4in diameter.
- Place a portion of the filling on each disc. Seal like a pouch and flatten each into a patty. Roll again into discs of 5cm/2in diameter.
- Heat a frying pan and fry the discs one at a time. Cook on a low heat till the underside is golden brown. Flip and repeat.
- Spread some ghee over each disc. Serve hot.

Shrikhand
(Milk Pudding with Dry Fruits)

Serves 4

Ingredients
1 tbsp raisins
1kg/2¼lb Greek yoghurt
1kg/2¼lb caster sugar
1 tbsp flaked almonds
½ tsp ground green cardamom
10 strands saffron

Method
- Soak the raisins in water for 1 hour. Drain and set aside.
- Whisk the yoghurt thoroughly with the sugar. Add the raisins and the remaining ingredients. Mix well.
- Serve chilled.

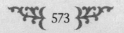

Rice Kheer
(Rice and Milk Pudding)

Serves 4

Ingredients
180g/6½oz basmati rice,
  soaked for 1 hour
  and drained
500ml/16fl oz water
1 litre/1¾ pints milk
180g/6½oz sugar
30g/1oz almonds, chopped
30g/1oz raisins, chopped
¼ tsp kewra essence*

Method
- Cook the rice with the water in a saucepan for 10 minutes on a medium heat. Stir the mixture occasionally.
- Add the milk and sugar. Simmer for 15 minutes, stirring frequently.
- Add half the almonds and raisins. Stir lightly. Remove from the heat and add the essence.
- Garnish with the remaining almonds and raisins. Serve chilled.

Gulab Jamun
(Dumplings in Sweet Saffron Syrup)

Makes 25-30

Ingredients
800g/1¾lb khoya*,
  crumbled
250g/9oz plain white flour
¼ tsp bicarbonate of soda
¼ tsp ground green
  cardamom
7-8 saffron strands,
  crushed
1.25kg/2¾lb sugar
60ml/2fl oz milk
Ghee for deep frying
500ml/16fl oz water

Method
- Sieve the khoya with the flour and bicarbonate of soda. Add the cardamom, saffron, 500g/1lb 2oz sugar and the milk. Mix well.
- Knead into a soft dough and divide the dough into walnut-sized balls.
- Heat the ghee in a saucepan. Fry the balls on a medium heat till they turn golden brown. Drain and set them aside.
- Boil the water with the remaining sugar in a saucepan on a medium heat. Cook till it achieves 1-thread consistency (see cooking techniques).
- Soak the fried balls in the syrup. Serve hot or cold.

Besan Laddoo
(Bengal Gram Flour Dumplings)

Serves 4

Ingredients
300g/10oz ghee
60g/2oz besan*
60ml/2fl oz milk
1 tbsp almonds, ground
1 tbsp raisins
500g/1lb 2oz caster sugar

Method
- Heat the ghee in a saucepan. Add the besan and fry it on a medium heat for 30 minutes. Stir the mixture frequently to avoid lumps.
- Add the milk, almonds and raisins. Mix well. Cook on a low heat for 5 minutes, stirring continuously.
- Cool the mixture and add the sugar. Knead well and divide into walnut-sized balls. Serve.

Sweet Potato Kheer
(Sweet Potato Pudding)

Serves 4

Ingredients
1 litre/1¾ pints milk
4 large sweet potatoes, peeled and grated
500g/1lb 2oz sugar
¼ tsp ground green cardamom
1 tbsp flaked almonds
A few saffron strands, soaked in 1 tbsp milk

Method
- Boil the milk in a saucepan on a medium heat for 5 minutes. Add the sweet potatoes and sugar. Simmer the mixture for 15 minutes, stirring occasionally.
- Add the cardamom and almonds. Stir the mixture well. Simmer for another 10 minutes.
- Add the saffron. Stir the mixture thoroughly. Serve chilled.

Sweet Sheera

(Semolina-based Sweet Dish)

Serves 4

Ingredients
2 tbsp ghee

300g/10oz semolina

250ml/8fl oz milk

250g/9oz sugar

250ml/8fl oz water

1 tbsp flaked almonds

½ tsp ground green cardamom

1 tbsp raisins, soaked in water

A few saffron strands, soaked in 1 tbsp milk

Method
- Heat the ghee in a saucepan and dry roast (see cooking techniques) the semolina on a medium heat till golden brown.
- Add the milk, sugar and water. Stir the mixture thoroughly. Simmer till the milk and water evaporate, stirring continuously.
- Add the remaining ingredients. Mix well. Serve hot.

Malai Kulfi

(Indian Ice cream)

Serves 4

Ingredients
1 litre/1¾ pints milk

180g/6½oz sugar

1 tbsp cornflour, dissolved in 60ml/2fl oz water

30g/1oz flaked almonds

1 tsp ground green cardamom

A few saffron strands, soaked in 1 tbsp milk

1 tbsp pistachios, crushed

Method
- Boil the milk in a saucepan on a medium heat for 7-8 minutes.
- Add the sugar. Continue to cook for 10 minutes, stirring lightly.
- Add the remaining ingredients. Mix thoroughly and simmer 10-12 minutes.
- Cool and pour into kulfi moulds or an ice tray. Refrigerate for 6-7 hours.
- Serve chilled.

Doodhi Halwa
(Bottle Gourd Confection)

Serves 4

Ingredients
2 large bottle gourds*, peeled and grated

1 tbsp ghee

1 litre/1¾ pints milk

250g/9oz sugar

1 tbsp flaked almonds

½ tsp ground green cardamom

1 tbsp raisins, soaked in water

Method
- Squeeze the excess moisture from the bottle gourd by pressing it between your palms.
- Heat the ghee in a saucepan. Add the bottle gourd and fry on a low heat for 5 minutes.
- Add the milk and sugar. Mix well and simmer for 10 minutes. Add the remaining ingredients. Stir lightly.
- Serve hot or cold.

Carrot Halwa
(Carrot Confection)

Serves 4

Ingredients
2 tbsp ghee

500g/1lb 2oz carrots, finely grated

500ml/16fl oz milk

250g/9oz sugar

10 almonds, blanched

Method
- Heat the ghee in a saucepan. Add the carrots and fry them on a medium heat for 3-4 minutes, stirring frequently.
- Add the milk and sugar. Mix well. Simmer for 10-15 minutes, stirring frequently.
- Garnish with the almonds. Serve hot or cold.

Sweet Rice

Serves 4

Ingredients
400g/14oz steamed rice
(see page 519)

250g/9oz sugar

2 tbsp ghee

3 cloves

5cm/2in cinnamon

3 bay leaves

A few saffron strands,
soaked in 1 tbsp milk

Method
- Mix the rice with the sugar. Set aside.
- Heat the ghee in a saucepan and add the cloves, cinnamon and bay leaves. Let them splutter for 15 seconds.
- Gently add the rice mixture. Cook on a low heat for 5-10 minutes stirring carefully. Add the saffron.
- Serve hot.

Phirni
(Creamy Rice Flour Pudding)

Serves 4

Ingredients
250g/9oz long-grained rice,
soaked for 1 hour

1 litre/1¾ pints milk

250g/9oz sugar

1 tbsp flaked almonds

½ tsp ground green
cardamom

Method
- Drain the rice and grind it coarsely. Set aside.
- Boil the milk with the sugar in a saucepan on a medium heat for 8-10 minutes. Add the rice. Simmer the mixture for 6-7 minutes, stirring frequently.
- Add the almonds and cardamom. Stir the mixture thoroughly. Serve chilled.

Soan Papdi

(Roasted Sugar Treat)

Makes 20

Ingredients
300g/10oz besan*
300g/10oz plain white flour
300g/10oz ghee
2 tbsp milk
600g/1lb 5oz sugar
360ml/12fl oz water
½ tsp ground black cardamom

Method
- Sift the besan and the flour together.
- Heat the ghee in a saucepan. Add the flour mixture and sauté on a low heat for 6 minutes. Set aside.
- Boil the milk with the sugar and water on a medium heat till it achieves 2½-thread consistency (see cooking techniques).
- Mix with the flour mixture. Whisk with a fork till the mixture forms thread-like flakes.
- Brush with ghee and garnish with the cardamom. Chop into 2.5cm/1in pieces.

NOTE: *This can be stored for up to 15 days.*

Coconut Barfi

(Coconut Fudge)

Makes 20-25

Ingredients
150ml/5fl oz water
250g/9oz sugar
250g/9oz fresh coconut, finely grated
Ghee for greasing

Method
- Boil the water with the sugar in a saucepan on a medium heat for 15 minutes. Set aside.
- Heat a saucepan. Dry roast (see cooking techniques) the coconut on a medium heat for 1-2 minutes.
- Add the sugar-water mixture. Mix well. Simmer till it achieves 2½-thread consistency (see cooking techniques).
- Spread on a greased dish and cool. Chop into 2.5cm/1in pieces.

NOTE: *This can be stored in a refrigerator for 3-4 days.*

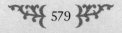

Kaju Barfi
(Cashew Nut Fudge)

Makes 20

Ingredients
75g/2½oz ghee
250g/9oz refined white flour
500ml/16fl oz water
300g/10oz sugar
150g/5½oz cashew nuts, powdered
1 tbsp ground green cardamom

Method
- Heat the ghee in a saucepan. Add the flour and fry on a medium heat for a minute, stirring frequently. Set aside.
- Boil the water with the sugar in a saucepan on a medium heat for 15 minutes.
- Add the flour mixture and simmer till the water evaporates, stirring continuously.
- Add the cashews and cardamom. Mix well. Cook till the mixture thickens.
- Spread on a greased dish. Cool and chop into squares. Serve.

Khajur Rolls
(Date Fudge)

Makes 40

Ingredients
400g/14oz can condensed milk
250g/9oz mixed nuts (almonds, cashew nuts, pistachios, etc.)
1kg/2¼lb seedless dates, roughly chopped
50g/1¾oz desiccated coconut
Ghee for greasing

Method
- Cook the condensed milk with the nuts and dates in a saucepan on a low heat for 10-12 minutes, stirring continuously. Ensure that it does not stick to the bottom. Set aside.
- Spread the coconut on a sheet of greaseproof paper greased with ghee. Spread the milk mixture over the coconut. Roll into 4 thick cylinders. Refrigerate for a few hours.
- Slice each cylinder into 10 pieces. Serve chilled.

Jalebi
(Sugar Spirals)

Serves 4

Ingredients
750g/1lb 10oz besan*
1 tsp dry yeast
240ml/6fl oz water
750g/1lb 10oz sugar
1 tsp ground cardamom
4-5 saffron strands
Ghee for deep-frying

Method
- Mix the besan and yeast with enough water to form a thick batter. Transfer this mixture to a piping bag. Set aside.
- Simmer the water with the sugar in a saucepan till it achieves 1-thread consistency (see cooking techniques). Add the cardamom and saffron to this mixture. Mix well. Set aside.
- Heat the ghee in a frying pan and squeeze the batter out of the piping bag in the shape of spirals.
- Fry these spirals on a low heat till they turn crisp. Drain and soak in the water-sugar mixture for 3-4 minutes. Drain.
- Serve hot.

Nankhatai
(Sweet Indian Cookies)

Makes 20-25

Ingredients
300g/10oz butter
500g/1lb 2oz caster sugar
750g/1lb 10oz plain white flour
25 glacé cherries, finely chopped
Ghee for greasing

Method
- Mix the butter and sugar and whisk till frothy. Gradually add the flour and knead to form a soft dough.
- Divide into 20-25 balls. Press a few cherry pieces into the centre of each ball.
- Grease a baking tray and arrange the cookies on it, making sure that they don't touch each other.
- Bake in a preheated oven at 180°C (350°F, Gas Mark 4) for 15 minutes. Serve at room temperature.

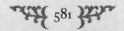

Chickoo Halwa
(Sapota Confection)

Serves 4

Ingredients
6 chickoos*, peeled,
  deseeded and mashed

120ml/4fl oz milk

200g/7oz khoya*

60g/2oz sugar

1 tbsp ghee

2 tbsp walnuts, chopped

Method
- Mix the chickoos with the milk. Simmer this mixture in a saucepan for 15 minutes. Stir occasionally.
- Add the khoya and simmer for 20 minutes, stirring continuously.
- Add the sugar and ghee. Continue to stir for another 7-8 minutes.
- Garnish the halwa with the walnuts. Serve warm.

Dhal Ka Sheera
(Lentil Confection)

Serves 4

Ingredients
600g/1lb 5oz masoor
  dhal*, soaked for 5-6
  hours

1kg/2¼lb sugar

750ml/1¼ pints water

3 tbsp milk

600g/1lb 5oz ghee

1 tsp ground green
  cardamom

A few saffron strands,
  soaked in 1 tbsp milk

30g/1oz mixed nuts,
  chopped

Method
- Drain the dhal and grind to a thick paste. Set aside.
- Cook the sugar and water in a saucepan on a medium heat for 20-30 minutes, stirring frequently.
- Add the milk. Bring the mixture to a boil and simmer till it achieves 1-thread consistency (see cooking techniques). Set aside.
- Heat the ghee in a saucepan. Add the dhal paste and fry it on a medium heat till it turns golden brown.
- Add the milk mixture, cardamom and saffron. Stir and cook for 6-7 minutes.
- Garnish with the mixed nuts. Serve hot.

Kalakand
(Milk Burfi)

Makes 25

Ingredients
2 litres/3½ pints milk

½ tsp citric acid, dissolved in 120ml/4fl oz water

180g/6½oz sugar

Ghee for greasing

Silver leaf, to decorate

3 tbsp mixed nuts, chopped

Method
- Boil half the milk with the citric acid mixture and sugar in a saucepan on a medium heat for 10 minutes.
- Remove from the heat, and let the curdled mixture settle. Strain through muslin, reserving both the curds and liquid.
- Squeeze any excess water from the curds and flatten them. Set aside.
- Simmer the strained liquid in a saucepan till its quantity reduces by half.
- Add the curds and the remaining milk. Mix well. Simmer till the mixture thickens. Stir the mixture continuously.
- Place on a greased tray, spread the silver leaf over it and sprinkle with nuts.
- Cool and chop into squares to serve.

Badam ka Sheera
(Almond Confection)

Serves 4

Ingredients
225g/8oz almonds, soaked overnight

300g/10oz ghee

750ml/1¼ pints hot milk

125g/4½oz sugar

Chopped mixed nuts, to decorate

Method
- Peel the almonds and grind to a fine paste.
- Heat the ghee in a saucepan and fry the paste on a medium heat. Stir continuously till it turns light brown.
- Add the milk and sugar. Simmer till thick, stirring continuously.
- Decorate with the chopped nuts. Serve hot.

Atte ka Sheera

Serves 4

Ingredients

2½ tbsp ghee
250g/9oz wholemeal flour
600ml/1 pint water
250g/9oz sugar
½ tsp ground green
  cardamom
½ tbsp pistachios, chopped
½ tbsp almonds, chopped

Method

- Heat the ghee in a saucepan and sauté the flour on a low heat till brown. Set aside.
- Boil the water with the sugar for 20 minutes on a medium heat. Stir the mixture frequently.
- Add the flour. Simmer till the water evaporates, stirring continuously.
- Add the cardamom. Mix well.
- Garnish the sheera with the pistachios and almonds. Serve hot.

Beetroot Halwa

(Beetroot Confection)

Serves 4

Ingredients

1kg/2¼lb beetroots, peeled
  and grated
1.5 litres/2¾ pints milk
1kg/2¼lb sugar
3 tbsp ghee
1 tsp ground green
  cardamom
4-5 saffron strands, soaked
  in 1 tbsp milk

Method

- Cook the beetroot with the milk in a saucepan for 30 minutes on a medium heat, stirring frequently.
- Add the sugar and simmer till thick. Stir the halwa continuously.
- Add the remaining ingredients. Continue to stir till the ghee separates from the mixture.
- Serve hot.

Rava Laddoo
(Semolina Dumplings)

Makes 8

Ingredients
2 tbsp ghee
100g/3½oz semolina
180g/6½oz caster sugar
½ tsp ground green
  cardamom
50g/1¾oz desiccated
  coconut
4-5 saffron strands, soaked
  in 1 tbsp milk
60ml/2fl oz milk

Method
- Heat the ghee in a saucepan and fry the semolina on a medium heat till light brown.
- Add the sugar. Stir for 3-4 minutes.
- Remove from the heat and add the remaining ingredients. Knead well.
- Divide into 8 equal portions and roll them into balls with greased palms. Serve.

Rossogolla
(Dumplings in Sugar Syrup)

Makes 12

Ingredients
1 litre/1¾ pints milk
½ tsp citric acid
1 litre/1¾ pints water
375g/13oz sugar
2-3 drops rose essence

Method
- Boil the milk with the citric acid in a saucepan on a medium heat for 10-15 minutes. Stir till the milk curdles. Set aside for 5 minutes.
- Strain the curdled milk through a piece of muslin cloth. Squeeze out the excess moisture from the curds and gently knead them into a soft dough. Divide into 12 balls. Set aside.
- Simmer the water and sugar in a saucepan for 30 minutes.
- Add the balls and cover the pan with a perforated lid. Continue to simmer for 15 minutes.
- Allow the mixture to cool, add the rose essence and refrigerate the rossogollas for 4-5 hours. Serve chilled.

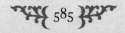

Pedas
(Thickened Milk Dessert)

Makes 36

Ingredients

750g/1lb 10oz caster sugar

750g/1lb 10oz khoya*

½ tsp ground green cardamom

Dash of yellow food colour

8-10 pistachios, finely sliced

Method

- Cook the sugar with the khoya in a saucepan on a low heat for 10-15 minutes, stirring continuously. Set aside to cool.
- Add the cardamom and food colour. Knead thoroughly. Divide into 36 portions and press into cookie moulds briefly to shape them.
- Remove from the moulds and press 2-3 pistachio slices on each peda. Serve.

Mawa Burfi
(Thickened Milk Fudge)

Makes 25

Ingredients

750g/1lb 10oz khoya*

750g/1lb 10oz caster sugar

1 tsp ground green cardamom

2 sheets silver leaf

Method

- Mash the khoya and knead it with the sugar.
- Cook in a saucepan on a low heat for 10-12 minutes. Stir the mixture continuously.
- Add the cardamom. Mix well. Continue to cook till the mixture resembles a thick lump.
- Spread the mixture on a flat platter so that it is 1cm/½in thick. Set aside to cool.
- Spread the silver leaf on top of the mixture.
- Chop into 2.5cm/1in square pieces. Serve.

Malai Laddoo
(Sweet Cream Dumplings)

Makes 8

Ingredients
300g/10oz unsalted soft
  goat's cheese, drained

120ml/4fl oz condensed
  milk

2-3 drops kewra essence*

¼ tsp yellow food colour

¼ tsp ground green
  cardamom

Method
- Cook the goat's cheese with the condensed milk in a saucepan on a low heat for 10-12 minutes, stirring the mixture continuously till it begins to leave the sides of the pan.
- Add the remaining ingredients. Mix well. Set aside to cool.
- Divide into 8 balls. Serve.

Coconut & Bread Sweetmeat

Makes 20-25

Ingredients
16 slices white bread

500g/1lb 2oz sugar

360ml/12fl oz water

2 egg yolks, whisked

1 large fresh coconut,
  grated

½ tsp ground green
  cardamom

½ tsp grated nutmeg

2 tbsp raisins

75g/2½oz cashew nuts

Method
- Cut the bread into small pieces. Set aside.
- Cook the sugar with the water in a saucepan on a medium heat. Stir till it achieves a 1-thread consistency (see cooking techniques).
- Using a dessert spoon, pour thin streams of the whisked egg yolks into the sugar-water mixture.
- When the egg strips begin to harden, remove them from the syrup carefully. Make sure they don't turn brown. Set aside.
- Add the bread pieces, grated coconut, cardamom, nutmeg, raisins and cashew nuts to the syrup. Stir till the syrup has been absorbed. Add the egg strips.
- Transfer to a greased dish and set aside to cool.
- Chop into square pieces to serve.

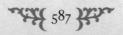

Culculs
(Sweet Conches)

Serves 4

Ingredients
125g/4½oz butter
500g/18fl oz plain white
  flour
2 eggs, whisked
¼ tsp salt
250g/9oz caster sugar
500ml/16fl oz coconut milk
Ghee for frying

Method
- Mix the butter with the flour. Crumble with your fingers.
- Add the remaining ingredients, except the ghee. Mix well. Knead to a stiff dough. Cover with a damp cloth and set aside for 1 hour.
- Divide into marble-sized balls. Press with the back of a fork to give a ribbed appearance, then roll into conch-like shells.
- Heat the ghee in a frying pan and fry the conches on a medium heat till brown. Serve at room temperature. The conches can be stored at room temperature for 15 days.

Gram Sweet

Makes 30

Ingredients
750g/1lb 10oz chana dhal*
1.5 litres/2¾ pints water
1kg/2¼lb sugar
1 large fresh coconut,
  finely grated
2 tbsp ground green
  cardamom
4 tbsp ghee

Method
- Cook the dhal with 1.2 litres/2 pints water in a saucepan on a medium heat for 45 minutes. Drain the dhal and grind to a fine paste. Set aside.
- Cook the sugar with the remaining water in a saucepan on a medium heat till it achieves 1-thread consistency (see cooking techniques).
- Add the cooked dhal and the remaining ingredients. Simmer till the mixture leaves the sides of the pan, stirring frequently.
- Transfer the mixture to a greased plate and set it aside to cool.
- Chop into diamond-shaped pieces. Serve.

Coconut Diamonds

Makes 20-25

Ingredients
200g/7oz semolina
1kg/2¼lb sugar
250ml/8fl oz water
¼ tsp salt
1 large fresh coconut,
  finely grated
1 tsp vanilla essence
4 tbsp ghee

Method
* Heat a frying pan and dry roast (see cooking techniques) the semolina on a medium heat for 3-4 minutes. Set aside.
* Cook the sugar with the water in a saucepan on a medium heat till it achieves 1-thread consistency (see cooking techniques).
* Add the semolina and the remaining ingredients. Stir lightly till the mixture begins to leave the sides of the pan.
* Transfer to a greased tray. Cool and chop into diamond-shaped pieces to serve.

Bebinca
(Traditional Goan dessert)

Serves 4

Ingredients
200ml/7fl oz water
350g/12oz caster sugar
450ml/15fl oz coconut milk
10 eggs, whisked
140g/5oz plain white flour
½ tsp grated nutmeg
2 tsp ground green
  cardamom pods
4 tbsp warm ghee

Method
* Mix the water and sugar thoroughly with the coconut milk.
* Add the remaining ingredients, except the ghee. Mix thoroughly to form a smooth batter.
* Pour 1 tbsp ghee into a 15cm/6in cake tin. Add a quarter of the batter and bake in a pre-heated oven at 200°C (400°F, Gas Mark 6) for 7-8 minutes.
* Spread another tbsp of ghee over this layer and add another quarter of the batter. Place under a grill for 7-8 minutes.
* Repeat the grilling procedure for the remaining batter.
* Set aside to cool. Cut into slices and serve.

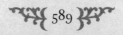

Madagane
(Yellow Gram and Coconut Milk Pudding)

Serves 4

Ingredients
150g/5½oz mung dhal*
75g/2½oz cashew nuts
1.5 litres/2¾ pints water
250g/9oz jaggery*
125g/4½oz rice flour
250ml/8fl oz coconut milk
2 tbsp ground green
  cardamom

Method
- Cook the dhal and cashew nuts with half the water in a saucepan on a medium heat for 25-30 minutes.
- Add the jaggery and the remaining water. Simmer for 10 minutes. Stir the mixture occasionally.
- Add the rice flour, coconut milk and cardamom. Continue to stir for 2-3 minutes.
- Serve hot.

Shankarpali
(Sugar-coated Fried Flour Crisps)

Makes 400g

Ingredients
250ml/8fl oz water
125g/4½oz sugar
75g/2½oz ghee plus extra
  for frying
375g/13oz plain white flour

Method
- Cook the water, sugar and ghee in a saucepan on a medium heat for 15-30 minutes.
- Remove from the heat and knead with the flour into a soft, pliable dough.
- Divide the dough into 4 parts and roll out each part into a thick disc.
- Chop each disc into diamond shapes with a cookie cutter. Set the shankarpali aside on a dry cloth for 1 hour.
- Heat the ghee in a frying pan and fry the shankarpali on a medium heat till golden brown. Drain and cool. Store in an airtight container.

NOTE: *This can be stored for 15 days.*

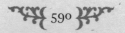

Besan Barfi
(Gram Flour Fudge)

Makes 12

Ingredients
85g/3oz ghee
250g/9oz besan*
300g/10oz sugar
120ml/4fl oz water
¼ tsp grated nutmeg

Method
- Heat the ghee in a saucepan and fry the besan on a medium heat till light brown. Set aside.
- Cook the sugar and water in a saucepan on a medium heat till it achieves 1-thread consistency (see cooking techniques).
- Add the besan. Simmer till the water evaporates, stirring frequently.
- Add the nutmeg. Continue to stir till the mixture leaves the sides of the pan.
- Spread the mixture on a greased plate and chop into square pieces when cool. Serve.

Rabdi

Serves 4

Ingredients
2.5 litres/4½ pints full fat milk
750g/1lb 10oz sugar
7-8 saffron strands
1 tbsp ground green cardamom

Method
- Boil the milk in a saucepan on a high heat for 15 minutes.
- Lower the heat and let a creamy film form over the milk. Move the film aside with a wooden ladle so that it sticks to the sides of the pan. Continue to do so until 80 per cent of the milk is a creamy mixture.
- Transfer the cream to a plate and set it aside to cool and harden. Reserve the remaining milk.
- Mix the remaining milk with the sugar. Slice the cream into square pieces. Soak the pieces of cream in the milk-sugar mixture.
- Add the saffron and cardamom. Serve chilled.

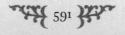

Sandesh
(Sweet Creamy Squares)

Makes 20

Ingredients
2.5 litres/4½ pints full-fat milk

Juice of 1 lemon

375g/13oz caster sugar

7-8 saffron strands

Method
- Heat the milk in a saucepan on a high heat. Remove from the heat before it boils.
- Add the lemon juice and stir till the milk starts to curdle. Separate the curds by straining through a muslin cloth. Discard the liquid.
- Squeeze out the excess moisture from the curds and set them aside for 30 minutes.
- Knead well with the remaining ingredients.
- Shape the sandesh using square moulds.
- Gently scoop out and serve.

Petha
(Sweet White Pumpkin Triangles)

Makes 15

Ingredients
500g/1lb 2oz pumpkin, peeled and deseeded

1.7 litres/3 pints water

4-5 saffron strands, soaked in 1 tbsp milk

1kg/2¼lb sugar

Silver leaf

For the filling:
300g/10oz paneer*

200g/7oz khoya*

250g/9oz sugar

1 tbsp pistachios, chopped

Method
- Chop the pumpkin into 5cm/2in pieces.
- Cook with 750ml/1¼ pints water in a saucepan on a medium heat for 10 minutes.
- Drain and sprinkle the saffron mixture on top. Set aside.
- Cook the sugar with the remaining water in a saucepan on a medium heat till it reaches 1-thread consistency (see cooking techniques). Soak the pumpkin pieces in the syrup for 5-6 minutes. Drain and set aside.
- Mix the filling ingredients together. Slit each pumpkin piece horizontally and stuff with the filling.
- Cut each piece diagonally into triangles and decorate with the silver leaf. Serve.

Puaas
(Sugary Pancakes)

Serves 4

Ingredients
250g/9oz caster sugar

250ml/8fl oz warm water

500g/1lb 2oz wholemeal flour

½ tsp ground fennel

1 tsp raisins

Dash of vanilla essence

Ghee for deep frying

Method
- Mix the sugar, water and flour thoroughly to form a smooth batter.
- Add the remaining ingredients, except the ghee. Mix well.
- Heat the ghee in a saucepan and drop in a large spoonful of the batter. Spread like a pancake and deep fry on a medium heat till golden brown.
- Repeat for the remaining batter.
- Serve hot.

Sago & Nut Kheer
(Sago and Nut Milk Pudding)

Serves 4

Ingredients
400g/14oz sago, washed

1.4 litres/2½ pints coconut milk

200g/7oz vermicelli, soaked for 15 minutes

75g/2½oz cashew nuts

30g/1oz raisins

250g/9oz sugar

100g/3½oz honey

Method
- Cook the sago in a saucepan with the coconut milk on a medium heat for 8-10 minutes.
- Add the remaining ingredients. Simmer for 10 minutes, stirring frequently. Serve hot.

Dry Fruit Rabdi

Serves 4

Ingredients
1 litre/1¾ pints milk
3 tbsp sugar
50g/1¾oz pistachios, finely chopped
25 almonds, finely chopped
20 cashew nuts, finely chopped
25 raisins, finely chopped
2 tbsp figs, finely chopped
10 apricots, finely chopped

Method
- Cook the milk and sugar in a saucepan on a low heat for 20 minutes. Stir the mixture frequently.
- Add the remaining ingredients. Mix well. Stir for 7-8 minutes. Serve chilled.

Perad
(Goan Guava Compote)

Serves 4

Ingredients
500g/1lb 2oz guavas, quartered and deseeded
300g/10oz sugar

Method
- Whizz the guavas in a blender till the mixture turns into a smooth pulp.
- Mix the pulp thoroughly with the sugar in a saucepan and cook for 15 minutes on a low heat, stirring frequently.
- Spread this mixture on a greased plate and set aside to cool. Cut into square pieces to serve.

Sweet Dosa

Serves 4

Ingredients

500g/1lb 2oz jaggery*, grated

500g/1lb 2oz wholemeal flour

½ tsp grated nutmeg

½ tsp ground green cardamom

Ghee for greasing

Method

- Mix all the ingredients, except the ghee, to form a thick batter.
- Grease a frying pan with the ghee and heat it. Pour a large spoonful of batter in it. Spread like a pancake.
- Cook on a low heat till the underside turns light brown. Flip and repeat.
- Repeat for the remaining batter. Serve hot.

Maida Barfi
(Flour Fudge)

Makes 12

Ingredients

85g/3oz ghee

250g/9oz plain white flour

180g/6½oz sugar

60ml/2fl oz water

120ml/4fl oz milk

5 green cardamom pods, ground

Method

- Heat the ghee in a saucepan and fry the flour on a low heat for 4-5 minutes. Set aside.
- Cook the sugar with the water in a saucepan on a medium heat till it achieves 1-thread consistency (see cooking techniques).
- Add the flour and milk. Simmer for 10 minutes, stirring the mixture frequently.
- Add the cardamom. Cook till the mixture begins to leave the sides of the pan.
- Spread on a greased dish. Cool for 10 minutes. Chop into square pieces. Serve hot or cold.

Mysore Pak

(Bengal Gram Fudge Squares)

Makes 20

Ingredients
125g/4½oz sugar
240ml/8fl oz water
250g/9oz besan*
300g/10oz ghee

Method
- Cook the sugar and water in a saucepan on a medium heat till it achieves 1-thread consistency (see cooking techniques).
- Add the besan 1 tbsp at a time, and mix well. Make sure it does not form any lumps.
- Add the ghee and cook the mixture on a low heat, stirring continuously till it begins to leave the sides of the pan.
- Transfer the mixture to a greased dish and press the surface flat with a spatula.
- Cool for 10 minutes and chop into square pieces. Serve hot or cold.

Meetha Khaja

(Deep Fried Sweet Gram Flour Pastry)

Makes 20

Ingredients
250ml/8fl oz water
125g/4½oz jaggery*
¼ tsp ground green cardamom
1 tbsp ghee plus extra for deep frying
375g/13oz plain white flour

Method
- Cook the water and the jaggery in a saucepan on a medium heat for 5-6 minutes. Strain the mixture and let it cool.
- Add the cardamom, 1 tbsp ghee and the flour. Knead the mixture into a pliable dough.
- Divide into 20 balls. Flatten them into discs of 10cm/4in diameter.
- Prick each disc with a fork.
- Heat the ghee in a saucepan. Add the discs. Deep fry on a medium heat till light brown. Drain and cool.
- Store the discs in an airtight container.

NOTE: *This can be stored for up to a week.*

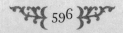

Boondi
(Sweetened Crisp Gram Flour Granules)

Makes 600g

Ingredients
125g/4½oz sugar
250ml/8fl oz water
1 tbsp milk
250g/9oz besan*
Ghee for deep frying
¼ tsp ground green
  cardamom
6-8 almonds, chopped

Method
* Cook the sugar, water and milk in a saucepan on a medium heat till it achieves 1-thread consistency (see cooking techniques). Set aside.
* Mix the besan with enough water to form a thick batter.
* Heat the ghee in a frying pan. Hold a perforated spoon over the ghee and pour the batter through it, allowing only small droplets to fall into the oil.
* Fry the granules till crisp. Drain and immerse in the sugar syrup for 3-4 minutes.
* Drain and mix with the remaining ingredients. Cool and store in an airtight container.

NOTE: *This can be stored for 2-3 days.*

Rava Barfi
(Semolina Fudge)

Makes 12

Ingredients
85g/3oz ghee
100g/3½oz semolina
250ml/8fl oz milk
500g/1lb 2oz sugar
½ tsp vanilla essence

Method
* Heat the ghee in a saucepan. Add the semolina. Fry on a medium heat for 2-3 minutes.
* Add the remaining ingredients. Stir the mixture on a low heat till it leaves the sides of the pan.
* Spread this mixture on a greased dish and let it cool for 10 minutes.
* Chop into square pieces. Serve.

Banana Shikran
(Mashed Banana Dessert)

Ingredients
4 large bananas, mashed
500ml/16fl oz whole milk
30g/1oz caster sugar
8 cashew nuts
8 raisins

Method
- Whisk all the ingredients together thoroughly for 10-15 minutes.
- Serve chilled.

Indian Bread Pudding

Makes 12

Ingredients
8 slices white bread
400ml/14fl oz whole milk
30g/1oz butter
45g/1 1/2oz sugar
6 saffron strands
1 tsp ground green cardamom pods
75g/2 1/2oz chopped cashew nuts or walnuts
2 eggs, whisked

Method
- Grease a round baking tin measuring 20cm/8in in diameter and arrange the bread slices in it.
- Mix the remaining ingredients together thoroughly and pour this mixture over the bread slices.
- Steam (see cooking techniques) for 30 minutes. Serve chilled.

Masala Doodh
(Spiced Milk)

Ingredients

750ml/1¼pt whole milk
300g/10oz sugar
60g/2oz ground almonds
60g/2oz ground pistachios
1 tsp ground green
  cardamom pods
Pinch of saffron

Method

- Boil the milk with the sugar in a saucepan on a medium heat for 15 minutes.
- Add the remaining ingredients and mix well. Simmer for 5 minutes, stirring continuously. Serve hot.

GLOSSARY

AMARANTH LEAVES: These have a taste similar to spinach. In India they are commonly referred to as chawli leaves.

AMCHOOR: Literally, 'mango powder', this is sun-dried unripe mangoes, ground into a powder. Amchoor has a distinct tart and fruity flavour. Frequently used as a souring agent, it can be substituted for lemon juice, vinegar or tamarind. It works well as dry seasoning or in a marinade too.

ANARDANA: Used as seasoning, anardana is dried and ground pomegranate seeds. They have a tangy flavour with a sweet aftertaste.

BESAN: Besan is also known as gram flour. When mixed with the right amount of water, it can be used as a substitute for egg in vegan cooking. It is commonly used to make batter.

BHAJI: In India, 'bhaji' is a generic term for any dish made with vegetables and spices. This is not to be confused with 'bhajiya', which are vegetable fritters.

BITTER GOURD: Extremely bitter, this vegetable commonly known as 'karela' evokes either love or hate in Indians. Highly beneficial for diabetes patients, the karela is chopped and fried or stuffed with spices and baked to stunning results.

BOMBAY MIX: A savoury mix of sev, peanuts, dried peas and many other condiments and spices.

BOONDI: A fried snack made of besan. It can be sweet or salty. It is made be dropping the besan batter through a slotted spoon into hot oil and frying the droplets.

BOTTLE GOURD: Similar to a pumpkin in texture, but firmer and crisper, the bottle gourd has a fresh, nutty flavour and is great for taking on diverse flavours.

CHAAT MASALA: A mix of amchoor, cumin, black salt, ground coriander, ginger powder, salt, pepper and asafoetida. Chaat masala is ubiquitous in India, sprinkled over all kinds of savouries, snacks and raitas to spice them up.

CHANA: Roasted kaala chana is referred to as 'chana' in India. It is usually eaten as a snack.

CHANA DHAL: A kind of lentil, also known as 'split Bengal gram'.

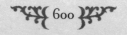

CHICKOO: Chickoo is a fruit with a grainy texture. Also known as sapota, it has a very sweet, nutty flavour, reminiscent of caramel.

COLOCASIA: Popularly known as *arbi*, the starchy root of this plant is eaten boiled or fried with spices. The plant's leaves are used for cooking, too.

DAIKON LEAVES: Indians cook the leaves of daikon radish as well as the root. They taste rather like watercress, but with a bitter tang.

DHANSAK MASALA: A classic Parsi spice blend made of a unique combination of numerous spices.

INDIAN DRUMSTICKS: Not to be confused with chicken drumsticks, these are long, unripe pods of the moringa tree and are commonly referred to as drumsticks in India. Their taste can be likened to that of asparagus.

JACKFRUIT: This fruit is eaten both raw and cooked in India. Green, or unripe, jackfruit is usually cooked in spicy sauces. Ripe jackfruit has a sweet flavour and is commonly eaten as fruit.

JAGGERY: Made of unrefined sugar, this sweetening agent is rich in iron and has a crumbly texture.

KAALA CHANA: Literally, 'black chickpeas', these are darker in hue and sometimes smaller than normal chickpeas. On boiling, they remain firm to the bite, creating texture.

KALI DHAL: A kind of lentil, also known as 'whole black gram'.

KALONJI SEEDS: Called nigella seeds in English, but known as kalonji seeds throughout India, these tiny seeds are triangular in shape and black in colour. They are commonly seen studded on naan bread.

KEWRA ESSENCE: Essence of pandanus flowers, kewra is used to flavour meats, desserts and beverages.

KHOYA: A milk product, khoya (or khoa) is made by thickening milk in an open pan. Khoya gives texture and adds to the consistency of many an Indian sweet. Unsalted ricotta cheese is a good substitute for khoya.

KOKUM: Native to the coastal regions of western India, kokum is also known as mangosteen. Its taste resembles that of tamarind, with a tangy, fruity flavour that particularly complements coconut-based curries. Kokum is usually dried and stored, and is infused in hot water

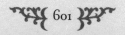

just before cooking.

KURMURE: Puffed rice, similar to crisped rice cereal.

MASOOR DHAL: Split red lentil.

MUNG BEANS: A kind of lentil, also known as 'green gram'.

MUNG DHAL: Dehusked mung beans. These are yellow in colour.

MELON SEEDS: Melon seeds are a common garnish in India. They are also popularly peeled and eaten on many a winter afternoon.

PANCH PHORON: A mix of five whole seeds – cumin, fennel, kalonji, mustard and fenugreek. Also known as Bengali five-spice, it is used to imbue curries with a fragrant, spicy-sweet aroma.

PANEER: Paneer is a firm, bland cheese that is usually available in big chunks that can be easily chopped. A close approximation would be tofu.

PAV BHAJI MASALA: A traditional blend of unique spices used to give pav bhaji its typical taste.

POHA: Beaten rice, commonly soaked and used for making snacks.

SAMBHAR POWDER: A traditional South Indian spice blend made of a unique combination of numerous spices.

SEV: Fried besan snack made by deep frying thin strands of the batter.

SEV PURIS: Small, crunchy puris made of wheat flour, usually deep fried.

SOY BEAN SEMOLINA: Semolina made with soy bean.

TOOR DHAL: A type of lentil, also known as 'split red gram'.

URAD BEANS: A kind of lentil, also known as 'whole black gram'.

URAD DHAL: A kind of lentil, also known as 'split black gram'.

WHITE PEAS: A type of lentil, also known as 'matra' or 'wataana'.

WHOLE MASOOR DHAL: A type of lentil, also known as 'red lentil'.

YAMS: The starchy roots of these vines are similar to sweet potatoes.

COOKING TECHNIQUES

BLANCHING TOMATOES

- In a saucepan, heat water on a high heat. When the water starts boiling, add the tomatoes to it and remove the pan from the heat. Set aside for 2-3 minutes. Discard the water and remove the tomato skins. They will come off quite easily.

CLEANING CLAMS

- Soak the clams in a large pot of water so that they are fully immersed. Set aside for 5-7 minutes.
- Scrub the shell to remove barnacles or any other debris. Rinse under running water.
- Drain all water and place the clams in a pan with a lid. Place the pan in the freezer overnight. This will make the shells open up.
- Next morning, place the clams outside the freezer and allow to thaw until they are at room temperature.
- Twist and break the shell with no meat away. Use the side with the flesh.

CLEANING CRABS

- Place the crab on a table, belly side up. Pull off the triangular belly flap or 'apron'.
- Turn the crab over. Inserting your thumb between the body and the shell at the rear, pull the shell up.
- Twist the claws and legs off. (They can also be cracked with a nutcracker.) Also pull off the spongy gills and small paddles at the front of the crab and discard them.
- Using a knife, cut the crab's body lengthwise into half, and then into quarters.

DRY ROASTING

- Heat a flat pan until almost smoking. Place the ingredients on the flat pan and keep gently stirring for about 2-3 minutes on a medium heat, until an aroma emanates from the ingredients.

PARBOILING RICE

- In a saucepan, bring the water to a boil on a high heat. Add the rice and lower the heat. Mix well and cook for 5 minutes. Drain the rice in a colander and set aside for 4-5 minutes.

ROASTING VEGETABLES (tomatoes, peppers and onions)

- Wrap the vegetables in aluminium foil and place in a pre-heated oven at 200°C (400°F, Gas Mark 6) for 15 minutes until the skin shrivels up and starts turning brown.

STEAMING

- Fill a pan with water to the extent that the level of water will be 2.5cm/1in below the bottom of the steamer. Heat the water on a high heat.
- Just before the water starts boiling, lower the heat to medium and carefully place the steamer, with the ingredients, into the pan.
- Cover the pan and cook on a medium heat for the time specified in the recipe. Be careful of the steam when you uncover the pan.

THREAD CONSISTENCY

- This technique is used to check whether the consistency of the sugar syrup is right for a particular dessert. It's a simple technique.
- Spoon some syrup out and let it cool for 5 seconds.
- Dip the tip of your forefinger into the syrup. Then touch your thumb and forefinger together and pull apart gently. Notice the number of syrup threads formed between your finger and thumb.
- The more you boil the syrup, the greater the number of threads will be. Keep simmering the syrup on a low heat until you reach the desired consistency. The stages progress fairly quickly, so check frequently.

WET GRINDING

- Mix water and the ingredients in the same proportion. Grind in a blender till smooth.

Index

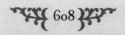

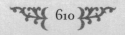

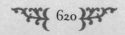

N

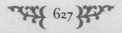

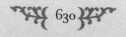

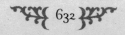

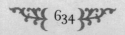

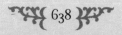